LIBRARY OF NEW TESTAMENT STUDIES

654

formerly the Journal for the Study of the New Testament Supplement series

Editor
Chris Keith

Editorial Board
Dale C. Allison, John M.G. Barclay, Lynn H. Cohick,
R. Alan Culpepper, Craig A. Evans, Robert Fowler, Simon
J. Gathercole, Juan Hernández Jr., John S. Kloppenborg,
Michael Labahn, Matthew V. Novenson, Love L. Sechrest,
Robert Wall, Catrin H. Williams, Brittany E. Wilson

Atonement and Ethics in 1 John

A Peacemaking Hermeneutic

Chris Armitage

LONDON • NEW YORK • OXFORD • NEW DELHI • SYDNEY

T&T CLARK
Bloomsbury Publishing Plc
50 Bedford Square, London, WC1B 3DP, UK
1385 Broadway, New York, NY 10018, USA
29 Earlsfort Terrace, Dublin 2, Ireland

BLOOMSBURY, T&T CLARK and the T&T Clark logo are trademarks of Bloomsbury
Publishing Plc

First published in Great Britain 2021
This paperback edition published 2023

Copyright © Chris Armitage, 2021

Chris Armitage has asserted his right under the Copyright, Designs and Patents Act, 1988,
to be identified as Author of this work.

For legal purposes the Acknowledgements on p. x constitute
an extension of this copyright page.

Cover design: Charlotte James

All rights reserved. No part of this publication may be reproduced or transmitted in any
form or by any means, electronic or mechanical, including photocopying, recording, or
any information storage or retrieval system, without prior permission in writing from the
publishers.

Bloomsbury Publishing Plc does not have any control over, or responsibility for, any third-
party websites referred to or in this book. All internet addresses given in this book were
correct at the time of going to press. The author and publisher regret any inconvenience
caused if addresses have changed or sites have ceased to exist, but can accept no
responsibility for any such changes.

A catalogue record for this book is available from the British Library.

Library of Congress Cataloging-in-Publication Data
Names: Armitage, Chris, author.
Title: Atonement and ethics in 1 John : a peacemaking hermeneutic / Chris Armitage.
Description: London ; New York : T&T Clark, 2021. | Series: Library of New
Testament studies ; 2513–8790 ; 654 | Includes bibliographical references and index. |
Summary: "Christopher Armitage considers previous theological perception of 1 John as
a text advocating that God abhors violence, contrasted with biblical scholarship analysis
that focuses upon the text's birth from hostile theological conflict between 'insiders' and
'outsiders', with immensely hostile rhetoric directed towards 'antichrists' and those who
have left the community"– Provided by publisher.
Identifiers: LCCN 2020054766 (print) | LCCN 2020054767 (ebook) | ISBN
9780567700742 (hardback) | ISBN 9780567700759 (pdf) | ISBN 9780567700773 (epub)
Subjects: LCSH: Bible. Epistle of John, 1st–Criticism, interpretation, etc. | Bible. Epistle
of John, 1st–Criticism, Textual. | Atonement–Biblical teaching. | Reconciliation–Biblical
teaching. | Ethics in the Bible. | Rhetoric in the Bible.
Classification: LCC BS2805.6.A8 A76 2021 (print) | LCC BS2805.6.A8
(ebook) | DDC 234/.5–dc23
LC record available at https://lccn.loc.gov/2020054766
LC ebook record available at https://lccn.loc.gov/2020054767

ISBN: HB: 978-0-5677-0074-2
PB: 978-0-5677-0078-0
ePDF: 978-0-5677-0075-9
ePUB: 978-0-5677-0077-3

Series: Library of New Testament Studies, volume 654
ISSN 2513–8790

Typeset by Integra Software Services Pvt. Ltd.

To find out more about our authors and books visit www.bloomsbury.com
and sign up for our newsletters.

Contents

Preface	viii
Acknowledgements	x
Abbreviations	xi
Introduction – Some Peacemaking Hermeneutical Approaches to 1 John	1
Genesis of This Study	1
René Girard	5
James Alison	10
Raymund Schwager	11
Willard Swartley	12
William Klassen	14
Pheme Perkins	15
Wayne Northey	16
Kharalambous Anstall	17
Glen Stassen, David Gunshee	17
John Howard Yoder	18
Gordon Kaufman	20
Stanley Hauerwas	21
Darrin W Snyder Belousek	21
Richard Hays	22
Richard Burridge	23
George Hunsinger	25
Hans Urs von Balthasar	26
Thomas Torrance	27
Gustav Aulen	28
Conclusion	29
1 The Background, Purpose, Literary Structure and Reception of 1 John	31
Introduction	31
The Background of 1 John	32
(i) Jewish Influence in 1 John	32
(ii) The Johannine Community – John and His Opponents	35
The Purpose of 1 John	41
Conflict in 1 John – Present or Past?	47

The Literary Structure of 1 John	54
Reception of 1 John in the Early Church	59
Conclusion	61
2 Ἱλασμός and Its Cognates in the Septuagint, the Intertestamental Literature and the Dead Sea Scrolls	63
Introduction	63
Ἱλασμός in the Septuagint	63
(i) Leviticus 25:9	64
(ii) Numbers 5:8	67
(iii) 1 Chronicles 28:20c	68
(iv) Psalm 130:4	69
(v) Ezekiel 44:27	70
(vi) Daniel 9	72
(vii) Amos 8:14	72
Cognates of ἱλασμός in the Septuagint	73
Conclusions on Usage of ἱλασμός and Its Cognates in the LXX	75
Atonement and Forgiveness in Some Intertestamental Pseudepigrapha	75
(i) 1 Enoch	76
(ii) Jubilees	78
Atonement and Forgiveness in the Dead Sea Scrolls	80
Conclusion	82
3 Ἱλασμός in 1 John	87
Introduction	87
Scholarship Review	89
(i) Expiation	89
(ii) Propitiation	98
(iii) Other Views	107
Conclusions from Scholarship Review	110
Exegesis of 1 John 2:2 and 4:10	111
(i) 1 John 2:2	111
(ii) 1 John 4:10	116
Conclusion	119
4 Σφάξω and ἀνθρωποκτόνος in 1 John	123
Introduction	123
Cain and Abel in the Hebrew Bible	125
Cain and Abel in the Septuagint	128
Cain and Abel in Some Intertestamental Literature	130

	(i) 1 Enoch	130
	(ii) Jubilees	131
	(iii) The Testament of Abraham	133
	Cain and Abel in Philo	134
	Cain and Abel in Josephus	138
	Historical Summary	141
	Σφάξω and ἀνθρωποκτόνος in 1 John	143
	Conclusion	150
5	Ἀγαπάω and ἀδελφός in 1 John	153
	Introduction	153
	Leviticus	154
	Deuteronomy	162
	Possible Influence of Leviticus and Deuteronomy on 1 John	168
	Conclusion	173
6	Peacemaking in 1 John	181
	Introduction	181
	John's Polemic against the Secessionists	183
	Ἱλασμός and Peacemaking in 1 John	188
	Σφαξω, ἀνθρωποκτόνος and Peacemaking in 1 John	190
	Ἀγαπάω, ἀδελφος and Peacemaking in 1 John	192
	Conclusion: A Peacemaking Hermeneutic of 1 John	194
Bibliography		197
Author Index		212
Index of References		216

Preface

Among biblical theologians who oppose violence, some have sought a corresponding hermeneutic grounded in the NT. They seek a hermeneutic of non-violence in the NT. Some refer to it more positively as a "peacemaking hermeneutic". I prefer this term for that reason. These interpreters, of widely varying theoretical standpoints, often use texts from 1 John as an epistemology of love, to borrow a phrase from the French anthropological philosopher René Girard, and of non-violence, relying particularly on the pejorative use by 1 John of the Cain and Abel story to condemn hatred. The problem about such uses, not fully faced in peacemaking theology, is that 1 John was written at a time of hot theological dispute. The author writes against what he sees as destructive and dangerous tendencies, which he identifies as a defective, seemingly docetic Christology and moral indifference, identified with opponents who have recently left his community. His rhetoric is strong, using strong terms of condemnation such as "antichrists". It may appear difficult to read 1 John, even through modern eyes far removed from the conflict, as a tract centred on love and peace. This study nevertheless argues that a peacemaking hermeneutic of 1 John is in harmony with its key ideas.

In short, this study contends that a peace-oriented reading of 1 John is generally viable in view of the "weapons" John deploys against his opponents – not hatred and combat, although he is deeply opposed to their theological ideas, but a "new commandment" which is yet an old one, of mutual love and avoidance of hatred, which leads ultimately to murder – the ultimate violence. On the surface, the castigation used against the author's opponents looks like hatred, but the overarching love he enjoins his community to practise as the antidote to the opponents' sectarian divisions is the dominant theme of the epistle.

The point of view of this study is that because 1 John was written in a milieu in which his audience, if not entirely comprised of converted Jews, were in general thoroughly familiar with the OT, echoes of it, beyond the explicit reference to Cain, are ever present in 1 John. I therefore examine central themes in 1 John, represented by five keywords, ἱλασμός, σφάζω, ἀνθρωποκτόνος, ἀγάπη and ἀδελφός, by looking at their background and use in the OT, in both the Hebrew and LXX versions, the intertestamental pseudepigrapha and the Qumran literature in order to cast light on their use in 1 John.

By so doing, this study argues that these central themes in 1 John presuppose a God whose primary engagement with the world is not assuagement of divine anger, nor ferocious defence of truth at the expense of love, but rather peace and avoidance of hatred, which leads to violence and death. First John, in its use of the OT ideas underlying the five keywords identified in this study keywords identified in this study, ἱλασμός, σφάζω, ἀνθρωποκτόνος, ἀγάπη and ἀδελφός, exposes the key connection drawn by the author between God's love in the gift of Jesus and the love he enjoins in his community as absolutely central to their understanding of God's own nature and purpose for the world. A peacemaking hermeneutic of 1 John is not only feasible, but integral to reading the epistle.

Acknowledgements

My debts in the preparation of this study are so manifold and profound that none can be fully acknowledged, much less repaid. First must come my senior colleague at St Mark's National Theological Centre in Canberra, Associate Professor David Neville. He made free with his profound scholarship and deep but not uncritical Christian faith in his encouragement and support of this project from the beginning. I also had the extraordinarily good fortune to have available to me at the Canberra campus Professor John Painter, who is of course a leading Johannine and indeed New Testament scholar of our time, and he too was prodigal with his time and encouragement of my project. My colleagues in the postgraduate seminar at St Mark's were always forthcoming with much-valued encouragement and constructive criticism of my work, particularly the then-director and chair of the seminar, Bishop Tom Frame. My colleagues Anastasia Webster-Hawes and Marie-Louise Craig provided much-needed encouragement and invaluable assistance with my Hebrew. The library staff at St Mark's were helpful and patient in their support for my research. My old friend Bishop Donald Cameron was there from the beginning, and his profound knowledge and love of Koinē Greek were a guiding light throughout my research. Needless to say, the views expressed in this study are mine alone, and any faults and deficiencies in it are my responsibility. I must thank Professors C Clifton Black, Paul N Anderson and Peter Rhea Jones for their helpful corrections and suggestions. Thanks are also due to Professor Chris Keith for accepting this study for publication and to Sarah Blake and the editorial team for their invaluable assistance. Since completion of this work I have formed a most productive connection with the Department of Ancient History at Macquarie University in Sydney, and with the Society for the Study of Early Christianity there, and with Emeritus Professor Alanna Nobbs in particular, who kindly read my manuscript and made a number of helpful suggestions. My thanks are also due to Bloomsbury, Prof Chris Keith, Sarah Blake, Viswasirasini Govindarajan, and my peer reviewers and copy editor for their assistance in publishing my manuscript. Last but not least my loving family, my late father John and mother Betty, my lovely daughters Lucy and Clare, and, most of all, my darling wife Maureen were a constant source of love, support and encouragement, a very present help in trouble, and endlessly tolerant of my frequent absences, physical or mental, from our household. Quite simply, without them I could never have done it.

Abbreviations

Bib	Biblica
B Sac	Bibliotheca Sacra
CBQ	Catholic Biblical Quarterly
CTM	Concordia Theological Monthly
DSD	Dead Sea Discoveries
Exp Tim	Expository Times
Euro J	*The* European Journal of Theology
Ev Q	Evangelical Quarterly
HTR	Harvard Theological Review
Int	Interpretation
JETS	Journal of the Evangelical Theological Society
JBL	Journal of Biblical Literature
JSJ	Journal for the Study of Judaism in the Persian, Hellenistic and Roman Periods
JSNT	Journal for the Study of the New Testament
JTS	Journal of Theological Studies
LXX	The Septuagint
Nov T	Novum Testamentum
NT	New Testament
NTS	New Testament Studies
Numen	Numen – International Review for the History of Religions
OT	Old Testament
SJT	Scottish Journal of Theology
Tyn Bul	Tyndale Bulletin
VT	Vetus Testamentum
ZNW	*Zeitschrift für die neutestamentliche Wissenschaft*

Introduction – Some Peacemaking Hermeneutical Approaches to 1 John

Genesis of This Study

First John, on the face of it, is a text riven with underlying conflict with opponents, displaying hostile rhetoric against them. Εἰρήνη ὑμῖν, the dominical, Johannine formula, "peace be with you" (John 20:19, 20:21, 20:26),[1] nicely taken up in the early church's liturgical Greeting of Peace, is not found in 1 John. Nor are the other uses of εἰρήνη in John's Gospel (John 14:27 [twice], 16:33). We find εἰρήνη in 2 John 3 and 3 John 15 in greetings, but it appears nowhere in 1 John. First John might seem the very last text on which to build a theology of peacemaking or non-violence.

Yet peace-oriented or non-violent hermeneutical approaches to 1 John are not uncommon in recent peacemaking theological and NT ethical studies. This poses the question whether such approaches are exegetically, or even hermeneutically, legitimate in light of the background and purpose of 1 John and indeed in light of the way it approaches the problem of dissension over theological differences in the community to which it is addressed. This study addresses that question. First, it examines the background and purpose of 1 John. Then it examines key ideas in 1 John, represented by certain Greek keywords in 1 John against the background of their use in the Septuagint (LXX) and in some intertestamental pseudepigrapha and Jewish historical texts written reasonably contemporaneously with 1 John. Finally, deploying its findings in earlier chapters, it presents an original peacemaking hermeneutical approach to 1 John.

This introduction presents a survey, which will be anything but exhaustive, of recent use of 1 John by those writing peacemaking theology. Some writers whose work is examined are theologians, and others are biblical scholars, but their work is written more from a theological perspective. Some other writers' work is presented, although they do not appeal to 1 John, in order to ask whether their argument may be supported by 1 John. Some writers would not identify themselves as peacemaking theologians, and some indeed oppose some of the ideas of that school, but they are included because their ideas harmonise in some areas with peacemaking theology.

---

[1] It was (and still is) the traditional, everyday greeting of Jews in Israel: George R Beasley-Murray, *John* (New York: Thomas Nelson Inc., 2nd ed., 1999), 378.

Here "peacemaking theology" refers to the work of writers in the Christian tradition who enjoin abstaining from violence and warfare and attaining peaceful reconciliation among families, communities and nations. The term "hermeneutic" is employed in the more modern sense of seeking to derive from the text theological principles which may be supported by a particular interpretation of the text itself.[2] What is *not* intended by the term "hermeneutic" in this study is a philosophical grid whereby an a priori hermeneutical principle is applied to a text, which is then made to fit that principle. Any hermeneutical enterprise encounters the problem of the "hermeneutical circle", whereby we bring to a text all kinds of predetermined understandings, used by us to shape our questions of the text, which then suggest the answers we derive from it.[3] Ricoeur seeks to avoid this by interpreting the outside world through the lens of the text: "For us, the world is an ensemble of references opened up by the texts."[4] An instructive example of this technique is Ricoeur's essay on the sixth Decalogue commandment, "thou shalt not kill", where he sets it against Genesis 22, in which the Lord's command to Abraham to kill his firstborn, Isaac, occurs: here Ricoeur shows that the ideal of "loving obedience" underlies God's relationship with humanity.[5] Following Ricoeur, may we exercise some leverage against the literal text of 1 John to derive an overarching ethic from it?

It is an age-old practice to ask of a text whether an overarching a posteriori hermeneutical principle can be derived from it. A good example is Augustine's standpoint that the love of God and of others is the proper perspective of a Christian in reading scripture, so that when adjudicating on competing interpretations of it, one must ask which is favoured by the hermeneutical rule of charity.[6] This study's methodology is similar: it asks whether various uses of 1 John in peacemaking theology to promote mutual love and oppose violence can be founded on its text, having regard to the theological aims and historical situation emerging from it.

Barth's well-known warning on this subject needs heeding here:

> The irremediable danger of consulting Holy scripture apart from the centre, and in such a way that the question of Jesus Christ ceases to be the controlling and comprehensive question and simply becomes one amongst others, consists

---

[2] For a good but brief discussion of this issue, see Werner Jeanrond, *Theological Hermeneutics: Development and Significance* (London: SCM Press, 1994), 1–5.
[3] Ibid, 5–6.
[4] Paul Ricoeur, *Hermeneutics and the Human Sciences: Essays in Language, Action and Interpretation* (ed. John B Thompson; Cambridge: Cambridge University Press), 202, quoted in Dan R Stiver, *Theology after Ricoeur: New Directions in Hermeneutical Theology* (Louisville/London/Leiden: Westminster John Knox Press, 2001), 33.
[5] Paul Ricoeur, "Thou Shalt Not Kill: A Loving Obedience" in *Thinking Biblically: Exegetical and Hermeneutical Studies* (ed. André LaCocque and Paul Ricoeur, trans. David Pellauer; Chicago and London: The University of Chicago Press), 111–40.
[6] Ibid, 23, referring to Augustine, *De Doctrina Christiana*, 3.54; see also Charles H Cosgrove, *Appealing to Scripture in Moral Debate: Five Hermeneutical Rules* (Grand Rapids: Eerdmans, 2002), 159; James A Andrews, *Hermeneutics and the Church: In Dialogue with Augustine* (University of Notre Dame, Indiana: Notre Dame Press, 2012), 87–130.

primarily in the fact that (even supposing a strict and exclusive scripture principle) scripture is thought of and used as though the message of revelation and the Word of God could be extracted from it in the same way as the message of other truth or reality can be extracted from other sources of knowledge, at any rate where it is not presumably speaking of Jesus Christ.[7]

Barth is speaking here of a "transition from biblical to biblicist thought" by the development in the "older Protestant orthodoxy" of the doctrine of the verbal inspiration of scripture, which, he said, was no doubt developed as a bulwark against rationalism, but which in fact was a product, not of "an over-developed faith of revelation", but of "rationalistic thinking – the attempt to replace faith and indirect knowledge with direct knowledge".[8] This study does not advocate an approach which *reifies* Holy scripture, which holds that scripture itself is not only its best, but its sole interpreter, any more than does Barth. Such an approach puts aside any solid attempt to employ the tools of sociological and even historical enquiry, which have cast so much light recently on the situation in which scripture was produced and on the communities from which it arose. It also deprives us of the opportunity to seek an overarching hermeneutic from a scriptural text which is anchored in it.

There is a corresponding danger in peacemaking theology of reading references to peace and mutual love in scripture literally, without attending to the genre of the text, the historical situation in which it was written, and its overall theological aims. In the case of 1 John, such a literalistic approach fails to give weight to the Christology of the letter, underlying the stigmatising of the opponents, thus missing the "question of Jesus Christ" which Barth holds to be central to any hermeneutical question asked of the NT in any field, including ethics, as in this study.

Obviously, the *whole* NT needs to be examined to see whether it provides support for a peacemaking hermeneutic, before one may claim to have developed a truly NT theology of peacemaking. That is beyond the scope of this study. But in such an endeavour the "difficult" NT texts need examination as well. First John may be one of these, because of its hostile rhetoric. The contribution this study aims to make is to examine some keywords, ἱλασμός, σφάξω, ἀνθρωποκτόνος, ἀγαπάω and ἀδελφὸς, often used in 1 John, which appear to stand for key ideas in the epistle, against the Jewish background against which it was written, and more particularly some of their uses in the LXX, to see if some recent peacemaking hermeneutical approaches to 1 John are supported by its text.

Peacemaking theology has often found support in the synoptic gospels, especially in Matthew and Luke. As but one example, Richard Hays, a NT biblical scholar and ethicist, has sought to show, in a careful exegesis of Matthew 5:38-48, that it teaches non-violent love of enemies as normative.[9] Similar uses of 1 John have been less common, but there

---

[7] Karl Barth, *Church Dogmatics*, IV/1 (trans. GW Bromiley; Edinburgh: T&T Clark, 1956), 368.
[8] *Ibid.*
[9] Richard B Hays, *The Moral Vision of the New Testament* (New York: HarperCollins, 1996), 319–29.

are still many, as we shall see. So the present study asks whether a peacemaking or non-violent hermeneutic built on citations of 1 John has sure foundations. The textual context, from which citations from 1 John are taken to support such theology, may or may not be consistent with their hermeneutical use.

Some uses of 1 John to support a peacemaking hermeneutic, particularly by theologians rather than biblical scholars, tend to avoid the more painful aspects of the letter – particularly the hostility the author shows to his secessionist opponents, and their ideas. In a theological work, where the main object is to engage with scripture to provide apt illustrations of themes which the author has developed in his or her cultural context, this is understandable. Other writers, often themselves biblical scholars, have used 1 John in a similar way. By the nature of their discipline, their examination of the text of 1 John is closer.

In biblical scholarship, however, the question still needs to be asked: are these uses of 1 John entirely appropriate in light of what we know, almost entirely from the text itself, about the conflict which engulfed the Johannine community, its causes and the antidote offered by its author to it? Before attempting an answer to this question in the chapters which follow, we must first examine how 1 John has been used in peacemaking theological and NT ethical studies, and the extent to which such uses may have passed over the difficulty of applying a hermeneutic of non-violence to a text replete with hostility, stemming from theological conflict. The purpose of this chapter is to identify some peacemaking hermeneutical approaches to 1 John. The question asked by it is whether 1 John supports or opposes such approaches.

Perhaps the most notable example of use of 1 John to support a theology of non-violence or peacemaking is René Girard's work, which will be examined first. After that, the work of some Girardian interpreters, including James Alison, Raymund Schwager and Willard Swartley,[10] using 1 John will be examined. Then this introduction will engage with non-violent interpretations of 1 John by other theologians, biblical scholars and Christian ethicists, including John Howard Yoder, Richard Burridge, Richard Hays and others. It will also examine J Denny Weaver's work on a non-violent, "narrative Christus Victor" atonement model, which builds on Girardian insights. It has also seemed appropriate to include in this chapter some brief analysis of the use of the thought of 1 John by two other theologians, Hans Urs von Balthasar and George Hunsinger, who have been critical of Girard, but whose work has to some extent arrived at a similar result – a peacemaking theology of non-violence – by a different route. What follows is a selective but representative sample of the work of some peacemaking theologians, NT ethicists and biblical scholars insofar as it relates to 1 John and of others who are relevant but who do not traditionally sit within the peacemaking tradition. Because of the focus of this study, it does not undertake an evaluation of their work as a whole.

---

[10] "Girardian interpreter" is a convenient but somewhat inadequate label for Swartley, as his work ranges well beyond Girardian interpretation, especially when dealing with the work of John Howard Yoder.

René Girard

René Girard, literary critic, anthropological philosopher and Christian convert, believes that humans desire, and mimic each other's longing for, a particular object. There is no sacred reality, no religion, no language before sacrifice. A "founding murder" (e.g. that of Abel by Cain) by one person of another who desires the same object gives birth to the sacred. The awe the victim provides in this crisis provokes worship. The original violent sacrifice gives birth to the development of culture – of myth and ritual, law and taboo. Propitiatory sacrifice is a device sanctified by religious practice to defuse violence otherwise arising between humans competing for the same object. A sacrificial victim or *scapegoat* is offered to a deity, to propitiate its anger, so the deity will smile on them and restore their fortunes. To Girard, the story in Genesis 27 of Jacob's theft of Esau's birthright shows *sacrificial substitution*.[11] A people thinks "the surrogate victim alone can save them; almighty violence may judge the 'guilty' parties to have been sufficiently 'punished'".[12]

Girard uses OT stories, including the Genesis account of Abel's murder by Cain[13] – referred to in 1 John 3:12-15 – to illustrate his proposal that violence arises from mutual envy by humans, in which both desire the same object, and one must destroy the other to secure it.[14] This desire, according to Girard, "does not arise because of the fortuitous convergence of two desires on a single object; rather, *the subject desires the object because the rival desires it*".[15] This is Girard's concept of "mimetic desire", from the Greek verb μιμέομαι, "to imitate".

To Girard, the origins of violence between humans lie in *mimetic desire*, competition for the same object by imitation of one another's deep wishes. People are brought to desire the same object, and into conflict when they both cannot attain it, because "in desiring an object the rival alerts the subject to the desirability of the object".[16] Using his concept of *mimetic doubling*, through OT stories and Graeco-Roman mythology – including the story of Cain and Abel[17] – Girard holds that an eternal, triangular struggle occurs in which both desire an object they cannot share, which can only end in the death of one or the other.[18] In fact the story of Cain and Abel is central to Girard's thought, because upon Cain's murder of Abel, and Cain's subsequent protection by God, who placed the "mark of Cain" on him to prevent others from killing him in turn (Genesis 4:15), there was founded a town, built by Cain and named after Enoch, his son. Thus, says Girard, was a civilisation, a culture, built on the founding murder of

---

[11] René Girard, *Violence and the Sacred* (trans. Patrick Gregory; New York and London: Johns Hopkins University Press, paperback edition 1979), 5.
[12] *Ibid*, 259.
[13] *Ibid*, 4.
[14] René Girard, *The Girard Reader* (ed. James G Williams; New York: Crossroad, 1996), 9.
[15] Girard, *Violence and the Sacred*, 145.
[16] *Ibid*, 145.
[17] *Ibid*, 61.
[18] *Ibid*, 62–3.

Abel by Cain.[19] However, one must remark in passing, for Israel the mark of Cain is ambiguous, because the Israelite genealogy in Genesis 5 is founded not on Cain, but on Seth, Adam's younger son, born "after he knew his wife again", who in turn had a son, also named Enoch (Genesis 4:25-26).

The resulting disorder, caused by rivalry between mimetic doubles, then threatens the society in which it occurs. That society's answer is that "the old pattern of each against one gives way to the united antagonism of all against one".[20] This is Girard's concept of *scapegoating* – one person or people is made responsible by a society for all the evils which beset it, so that person or people becomes a *surrogate victim*.

Because this pattern entrenches violence in a community, it is then transmuted and re-enacted in religious sacrifices, in which a victim, originally an animal, is sacrificed, and in which the object of the rite "assumes, not some vague and ill-defined sins, but the very real (though often hidden) hostilities that *all the members of the community feel for one another*".[21] The object of the ritual becomes a *substitute* for the surrogate victim. Girard explains:

> All sacrificial rites are based on two substitutions. The first is provided by generative violence, which substitutes a single victim for all the members of the community. The second, the only strictly ritualistic substitution, is that of a victim for the surrogate victim.[22]

Deutero-Isaiah predicts the "innocent servant", one whose death initially renders him "similar to a certain type of sacrificial victim within the pagan world".[23] The servant would have "no connection with violence and no affinity with it", the one of whom Isaiah said, "We accounted him stricken, struck down by God, and afflicted" (Isaiah 53:4), which signifies that "it was not God who smote him; God's responsibility is implicitly denied".[24] Crucially, Matthew places Psalm 78 in Jesus' mouth, where he predicts that he will "utter what has been hidden from the foundation of the world" (Matthew 13:35),[25] reading καταβολῆς there as signifying the foundation of the world.[26]

Girard sees Jesus' tomb as a *metaphor* for the "mythic process of conjuring away man's violence by endlessly projecting it upon new victims": murder "calls for the tomb", which "is built around the dead body it conceals", so that the tomb is "the prolongation and perpetuation of murder" (citing Luke 11:47-48).[27] For Girard, the meaning of Jesus' passion is not that "the victim should inherit all of the violence

---

[19] René Girard, *Things Hidden since the Foundation of the World* (trans. Stephen Bann and Michael Metteer; Stanford, California: Stanford University Press, 1987), 144–6.
[20] *Ibid*, 78.
[21] *Ibid*, 99. Italics in original.
[22] *Ibid*, 269.
[23] Girard, *The Girard Reader*, 156.
[24] *Ibid*, 157.
[25] Providing Girard with the title of his book *Things Hidden since the Foundation of the World*!
[26] Girard, *The Girard Reader*, 159.
[27] "Woe to you! For you build the tombs of the prophets whom your ancestors killed. So you are witnesses and approve the deeds of your ancestors; for they killed them, and you build their tombs."

from which the victim has been exonerated", but that the text "lets the violence fall upon the heads of those to whom it belongs", so that the "founding murder" (i.e. of the innocent Abel) is repeated.[28] Girard writes that "there is nothing in the Gospels to suggest that the death of Jesus is a sacrifice, whatever definition (expiation, substitution, etc.) we may give for that sacrifice".[29]

Girard identifies 1 John as a "genuine epistemology of love", citing 1 John 2:10-11. The love of which John[30] speaks here "reveals the victimage processes that underlie the meanings of culture"; it is "no purely 'intellectual' process", because "the very detachment of the person who contemplates the warring brothers is an illusion".[31] So "love is the only true revelatory power because it escapes from, and strictly limits, the spirit of revenge and recrimination",[32] and "only Christ's perfect love can achieve without violence the perfect revelation to which we have been progressing – in spite of everything – by the dissensions and divisions that were predicted in the gospels".[33] Thus, 1 John 3:15, "all who hate a brother or sister are murderers", shows that "every negation of the other leads … towards expulsion and murder".[34]

Girard's linkage of 1 John's contrast between love and hatred towards a brother (2:10-11), and John's use of the Cain and Abel analogy to demonstrate the end result of hatred (3:12), with the "founding murder" of Abel by Cain, on which an unredeemed, warring civilisation has been built, and to which the love command is the antidote, is central to his thinking. It is an insight of pure genius. Only a truly original thinker could paint on so large a canvas a picture of an OT culture built on rivalry, hatred and murder, redeemed by God's love in Jesus, redeeming and saving us from our own mutual envy, hatred and warfare. But such a proposal may be problematical in view of the "rivalrous" relationship it sets up between the OT and NT, and in the standpoint Girard adopts as to Jesus' historical role, not least in view of Matthew, that most Jewish of gospels, where at 5:17 Jesus proclaims that he has come, not to abolish but to fulfil *Torah*, the law. It must also be said that Girard engages not so much with the hostility evident in 1 John towards its opponents, but with the antidote, the "new commandment" the author gives to his community, to protect itself against the defective Christology and ethical indifference of the secessionists: that as in Jesus the love of God has reached full perfection (1 John 2:5), they must love their brothers and sisters and live in the light (1 John 2:10).

Certainly Girard recognises that hatred, love's opposite, leads to violence and murder (1 John 3:14-15). And he sees that Jesus is the "model of holiness" whom we must imitate, but whose "denunciation of sacrificial mechanisms constantly exacerbates

---

[28] Girard, *The Girard Reader*, 168.
[29] Girard, *Things Hidden*, 180; similarly René Girard, *The Scapegoat* (trans. Y Freccero; Baltimore: Johns Hopkins University Press, 1986), 199–200.
[30] In what follows, the author of 1 John will on occasions be referred to as John, for convenience. No assumption as to his identity is implied, as the authorship of 1 John, and of common authorship with John's Gospel, is outside the scope of this study.
[31] Girard, *Things Hidden*, 277.
[32] *Ibid.*
[33] *Ibid.*
[34] *Ibid*, 214.

violence by those outraged by it".³⁵ Girard sees that John's Gospel condemns imitation of the devil in his desires and that those who acknowledge God's fatherhood will love Jesus himself (John 8:42-44).³⁶ This is a linkage almost identical to that in 1 John 2:15.

As one might expect – writing as an anthropological philosopher – Girard does not, in his citations of 1 John, exegete its polemical tone towards opponents, and the theological "warfare" this implies. His use of 1 John unfolds an alternative universe in which mimesis of Jesus' love might abolish rivalry and death-bringing hatred. A criticism is that this may unintentionally divert attention from the very real hostility 1 John displays towards its secessionist opponents, and indeed on occasions towards "the world" (ὁ κόσμος) in general (cf. 1 John 2:15-17; 3:13; 4:9), and from the possible negative implications of this outward-directed hostility for the practice of love outside John's community, rather than inside.

To be fair, Girard has engaged more directly with hostility to opponents evident in 1 John where he uses the term "antichrist" to denote "the ideology that attempts to outchristianize Christianity, that imitates Christianity in a spirit of rivalry", referring here to what he terms the "totalitarianisms of the right", which find Christianity "too soft on victims", and those of the left, which attempt to "outflank" it, both of which he sees as "ultrachristian" caricatures,³⁷ noting the use of "antichrist" in 1 John 2:18-19 and 2 John 7.³⁸ This may be a rather strained linkage. Furthermore, as 1 John 2:18-19 warns the faithful remainder in the Johannine community against "antichrists" among the secessionists from the author's community who may deceive them, Girard refers to the danger that totalitarian ideologies may occasionally mask themselves in the language of Christian apologetics. Thus Christian believers might think such ideologies are "from God", that is fulfilling the divine purpose, when they are really not so (cf. 1 John 4:3). In that way, one must concede, Girard implicitly acknowledges that 1 John, too, was written in a time of ideological crisis, with deceptive opponents at the door, although he does not address the *manner* in which this crisis is met.

Girard's view of murder as the end result of hatred, bolstered by his reference to 1 John, is better understood in light of his explanation of John 8:42-44. There, in the context of a discourse with "the Jews who had believed in him" (8:31), but who questioned his teaching and protested their sonship from Abraham (8:39), Jesus accuses them of being descended from Satan, who "was a murderer from the beginning" and "a liar and the father of lies" (8:44), to Girard, these Jews took the devil as the model for their desires, rather than God: God and the devil are two "arch-models". Thus, if people do not imitate Christ in their desires, but rather Satan, they "become the playthings of mimetic violence".³⁹ We see a linkage in Girard's thought between mimetic desire

---

[35] Réne Girard, *Battling to the End: Conversations with Benoît Chantre* (trans. Mary Baker; East Lancing: Michigan State University Press, 2010), 105.
[36] Réne Girard, *I See Satan Fall like Lightning* (trans. James G Williams; Maryknoll, New York: Orbis Books, 2009), 39.
[37] René Girard with Pierpaolo Antonello and João de Castro Rocha, *Evolution and Conversion: Dialogues on the Origin of Culture* (London: T&T Clark, 2007), 236.
[38] *Ibid*, 263, n.6.
[39] Girard, *I Saw Satan*, 39–40.

directed towards Satan and both violence and murder. To Girard, mimesis of Cain has the same end result, as 1 John 3:13-15 shows. In 1 John 3:8-10, in the preceding pericope, the children of God and those of the devil are also brought into opposition in typically Johannine dualistic terms.

Nevertheless the question must still be asked: Is 1 John an appropriate vehicle to convey and support Girard's overarching message of liberation from rivalry, hatred and murder, if it was in fact written against theological rivals towards whom the author obviously feels great hostility? The antidote offered by the author of 1 John is a Christology and soteriology which gives proper weight to Jesus' humanity and identification with, and love for, us and a consequent command that we love one another as he has loved us. May this be extended hermeneutically – if not exegetically – to embrace all humanity? If so, Girard's use of 1 John is supportable, even taking into account its author's hostility towards opponents. In particular, Girard's interpretation of 1 John 3:12 may be supported if in v.12c the text, ὅτι τὰ ἔργα αὐτοῦ πονηρὰ ἦν, τὰ δὲ τοῦ ἀδελφοῦ αὐτοῦ δίκαια, "because his own deeds were evil but those of his brother were righteous",[40] connotes brotherly rivalry. Some answers to these questions will be offered, after an exegesis of 1 John's use of a number of keywords, in this case ἀγαπάω ἀδελφός and their derivatives.

Girard's system is attractive. One does not have to be convinced that it is a universal answer to human violence to see that it is one of the major contributions in the last century to the theological debate concerning the meaning of the death of Jesus and its implications for Christian ethics. Many of Girard's critics have concentrated on what they see as the deficiencies of Girard's atonement theology. Having concluded that his atonement ideas are deficient, they then suggest that the ethical implications said by Girard to flow from the unmasking of human mimetic violence in the death of Jesus, centring on deliverance from envy and hostility between humans, cannot be validly inferred from the religious mechanism Girard identifies and Jesus' final exposure of it. Does this follow? It is legitimate to ask whether deficiencies in Girard's atonement theology necessarily mean that his whole system collapses.

Crucial to Girard's argument is his identification of Cain's murder of his brother Abel as the "founding murder" upon which all sacrificial violence and therefore all "religion" as the very basis of civilisation have been built. As we shall see, that event forms a central plank in the argument of the author of 1 John. Furthermore, the meaning of the atonement is directly addressed in 1 John, as is the connection between Jesus' death and John's love command, in terms of love as being constitutive of the very nature of God. Clearly 1 John is crucial to Girard's argument, and close exegesis of some key terms in the epistle may provide support for it.

---

[40] Here and elsewhere, the translation of the OT and NT is the author's own – though on occasions it mirrors that of the *NRSV* where it cannot be bettered! The non-gender-specific translations of the *NRSV* have been avoided for accuracy, not from any opposition to its laudable aim of showing that all are "one in Christ": Galatians 3:28.

James Alison

James Alison, a theologian and one of Girard's foremost interpreters, sees the apostolic witness as casting unredeemed human desire as a *skandalon*, a stumbling block, "by which we receive death from each other and mete out death to each other by our involvement in mutual victimisation".[41] So, therefore, in 1 John 2-3 love is defined as "a reciprocal relationship between brothers" and the stumbling block as "the relationship of hatred between brothers" (2:7-11), which is then shown in the hatred of Cain leading to murder (3:11-15). So "this is the real content of the sin of the devil from the beginning: hatred between brothers leading to murder", from which *scandalon* Jesus has come to set us free.[42] Thus, as does Girard, Alison picks up the connection between Satan, the murderer from the beginning, and hatred between brothers and its end result, illustrated in 1 John by the Cain and Abel example. Elsewhere Alison portrays a fearful Cain wandering the earth (Genesis 4:18) "only half-protected" by the law God gave (Genesis 4:19) to "contain the violence of reciprocal vengeance".[43] In this way Alison seeks to demonstrate the self-perpetuating nature of violence, and of the fears it generates, with these fears themselves then leading to further violence.

Alison argues that there is a crucial difference between this "foundational mentality" which is at its root an "envious culpabilisation of some other" and the new one in 1 John 3:2, "we are all God's children now; it does not yet appear what we shall be, but we know that when he appears we shall be like him, for we shall see him as he is".[44] To Alison, the self-giving nature of God is shown in 1 John 4:7-11, in that God's love was made manifest in sending God's son into the world as the expiation for our sins.[45] Thus Alison found his use of 1 John on its intimate connection between ethics on the one hand and Christology and soteriology on the other: "As God has loved us so much, so we must love one another."[46]

Alison writes as a theologian, but the biblical scholar needs to ask how the God who has wrought this potential fundamental reorientation of human desire and destiny is portrayed in relation to the hostile rhetoric against opponents in 1 John. Is God's wrath called down upon the opponents? Or is the Christology and soteriology of 1 John a clue that God as portrayed in 1 John loves the whole world in Jesus and extends his salvation to all? May the love command the author pronounces therefore extend hermeneutically to all humanity, even given his attitude to his opponents? If Jesus died for the sins περὶ ὅλου τοῦ κόσμου, "of the whole world" (1 John 2:2b), does this ultimately govern the scope of the author's love command? If so, Alison's use of 1 John may be both legitimate and persuasive. If not, any support for his peacemaking

---

[41] James Alison, *The Joy of Being Wrong: Original Sin through Easter Eyes* (New York: Crossroad, 1998), 146.
[42] *Ibid.*
[43] James Alison, *Raising Abel: The Recovery of the Eschatological Imagination* (New York: Crossroad, 1996), 132.
[44] *Ibid*, 170.
[45] James Alison, *Knowing Jesus* (Springfield, Illinois: Templegate Publishers/London: SPCK, 1993), 50.
[46] 1 John 4:11.

theology from 1 John falls away. An answer to this question is offered later in this study after exegesis of 1 John's use of ἱλασμός in 1 John 2:2 and 4:10.

Alison is one of many theologians whose use of 1 John is, by the very nature of his discipline, hermeneutical rather than exegetical. That is to be expected. As with Girard, his vision of human brotherhood and sisterhood, united with Jesus and with each other through the love of God as constitutive of God's own nature, seems to fall naturally from the pages of 1 John. But does it? The situation of the epistle is one in which hostility and seductive argument from John's secessionist opponents, who were originally part of his community but who are now outside it, create the need for internal solidarity within the remaining community. Intuitively, one might expect that any explanation of Jesus' death written for this purpose might encourage the belief that it was of benefit to those inside the community, to the exclusion of those outsiders who opposed it. One might expect that any command to love one another might be restricted to that community, with hostility and resistance being directed to those outside it. As we shall see from our exegesis of this love command later, much ink has been spilled on these questions. Until we answer them, we may not hazard whether 1 John truly supports the sort of ideas Alison's theology presents.

Raymund Schwager

With Girard himself, Raymund Schwager, another eminent Girardian interpreter and theologian, finds a connection between John 8:44, where Jesus condemns Satan as a "murderer from the beginning" and "the father of lies", and 1 John 3:11-12. To Schwager, John 8:44 shows that "perpetrators of violence always try to hide the truth of their actions from others as well as from themselves".[47] Elsewhere Schwager points out that John 8:44 is not in itself anti-Semitic, since it is addressed to "the Jews that had believed in him", but is "nevertheless directed in the first place inward",[48] which is an important insight, for otherwise John could be seen as advocating violence towards the Jews – a common modern perversion of this verse. So to Schwager, it would be "astonishing" if John's Gospel did not refer to "the same murderous spirit" when speaking of the hatred of the world; 1 John also shows "an explicit relationship between hatred and murder", which are "identical".[49]

Thus, Schwager writes that the Cain allusion in 1 John 3:11-12 teaches that hatred is the opposite of love; fratricide is directly opposed to it. And, he points out, 1 John 3:15 shows that hatred and murder are indeed ultimately identical. Hatred is never "a purely psychical affair", and the statement in 1 John 3:14 that everyone who does not love remains in death is "much more than a noncommittal, rhetorical image".[50]

---

[47] Raymund Schwager, *Must There Be Scapegoats? Violence and Redemption in the Bible* (trans. Maria L Assad; New York: Gracewing, 1987), 159.
[48] Raymund Schwager, *Jesus in the Drama of Salvation: Towards a Biblical Doctrine of Redemption* (trans. James G Williams and Paul Haddon; New York: Crossroad, 1999), 148.
[49] Schwager, *Must There Be Scapegoats*, 162.
[50] *Ibid.*

As does Alison, Schwager rightly sees in 1 John the very kernel of Jesus' teaching about violence and its antidote, love, in imitation of the godhead in giving God's Son to save us. However, Schwager's use of the epistle, to derive from it a universal ethic of love and non-violence, still may be seen to conflict with the letter writer's aim to confute and isolate theological opponents who had once been part of his community.

If, as suggested by Schwager, 1 John's Christology and ethics can be seen, hermeneutically if not exegetically, as aimed at all humanity, rather than the author's own remaining community, Schwager's project may possibly receive the support he seeks from the letter. Again we note that 1 John 2:2c affirms that Jesus died for the sins περὶ ὅλου τοῦ κόσμου. Again, exegesis of 1 John's use of ἱλασμός in 1 John 2:2 and 4:10 will help to answer these questions.

Schwager's observation that 1 John 3:14 contains more than a rhetorical image, where it affirms that everyone who does not love remains in death, is extremely significant. It connects Christian ethics with eschatology, in that it concerns the divine future of those who love and those who do not. One may see in Schwager's insight an implicitly Trinitarian idea, in that it suggests a connection between God's love in and towards Jesus and the mimetic conduct of the true disciple, and the consequences of failure to conduct oneself in this way. Looking at the emergence of these ideas in 1 John through exegesis of some central ideas connoted by certain keywords may illuminate and provide some support for the ideas Schwager presents.

Willard Swartley

Willard Swartley, New Testament scholar and Girardian interpreter, brings biblical scholarship to bear on the work of Girard and others in writing peacemaking theology. He writes specifically of the conflictual ethos in the Johannine corpus, including 1 John, and derives from it a vision of an alternative community as a foundation for peace.[51] Unsurprisingly, his use of 1 John is extensive.

Swartley in his work *Covenant of Peace* characterises love as the mark of the Johannine community, referring inter alia to 1 John 4:21 and writing:

> In John's narrative world and community, love for one another makes peace in the community first of all. That peace includes the shalom of the neighbour in need, as extended homilies in 1 John make clear (3:14-18; 4:19-21). This love for the neighbour extends to its ultimate expression, laying down one's life for the brother or sister (1 John 3:16; 4:11 in the context of Jesus giving his life as an atoning sacrifice and the model of the good shepherd in John 10:11-18; cf. 15:13).[52]

But who is the neighbour to whom the peace extends? Swartley does not shrink from that difficult question, acknowledging that these "homilies" enjoin love within

---

[51] See the title to chapter 10, Willard M Swartley, *Covenant of Peace: The Missing Peace in New Testament Theology and Ethics* (Grand Rapids, Michigan: Eerdmans, 2006), 276.
[52] *Ibid*, 296.

the community and asking whether they "serve a positive or negative function in relation to the world, specifically those beyond the borders of the community".[53]

Swartley's answer is to employ John's Gospel in a hermeneutical, rather than strictly exegetical explanation of the scope of the love commandment in 1 John. For example, he places alongside one another John 3:16 and 6:51 and 1 John 4:7-11, 16, 19 as demonstrating how the model of shared love between Father and Son is a gift to the community, so that "to answer the question whether love for one another extends to those outside the community, the model of God's love for the world set forth in the gift of the Son says yes".[54]

Whether such a hermeneutical move is supportable in light of the theology of 1 John will be examined in detail in this study, by examining the picture of atonement and ethics presented in 1 John by a study of some keywords presenting central theological concepts in the letter, in particular ἱλασμός and ἀδελφός.

Swartley says Girardian imitation, "good mimesis" of Jesus' own behaviour as enjoined by 1 John, endorses John Howard Yoder's work in identifying "texts that speak of believers sharing the divine nature" in "light and purity", referring to 1 John 1:5-7, 3:1-3 and 4:17.[55] He also notes Yoder's citing of 1 John 1:6 as showing that the disciple participates in the life of Jesus,[56] exampling Yoder's citation, inter alia, of 1 John 3:11-16 as portraying the disciple "loving as Christ loved, by giving himself".[57] Swartley then brings together his understanding of "good mimesis" in imitation of Christ with Girardian theory:

> My contribution, which examines the NT teaching on "imitation of Christ" as well as Jesus' teachings on discipleship, shows clearly that Jesus in his revelation of God presents a model of desire and imitation that does not lead to rivalry and violence.[58]

But how can this model sit alongside the hostility to theological opponents that leaps from the pages of 1 John? Is there rivalry and violence in John's treatment of his opposition? These questions are raised regretfully, given the appeal of Swartley's vision of "good mimesis" as our deliverance from mimetic violence. But they can only be answered by a detailed study of 1 John's picture of the atonement and of the love command as the antidote to hatred in his community – and possibly outside it.

These same questions are prompted by Swartley's fruitful use of 1 John in his earlier essay "Discipleship and Imitation of Jesus/Suffering Servant", placing at the beginning of his essay Girard's use of 1 John 2:6 to illustrate "good mimesis".[59] Swartley's thesis

---

[53] Ibid, 296–7.
[54] Ibid, 297.
[55] Ibid, 371.
[56] Ibid, 371–2.
[57] Ibid, 372.
[58] Ibid, 381.
[59] Willard M Swartley, "Discipleship and Imitation of Christ/Suffering Servant: The Mimesis of New Creation" in *Violence Renounced: René Girard, Biblical Studies and Peacemaking* (ed. Willard M Swartley; Telford, Pennsylvania: Pandora Press U.S., 2000), 218–45, 218.

is that Luther's negative reaction to *imitatio Christi* as undermining justification by faith through a "works theology" is unjustified, because, by atonement theology that separates Jesus' death as "so unique to the salvific purpose", it "disconnects discipleship from salvation".[60] Was this link ever broken in the atonement theology of 1 John? Does it not intimately connect Jesus as atoning sacrifice for us (1 John 2:2, 4:10) with the command to love one's brother, which marks that we are in the light (1 John 2:10) and born of God and knowing God (1 John 4:7)? These questions will receive attention later in this study.

Swartley's vision of universal brotherhood and non-violence in 1 John is attractive. Its use of 1 John, supporting an ethic of love for one's neighbour, not traditionally associated with the Johannine corpus, as opposed to the synoptic Gospels, especially Matthew and Luke, is worth exegetical exploration against our key ideas in 1 John.

William Klassen

William Klassen uses a detailed critique of Bultmann's view that the love command in 1 John is universal and includes love of neighbour and of enemy, to show that a scholarly consensus rejects this view, but the evidence supports it.[61] Klassen, also a biblical scholar, argues that while the commandment to love the enemy is not found in 1 John, the injunction against hating the brother is strong, finding in its reference to Cain (1 John 3:12) a joinder of hatred and manslaughter, which he connects to Matthew 5:22, where Jesus himself consigns to Gehenna anyone who calls his brother a fool.[62] Is this linkage of 1 John's prohibition on hatred for the brother with Matthew's gospel, where there is an undoubtedly universal command to love the enemy (Matthew 5:43-48), permissible? The answer may lie in the scope of 1 John's love command. If it is universal, it then becomes legitimate to argue that there is in 1 John a correlative prohibition of hatred which is also universal in its scope.

Klassen finds in 1 John 3:16 a direct relationship between Jesus' laying down of his life and "the believer's response to the brother or sister in material need"; he notes that 1 John 3:16 affirms that those who do not love their brother[63] are not from God, interpreting this as meaning that "love and doing justice reveals whether we have our origin in God or in the devil".[64] Granted, 1 John 3:17 may support emphasis on "doing justice", which may imply a universal command. But is the "brother" the neighbour in general or one's fellow in a Christian community? Exegesis of 1 John's use of ἀδελφός will help to answer this.

---

[60] *Ibid*, 219.
[61] William Klassen, "'Love Your Enemies': Some Reflections on the Current Status of Research" in *The Love of Enemy and Nonretaliation in the New Testament* (ed. Willard M Swartley; Louisville, Kentucky: Westminster/John Knox Press, 1992), 1–31, 14.
[62] *Ibid*, 15.
[63] Klassen uses "brother" in a generic, non-gendered sense, to include "sister". This study adopts the same usage, where "brother" is required for textual accuracy.
[64] *Ibid*, 15–16.

Klassen argues that in 1 John 4:7-21 we find an affirmation of God's very nature as ἀγάπη – the Spirit, he argues, is our guarantee of this (4:13) and that we have seen and testify that God has sent his Son as saviour (4:14).[65] So love marks God's nature and the unchanging way God deals with the community and the whole world (5:2).[66] Klassen therefore argues that "John's agenda is to restore love as the central reality of his community" and that those who have left (the secessionists) are not therefore condemned to damnation or told they cannot return; rather, John addresses the topic most pressing at the moment, while affirming that the *whole* world can be redeemed (2:2) and that God sent his Son into the world so we may live (4:9).[67]

This reasoning might be supported by 1 John 5:1-5, where we find in 5:4a ὅτι πᾶν τὸ γεγεννημένον ἐκ τοῦ θεοῦ νικᾷ τὸν κόσμον, "for that which is born of God conquers the world", and in 5:5, ὅτι Ἰησοῦς ἐστιν ὁ υἱὸς τοῦ θεοῦ, "that Jesus is the Son of God". What is the effect of ἡ πίστις ἡμῶν, "our faith", in 5:4b? It is that ὁ μένων ἐν τῇ ἀγάπῃ ἐν τῷ θεῷ μένει καὶ ὁ θεὸς ἐν αὐτῷ μένει, "those who abide in love abide in God, as God does in them" (4:16b). So, it may be argued, John may be read as affirming here that love conquers the world, in Jesus. How? By those who confess Jesus as Son of God abiding in love, that is, loving the "brother", whoever he or she be, inside or outside one's community. Again, whether this interpretation is defensible can be answered only by detailed exegesis of 1 John's use of ἀγάπη and ἀδελφός in their scriptural context, later in this study.

Klassen's connection through 1 John 3:16 between atonement theology and Christian ethics is an all-important insight. But may we find exegetical support in 1 John for Klassen's advocacy of universal love and non-violence towards humanity as a whole? On the face of it, the hostility to outsiders in the epistle might contraindicate this. A closer look at some of the keywords the author uses to express prominent ideas in his epistle will advance this inquiry.

Pheme Perkins

Pheme Perkins, another biblical scholar, notes that neither John's Gospel nor the Johannine epistles repeat Jesus' teaching on love of enemies and holds that the epistles portray plainly sectarian conflict in the communities claiming the Johannine heritage.[68] To Perkins, the author's dualistic language, defining the church over against "the world", ὁ κόσμος, as a place of hatred and death (1 John 3:14-15), is a clear indication that the love command extends only to fellow Christians within the church (1 John 2:9-11; 4:20-21), so the language of communal encouragement is the rhetoric

---

[65] *Ibid*, 16–17.
[66] *Ibid*, 17.
[67] *Ibid*, 17–18.
[68] Pheme Perkins, "Apocalyptic Sectarianism and Love Commands: The Johannine Epistles and Revelation", in *The Love of Enemy and Nonretaliation in the New Testament* (ed. Willard M Swartley; Louisville, Kentucky: Westminster/John Knox Press, 1992), 287–96, 290.

of apocalyptic condemnation with the secessionists' false teaching equated with false prophets leading people astray in the end time.[69]

Perkins replies to some scholars' attempt to ameliorate John's restricted love command by noting that 1 John nowhere counsels hatred of the secessionists; she argues that "hate language" refers to the community's experience of the world and to the Christian community member who does not love fellow Christians.[70] Perkins therefore argues that for the author, the secessionists' identification with the lawlessness of the last days (1 John 2:18, 22; 4:1-5) means they cannot be the object of love – and that therefore the author's focus is on love between believers, not love of outsiders.[71] Perkins states an acute problem for Christian ethicists and for any peacemaking theology founded on 1 John: how can a love command intended for the remaining Johannine "insiders" extend to all humanity? Perkins is firmly of the opinion that this conflict is insoluble – it is simply *there*. Can it be resolved?

Perkins' opposition to any universal love hermeneutic in 1 John, and to any universal ethic of non-violence in it, may usefully be brought into conversation with the views of those who advocate such an approach. Her closely argued theses need evaluation and testing against more optimistic views as to the scope of 1 John's love command.

Wayne Northey

Wayne Northey, another theologian and Girardian interpreter, thinks differently, sharing Girard's view that seeing Jesus' death as a blood sacrifice in our stead misreads the NT, finding support in 1 John 2:2, read in light of 1 John 2:3-11.[72] To Northey, Jesus' death is "effective in all humanity", harmonising love doing no harm to its neighbour as the fulfilment of the law (Romans 13:10) with 1 John's love command (1 John 4:20-21); these texts show that "the biblical test case for love of God is love of neighbour" and "failure to love the enemy is failure to love God".[73]

With Girard, Northey presents an inspiring picture of a God who does not demand retribution from humankind, sated by the death of God's own Son, but rather loves humankind and gives that Son as innocent victim to rid the world of hatred and violence. The obvious problem about such harmonising is that it fails to give due weight to the context of John's love command and evades the question of whether John directs it to – and within – the community to whom he writes or whether it is universal. Again, this underlines the need for close examination of 1 John's love command in its context to answer this question. This will occur later in this study.

---

[69] *Ibid*, 290-1.
[70] *Ibid*, 290.
[71] *Ibid*.
[72] Wayne Northey, "The Cross: God's Peace Work – Towards a Restorative Peacemaking Understanding of the Atonement" in *Stricken by God? Nonviolent Identification and the Victory of Christ* (ed. Brad Jersak and Michael Hardin; Grand Rapids: Eerdmans), 356-77, 372.
[73] *Ibid*, 373.

Kharalambous Anstall

Kharalambous Anstall, an Orthodox theologian, argues that the Orthodox tradition has never taught a juridical, price-paying model of the atonement. He condemns the use in the Latin tradition of the sign of the cross merely as a reminder of Jesus' suffering, to teach us of the ransom, the "blood money", paid for us by him.[74]

Anstall presents God as love through 1 John 4:8, 4:16, and 4:7; to be godlike we must love God, who is love, and also one another, because God in a *kenosis* has descended to our level and offered the Son for us to save us from our selfishness.[75] To Anstall it is "oxymoronic" and "shocking" to the Orthodox mind that such a God should be presented as "cruel, capricious, judgmental and vindictive".[76]

But is 1 John inherently vindictive towards the secessionist opponents against whom its author writes? Is his love command primarily intended to bolster his community against false teaching from without? Any hermeneutic of universal love and non-violence as godlike derived from 1 John must wrestle with these questions.

Glen Stassen, David Gunshee

Glen Stassen, a much-mourned Christian ethicist and peacemaking theologian, and David Gunshee, philosopher and Christian ethicist, use 1 John to argue from 1 John 4:7-11 that "the once-for-all drama of the cross has far deeper meaning than any one interpretation of the meaning of the atonement can exhaust", so that "there is spiritual and experiential meaning in all the classical interpretations of the atonement", including "the *Christus Victor*, satisfaction, penal substitution, moral, governmental and ransom theories".[77] But understanding *agapē* as delivering love "sets the cross in the context of the incarnation", in that in bringing love, God breaks down the barriers between us and God, and between each other, "establishing fellowship and presence with us on our side of the walls, since we cannot climb over them to God" (1 John 4:9-11), and "Jesus did not die merely for the sake of sacrifice, but to deliver us *into community* with himself."[78]

These are deep sayings indeed, but it may be argued that they do not engage sufficiently with the contradictory portrayals of the divine nature inherent in penal substitutionary atonement theory, as against others more centred on God's love in sending the Son as a demonstration of divine love for humankind, to cleanse it from

---

[74] Kharalambous Anstall, "Juridical Justification Theology and a Statement of the Orthodox Teaching" in *Stricken by God? Nonviolent Identification and the Victory of Christ* (ed. Brad Jersak and Michael Hardin; Grand Rapids: Eerdmans), 482–503, 496.
[75] *Ibid*, 497–8.
[76] *Ibid*, 498.
[77] Glen H Stassen and David P Gushee, *Kingdom Ethics: Following Jesus in Contemporary Context* (Downers Grove: IVP, 2003), 342.
[78] *Ibid*, 342–3.

sin and bring about reconciliation between humans and God and with one another. This study will seek to grapple with this difficult question.

Stassen and Gushee observe that followers of Jesus know the truth (1 John 2:21; 4:6), and the truth abides in them (1 John 1:2), in the context of an argument that God is reliable and trustworthy, that Jesus is the ultimate bearer and communicator of truth and that therefore failure to "live the truth" by people raises doubts about whether the truth exists in such persons (1 John 1:8; 2:4). The authors frankly face the fact that in a battle over contradictory truth claims, John was adamant that he and his community were "in the truth" and their adversaries were not. Nevertheless they argue that for today, the truth is not simply a matter of intellectual conviction, but something that dwells in one's inner being, and may be verified by deeds.[79] Therefore, they contend, "The inbreaking of the kingdom heightens the urgency of participation in God's redemptive will as taught by Jesus Christ."[80] Their larger argument is that truth-telling can involve resistance to political oppression, even to the point of death, without compromising the truth of the Gospel by participating in acts of deception to justify repression or war.[81]

True it is that Stassen and Gushee acknowledge the situation of theological conflict in which 1 John was written, but their use of it poses the difficult question, whether it is a suitable foundation for an ethic of non-violent truth-telling in opposition to repression and violence when 1 John's own polemic in condemning opponents is so vehement and, arguably, sectarian. This study will engage with this difficulty.

John Howard Yoder

John Howard Yoder, a pre-eminent recent Mennonite theologian, uses 1 John, among other biblical texts, in *The Politics of Jesus* to illustrate what he means by the strand of the apostolic ethical tradition which he terms "correspondence", whereby the believer's attitude corresponds to or reflects or partakes in the same nature as that of their Lord, by following after or learning from that person.[82]

Yoder cites, with other texts, 1 John 1:5-7 and 3:1-3 to support the notion that what is in the OT a universally presupposed concept, following God, becomes in the NT "a new reality with the Holy Spirit".[83] He puts aside notions of sinless perfection as Hellenistic and mediaeval importations into scripture, and both impossible and crushing, citing the simplicity of the gospel demand that because God does not discriminate in the object of God's love, neither should we.[84] To illustrate the inclusive nature of this demand, he cites 1 John 4:7-12.[85]

---

[79] *Ibid*, 378–9.
[80] *Ibid*, 279.
[81] *Ibid*, 380–8.
[82] John Howard Yoder, *The Politics of Jesus* (Grand Rapids: Eerdmans, 2nd ed., 1994), 113.
[83] *Ibid*, 114–15.
[84] *Ibid*, 116–17.
[85] *Ibid*, 117.

One might reflect here that as God's atonement for sin through Jesus is universal, περὶ ὅλου τοῦ κόσμου (1 John 2:2b), may one argue, building on Yoder, that the proper function of the word πᾶς in 1 John 4:7b is to signify that the part-verse embraces as ἐκ τοῦ θεοῦ γεγέννηται καὶ γινώσκει τὸν θεόν, "born of God and knowing God", *everyone* who is truly ὁ ἀγαπῶν, "the one who loves"? Surely to argue that it means the converse, that to love one must first be a child of God, stands the verse on its head! When we pass to a detailed exegesis of 1 John's use of ἀγαπάω and its derivatives, this possibility will be evaluated. It requires one to take into account the author's hostility to the opponents against whom he is writing. Does he condemn them for lack of love, a universal command, or does he seek to "arm" his community with love *only* for one another, as a defence against opponents?

Yoder speaks of "being in Christ as the definition of human experience", citing 1 John 2:6,[86] and of "loving Christ as Christ loved, giving himself", citing 1 John 3:11-16, comparing it to 4:7-10, to be discussed later.[87] He writes that it is a mistake to say that the key statement of the Christian ethic is the "golden rule" of doing unto others what you would have them do unto you, which Jesus defines as the cornerstone of the Law, not the sum of his own teaching; he says Jesus, by contrast, offers a "new commandment", citing John 13:34 and 1 John 2:18, meaning "do as I have done for you" or "do as God has done for you in sending his Son".[88]

Looking at 1 John 3:11-16, again building on Yoder, might one argue that because in 3:13 the author defines his community over against the world, and urges them μὴ θαυμάζετε, ἀδελφοί, εἰ μισεῖ ὑμᾶς ὁ κόσμος, "do not be surprised, brothers, if the world hates you", he does not counsel reciprocal hatred – quite the reverse? Does the author's love command (3:13) extend to ὁ κόσμος, for whom Jesus died (2:2)? Again, to answer this question properly, one must pay serious regard to John's condemnation of the opponents' theology: does this extend to the opponents themselves? Later we shall attempt to answer this question after examining 1 John's use of ἀγαπάω and its derivatives.

Yoder notes that 1 John 3:16, like Ephesians 5:1-2, commands that we give our lives for others, as Jesus did, combining this with the suggestion that Jesus requires suffering servanthood, not dominion, and argues that these imperatives are founded, not on Jesus' imminent self-sacrifice, but on his posture in his earthly life as a servant.[89] Yoder writes elsewhere, citing 1 John 4:17, that "'as he is, so are we in this world' cannot be said without including reference to the earthly life of Jesus".[90]

This argument seems somewhat problematic at first sight, when linked with 1 John 3:16, which relates to imitation of Jesus *after* – and indeed resulting from – his death, although to be fair, Yoder deploys other gospel citations to suggest that Jesus' servanthood acts as an example to the church after his death.[91] But may we say from 1

---

[86] *Ibid*.
[87] *Ibid*, 118.
[88] *Ibid*, 119.
[89] *Ibid*, 123.
[90] John H Yoder, *The War of the Lamb: The Ethics of Nonviolence and Peacemaking* (ed. Glen Stassen, Mark Theissen Nation and Matt Hamsher; Grand Rapids: Baker Publishing Group, 2009), 169.
[91] Yoder, *Politics of Jesus*, 124.

John 3:16b that ἡμεῖς ὀφείλομεν ὑπὲρ τῶν ἀδελφῶν τὰς ψυχὰς θεῖναι, "we should lay down our lives for our brother", so that in identifying with Jesus' non-resistance to his violent death, we may in defence of others offer only non-violent resistance?[92]

Is this compatible with the situation of conflict with the secessionists in which 1 John was written? Is active resistance to violence in defence of one's loved ones – or for that matter of one's country – permissible? Later in this study, after an exegesis of ἀγαπάω and ἀδελφός and their derivatives, and some hermeneutical reflection on 1 John alongside John's Gospel, some answers to these questions will be offered.

Gordon Kaufman

Gordon Kaufman, who would vie with Yoder for the title of "pre-eminent modern Mennonite theologian", and certainly a theologian of non-violence, has as his central thesis that "God", the symbol, to whom we attach anthropomorphic qualities such as "all-powerful", "sovereign" and "king of the universe", is to be contrasted with the reality of God, who is transcendent, infinite, eternal and all-powerful – insofar as we can describe God at all – and that these are descriptors which themselves emphasise that the reality of God is beyond our comprehension or understanding.[93]

Thus Kaufman cites 1 John 4:12, "no-one has ever seen God", as proof that even to the early Christians, God was not directly experienced by humanity: he cites 1 John 4:13 to show that we experience God as abiding in us when we love one another: hatred of the brother (1 John 4:20) is proof that God's spirit is absent from us.[94]

Kaufman also cites 1 John 4:7-8 and 12 to show that love, as a quality of life present within a Christian community, is itself identified as "the very presence of God".[95] So to Kaufmann, "it is finally possible to conceive of God as love (1 John 4:7-12) in a very radical sense", which is "non-resistance to all aggressive power", citing also Matthew 5:39-48.[96] This is a direct linkage between the Sermon on the Mount and 1 John's moral preaching, directed at "my little children", τεκνία μου, in 1 John 2:1.

Is this hermeneutical move defensible? Perhaps John's attitude to ὁ κόσμος may be seen to shift here – is it possible to see him as affirming the world as worthy of love, through Jesus as ἱλασμός (1 John 2:2, 4:10) for ὅλου τοῦ κόσμου (2:2)? Exegesis later in this study of ἱλασμός in 1 John may provide some answers.

---

[92] See John H Yoder, *Christian Attitudes to War, Peace and Revolution* (ed. Theodore J Koontz and Andy Alexis-Baker; Grand Rapids: Baker Publishing Group, 2009), chapter 23, "The Lessons of Non-Violent Experience", 353–68 for Yoder's reflections in conversation with other writers on this very stance.

[93] Gordon D Kaufman, *In Face of Mystery: A Constructive Theology* (Cambridge, Massachusetts: Harvard University Press, 1993), 4–7.

[94] *Ibid*, 333.

[95] *Ibid*, 406; see also Gordon Kaufman, *God, Mystery, Diversity: Christian Theology in a Pluralistic World* (Minneapolis: Fortress Press, 1996), 122; Gordon Kaufman, *In the Beginning ... Creativity* (Minneapolis: Fortress Press, 2004), 104.

[96] Kaufman, *God, Mystery, Diversity*, 150.

Stanley Hauerwas

Stanley Hauerwas in his work in the theology of non-violence cites 1 John 4:13-21 to illustrate his thesis that "because we Christians worship a resurrected Lord, we can take the risk of love".[97] So, he argues, we are a forgiven people, who "have learned not to fear one another", because "love is the non-violent apprehension of the other as other", as opposed to seeing others as frightening, challenging our way of being.[98]

This has some Girardian echoes, although Hauerwas is no Girardian! Fear of the other leads to rivalry, and rivalry to conflict. How does the author's teaching that ἡ τελεία ἀγάπη ἔξω βάλλει τὸν φόβον, "perfect love casts out fear", in 1 John 4:18a stands alongside his evident hostility to the secessionists who "went out from us" (1 John 2:18)? Does John hate or fear the secessionists? Exegesis of ἀγάπη as used in 1 John, especially at 4:18-19, may answer this question. Hauerwas is a very fine writer, and his theology is deep indeed, but the difficult question of 1 John's hostility to the secessionists, which reflects the situation in which it was written, means that one must ask if the texts Hauerwas uses really support his argument.

Darrin W Snyder Belousek

Darrin W Snyder Belousek sets out to demolish a penal substitutionary model of the atonement and draws out the implications of a sacrificial and cleansing model (which is adopted in this study) for peacemaking theology, and for a model of restorative, rather than retributive justice.[99]

His uses of 1 John are many and there is space here only for some. For example, he asserts that in 1 John 2:2, the use of the term ἱλασμός is connected to the statement that Jesus' blood cleanses us from sin (1:7), and its use here parallels that in Ezekiel 44:27 where it is used to connote purification from sin, not divine propitiation.[100] We shall see later that there are other OT uses of this term with similar meanings.

Belousek refers again to the use of ἱλασμός in 1 John 2:2, and in 4:10, comparing it to the use of ἱλασμός cognates in Hebrews 2:17 and Romans 3:25 and contending that in each case, Jesus' life and death effect e*xpiation* rather than propitiation of human sin. He says the statement in 1 John 2:2 that Jesus is the ἱλασμός, "atoning sacrifice" for the sins περὶ ὅλου τοῦ κόσμου, "of the whole world" refutes a Calvinist atonement, which only effects forgiveness of the sins of the "elect".[101]

Belousek notes that the divine motivation for redemption of the world is solely *love*, comparing John 3:16 and 1 John 4:9 with Romans 5:8, suggesting that Jesus' death for

---

[97] Stanley Hauerwas, *The Peaceable Kingdom: A Primer in Christian Ethics* (London: SCM Press, 1983), 90–1.
[98] Ibid, 91.
[99] Darrin W Snyder Belousek, *Atonement, Justice and Peace: The Message of the Cross and the Mission of the Church* (Grand Rapids/Cambridge, UK: Eerdmans, 2012), 3–8.
[100] Ibid, 248.
[101] Ibid, 333, 500–1.

us was not to fulfil some legal requirement, because God's wrath demands propitiation, but a revelation of divine love for creation and for God's creatures.[102]

Belousek's project is not dissimilar to our own. The additional contribution it seeks to make is to draw out further the OT background against which 1 John was written, suggesting that not only ἱλασμός but other Greek keywords in the LXX supply clues that a peacemaking hermeneutic is integral to a proper reading of 1 John.

Richard Hays

Richard Hays, a NT ethicist, seeing John's Gospel and 1 John as "a common stream of tradition", even if not written by the same person, maintains that in both, the love command is applied only within the Johannine community, noting that this has led some scholars to label the Johannine tradition morally deficient in this respect.[103] He asks whether this is fair, and whether in Johannine studies, ethics have been "crowded out" by Christology.[104]

Hays notes elements of the portrait of Jesus in John's Gospel in his supernatural knowledge of people's hearts (John 2:23-25), his lack of hunger for material food (John 4:31-34), his mysterious disappearance from hostile crowds (John 7:30, 8:59), his employment of Lazarus' death as a "useful teaching aid" for his disciples (John 11:14-15), his miracles as "signs" triggering long meditative interpretations (e.g. the "bread of life" discourse in John 6), and his many Christological discourses proclaiming his identity and oneness with God.[105]

But, Hays argues, the author of 1 John stigmatises "docetic schismatics" who "took their cues" from these elements in John's Gospel as denying that Jesus Christ has come in the flesh (1 John 4:2-3), noting that John therefore claims to have touched the Word of Life "with our hands" (1 John 1:1) and that indeed in John's Gospel there are anti-docetic elements: Jesus thirsts and asks a Samaritan woman for drink (John 4:7), weeps at Lazarus' grave (John 11:35), washes the feet of the disciples (John 13:3-5) and is "the word made flesh" (John 1:14).[106] Thus to Hays, the Johannine tradition claims for Jesus many Christological titles and supernatural roles, yet proclaims him as a historical person who lived an earthly life and whose flesh could be handled and wounded.[107] Rightly, Hays does not set John's Gospel and 1 John over against each other as conveying opposing views of Jesus' nature.

Against this background, Hays refers to the "new commandment" in John 13:34 and then yokes it to 1 John 3:11 and 3:16-18, noting that this identifies such love as a matter of action, not of mere warm feelings.[108] To Hays, this admonition to love within

---

[102] *Ibid*, 609.
[103] Hays, *The Moral Vision of the New Testament*, 139.
[104] *Ibid*, 140.
[105] *Ibid*, 141.
[106] *Ibid*.
[107] *Ibid*, 141–2.
[108] *Ibid*, 145.

the community is not trivial and is a good place to start discussing Christian ethics.[109] Thus the historical setting of this commandment is that within a closely knit group of Jewish Christians, tensions over the continued observance of Jewish festivals emerged, leading to expulsion from the synagogue (John 9:22; 12:42; 16:20), so the Johannine community was led to define itself against the synagogue and "the world", expecting its hatred (1 John 3:13-14; 5:19), warning itself not to love the world (1 John 2:15), so that love within the community became a guarantee of its preservation, excusable as a "response to a communal crisis of identity".[110]

In response to Hays here, while conceding that in 1 John 3:13 the author defines his community over against the world, and urges them μὴ θαυμάζετε, ἀδελφοί, εἰ μισεῖ ὑμᾶς ὁ κόσμος, "do not be surprised, brothers, if the world hates you", one must again ask whether his love command extends to ὁ κόσμος, for whom Jesus died (2:2). Because the author does not in 3:13 counsel reciprocal hatred for ὁ κόσμος, might there be a creative tension between Jesus' love *for* ὁ κόσμος and John's admonition to his community not to be surprised by hatred stemming *from* ὁ κόσμος, just as there is a creative tension between the Johannine tradition's affirmation of Jesus' divinity and of his humanity, as Hays indeed identifies? Might the author's love command extend beyond his community, towards ὁ κόσμος, while at the same time he remains conscious of the moral degradation into which it has fallen, and of its enmity towards his community? Or is the thought in 1 John 3:13 simpler, and similar to that in John 1:13, that just as ὁ κόσμος did not receive Jesus, his followers should be unsurprised if they encounter similar hostility? Some answers may appear after an exegesis of 1 John's use of ἀγάπη and its derivatives later in this study.

To Hays, 1 John 3:14 portrays a community living in the fullness of eschatological life, having passed from death to love because they love one another, and failures of love and schisms within the community threaten this realised eschatology.[111] Hays sees this as a reason for the author to confine the love command to his community. Might one not argue the opposite, that this verse also invokes future eschatology, a future in which ὁ κόσμος, for whom Jesus died (2:2), is brought from death into life by universal love? Again, an exegesis of 1 John's use of ἀγάπη may clarify this.

Richard Burridge

Richard Burridge, NT scholar and Christian ethicist, in a chapter on Johannine ethics, appeals to 1 John as evidence for the need for Christian love. He notes 1 John's use of "paraclete", παράκλητος in 1 John 2:1, linking this to its use in John 14:16 to show that as Jesus has lived among us as a manifestation of divine love, so ἄλλον παράκλητον, "another advocate" (John 14:16), will later offer that love.[112]

---
[109] *Ibid*, 145–6.
[110] *Ibid*, 146–7.
[111] *Ibid*, 150.
[112] Richard Burridge, *Imitating Jesus: An Inclusive Approach to New Testament Ethics* (Grand Rapids/Cambridge, UK: Eerdmans, 2007), 301–2.

Building on this, might it be argued that the usage of παράκλητος to depict Jesus in 1 John 2:1 is to show not only that if *we* sin, παράκλητον ἔχομεν πρὸς τὸν πατέρα, "we have an advocate with the Father", but that "if *anyone* sins", ἐάν τις ἁμάρτῃ, the παράκλητος, Jesus himself, can be trusted to cleanse, deal with that sin: τὸ αἷμα a Ἰησοῦ τοῦ υἱοῦ αὐτοῦ καθαρίζει ἡμᾶς ἀπὸ πάσης ἁμαρτίας, "the blood of Jesus his Son cleanses us from all our sin" (1:7b)? Therefore, it might be argued, wreaking vengeance on others for sins against us is inappropriate for Christians, because we should forgive as God forgives, by cleansing, through Jesus the παράκλητος.

Burridge at first asserts that the love commandment of 1 John is not new, instancing Leviticus 19:18 on loving one's neighbour as oneself.[113] But he then notes that in 1 John 4:19 the love we are to have for one another is "based on the prior love of Jesus himself", noting that the "essential novelty" of the Johannine love commandment is "the Christological reference".[114] Precisely! But one must surely be careful in equating this commandment with love of neighbour *simpliciter*, for this may obscure the question whether the Johannine love command is universal. Again, this will be dealt with later in this study by exegesis of our keywords in 1 John.

Burridge passes to the idea of imitation of Jesus, pointing out that John's Gospel is the only one to use the word ὑπόδειγμα, "example", at the footwashing (John 13:15): he links this 1 John 2:6 and 3:3, 7 and 16, using Girard's word, *mimēsis*, and notes examples in the Apocrypha of exemplary death (2 Maccabees 6:28 and 6:31; 4 Maccabees 17:22-23).[115] Might it be argued that in 1 John 3:16b the admonition that ἡμεῖς ὀφείλομεν ὑπὲρ τῶν ἀδελφῶν τὰς ψυχὰς θεῖναι, "we should lay down our lives for the brother", another exemplary death, is portrayed? Exegesis later of our key ideas in 1 John might clarify this.

Burridge cites Archbishop Desmond Tutu's reliance, in his defence in 1982 of his actions before a commission of inquiry in Apartheid-era South Africa, on 1 John 3:15-18, among other texts, as showing that practical action was – and is – needed to reconcile all people to each other as beloved children of God.[116] This text seems to speak to us loudly in just the way Desmond Tutu interpreted it – but again a difficult question cannot be dodged: who is the ἀδελφός in 1 John? And can this keyword in 1 John be interpreted as a reference to all humanity? This requires later examination.

As Burridge says, the mimetic aim, found among others in the NT text, is made clear, inter alia, in 1 John 2:2 and 3:3, 7.[117] And, as he says, 1 John 3:11-24 encourages us to live in love as Jesus loved us.[118] But is the mimesis advocated in 1 John simply a defence against opponents or a stance advocated towards all humanity? Again, exegesis of our keywords in 1 John will help answer this.

---

[113] *Ibid*, 326.
[114] *Ibid*, 327.
[115] *Ibid*, 344.
[116] *Ibid*, 373–4.
[117] *Ibid*, 391.
[118] *Ibid*, 392.

George Hunsinger

Hunsinger is a vigorous critic of Girard. He says that because it is a consequence of Girard's view of the crucifixion, as the final revelation of human violence and of God's non-violent nature, "sacrificial motifs must simply be purged from the Gospels if Girard is to maintain his thesis", so that "resorting to statements that are as sweeping as they are untenable, he thus proceeds to purge them".[119] Therefore, Girard offers "a 'Pelagian' solution to an 'Augustinian' problem".[120] The problem is Augustinian, says Hunsinger, because it roots the problem of "covetousness" (the biblical name for "mimetic desire") in the perversity of the human heart.[121] Hunsinger stigmatises Girard's solution as "Pelagian" because, he says, all Girard offers is the unmasking of the scapegoating mechanism, the expulsion of violence by violence, which is then rendered impotent by the very fact of its unmasking, so that the Gospels' message is that loving one's brother completely is the antidote to mimetic violence.[122] He characterises Girard's solution as Pelagian also because it relies on humanity to "do the rest", as it were, once mimetic violence is unmasked by Jesus' complete love in his self-offering on the Cross.[123] Thus what we are left with is a "low" Christology which reduces Jesus to "little more than a moral exemplar".[124]

This may be a vast over-simplification of Girardian theory. But again it raises what is signified by ἀγάπη and ἱλασμός in 1 John. Does ἱλασμός signify a "transaction" between God and the Son in which the Son offers to placate an angry God, who is bound by God's own system to punish humanity for its sins unless someone else pays the price? Or is the verb καθαρίζw in 1 John 1:7 and 9 a clue that *God* is the actor here and that God's love for the world, not punishment for sin, is the main focus here? Exegesis of ἀγάπη and ἱλασμός in 1 John will help resolve this.

Hunsinger looks at atonement doctrine in Von Balthasar's writings, showing how Von Balthasar trenchantly criticises what he sees as Girard's failure to come to grips with the connection between the "vertical", Christological dimension of Trinitarian theology, and the "horizontal" dimension or historical aspects of the cross.[125] Next Hunsinger shows how Torrance, in a reflection on Jesus as prophet, priest and king, shows how Jesus breaks our bondage to sin and death by objectively removing the guilt which separates us from God.[126] Hunsinger agrees with Von Balthasar, using Torrance's insights to critique Girard's atonement theology, preserving some of Girard's insights, but avoiding what he sees as Girard's deficiencies.[127]

---

[119] George Hunsinger, "The Politics of the Non-Violent God: Reflections on Rene/Girard and Karl Barth", *SJT* 51:1 (1998), 61–85, 66.
[120] *Ibid*, 69.
[121] *Ibid*.
[122] *Ibid*, 69–70.
[123] *Ibid*, 70–1.
[124] *Ibid*, 71.
[125] *Ibid*, 71–4.
[126] *Ibid*, 74–7.
[127] *Ibid*, 71.

To Hunsinger, "enemy love in Karl Barth's theology is at the heart of the Gospel".[128] Hunsinger appropriates Barth's notion that in the Cross, God makes God's own self vulnerable to enemies: he cites Barth's well-known statement that "in giving Him – and giving Himself – He exposes Him – and Himself – to the greatest danger" and that "He sets at stake His own existence as God".[129] He quotes Barth as asserting that "in this radical sense God has loved first (*prōtos*, 1 John 4:19)".[130] So God does not meet God's enemies by brute force, but by "the mystery of suffering love".[131]

This draws a nexus between 1 John and Barth's theology of enemy-love, as seen by Hunsinger. In 1 John 4:19 we read that God has loved us first, πρῶτος. Exegesis of 1 John's use of an ἀγάπη derivative here, in showing the *priority* of God's love, how it *preceded* God's people's love for God, with the consequence that our love for God must be essentially *mimetic*, will illuminate whether Hunsinger's characterisation of Barth's theology as non-violent, and rooted in enemy love, has support in 1 John. Hunsinger's reliance on Von Balthasar and Torrance leads us naturally into a brief examination of how these writers either use 1 John or reflect the ideas in it.

Hans Urs von Balthasar

Hans Urs von Balthasar's critique of Girard is that he is dismissive of Jesus' death as sacrificial. Von Balthasar poses a stark dilemma: how can it be said that Jesus' self-surrender is offered to the Father if "the latter, no longer an Old Testament God, has 'no pleasure' in it, since he did not *want* the cross, and even less *commanded* his son to accept it"?[132] Girard allows a sacrificial interpretation of Jesus' death, but only "on condition that we maintain the abyss between this latter self-sacrifice and the old ritual sacrifice, which is intended to placate a god who requires violence".[133]

One of Von Balthasar's criticisms of Girard's system is that for Girard the concept of sin is secondary, so that it is not clear how Jesus, the ultimate scapegoat, may bear the sin of the world, unless the world itself loads it onto him.[134] Thus, he says, to Girard what happens on the cross is the transferral *by* the world of its guilt onto Christ, while a powerless God demands nothing by way of "atoning sacrifice".[135]

Here Von Balthasar uses the ἱλασμός language of 1 John 2:2 and 4:10. His critique of Girard is that in some way Jesus being a ἱλασμός for the whole world, περὶ ὅλου τοῦ κόσμου (1 John 2:2), involves a sacrifice which is *something more* than self-giving which "unmasks" the Satanic notion of scapegoating, which formed the basis of all religion until that time. Exegesis of ἱλασμός in 1 John may cast light on this.

---

[128] *Ibid*, 77.
[129] Barth, *Church Dogmatics*, IV/1, 72, quoted in Hunsinger, "The Politics of the Nonviolent God", 78.
[130] Hunsinger, "The Politics of the Nonviolent God", 78.
[131] *Ibid*.
[132] Hans Urs von Balthasar, *Theo-Drama: Theological Dramatic Theory*, Vol IV, "The Action" (trans. G Harrison; San Francisco: Ignatius Press, 1994), 307.
[133] *Ibid*, 310.
[134] *Ibid*, 309.
[135] *Ibid*, 309–10.

Von Balthasar also criticises Schwager, pointing out that for him, the only answer to the question "why the Cross?" is that in order to get rid of their sin, humankind must transfer their hostility to God concretely to Jesus through the crucifixion by unloading "their innermost desires on Jesus".[136] Von Balthasar asks, "why the Cross, if God forgives in any case?" and criticises Schwager's answer as concerning only humanity's attitude to Jesus, not God's attitude to him.[137] God's forgiveness and Christ's bearing of sin in the cross cannot be left in isolation, and that while Schwager's "discovery" that not only the punishment for sin but also the *sin itself* is transferred to Jesus in the Cross brings "the final element in the drama of reconciliation", it does not provide a satisfying answer.[138]

Von Balthasar does not specifically quote 1 John, but he is very close to the idea in 1 John 4:10 that God's love, ἀγάπη, is shown in his sending of his Son to be the ἱλασμός for our sins. The plural ἁμαρτιῶν here may connote not a *state* of sin, but specific acts of rebellion against God by humanity. If so, God's ἱλασμός in Jesus is to be seen as a bearing of *all* humanity's acts of rebellion rather than an assumption simply of humanity's brokenness, its mortal clay, its inevitable tendency to sin, to rebel. In that Schwager speaks of the sin of humanity *itself*, as well as the punishment for it, being assumed in the Cross, he may give insufficient weight, in light of 1 John 4:10, to Jesus as bearer of the *sins* of humanity. This need not be resolved now, but later on in exegesis of ἱλασμός and ἀγάπη in 1 John.

Thomas Torrance

In a huge statement, Thomas Torrance holds that to understand the atonement we must see that "through the Son and in the Spirit God *has given himself to us*".[139] Earlier he explains what this means: no explanation is ever given in the NT, or for that matter in the OT, why atonement for sin *requires* the blood of sacrifice, so God's atoning act, as with God's love, "knows no 'Why'".[140] Therefore:

> In him priest and sacrifice, offering and the offeror are one, so that he constitutes in himself the new and living way opened up for us into God's immediate presence. He is our Forerunner, our High Priest, in whom our hope is lodged as an anchor sure and steadfast that reaches beyond the veil of sense and time into the heavenly world. In him God has drawn near to us, and we may draw near to God with complete confidence as those who are sanctified together with Jesus, and who are included in his eternal self-presentation through the Spirit to the Father.[141]

---

[136] *Ibid*, 311; and see Schwager, *Must There Be Scapegoats?*, 214.
[137] Von Balthasar, *Theo-Drama* Vol IV, 312.
[138] *Ibid*, 312–13.
[139] TF Torrance, *The Mediation of Christ* (Edinburgh: T&T Clark, 1992), 123.
[140] *Ibid*, 114.
[141] *Ibid*, 114–15.

Torrance does not cite 1 John, but 1 John 4:10-12 comes to mind: God has sent his Son, Jesus Christ, as ἱλασμός for our sins, and as he loved us, so we ought to love one another: the unseen God may live in us so God's love may be perfected in us.

With Torrance, one may say that any attempt to *define* a precise mechanism by which God extends forgiveness to us through the atoning gift of God's own Son in his Incarnation, life and death runs the risk Barth foresaw when he spoke, as we have seen, of the situation where

> scripture is thought of and used as though the message of revelation and the Word of God could be extracted from it in the same way as the message of other truth or reality can be extracted from other sources of knowledge, at any rate where it is not presumably speaking of Jesus Christ.[142]

So God's atonement in Jesus is at bottom a mystery, as is Jesus' own nature, truly God and true human. This, we shall see, is also the final viewpoint of 1 John.

Gustav Aulen

Gustav Aulen – and in this important respect he is foresquare with Barth – holds that the atonement is at all times to be seen as God's work alone.[143] He seeks to retrieve, from mediaeval speculation about God's "justice" being "satisfied" by Jesus' atoning death for human sin, which to him is the "classic" view of the atonement.

Aulen explains that this "classic" idea may be described as a drama, in which the evil powers of the world are vanquished by Jesus as *Christus Victor*, so that in his victory over the "tyrants" under which humankind is suffering, God reconciles the world to God's own self.[144] To Aulen the background of this idea is dualistic: Jesus' victory is over powers of evil that are hostile to God's will, and this victory brings to pass in a cosmic drama a relation of *reconciliation*,[145] that is between God and humanity.

Aulen sees this view of the atonement as "classic" because it appears in Irenaeus' *Recapitulation*, in which, as Aulen sets out from Irenaeus' *Adversus Haereses*, Irenaeus answers the question, *ut quid enim descendebat?*[146] by the propositions that

> man had been created by God hat he might have life. If now, having lost life, and having been harmed by the serpent, he were not to return to life, but were to be wholly abandoned to death, then God would have been defeated, and the malice of the serpent would have overcome God's will. But since God is both invincible and magnanimous, He showed His magnanimity in correcting man, and in proving all

---

[142] Barth, *Church Dogmatics*, IV/1, 368.
[143] Gustav Aulen, *Christus Victor: An Historical Study of the Three Main Types of the Idea of Atonement* (trans. AG Hebert; London: SPCK, 1931; repr. Eugene, Oregon: Wipf and Stock, 2003), 5.
[144] *Ibid*, 4.
[145] *Ibid*, 4–5.
[146] "For what purpose did Christ come down from heaven?": *Ibid*, 18.

men, as we have said, but through the Second Man he bound the strong one, and spoiled his goods, and annihilated death, bringing life to man who had become subject to death. For Adam had become the devil's possession, and the devil held him under his power, by having wrongfully practised deceit on him, and by the offer of immortality made him subject to death. For by promising that they should be gods, which did not lie within his power, he worked death in them. Wherefore he who had taken men captive was himself taken captive by God, and man who had been taken captive was set free from the bondage of condemnation.[147]

This quotation has been rendered in full as it reveals how Irenaeus creates a dramatic picture of the action between the *dramatis personae* in his atonement theology. Aulen then traces how this "dramatic" idea of the atonement was taken up by the Fathers in both east and west, exampling Origin, Athanasius, Basil the Great, Gregory of Nyssa, Gregory of Nazianzus, Cyril of Alexandria, Cyril of Jerusalem and John Chrysostom.[148]

One may detect how congenial Johannine dualism might have been to such an idea. Indeed Aulen notes its prominence in Johannine writings, in particular 1 John where in 5:19 it is said that "the whole world lies under the power of the evil one", so that "the purpose of Christ's coming is summed up in 1 John iii.8: 'To this end was the Son of God manifested, that He might destroy the works of the devil'".[149]

As we have seen, a *Christus Victor* model of the atonement has found favour with some peacemaking theologians, Weaver in particular, and there are at least echoes of it in Girard himself. Is 1 John congenial to it? How may it avoid a picture of a violent, retributive God, if at all? Our contextual exegesis of keywords underlying the principal ideas in 1 John will provide some answers to these questions.

Conclusion

We have seen a tendency discernible in the work of peacemaking theologians who advocate a non-violent approach both to the atonement and to ethics to cite the more general statements and injunctions, somewhat as proof texts, in 1 John, such as "God is love" and "love one another", without tying them to the context in which the epistle was written, and thus to its proper exegesis. This is totally understandable in eminent writers whose concern with 1 John, and indeed with scripture as a whole, is hermeneutical and illustrative, rather than in any way exegetical. Some biblical scholars, as we have also seen, approach hermeneutical questions prompted by the keywords in 1 John identified above in greater exegetical depth, as one would expect of their calling. But most citations of 1 John by biblical scholars identified above, again in service of a peacemaking or non-violent approach to scripture, have been incidental. The wider projects undertaken by these scholars, in the works where these citations

---

[147] *Ibid*, 19–20, quoting Irenaeus, *Adversus Haereses*, II., 23.1.
[148] See *ibid*, chapter 2, "The Fathers in East and West", 38–60.
[149] *Ibid*, 74–5.

occur, have themselves no doubt prevented close exegesis of them to see if they support the hermeneutic in support of which they are deployed.

We have seen too that Von Balthasar and Hunsinger in their critiques of Girard and his interpreters have relied in part on 1 John in their atonement theology and that Barth himself has been so reliant. Their use of 1 John differs radically from that of Girard and his interpreters. One possibility is that Girard's critics might stand together with Girard and his supporters in justifying, in different ways, a peacemaking theology derived from 1 John. Exegesis of some keywords in 1 John, having regard to the situation of John's community, will help decide whether a peacemaking hermeneutic of 1 John holds water.

What is at stake here is not only the proper use of scripture but our very picture of God. But one must not approach Holy scripture in general, and 1 John in particular, as if it were a quarry, with the anterior, hermeneutical motive of proving that a peacemaking, non-violent picture of God, with consequences for our picture of the atonement and Christian ethics, may validly be found there. One must approach scripture empirically, with an open mind, to see if it will bear such a hermeneutic. This may only be done through an open and honest view of the situation in which 1 John was written and by bringing this to bear on the exegesis of some keywords in 1 John which we have already identified. Exegetical study abounds in all schools of biblical scholarship, but without any attempt at deriving meaning from the circumstances in which a particular text was written, one is limited to simple word studies, which examine the use of particular language in a text in one tradition, such as the Johannine corpus, and then infer that a similar usage is intended in another text within that tradition.

This sort of wider exegetical enquiry into the circumstances within which 1 John was written, as revealed in its text, is what is needed if we are to determine whether a peacemaking hermeneutic may be derived from 1 John. What the author really meant is obviously not the end of the hermeneutical enquiry; the so-called intentional fallacy is an ever-present danger. But if it can be shown that the author meant the precise reverse of what is portrayed by hermeneutical use of his words in service of a peacemaking theology, in both atonement and NT ethical studies, there is a very large problem. This study aims to elucidate whether or not such a problem exists, and if it does, to attempt to solve it.

1

The Background, Purpose, Literary Structure and Reception of 1 John

Introduction

Writers advocating a peacemaking or non-violent hermeneutic of the NT make much use of 1 John. This study asks whether it is exegetically legitimate, or even possible, to do so. The following chapters of this study will suggest an answer, by undertaking an exegesis of some keywords standing for central ideas in 1 John. But before beginning that project we must first ask, and attempt to resolve, a number of broad preliminary questions. To whom and why was 1 John written? Is the conflict with opponents seen in it present or past? What is its literary structure? When and how was it received in the early church? Put simply, we must examine, in a survey of some representative scholarship, the background, purpose, literary structure and reception of 1 John.

Why is this needed in a study of the present type? As we shall see, the broad scholarly consensus, with some exceptions, is that 1 John was written as a response to tendencies within the Johannine community to adopt too high a Christology. This may have occurred in response to statements in John's Gospel as to Jesus' heavenly origin and nature, the purposes of which may have been in part to refute an overly low Christology, though not specifically to refute Ebionite tendencies.[1] These may have led some in the Johannine community to over-spiritualise Jesus' teaching and to downplay the importance of his humanity and life on earth and of the necessity for mutual love as the basis of a Christian ethic in response to Jesus' earthly life and his saving work in his death and resurrection. We must examine, therefore, how the general consensus as to the background, purpose, literary structure and reception of 1 John has been formed. This study does not pretend to resolve these much-disputed questions. All that is attempted in what follows is a survey of but a few answers to these questions in the literature and an indication of the stance adopted concerning these debates by this study, which underlie its later consideration of peacemaking theology and its relevance to 1 John.

---

[1] Raymond Brown, *The Gospel According to John, I–XII* (New York: Doubleday, 1966), lxxvi.

The Background of 1 John

(i) Jewish Influence in 1 John

It seems that a "parting of the ways"[2] occurred between early Jewish Christian converts and what became Rabbinic Judaism, perhaps as early as the first century, occasioned by early Christian teaching about the inauguration of the eschatological kingdom of God in the public ministry of Jesus.[3] A second "parting of the ways" is also evident between Jewish Christian groups, consisting entirely of Jewish converts to "the way", as portrayed for in Acts 2:37-42, and Gentile converts, depicted in Acts 10:44-48. A short summary of some representative scholarship will suggest a broad scholarly consensus that there is considerable Jewish influence in 1 John.

Lieu asks whether this parting is a theological construct or an historical reality.[4] She concludes that it was the latter, with the formation of separate identity and development, based on the literature of a number of brief case studies of early Christian communities in various places in the eastern Mediterranean area.[5]

Writing in the early twentieth century, Law finds in 1 John 5:18-21 "alternating tristichs and distichs", observing that while this may not represent conscious imitation of Hebraic forms, "no-one could have written as our author does whose whole thought and style had not been unconsciously formed on Old Testament models".[6] As we shall see in a moment, this view is persuasive.

A difficulty for those arguing for Jewish influence on 1 John is that the only overt OT reference in John is the Cain analogy in 3:12 and that it contains no OT quotations. This may well indicate that the membership of the Johannine community was not predominantly of Jewish background. But we should not jump to the conclusion that this is evidence of absence of Jewish influence on 1 John. To Brown, the Cain reference shapes a whole section of 1 John, 3:12-24, and OT covenant themes have a strong influence on its ethical outlook.[7] This is cogent: 3:11 refers to a message ἀπ' ἀρχῆς,[8] "from the beginning"; 3:22 speaks of receiving whatever we ask because of obedience to τὰς ἐντολὰς αὐτοῦ, "his commandments"; 3:23 speaks of an ἐντολὴ, "commandment", to love one another; and 3:24 says all who obey τὰς ἐντολὰς αὐτοῦ, "his commandments", abide in him and he in them.

---

[2] For a good survey of scholarly use of this phrase see Judith M Lieu, *Neither Jew Nor Greek?* (London & New York: T&T Clark, 2002), 11–29; see also Lydia Gore-Jones and Stephen Llewellyn, "The Parting of the Ways" in *Into All the World: Emergent Christianity in Its Jewish and Greco-Roman Context* (ed. Mark Harding and Alanna Nobbs; Grand Rapids: Eerdmans, 2017), 158–83.

[3] John McHugh, "'In Him Was Life': John's Gospel and the Parting of the Ways" in *Jews and Christians: The Parting of the Ways* (ed. JDG Dunn; Grand Rapids: Eerdmans, 1992), 123–58, 124.

[4] Lieu, *Neither Jew nor Greek*, 11.

[5] *Ibid*, 27–9.

[6] Robert Law, *The Tests of Life* (Edinburgh: T&T Clark, 1909), 4.

[7] Raymond E Brown, *The Epistles of John* (New Haven and London: Yale University Press, paperback ed., 2006), 28; similarly Birger Olsson, *A Commentary on the Letters of John: An Intra-Jewish Approach* (trans. Richard J Erickson, Eugene, Or.: Pickwick Publications, 2013), 116–17.

[8] The Greek NT text in this study is taken from *Novum Testamentum Graece* (ed. Barbara and Kurt Aland, Johannes Karavidopoulos, Carlo M Martini, Bruce M Metzger; Deutsche Bibelgesellschaft: Münster/Westphalia, 28th rev. ed., 2012).

Brown notes others' views that the "from the beginning" formula used here is consistent with early Christian baptismal catechesis,[9] but the better view is that in its context by virtue of its association with ἐντολὴ, "commandment", this formula reflects OT covenant theology. Exodus 24, where we see the people's promise of obedience to all that the Lord has spoken (24:3, 8) – itself a reiteration of Exodus 19:8[10] – and Moses' offering of the blood of the covenant (24:1-8), also relates Moses' receipt from the Lord of the tablets of stone containing the Decalogue, with "all the law and the commandments" (24:12). "Commandment" translates the Hebrew hwfc:mi, which is translated in the LXX here as ἐντολὰς, "commandments", the same word used in 1 John 2:7-8 and 3:22-24. It is indeed likely that the author of 1 John had this same idea of divinely initiated law and covenant in mind here.

Brown argues for Jewish influence on 1 John in parallel with the Dead Sea Scrolls. *IQS* (the Rule of the Community) warns that no one can enter the community who does not walk in the ways of God, "if seeking the ways of light, he turns towards darkness" (3:3): such a person cannot be purified by atonement or cleansed by purifying waters (3:4), and only the person who walks in the ways of God receives the true teaching, and is cleansed of sin, and is accepted by a pleasing atonement before God and becomes part of the covenant of eternal communion (3:11-12). As Brown argues, these ideas are similar to those in 1 John 1:5-7 and 2:8-11.[11] There are parallels between the ideas in *IQS* 3:17-22, where it refers to "two spirits in which to walk" and the "generations of truth" which "spring from a fountain of light" and "the generations of iniquity from a source of darkness", and "the sons of righteousness under the rule of the prince of light" and "the sons of darkness under the rule of the angel of darkness", and those in 1 John 2:8-11 and 3:12.[12]

Goff says of the themes of the "two spirits" in *IQS* 3:17-22 that "they are combined in various ways that the human being is the context of a cosmological drama in which various supernatural agents, both good and evil, vie against one another".[13] This would not be an inapt way to describe the themes of darkness and light in 1 John.

Similarly Eynikel, while making the point that Johannine ethical thought, in contrast to Qumran, generally sees light as God himself, and darkness as personified by Satan, notes that in 1 John especially, there is similarity to the Dead Sea Scrolls,

---

[9] *Ibid*, 90.
[10] Walter Brueggemann, *Old Testament Theology* (Nashville: Abingdon Press, 2008), 53; *contra* Udo Schnelle, "Ethical Theology in 1 John" in *Rethinking the Ethics of John* (ed. Jan G Van Der Watt and Ruben Zimmerman; Tübingen: Mohr Siebeck, 2012), 321–39, 329.
[11] Brown, *Epistles of John*, 242–3.
[12] *Ibid*, 243; similarly IH Marshall, *The Epistles of John* (Grand Rapids: Eerdmans, 1978), 49–51; see also *The Dead Sea Scrolls Study Edition* Vol 1 (ed. & trans. Florentino García Martínez and Eibert JC Tigchelaar; Brill: Leiden/Boston/Köln/Grand Rapids/Cambridge, UK: Eerdmans, paperback ed., 2000), 74–5; Geza Vermes, *The Dead Sea Scrolls: Qumran in Perspective* (London: Collins, 1977), 90; Erik Eynikel, "The Qumran Background of Johannine Ethics" in *Rethinking the Ethics of John* (ed. Jan G Van Der Watt and Ruben Zimmerman; Tübingen: Mohr Siebeck, 2012), 102–13, 109–10.
[13] Matthew Goff, "Male and Female, Heaven and Earth: Claude Lévi-Strauss's Structuralist Approach to Myth and the Enochic Myth of the Watchers" in *The Dead Sea Scrolls and the Study of the Humanities* (ed. Pieter B Hartog, Alison Schofield and Samuel I Thomas; Leiden/Boston: Brill, 2018), 77–91, 90.

instancing 1 John 4:1-6, speaking of testing of spirits and conflict between the two spirits of truth and error.[14]

To Schnackenburg, many ideas in 1 John "can come only from a Jewish background", suggesting that its author "had his roots in Judaism"; he refers to ideas such as sin as transgression of God's commandments, atonement through the shedding of blood, and final judgement, arguing that even if the author was "indebted primarily to Christian *kerygma* and the Church's catechesis", nevertheless "the acceptance and continuation of these ideas from Judaism is taken for granted".[15] This too is cogent. The similarity between the usage of ἐντολή, "commandment", in 1 John 2:7-8 and 3:22-24 and in the LXX in Exodus 24:12 is but one illustration of this phenomenon. Schnackenburg rightly sees a similarity between the Qumran texts and the Johannine writings, both linguistically and theologically, while conceding that it is unclear whether this is because of a common milieu, the world of first-century Judaism, or whether the author of 1 John had contact with the Qumran community.[16]

Painter refers to the "non-Jewish context" of John's letters, pointing to their lack of OT quotations and the warning to guard against idols (1 John 5:21).[17] He argues that Jewish elements can occur in a text for different reasons: the subject may be Jewish, or the author may be Jewish, or he may be writing to a Jewish audience, although he concludes that the lack of OT quotations in 1 John contraindicates the latter.[18] As early as Westcott, the "thoroughly Hebraistic" tone of 1 John's writing was noted.[19] Painter is less impressed by the linguistic similarities between 1 John and the Qumran texts: he notes them but concludes that John's letters were written to believers at a time when they were independent from Judaism and that they reflect no specifically Jewish problems.[20] He suggests that the Johannine letters were written to a predominantly Gentile readership and so do not use specifically OT language or thought.[21] If this be so, the use of the Cain analogy is curious: it appears more likely that in this connection at least, the author assumed some knowledge of the OT in his readership. Painter sees the Cain reference as developing the tradition found in John 8:39-44 and refers to Philo's sustained treatment of Cain, traced in Chapter 4 of this study.[22] Granted, 1 John does not deal with specifically Jewish problems, and 1 John's author may or may not have been a Jew, but his awareness of Jewish tradition concerning Cain still suggests that he was steeped in the Jewish faith and literature of his time.

To Lieu, 1 John is not more "Hellenistic" than John's Gospel: even if Gnosticism was in view as the enemy, it was as much a Jewish as a Greek phenomenon.[23] She points

---

[14] Eynikel, "The Qumran Background of Johannine Ethics", 109–10.
[15] Rudolf Schnackenburg, *The Johannine Epistles* (trans. R and I Fuller; New York, Crossroad, 1992), 27.
[16] *Ibid*, 28.
[17] John Painter, *1, 2, and 3 John* (Collegeville, Minnesota: Liturgical Press, 2008), 1.
[18] *Ibid*, 19.
[19] Brooke Foss Westcott, *Epistles of St John* (Cambridge & London: Macmillan & Co., 1886), xl.
[20] Painter, *1, 2, and 3 John*, 12–13.
[21] *Ibid*, 77–8.
[22] *Ibid*, 233.
[23] Judith Lieu, *I, II, & III John* (Louisville/London: Westminster John Knox Press, 2008), 23.

to the parallels between contemporaneous Jewish writings and 1 John, citing also *The Rule of the Community* (*IQS*) in the Dead Sea Scrolls, which speaks of the two spirits that govern human behaviour (*IQS* 3.13-4.7).[24] That passage has some similarities to 1 John, especially in 2:8-11 and 3:12. Lieu's reliance on another contemporary Jewish text, *The Testaments of the Twelve Patriarchs*, as a possible influence on 1 John, is more problematical because, as she herself notes, unlike the Dead Sea Scrolls it survives only by Christian transmission, and similarly problematic are proposals which seek to identify a "Jewish substratum" to 1 John, added by Christian editing.[25] To Lieu, while 1 John cannot be given the label "Jewish Christian", itself of little use, it can validly be said to reflect a thought pattern which is Jewish in ethos, even if it does not address the disagreements between Jews who believed in Jesus and those who did not.[26]

In summary, the better view is that 1 John was probably written by someone steeped in Jewish scripture – even if he did not address specifically Jewish problems – and who wrote using Jewish thought patterns, one who did not hesitate to reach for the one OT allusion in 1 John, the story of Cain and Abel, as an example of deadly hatred which would be familiar to his audience. Those to whom he wrote may or may not have been predominantly Jewish converts, but they were probably familiar enough with Jewish scripture for such an example to be meaningful.

(ii) The Johannine Community – John and His Opponents

Martyn finds in John 9, particularly in 9:22, referring to excommunication from the synagogue, indications of a Jewish Christian community confessing Jesus as Messiah which was formally expelled from the synagogue some time before John wrote.[27] He finds similar indications in John 16:1-2, the warning about exclusion from the synagogue, that some members of the Johannine church had come to it from the synagogue through exclusion from it.[28] He finds in John 12:42 a picture of those among the authorities who remain secret believers in Jesus, for fear of exclusion from the synagogue, implying an authoritative decision by that body, before the time of writing, to exclude those confessing belief in Jesus.[29]

Building on Martyn's work, Brown maintains that a separate Johannine community later arose, traditionally associated with the "beloved disciple" of John's Gospel, its hero.[30] Dissensions and consequent splits, the subject of John's first letter, then occurred in it. Based on earlier work on John's Gospel by Martyn, Brown postulates that this Johannine community consisted originally of Jews who held to a relatively low Christology, involving use of titles not specifically implying Jesus' divine origin and

---

[24] *Ibid*, 24; see also *The Dead Sea Scrolls Study Edition* Vol 1, 74–7.
[25] *Ibid*, 24–5, citing JC O'Neill, *The Puzzle of 1 John* (London: SPCK, 1966).
[26] *Ibid*, 25. See generally also Stephen S Smalley, *1, 2, 3 John* (Waco, Texas: Word Books, 1984), xxiii.
[27] J Louis Martyn, *History and Theology in the Fourth Gospel* (Louisville, Kentucky: Westminster John Knox Press, 3rd ed., 2003), 46–7.
[28] *Ibid*, 48.
[29] *Ibid*, 49.
[30] Raymond E Brown, *The Community of the Beloved Disciple* (London: Geoffrey Chapman, 1979), 31.

destiny, but that this community later developed a higher Christology which brought it into direct conflict with Jews, who saw it as blasphemy.[31]

This view of 1 John, as being the later product of a separate Johannine community, has not gone unchallenged. Bauckham makes a textual argument that the "we" of John 21:24 reveals the authorship of the apostle John, the "beloved disciple", in that it is a "we" of authority, which stands for "I".[32] As part of his argument, he proposes that the "we" in 1 John 1:1-5 is traceable to its use in 3 John 9-10, 12. He argues that the "our" and "us" of 3 John 9 and 10 must be different from the "brothers" of v.10, apparently travelling missionaries associated with the Elder, and that the "we" of v.12 must be different from the "all" used there, referring apparently to all Christians in the author's and Gaius' community.[33] It is easiest, Bauckham concludes, to see the first-person plural in all three verses as a substitute for "I".[34] He then argues from this usage in 3 John that the "we" in 1 John 1:1-5 is not associative (including John with his audience in the one group) but rather an authoritative "we" representing eyewitness testimony, introduced in 1 John 1:6-10.[35]

There are three problems with this analysis. First, granted that the πάντων in 3 John 12 must be different from the ἡμεῖς, as shown by the δὲ, one cannot assume that the ἡμᾶς of vv.9 and 10 is different from the ἀδελφοὺς of v.10. It may just as validly be interpreted associatively, just as the elder associates himself with the ἀδελφῶν in v.3.

Second, the change from an authoritative "we" and "our", ἡμῶν, representing "I", in 1 John 1:1, and in vv.2-5, to an associative "we" in vv.6-10 is harder to accommodate than the simpler proposition that an associative "we" is intended throughout vv.1-10, meaning that the proclamation of what "we" must believe in vv.6-10 comes directly from what "we" have heard from the beginning in vv.1-5. It is only by interpreting "what we have seen with our eyes, what we have looked at and touched with our hands" in v.1 literally, as indicating eyewitness testimony by John, the beloved disciple himself, that the "we" in vv.1-5 becomes an authoritative "I". But this would crucially weaken the sense of the whole passage from vv.1-10, the whole point of which is to tie the theology of vv.6-10, which must be addressed to an associative "we", including John himself, to what the same "we" have heard from the beginning in vv.1-5. Of course it is not impossible that the beloved disciple himself wrote 1 John and/or 2 and 3 John, but it may not be possible by the textual arguments Bauckham raises to prove that he did.

Third, the associative "we" is also seen in John's Gospel at 21:24b: those affirming καὶ οἴδαμεν ὅτι ἀληθὴς αὐτοῦ ἡ μαρτυρία ἐστίν, "and we know that his testimony is

---

[31] Ibid, 25–51.
[32] Richard Bauckham, *Jesus and the Eyewitnesses: The Gospels as Eyewitness Testimony* (Grand Rapids: Eerdmans, 2006), 371. Similarly Richard Bauckham, "The Fourth Gospel as the Testimony of the Beloved Disciple" in *The Gospel of John and Christian Theology* (ed. Richard Bauckham and Carl Mosser; Grand Rapids: Eerdmans, 2008), 120–39, 131.
[33] Bauckham, *Jesus and the Eyewitnesses*, 372–3.
[34] Ibid, 373.
[35] Ibid, 374–5.

true", are referring, not directly to ἡ μαρτυρία of Jesus, but to ὁ μαθητὴς ὁ μαρτυρῶν περὶ τούτων, "the disciple who is testifying to these things", in 21:24a.[36]

This is of course a brief summary of but a small part of Bauckham's argument and it cannot do full justice to it. But by suggesting that 1 John was the product of the beloved disciple himself, rather than an author writing within a community, perhaps originally gathered around the beloved disciple, it unacceptably downplays the extent to which the epistle responds to conflict faced by the Johannine community.

Apart from these textual arguments, even a cursory examination of the themes of 1 John reveals polemic directed towards opponents, relating both to direct theological, Christological questions – who was Jesus and what were his origin(s) and destination and purpose – and to ethical disputes – what is the controlling principle of Christian ethics, and what is their level of importance? This strongly suggests conflict between an "orthodox" group and a secessionist, dissident group, both originally belonging to one community but later experiencing schism. What was the nature of the split between the author of the letter and his opponents, both as to the identity of the opponents and whether they were without or within the community to which the letter is addressed? What were the views they held and which the author confronted?

To Westcott, the object of 1 John was to confront external, Cerinthean error.[37] But it was not long before scholars saw that it confronts Christian opponents, perhaps antinomian, or "docetic in doctrine and antinomian in practice".[38]

Brooke sees it as aimed at those holding a "mixture of Jewish and Gnostic ideas which must have formed the most pressing dangers to the moral and spiritual life of a Christian community towards the end of the first century or the beginning of the second, or perhaps even later".[39]

Dodd views the opponents confronted in John's first letter as associated with that tendency in the religious life of the time which is known as "Hellenistic mysticism" or "the higher paganism", especially in its "near-Christian dress", as "Gnosticism".[40]

---

[36] See Beasley-Murray, *John*, 413–15 for a summary of the arguments for the use of the editorial "we" by the Gospel author himself here, versus the view that it represents the elders of the church at Ephesus. For present purposes it is sufficient to say that the second of these solutions seems more plausible in relation to John 21:24; so Francis B Moloney, *The Gospel of John* (Collegeville, Minnesota: Liturgical Press, 1998), 561; similarly Rudolf Bultmann, *The Gospel of John: A Commentary* (trans. GR Beasley-Murray; Oxford: Basil Blackwell, 1971), 717–18; Barnabas Lindars, *The Gospel of John* (London: Marshall, Morgan and Scott, 1972), 641; Leon Morris, *The Gospel According to John* (rev. ed.; Grand Rapids: Eerdmans, 1995), 777, Olsson, *A Commentary on the Letters of John*, 82, 294–5, 302, Karen H Jobes, *1, 2, and 3 John* (Grand Rapids, Mi: Zondervan, 2014), 50–1; *sed contra*, Gordon H Clark, *First John: A Commentary* (Jefferson: Trinity Foundation, 1980), 21–2, Daniel A Akin, *1, 2, 3 John* (Nashville: Broadman & Holman Publishers, 2001), 26–7, Craig S Keener, *The Gospel of John: A Commentary, Vol II* (Peabody, Massachusetts: Hendrickson Publishers, 2003), 1240, Bruce C Schuchard, *1–3 John* (Saint Louis, Concordia Publishing House, 2012), 89, Douglas Sean O'Donnell, *1–3 John* (Phillipsburg, NJ: R&R Publishing, 2015), 8, Constantine R Campbell, *1, 2 and 3 John* (Grand Rapids: Zondervan, 2017), 23–4.
[37] Westcott, *The Epistles of St John*, xxxv–xxxvi.
[38] Law, *Tests of Life*, 26.
[39] AE Brooke, *A Critical and Exegetical Commentary on the Johannine Epistles* (Edinburgh: T&T Clark, 1912, repr. Forgotten Books, 2012), liii.
[40] CH Dodd, *The Johannine Epistles* (London, Hodder & Stoughton, 1946), xx.

Bultmann sees 1 John as written in conflict with Gnostic opponents, although derived in part from a Gnostic source.[41] However, commenting on 1 John 2:25, he contrasts the Gnostic position that "life" is "an assured possession" with John's view that for the Christian, one is "on the way" to eternal life.[42] Bultmann's position is nuanced, but commenting on 2:19, he claims the opponents never stemmed from John's community and were not truly part of it.[43]

Strecker, however, considers that from 1 John 2:19 it may be seen that the author presumes that the false teachers originally belonged to the Johannine community, "no matter how much they 'did not belong to us' by their very nature".[44] In addition, he says, "It is presumed that the opponents separated from the Johannine community before the composition of 1 John."[45]

Schnackenburg postulates a community in an "advanced stage of development" lying behind 1 John, with the author "fighting on a single front" against "antichrists" (2:18) or "false prophets" who are "united in their denial of the church's Christological confession (2:22; 4:2-3)".[46] He postulates heretical opponents who present both Christological error and a false ethic (1:5–2:11; to be inferred also from 3:4-24, 4:20-5:3) which come from the same source and form a united un-Christian stance.[47] He thinks the opponents evidently came from a "Gentile Christian milieu", judging from John's argument that "Son of God" is the preferable title for Jesus, which uses no scriptural OT proofs[48] – unlike "Son of Man" or "Messiah".

Some earlier scholars, as noted above, acknowledge that John's opponents may have been originally from his own community, if not a genuine component of it. Brown undertakes a detailed reconstruction of stages in the development of the Johannine community to demonstrate how John's opponents seceded from it and thereafter threatened to subvert its Christological beliefs and ethical practice. Brown postulates four stages in the development of the life of the Johannine community from which John's Gospel (and indeed 1 John) sprang, based on his reading of John's Gospel itself. First is the pre-Gospel period, in which the community originated, which involves its relationship to mid-first-century Judaism.[49] Next is its situation at the time the Gospel of John was written, in about 90 CE according to Brown.[50] Next is the situation in the now-divided communities in which the Letters of John were written, in about 100 CE in Brown's estimation.[51] Last is the dissolution of the Johannine groups after the

---

[41] R Bultmann, *The Johannine Epistles* (trans. PP O'Hara with LC McGaughy and RW Funk; Philadelphia: Fortress Press, English translation 1973 from the 2nd German edition, 1967), 28 n.21, 38 ("the doctrine of the heretics is rooted in the duality of Gnosticism").
[42] Ibid, 40.
[43] Ibid, 36.
[44] G Strecker, *The Johannine Letters* (trans. LM Maloney; Minneapolis: Fortress Press, English translation 1995 from the German edition, 1989), 70.
[45] Ibid.
[46] Schnackenburg, *Johannine Epistles*, 17.
[47] Ibid, 18.
[48] Ibid.
[49] Brown, *The Community of the Beloved Disciple*, 22.
[50] Ibid, 23.
[51] Ibid.

Johannine letters were written with the final departure of all the secessionists from the main community in the early second century.[52]

Against this background, Brown postulates that John's adversaries in his letters were distinct from his own group yet were still a threat through their propagandists, who claimed to be teachers.[53] He thinks there was most likely one adversary group rather than many, because the text of 1 John gives the impression that the Christological and ethical errors stigmatised in it were closely related. He cites 1 John 3:23 as yoking together both species of error: "Now this is God's commandment: we are to believe the name of his Son, Jesus Christ, and we are to love one another just as he gave us the command." Brown points to the same language of lying and deceit being used to condemn both Christological and moral error.[54] He infers that John was attacking those who held too high a Christology, which stressed Jesus' pre-existence to the point of neglecting his flesh or humanity, and who therefore had difficulty with the belief that Jesus, the earthly man, was the Christ, the Son of God.[55] As we have seen, Brown's view is that this Johannine community consisted originally of Jews who held to a relatively low Christology, but that it later developed a higher Christology which brought it into direct conflict with Jews.[56]

Painter sees Brown's reconstruction as "generally convincing", although he sees the Johannine community's "higher Christology" as not necessarily developing later; it was more likely to be a contribution of the evangelist himself in dialogue with the synagogue.[57] Importantly, he adds that the break from the synagogue "almost certainly opened the community to Gentiles" who understood the Johannine community's tradition differently, which may have contributed to its later division.[58] He traces first the development of a group among Jewish converts, loosely described at the "Johannine School", then, after a break with the synagogue, the shaping of a group of Christian Jews, gathered around the evangelist himself, into the "Johannine community".[59] He postulates that at the break with the synagogue, reflected in John 9:22 and 12:42 (and, one might add, in John 16:2), some in the now-separate community of Jewish Christians "were wavering, undecided which way to turn".[60] One can readily see in this picture, of wavering Jewish Christians facing the influx of Gentile converts, the seeds of future conflict within the new Johannine community.

Since Brown wrote in 1979, there seems a broad scholarly consensus that John's opponents were from within his community. Smalley speaks of a situation seen first in 1 John 2:18-19 where John's doctrinal and ethical opponents "withdrew" – after this, in 2 John 7, there are "many deceivers" defecting from John's community.[61]

---

[52] *Ibid*, 24. For a fair summary of Brown's method see John Painter, *The Quest for the Messiah* (Edinburgh: T&T Clark, 2nd ed., 1993), 67-8 n.101.
[53] Brown, *Epistles of John*, 49.
[54] *Ibid*, 50.
[55] *Ibid*, 53-4.
[56] Brown, *Community*, 25-51.
[57] Painter, *The Quest for the Messiah*, 67.
[58] *Ibid*.
[59] *Ibid*, 71; see also Painter, *1, 2, and 3 John*, 75-7.
[60] Painter, *The Quest for the Messiah*, 72.
[61] Smalley, *1, 2, 3 John*, xxx.

Grayston presents the letters as a product of the "third stage" of an episode in John's community, the stages being dispute, secession and realignment.[62]

Loader speaks of John writing in the letters to "a community which has experienced schism" and addressing the needs and concerns of those who remain.[63]

Johnson writes of schism with a "large and influential group" leaving the original fellowship; the issues between them and John were both doctrinal and ethical.[64]

Rensberger also sees John as responding in his first letter to a crisis caused by people from within his own community, wrestling with issues in Johannine theology which the opponents have brought into focus.[65] He sees the conflict with present opponents evident in Johannine rhetoric in 1 John as lying in "translating its message in various ways into the 'cultural languages' it encountered", once the early church moved beyond the boundaries of Judaism, particularly in 1 John 4:1-6.[66] He maintains that the opponents used the language of Hellenistic dualism to express the good news of eternal life, portraying it as redemption from the flesh, whereas to the author of 1 John, this surrendered the depth of divine love and sacrifice, and the possibility of a divinely ordered life "within the human condition".[67]

To Jones, 1 John was written during a historical crisis in a "splintering church", to forge unity and fellowship in like-minded groups when schismatics "denied a corporeal Christ".[68]

Others deny that John was responding to opponents who were now outside his community. For example, Perkins writes that the letters do not "reply to the external pressures of Jews or Jewish Christians" but arise from differing interpretations of the fourth Gospel's picture of Jesus (assuming that it preceded the letters).[69] This view has its difficulties, as we shall see.

There has been more recent criticism of Brown's and Painter's approach on a different basis: that it focuses unduly on the historical background of the text of 1 John, in particular the situation within and without John's community, at the expense of its rhetoric, which is "flattened out" in the process.[70] Such criticism is misplaced, partly because 1 John's rhetoric must be viewed through the prism of its historical situation in order for its vehemence to be understood and partly because Brown and Painter both give ample attention to the literary structure and rhetoric of 1 John.[71]

For reasons we have outlined, this study adopts as broadly correct Brown's analysis of the conflict reflected in 1 John as being with opponents originally from within his

---

[62] K Grayston, *The Johannine Epistles* (London: Marshall, Morgan & Scott, 1984), 12.
[63] W Loader, *The Johannine Epistles* (London: Epworth Press, 1992), xvi.
[64] TF Johnson, *1, 2, and 3 John* (Peabody, Massachusetts: Hendrickson, 1993), 5–6.
[65] D Rensberger, *1 John, 2 John, 3 John* (Nashville: Abingdon Press, 1997), 21.
[66] D Rensberger, "Conflict and Community in the Johannine Letters", *Interpretation* 60:3 (2006) 278–91, 291.
[67] *Ibid.*
[68] Peter Rhea Jones, *1, 2 and 3 John* (Macon, Georgia: Smith and Helwys, 2009), 1.
[69] Pheme Perkins, *The Johannine Epistles* (Dublin: Veritas Publications, 1979), xiv.
[70] Deitmar Neufeld, *Reconceiving Texts as Speech Acts: An Analysis of 1 John* (Leyden/New York/Köln: EJ Brill, 1994) 37–9; similarly Matthew D Jensen, *Affirming the Resurrection of the Incarnate Christ: A Reading of 1 John* (Cambridge: Cambridge University Press, 2012), 7–10.
[71] See Brown, *Epistles of John*, 116–30, Painter, *1, 2 and 3 John*, 84–7.

own community and his delineation of the origin of, and the stages in the development of, the Johannine community. It creates difficulties for a peacemaking or non-violent hermeneutic of 1 John, which this study will have to face squarely.

The Purpose of 1 John

As we have seen, Brown postulates that the conflict addressed in 1 John occurred when, as reflected in 1 John 2:19, a group went out or seceded from the Johannine community.[72] This study adopts that widely accepted view. But who were they? The author's purpose cannot be defined without identifying the position(s) of his opponents. As Brown observes, one can only ascertain their beliefs by reconstructing them from the opinions inveighed against by John himself, a mirror-reading which has its perils, in that we cannot assume that every opinion John opposes was held by the secessionists.[73] Similarly we cannot assume that a single set of opponents had a "single tightly held logical position" or that 1 John is "intelligible entirely in the light of the threat of the opponents".[74]

There was a past tendency to identify the secessionists with Gnosticism, as for example Dodd and Bultmann did.[75] Houlden's position is more nuanced, seeing the opponents as unable to accept that the Messiah was identical with the human Jesus who suffered death.[76] He does not openly assert that John's opponents were Gnostic.

Law, writing much earlier, is of similar opinion, identifying John's opponents with Docetism.[77] He distinguishes two types: the first is the "crude, unmitigated" version Ignatius of Antioch describes, which held that Jesus only appeared to be a human being, but was not.[78] The second is the type Irenaeus linked with Cerinthus, denying Jesus' virgin birth and Incarnation altogether, and that he was the Christ, holding that the Christ descended on him at his baptism and left him at his death.[79] Thus this second view alone is sufficient to explain the Christological refutations in 1 John.[80]

Brooke links the opponents' "Christological and ethical laxity". He considers that "they could not tolerate a sharp distinction between Christian and unchristian in belief and practice". He identifies at least nine "tests" offered by John as assuring his readers of the truth of their Christian position. He identifies the opponents as Gnostic.[81] As

---

[72] Brown, *The Community of the Beloved Disciple*, 103.
[73] Ibid, 103–4.
[74] Painter, *1, 2 and 3 John*, 94.
[75] Cf. Dodd, *Johannine Epistles*, xviii–xxi; Bultmann, *Johannine Epistles*, 38.
[76] JL Houlden, *A Commentary on the Johannine Epistles* (London: A & C Black, 1973), 35.
[77] Law, *Tests of Life*, 92–3.
[78] Ibid, 92.
[79] Ibid, 93.
[80] Ibid, 93–4.
[81] Brooke, *Johannine Epistles*, xxviii.

we have seen, Bultmann sees 1 John as written in conflict with Gnostic opponents, although derived in part from a gnostic source.[82]

Strecker's view is more circumspect than those who identify John's opponents as either Gnostic or docetic. To him, Docetism, from the Greek δόκησις/δόκεσῖς, separated the earthly Jesus who suffered and died on the cross from the heavenly being of divine origin who ascended into heaven. So, "no doubt there was also a Gnostic Docetism, but Gnosis and Docetism should not be equated".[83] He says we should not assume that John's opponents thought themselves sinless or were "libertines" who promoted an unethical way of life, seeing the split in the Johannine community as caused by the secessionists' offence against the commandment of ἀγάπη, seen by the author of 1 John as the determining principle of Christian life.[84]

Schnackenburg is even more circumspect. He too identifies the position of the opponents by the formulae John uses against them.[85] He notes John's references to the message they had heard "from the beginning", citing 1 John 2:7 and 24, and 3:11. He postulates that the secessionists were evidently from a Gentile milieu, but that there is no trace in 1 John of the characteristic Gnostic "charismatic enthusiasm" threatening the life of the Johannine community.[86] Schnackenburg identifies the basic Christological tenets of the opponents or secessionists by the opposing formulae adopted in 1 John itself, in 4:2, "by this you know the Spirit of God: every spirit that confesses that Jesus Christ is come in the flesh is from God", and 5:6, "this is the one that came by water and blood, Jesus Christ".[87]

Schnackenburg's point here is that John marks out the opponents as those who reject the central Christological tenets which are central to the faith he is defending. However he doubts that John opposed the Cerinthean notion of a Christ temporarily associated with Jesus.[88] He finds in 1 John no trace of the Gnostic notion of two deities, a superior and inferior power.[89] He prefers the view that Ignatius' docetic opponents, who denied Christ's Incarnation, were identical with those opposed by John, finding striking similarity in the polemical language used by the martyr-bishop in his *Letter to the Smyrnians* and by John.[90]

Schnackenburg also sees the opponents' ethical deficiencies in this way: like John's opponents, Ignatius' heretics "cared nothing about *agapē* or about the widows and orphans, the afflicted, the prisoners, the hungry and the thirsty", and "here we find the same connection between Christological heresy and moral indifference, the same neglect of fraternal love",[91] a very important linkage, followed by later scholars.

---

[82] Bultmann, *Johannine Epistles*, 28 n.21, 38 ("the doctrine of the heretics is rooted in the duality of Gnosticism").
[83] Strecker, *Johannine Letters*, 71.
[84] Ibid, 75.
[85] Schnackenburg, *Johannine Epistles*, 17.
[86] Ibid, 18.
[87] Ibid, 18–19.
[88] Ibid, 20.
[89] Ibid, 21.
[90] Ibid, 21–2.
[91] Ibid, 22.

Brown sees 1 John 4:2 and 5:6 as key indicators of the opponents' deficient Christology, 4:2 as showing that they did not accept Christ's coming *in the flesh*, and 5:2 as signifying the crucifixion, in an echo of John 19:34, the salvific work of which the opponents denied.[92] But he does not go so far as to identify the opponents with the "radical Docetism" opposed by Ignatius of Antioch; they did not deny the humanity of Jesus per se, but rather the "salvific importance of the flesh and the death of Jesus".[93] He also distinguishes the possible positions of the opponents from full-blown second-century Gnosticism.[94] Importantly, Brown traces the same connection as Schnackenburg does between Christological error and moral laxity in John's opponents: "A theory that one's moral behaviour has no salvific importance could flow from a Christology in which the earthly career of Jesus, the way he lived and died, had no great importance."[95] So "the author's insistence of love of brethren ... also makes sense in light of a theory that the adversaries were (former) Johannine Christians of too high a Christology".[96] In other words, devaluing Jesus' humanity led to a devaluation of the moral importance of people's earthly deeds.

A radical deviation from the emerging consensus that John's opponents were Christian – Gnostic or not – is O'Neill's thesis that John's opponents were members of a Jewish sect who had failed to follow their fellows into the Christian community, as shown by self-contained sections in 1 John corresponding to "twelve poetic admonitions", each reflecting a distinct source with its own pre-Christian theology.[97] Painter's objection to this thesis, following Barrett, that Jewish material may appear in 1 John for many other reasons, because the subject matter is Jewish, as were the author and his audience,[98] seems conclusive. Brown's rebuttal of O'Neill's thesis on the basis of 1 John 2:19, "it was from our ranks that they went out",[99] is convincing.

Painter draws a somewhat more radical picture than does Brown of the opponents' Christological views. He builds on the work of Law, Brooke, Dodd and Schnackenburg among others.[100] He postulates that 1 John 2:22ff. suggests that the opponents indeed denied that Jesus was the Christ, by adopting the Cerinthian view, as described by Irenaeus and later by Law, that the higher power, "Christ", came upon Jesus at his baptism and left him at his death.[101] He directly says that the opponents denied the Incarnation, that Christ had come in the flesh.[102] Painter identifies that "their denial of the author's Christological confession shows that their faulty Christology was the basis for their defective understanding of God and their failure to acknowledge the obligation to love the brother".[103]

---

[92] Brown, *Epistles of John*, 76–7, and see also Brown, *The Community of the Beloved Disciple*, 110–12.
[93] Ibid, 58–9.
[94] Ibid, 59–60.
[95] Ibid, 55.
[96] Ibid.
[97] O'Neill, *Puzzle of 1 John*, 6–7.
[98] Painter, *1, 2 and 3 John*, 19.
[99] Brown, *Epistles of John*, 46.
[100] Painter, *1, 2 and 3 John*, 13.
[101] J Painter, *John: Witness and Theologian* (Melbourne: Beacon Hill Books, 3rd ed., 1986), 116.
[102] Painter, *1, 2 and 3 John*, 91–2.
[103] Ibid, 92.

Painter further writes (referring to 1 John 2:9-11) that "the claim to be in the light is falsified by hating the brother or the sister, behavior that exposes a person who is in the darkness", whereas "the person loving his or her brother or sister is in the light".[104] This too delineates the crucial connection in 1 John between theological and moral error. Building on the work of Law, Brooke and Schnackenburg, Painter sees the position of the author's opponents in 1 John as shown by slogan-like assertions, seen in the "if we say" formula in 1 John 1:6, 8 and 10; the "he who says" formula in 1 John 2:4, 8 and 9; and the "if anyone says" usage in 1 John 4:20. To him, these slogans show a coherent picture of the opponents.[105]

Painter's views are cogent. What is opposed in 1 John 1:6, 8 and 10 is moral indifference, and any assertion of fellowship with God while remaining in darkness, in sin. In 1 John 2:4, 8 and 9, claiming to "know" God but not obeying God's commandments and claiming to be "in the light" while hating a brother are stigmatised. In 1 John 4:20, those claiming to love God but hating a brother are condemned as liars. Tied to this is the testing of the spirits in 1 John 4, where in vv.2-3 the spirit that confesses that Jesus Christ – significantly, his full title is used here – is from God, whereas the spirit that does not confess Jesus is not from God.[106]

As Von Wahlde writes, the symbols of light, correct belief, love and ethics structure the letter around the two elements of the tradition attacked by the secessionists.[107] The picture of the opponents emerging here is of a group that denies both the ethical importance of love of the brother (or sister) and the true humanity of Jesus, denials which are essentially an illegitimate extension of the high Christology of the Gospel, especially in its prologue, in the direction of devaluing the Incarnation and Jesus' ethical teaching during his earthly life. And as Kysar says, 1 John "emphasizes the reality of the humanity of Jesus against a Christology which apparently did not take the Incarnation as seriously as it should".[108]

Importantly, as Klauck notes, 1 John 2:19 affirms that it was the secessionists who "went out from us", that is, from the remaining Johannine group to whom John writes, not the other way about: it points to a preceding shared history.[109] John's stance here may therefore be seen as defensive, not offensive, so that the trajectory of 1 John is not to seek to obliterate the opponents and their views, but rather to point out the dangers

---

[104] *Ibid*, 91.

[105] *Ibid*, 90.

[106] As Burge says, πνεῦμα in 1 John is the "litmus test of the orthodox faith": Gary M Burge, *The Anointed Community: The Holy Spirit in the Johannine Tradition* (Grand Rapids: Eerdmans, 1987), 171; see also Gary M Burge, "Spirit-Inspired theology and Ecclesial Correction: Charting One shift in the Development of Johannine Ecclesiology and Pneumatology" in *Communities in Dispute: Current Scholarship on the Johannine Epistles* (ed. R Alan Culpepper and Paul N Anderson; Atlanta: SBL Press, 2014), 179–85, 183.

[107] Urban C Von Wahlde, *The Johannine Commandments: 1 John and the Struggle for the Johannine Tradition* (New York/Mahwah: Paulist Press, 1990), 202.

[108] Robert Kysar, *John: The Maverick Gospel* (Atlanta: John Knox Press, 1976), 115, referring to 1 John 4:2 and 2:22.

[109] Hans-Josef Klauck, "Internal Opponents: The Treatment of the Secessionists in the First Epistle of John" in *Truth and Its Victims* (ed. Wim Beuken, Sean Freyne and Anton Weiler, English language editor James Aitken Gardiner; Edinburgh: T&T Clark, 1988), 55–65, 56.

in their theology and ethics to those remaining within John's group. His advocacy of love, and the connection between Jesus' divine love and that commanded of his followers, falls into place in this context and is in accord with John's Gospel (John 13:1, 14:18-24, 15:9-10, 16:27, 17:22-26) but is still remarkable for its lack of overt aggression. Even if John does not extend the love command to the opponents, he does not counsel hatred of them. We shall come to the significance of this observation for a peacemaking, non-violent hermeneutic of 1 John later.

The resemblance of Painter's views to Brown's is obvious. Like Brown, he sees differences in ideas and vocabulary between John and 1 John as accounted for by differences in genre, situation and intention, so that although their authors may be different, their theological ideas and motifs are still similar. And, like Brown, Painter sees 1 John's author, who is probably not the author of the Gospel but shares the principal features of his vocabulary and theological outlook, as writing after the Gospel and opposing an overly high Christology which secessionist opponents had built on that of the Gospel, so as to unbalance it and to render ethics – mutual love, in imitation of Jesus' love for us – of minimal importance.

Lieu, however, is unconvinced of Brown's and Painter's views. She writes of the situation in which 1 John was written that it "seeks to win its reader(s) in the face of a threat that challenges the author's own standing" and that "this threat is one that had its origins in a recent schism".[110] She considers that the author "apparently understands the problem to be centred on the proper acknowledgement of Jesus", but that "whether Christology was the overt cause of conflict and would have been identified as such by the other side is less certain since the letter never reveals what they did claim, although it is widely supposed that it was so".[111]

This, it must be acknowledged, is a sober and conservative view, which avoids pressing the text beyond its limits in order to define a conflict by inference from the views condemned in it. For example, speaking of the ὁ λέγων [ὅτι] statements at 2:4, 2:6 and 2:9, Lieu says that there is "no suggestion that there were those who did make these statements, and whom the author is concerned to expose and refute".[112] She sees these statements simply as engaging in debate within the author's community, not with those without it.[113] Of the ἐάν τις εἴπῃ formula at 4:20, Lieu contrasts it to the more direct "if we say" formula in the debate about sin in 1 John 1:6-10 and writes that "the more neutral 'if anyone says' carefully dismisses such a possibility from the actual experience of his readers".[114]

In this Lieu follows Perkins, who writes that the slogan "I have known God" in 1 John 2:4 is not a slogan of the author's opponents at all, but rather one that had developed within the Johannine tradition.[115] To Perkins, 1 John 4:20 too does not

---

[110] Lieu, *1, II and III John*, 9.
[111] *Ibid*, 9–10.
[112] *Ibid*, 67.
[113] JM Lieu, *The Theology of the Johannine Epistles* (Cambridge: Cambridge University Press, 1991), 30.
[114] Lieu, *I, II and III John*, 197.
[115] Perkins, *Johannine Epistles*, 23.

stigmatise opponents having a piety of direct vision of God, so undermining the teaching about love for fellow Christians, because the evidence is too weak.[116]

But the strength of Brown's and Painter's view is that it does not press the text beyond its limits either. It is difficult to believe that the ὁ λέγων [ὅτι] statements at 2:4, 2:6 and 2:9, and the ἐάν τις εἴπῃ formula at 4:20, particularly alongside the vehement ψεύστης, used *five times* in 1:10, 2:4, 2:22, 4:20 and 5:10, are mere literary devices to reinforce condemnation of views held only within John's community. It is harder still to accept that they are not addressed to, or do not even refer to, real people who had seceded and were alive and active in opposing that community and its views. Brown and Painter simply define the views against which John contends by the slogans defined by these formulae. This is based solidly on the work of Law, Brooke and Schnackenburg in defining them.

Other recent scholars are in broad agreement with Brown and Painter here. Smalley speaks of John addressing what he saw as deviant Christologies arising originally in his own community which had moved either in a low, Ebionite direction, tending to deny Jesus' divinity, or in too high a direction, denying Jesus' humanity, with a corresponding indifference to right conduct, because of a dualist view of the material, earthly dimension of human life as inherently evil, which he describes cautiously as a "Gnosticising tendency".[117]

Marshall is reluctant to characterise John's opponents as Cerinthean, because there is no echo in 1 John of the Cerinthean view that Jesus is the son of an inferior creator-God, nor of a "developed Gnostic cosmological myth with a series of aeons".[118]

Contra Smalley, Rensberger doubts that John's opponents denied Jesus' divinity or that Cerinthus actually taught that he did not come in the flesh, but he still sees John's opponents only as *forerunners* of later Cerinthean and Gnostic groups.[119] He warns against identifying John's opponents as Gnostics and then interpreting 1 John "in terms of Gnostic traits which it does not even mention".[120]

Johnson still identifies the opponents as "Gnostics".[121] Loader asserts simply that they denied Jesus' coming by "blood", that is his suffering in the crucifixion.[122]

Rhea Jones says the "critical Christological confession", explicit in 1 John 4:2 and implicit at 4:3, indicates docetic denial by the opponents of Christ's "fleshliness".[123]

The majority modern view, which seems correct, seems to be that it is wrong to identify John's opponents as Gnostic per se, but rather that they probably did embrace a docetic viewpoint, although there is disagreement as to its exact type. It sees their ethical deficiencies as related to their defective Christology. This meant that they tended to place lesser importance on ethical conduct because of a view that Jesus' earthly life and

---

[116] *Ibid*, 57.
[117] Smalley, *1, 2, 3 John*, xxiii–xxiv.
[118] Marshall, *Epistles of John*, 18.
[119] Rensberger, *1 John, 2 John, 3 John*, 23–4; similarly Grayston, *Johannine Epistles*, 16.
[120] *Ibid*, 24.
[121] Johnson, *1, 2 and 3 John*, 8.
[122] Loader, *Johannine Epistles*, xv.
[123] Rhea Jones, *1, 2 and 3 John*, 165.

his loving relationships in particular were of lesser significance. The conflict evident in 1 John with those of that view may pose difficulties for a peacemaking hermeneutic.

Conflict in 1 John – Present or Past?

Was the controversy reflected in 1 John, between the author and his opponents, present or past at its time of writing? Scholarly division on this topic must be examined to evaluate properly whether the ethical injunctions in 1 John, the love command in particular, are likely to have been addressed only to those within John's community or to the Christian world in general. If this conflict was past and over, and 1 John was not written in the heat of battle, it becomes easier to see John's ethics – and the love command in particular – as written in a more reflective frame of mind, with the needs of humanity in general, and not just John's own beleaguered community, in mind. However, Brown and Painter are firmly of the view that this conflict, though past, gave rise to painful differences which were still present and raw at the time 1 John was written, as will shortly be traced.

This view has early antecedents and much support in more modern scholarship. Westcott's opinion is that after the destruction of Jerusalem, "outward dangers were overcome", and "the world was indeed perilous, but it was rather by its seductions than by its hostility", and that "now the temptations are from within".[124] He implies that John was indeed battling with heretical opponents who were still active at the very time he wrote. However, Westcott tends to tone down John's polemic, holding that "his object is polemical only so far as the clear unfolding of the essence of right teaching necessarily shews all error in its real character".[125]

Law writes that "there is no New Testament writing which is more vigorously polemical in its whole tone and aim" and that the church or churches addressed "had lapsed into Laodicean lukewarmness", so "for them the absolute distinction between the Christian and the unchristian in life and belief had become blurred and feeble."[126] Sharp and present conflict between John and his opponents is envisaged here.

With Westcott, Brooke considers that the real object of the Johannine epistles is not exclusively, or even primarily, polemical, because edification of his "children" in the true faith and life of Christians is the author's main purpose.[127] But, Brooke writes, for John "the victory has been won, if only after a hard-fought battle", and the opponents, whose errors have been unmasked, "have gone out from among us", or at least the leaders of the movement have withdrawn or been expelled, but "there is still strong sympathy for their views, and perhaps some acute danger of their return to power."[128] John's battle may have been won in the short term, but theological war with active, dangerous opponents was still being waged.

---

[124] Westcott, *Johannine Epistles*, xxxiii.
[125] *Ibid*, xxxix.
[126] Law, *Tests of Life*, 25.
[127] Brooke, *Johannine Epistles*, xxvii–xxviii.
[128] *Ibid*, xxviii.

To Dodd, the rise of "heretical Gnostic sects" occurred in a "tunnel" period of church history after the apostolic age, and "what is not altogether clear is the process whereby this situation came about", but "the First Epistle of John appears to reflect a critical moment in the early stage in the process".[129] Thus those who taught "new doctrines" seceded after failing to carry the church with them and "found a wide hearing – indeed, a wider hearing than the orthodox teachers could command".[130] Thus "the fellowship of the church was rent" and "the rank and file may well be disturbed or perplexed", and "it is to this situation that the epistle is addressed."[131]

Houlden similarly sees the Johannine letters are "part of a campaign to put a brake on those who would 'gnosticise' the Johannine tradition", when the developing church still lacked leaders in authority who "by their very position could at least claim a right to discipline those whose teaching deviated from the approved lines".[132]

Schnackenburg too regards 1 John as reflecting a situation where "the apostasy and departure of the antichrists (2:19)" and "the intense activity of the false prophets (4:1)" have been followed by "the believing community's fight for survival (4:4-6)",[133] while the "gnostic movement is in the ascendant".[134] As noted previously, he speaks of the author of 1 John "fighting on a single front" against "antichrists or false prophets" who, though diverse, are "united in their denial of the church's Christological confession (2:22; 4:2-3)".[135]

Again Perkins' is a different voice. She deals at some length with what she sees as the oral character of John's mode of address to his readers. She writes that we must be careful not to read back the results of the NT canonical process to the period of John's letters.[136] We must remember that to John's readers, texts only had life as they were read aloud, with no more authority than other words spoken solemnly in liturgy or preaching.[137] Therefore, she says, "Scholars who are not sensitive to the language of oral cultures often misinterpret statements about opponents in ancient writings", and that "you would get the impression from reading some of the modern interpreters of the Johannine letters that the community was being violently ripped apart by the debate to which the author refers".[138] Despite John's reference to the opponents having left the community, she sees his hostile language towards them as simply typical of the fierce rhetoric of the time[139] and finds "no indication that [the opponents] have really set up an opposition church".[140]

---

[129] Dodd, *Johannine Epistles*, xviii.
[130] *Ibid*, xviii–xix.
[131] *Ibid*, xix.
[132] Houlden, *Johannine Epistles*, 18.
[133] Brown, *Epistles of John*, 48.
[134] Schnackenburg, *Johannine Epistles*, 17.
[135] *Ibid*.
[136] Perkins, *Johannine Epistles*, xviii.
[137] *Ibid*, xviii–xix.
[138] *Ibid*, xxi.
[139] *Ibid*, xxii.
[140] *Ibid*, xxiii.

Brown argues that the hypothesis that John and the secessionists were writing against each other, "making the claim that their interpretation of the Gospel was correct", explains both the secessionists' views and "the author's style of argumentation".[141] He points to 2 John 10-11, castigating secessionist emissaries for their deficient teaching, although he does not see Diotrephes in 3 John as a secessionist.[142] Brown reconstructs a portrait of John's adversaries, holding that they lay within one organised group, in that as Schnackenburg thought, John was fighting on only one front, based on suggestions in the text that John's opponents' Christology is at fault, that they refuse to listen to him, that they have left his community, and that they represent a threat through propagandists who claim to be teachers.[143] He resists Perkins' view that the rhetoric of 1 John does not reflect present conflict with opponents, referring to 1 John 5:16 where, he says, John refuses prayer for those secessionists who have committed mortal sin.[144] The solution "may not lie in reducing it all to rhetoric with little foundation in reality".[145]

Painter finds "strong affinity" between Law and Schnackenburg,[146] noting that though published in German much earlier, Schnackenburg's commentary on 1 John did not receive due recognition among English-speaking scholars until its English edition was published much later and that Brown's work, built on Schnackenburg's, was not fully appreciated.[147] To Painter, Brown's view that John was fighting vigorously on one front against present opposition which threatened the theological and ethical integrity of his community, is prefigured in, and strengthened by, strong earlier scholarship from Law, Brooke and Schnackenburg.[148]

Painter agrees with Schnackenburg that the polemic in 1 John was primarily addressed to those still within the author's community after the secessionists had left, to discourage them from following them into schism, and to provide encouragement in the trauma left by the schism. So the letter is both didactic and polemical, directed against the opponents (cf. 1 John 1:6-10) and also homiletic and paraenetic, addressed to the remaining community.[149] Painter notes that Law, Brooke and Schnackenburg "have made the point of the pervasive evidence of the conflict with schismatics in 1 John", which was a "bitter and painful event", so there is "polemic against their position".[150] To Painter, the opponents in 1 John had "seemingly been converted but held beliefs incompatible with the Christian faith",[151] and "the conflict with the 'opponents' runs through 1 Jn from the beginning, in the refutation of their boasts, to the end where the author opposes their position with antithetical statements".[152]

---

[141] Brown, *The Community of the Beloved Apostle*, 107.
[142] Brown, *Epistles of John*, 107.
[143] *Ibid*, 49–50.
[144] *Ibid*, 48.
[145] *Ibid*, 49.
[146] Painter, *1, 2 and 3 John*, 9.
[147] *Ibid*, 14.
[148] *Ibid*, 13–14.
[149] *Ibid*, 78, citing Schnackenburg, *Johannine Epistles*, 13–15.
[150] *Ibid*, 16.
[151] Painter, *Witness and Theologian*, 116.
[152] Painter, *Quest for the Messiah*, 444.

Painter sees a "trend to minimise the controversial nature of 1 John by arguing that although there was a schism, it was of minor significance, past and over by the time the epistles were written".[153]

As Painter says, this trend may be seen in Perkins' views which we have already noted. Perkins elsewhere offers an example to demonstrate her point: while the love command in 1 John "refers only to people within the church", citing 1 John 2:9-11 and 4:20-21, this exhortation "treats the failure of love as 'hatred'" and as "evidence that such persons lack eternal life".[154] She sees Johannine Christians as "accustomed to read their sociological experience in theological terms".[155] So "the sociological correlation of Johannine symbolism is also evident in the use of apocalyptic images to describe the opponents in 1 and 2 John".[156]

Like Perkins, Lieu refers to rhetoric in 1 John which is aimed at "the dangers in his own pattern of thought with its strong emphasis on assurance that those who believe should experience", so "there is no need to suppose that there were others that were making such claims but failing in appropriate behaviour: the argument is not directed outside (to supposed opponents) but within".[157] Lieu sees problems in viewing 1 John purely as polemic against opponents who seceded, seeing circularity in reconstructing their beliefs from John's polemic, then using these beliefs to reconstruct the debate with them.[158] She is not the only one to raise this potent point. But, problematic as this may be, how else can we reconstruct the views of John's opponents at all if his literature, not theirs, is the only surviving source? Lieu says that viewing John's rhetoric in the literary context of its time, rather than as necessarily aimed at present opponents, springs from a more "text-centred" reading of 1 John.[159] She says the results of rhetorical analysis of 1 John have so far been "meagre".[160] But as will be seen, rhetorical analysis of 1 John has not led entirely in the one direction, that John's polemic is to be explained by the rhetorical conventions of the time, rather than by a fierce struggle with secessionist opponents who were still alive and threatening.

Griffith has attempted an entirely non-polemical reading of 1 John, to try to dispel the consensus that John's rhetoric is aimed at opponents outside his community, both in its theological and moral dimensions.[161] He argues that, contra Brown, the "slogans" or "boasts", "if we say/claim", ἐὰν εἴπωμεν ὅτι, at 1 John 1:6, 1:8 and 10; "whoever says/claims", ὁ λέγων [ὅτι], at 2:4, 2:6 and 2:9; and "if anyone says", ἐάν τις εἴπῃ ὅτι, at 4:20

---

[153] Painter, 1, 2 and 3 John, 16.
[154] Pheme Perkins, "Apocalyptic Sectarianism and Love Commands", 289.
[155] Pheme Perkins, "Koinōnia in 1 John 1:3-7: The Social Context of Division in the Johannine Letters", CBQ 45:4 (1983): 631–41, 632.
[156] Ibid, 633.
[157] Lieu, I, II and III John, 16.
[158] Lieu, Theology of the Johannine Epistles, 15–16.
[159] JM Lieu, "Us or You? Persuasion and Identity in 1 John", JBL 127, no 4 (2008): 805–19, 806.
[160] Ibid. There she cites at n.6, as examples of rhetorical analysis of 1 John, Duane F Watson, "1 John 2:12-14 as Distributio, Conduplicatio, and Expolitio: A Rhetorical Understanding", JSNT 11 (1989): 97–110, and Duane F Watson, "Amplification Techniques in 1 John: The Interaction of Rhetorical Style and Invention", JSNT 16 (1993): 99–123.
[161] Terry Griffith, "A Non-Polemical Reading of 1 John: Sin, Christology and the Limits of Johannine Christianity", Tyn Bul 49:2 (1998): 253–76.

are contradicted by a "counterclaim". This is related implicitly or explicitly to ethical conduct, and far from their being polemic aimed at opponents and their claims, "it is far more likely that 1:5–2:11, indeed the whole of 1 John, has a pastoral rather than a polemic outlook, since nowhere are the views of opponents positively stated or refuted".[162]

Griffith argues that the formula, "if we say/claim", ἐὰν εἴπωμεν ὅτι, is a *pluralis sociativus* often used in Greek literature to confront readers with their own actions.[163] He offers apparently compelling instances of "Johannine"-type rhetoric, for example, the use of the ἐάν τις εἴπῃ, "if anyone says", formula in Philo's writings,[164] to show that use of this and similar formulae by John need not lead us to presuppose present secessionist opponents. Griffith quotes Lieu's view that the moral debate in 1 John is not explicitly related to the schismatics and need not be seen as a reaction against them and that by rhetorical persuasion the author seeks to lead his readers to conclusions made inevitable by his chosen starting point.[165]

How may we resolve the scholarly conflict we have traced? And of what significance is the solution for a peacemaking hermeneutic of 1 John? Divining who the author's opponents were when 1 John was written, and whether his rhetoric is used in the heat of conflict, or when such conflict was long past, so that the heat of the rhetoric is to be explained by the style and techniques of the time, is fraught with difficulty. Despite the confidence with which proposals are offered in the literature, the impression is unavoidable that any conclusions must be tentative, since they are based on analysis of the text of 1 John itself. The obvious danger is circularity, using the text to infer who the opponents were and whether the conflict was finished or still raging, and then analysing the text in light of one's conclusions.

That said, there appear to be two problems with Perkins, Lieu and Griffith's arguments. The first is John's denunciation at 1 John 2:18-25 of the "antichrists" who "went out from us" (2:19). The use of the aorist for "went out", ἐξῆλθαν, as Brown notes, "suggests a specific action"; although there may have been "constant leakage" from John's community, this usage suggests a "major rift" bringing the secessionist group into existence.[166]

But does the use of the perfect, "have gone out", ἐξεληλύθασιν, in 4:1d, "for many false prophets have gone out into the world", contradict Brown's analysis? Lieu argues that the use of the perfect here, while it "might refer to their departure", probably emphasises more "the evident fact of [the false prophets'] presence".[167] Brown's reply is convincing: despite the change of tense between 2:19 and 4:1d, John phrases the false prophets' departure in this way "because he wishes to underline their choice of the world, theologically understood as the enemy of Christ".[168] The reference at 2:19

---

[162] *Ibid*, 254–5.
[163] *Ibid*, 256.
[164] *Ibid*, 259.
[165] *Ibid*, 256–7.
[166] Brown, *Epistles of John*, 338.
[167] Lieu, *1, 2 and 3 John*, 165.
[168] Brown, *Epistles of John*, 490.

to those who "went out from us" more probably colours the whole denunciation of "antichrists" extending from 2:18 to 2:25, and the paraenesis on "testing the spirits" at 4:1-6.

Lieu's explanation that the constant use of "us" in 2:19 signifies that the problem only occurred *within* John's community, not with secessionists who had left it,[169] does not take sufficient account of the aorist reference to those who "went out", ἐξῆλθαν, from "us". This may suggest a definite past event – that is, an actual schism.

Perkins' view, that John's concern in 2:19, to assure his audience that those stigmatised were not really "from us" (2:19c), "shows that they have not established a completely independent sect", is vulnerable to the same criticism.[170] In 2:19, the aorist, ἐξῆλθαν, does not contraindicate, but indeed suggests, real and present conflict with a group who had left the fellowship at the time John wrote and threatened to attract further membership from it.

The second problem with Perkins, Lieu and Griffith's views is that the "slogans" or "boasts" really do appear to be aimed at *real people*. The most obvious and natural interpretation of "whoever says/claims", ὁ λέγων [ὅτι], at 2:4, 2:6 and 2:9, and "if anyone says", ἐάν τις εἴπῃ ὅτι, at 4:20 is that John is here arming his audience against arguments from *actual opponents*, who might imminently present these claims to them. It presses rhetorical arguments too far to suggest that merely because the use of this kind of language was undoubtedly common in Graeco-Roman rhetoric, no actual opponents need to be presupposed. This argument is strengthened if the same author wrote 2 John, where in v.7 we read of "many deceivers" who "have gone out into the world, who do not confess that Jesus Christ has come in the flesh" and that "any such person is the deceiver and the antichrist [ἀντίχριστος]" – a direct echo of ἀντιχρίστου in 1 John 4:3. The issue of common authorship of 1, 2 and 3 John, however, is beyond the scope of this study.

As Brown says, there is parallelism in the use of "liars", ψεύστης, in relation to those portrayed in 4:20, "those who say 'I love God' and hate their brothers": this is an "adversary statement" similar to the same use of ψεύστης in 2:4, "whoever says 'I have come to know him' but does not obey his commandments", suggesting John "is thinking of the secessionists and not simply enunciating a general maxim".[171]

Perkins does not disagree that the views opposed by the author of 1 John and 2 John (and one might point here to 2 John 7) were developed from the Christology of John's Gospel.[172] But her proposal is that at 2:4 "I have known God" was not a slogan of the opponents but one "developed in the Johannine tradition", based on John 14:7, where Jesus says to Thomas, "If you had known me, you would have known my Father also."[173] She says that 4:20 is to be accounted for by simply saying that "the distinction between 'saying that one loves God' and actually loving fellow Christians is the Johannine formulation of the common paraenetic distinction between saying and actually doing

---

[169] Lieu, *1, 2 & 3 John*, 101.
[170] Perkins, *Johannine Epistles*, 35.
[171] Brown, *Epistles of John*, 533.
[172] Perkins, *Johannine Epistles*, xiv.
[173] *Ibid*, 23.

(cf. 1 Jn 3:18)".[174] The objection to this lies in the personal tone of the ὁ λέγων [ὅτι] designation at 2:4, repeated in 2:6 and 2:9, and the "if anyone says", ἐάν τις εἴπῃ ὅτι, formula at 4:20. Actual opponents, rather than theological possibilities, are a more compelling explanation of such rhetoric.

Lieu's arguments are that in 2:4, 6 and 9 the "whoever says" or equivalent formula "remains a hypothetical or rhetorical possibility"[175] and that in 4:20-21 John is simply "proposing scenarios only to dismiss them as self-evidently flawed" and "drawing [his readers] into a pattern of logical necessity".[176] As with Perkins' arguments, these proposals take insufficient account of the ferocious tone of personal address evident in the ὁ λέγων [ὅτι] statements at 2:4, 2:6 and 2:9, and "if anyone says", ἐάν τις εἴπῃ ὅτι, formula at 4:20, particularly alongside the vehement ψεύστης in 2:6 and 4:20.

One must also remember the similar use of ψεύστης in 2:22a, "who is the liar but the one who denies that Jesus is the Christ?", where it is used, not merely in an ethical argument, but in a directly theological and indeed a Christological context. Again, the existence of actual opponents threatening the author's community and its stability, this time in its Christological beliefs, rather than hypothetical rhetorical possibilities, would seem the most natural inference to draw from such vehement, personalised language.

Griffith's argument, that John's use of rhetorical figures and techniques common in literary argument in the ancient world undercuts any inference that 1 John was written in the heat of conflict with secessionists still threatening his community, may be answered by Watson's analysis, already noted, of 1 John's rhetorical techniques, for example, amplification,[177] including such figures as augmentation and comparison,[178] as well as *expolitio*,[179] *regression*,[180] *conduplicatio*,[181] *distributio*,[182] *synonymy*[183] and *epanaphora*,[184] along with other techniques. After this exhaustive examination, Watson speaks of the "rhetorical situation" in 1 John as one where the "rheator" is "a member of the Johannine school", prompted to write by "a schism within the Johannine community which has resulted in secessionists leaving the rheator's audience to form their own community (2.18-19, 2 Jn 7)", the schism being "rooted in different understandings of Christology and ethics within the Johannine tradition (3.23; cf. 2 Jn 9)".[185] Watson remarks that "the use of amplification indicates a careful working of the material and the need to be emphatic and clear in the face of the secessionist doctrine and practice to which his audience is subject".[186]

---

[174] *Ibid*, 57.
[175] Lieu, *1, 2 and 3 John*, 70.
[176] *Ibid*, 197.
[177] Watson, "Amplification Techniques", 100–18.
[178] *Ibid*, 102.
[179] *Ibid*, 103–8.
[180] *Ibid*, 108–9.
[181] *Ibid*, 109–10.
[182] *Ibid*, 110–11.
[183] *Ibid*, 111–12.
[184] *Ibid*, 112–13.
[185] *Ibid*, 118.
[186] *Ibid*, 122–3.

Contra Griffith, Watson sees no reason to infer from John's use of rhetorical techniques of the time that he was not writing against present secessionist opponents threatening his community's beliefs and ethical practice. This is sound. Why, one might ask, would John not have used emphatic rhetorical techniques from his time as the most potent weapon available to him in order to confront present opponents in a live theological struggle?

This study therefore adopts the view adopted by Brown, Painter and others that the rhetoric in 1 John is aimed at real opponents who had seceded from his community and threatened to take others with them and that the conflict reflected in it is present rather than past. John's "love command" as the antidote to pressures from without is more remarkable, given that it arose in the heat of present conflict, than it would be if it were simply part of a rhetorical response to tendencies espoused by past opponents who had already suffered defeat. It may be that a non-violent reading of 1 John is more, rather than less, cogent if John's response to present, fierce conflict consists only of simple injunctions to his remaining community to hold to right belief and to love one another and avoiding hatred as the begetter of violence.

The Literary Structure of 1 John

The literary structure of 1 John has long presented a problem. It has no scheme of logical development of a single theme, but rather multiple themes which collide, in the manner of a fugue, being brought into contrapuntal relationship with one another. It lacks a connected plot – it is called a letter, after all, although there is no salutation or subscription, nor the ending one would expect of a letter.[187] Yet it cannot be read out of the context of its time, and it seems to have a concrete motive, stemming from a split in the community in which it was written.[188] Nevertheless, one also finds in 1 John the theme of universal healing wrought by Jesus' sending by God into the world, despite the epistle's concentration on the Johannine community.[189] The aphoristic character of the writer's "meditations" may mean that any endeavour to analyse the Epistle's structure is "useless".[190]

But what possible significance can the literary structure of 1 John have for the application of a peace-oriented, non-violent hermeneutic to the epistle? First John's underlying themes of faith in Jesus' coming in the flesh and mutual love are deliberately yoked together by the author in the literary structure of his letter, which primarily serves that connection. It therefore becomes clear that the epistle teaches that an ethic of mutual love and forbearance is compelled by faith in Jesus as truly incarnate in human flesh, because in his behaviour and teaching in his earthly life and death, he is the exemplar of this ethic.

---

[187] Theo C Heckel, "Die Historisierung der Johanneischen Theologie im Ersten Johannesbrief", *NTS* 50.3 (2004): 425–43, 428.
[188] *Ibid.*
[189] Hansjörg Schmid, *Gegner im 1. Johannesbrief?* (Stuttgart: Verlag W Kohlhammer, 2002), 262.
[190] Painter, *1, 2 and 3 John*, 116, following Brooke.

To Westcott, 1 John is in form a letter, but with no address or subscription and no evident destination, unlike even James, Ephesians or Hebrews, but personal in tone, speaking "in teaching and in counsel with the directness of personal experience".[191]

Law speaks of 1 John's simplicity of syntactical structure, the absence of connecting particles and "the generally Hebraic style of composition".[192] But to him it lacks logical structure or ordered progression of thought. Its small number of themes, righteousness, love and belief, are introduced many times and brought into every conceivable relationship.[193] The key to its interpretation is that it uses tests to evaluate whether the reader is "begotten of God".[194]

Brooke sets out Hort's scheme, which to some extent follows Häring's earlier one, which Brooke himself recommends.[195] It is as follows:

1:1-4 Introduction
1:5–2:17 God and the true light; goodness, not indifference.
2:18–3:24 Sonship to God, and hence likeness to His Son, and abiding in him.
4:1–5:17 Faith resting on knowledge of the truth the mark of the divine Spirit, not indifference.
5:18-21 Conclusion. The Christian knowledge, the true and the false.

Schnackenburg sets out a similar structural outline, also reliant on Häring. Schnackenburg is sceptical of its value, noting the strong caesura at 3:24: to him, the warning by those who find only a loose articulation in the epistle, that such analyses are purely subjective, is well taken.[196]

Schnackenburg's scheme is as follows:

Prologue: 1:1-4
   A. 1. Ethical thesis: 1:5–2:17 – Walking in the light as the true sign of fellowship with God.
      2. Christological thesis: 2:18-27 – Faith in Jesus as the Christ serving as the basis for fellowship with God.
   B. 1. Ethical thesis: 2:28–3:24 – Righteousness of life as a sign of being begotten of God.
      2. Christological thesis: 4:1-6 The Spirit proceeding from God confesses that Jesus Christ is come in the flesh
   C. The two theses combined:
      4:7-21 – Love as the basis for faith
      5:1-12 – Faith as the basis of love.
   Conclusion: 5:13-21.

---

[191] Westcott, *Epistles of St John*, xxix–xxx.
[192] Law, *Tests of Life*, 2.
[193] *Ibid*, 5.
[194] *Ibid*, 6.
[195] Brooke, *Epistles of St John*, xxxvii–xxxviii.
[196] Schnackenburg, *Johannine Epistles*, 12.

This scheme perhaps suggests more logical connections between themes than the epistle truly possesses, but it is useful. A possible criticism of it, which Schnackenburg concedes, is that it ignores the strong caesura at 1 John 3:24.[197]

That point too is well taken. After 3:24 there is an obvious change of subject at this point from "commandments", ἐντολὰς, in 3:24, to which the preceding discourse at 2:7–3:24 relates, from the first mention of ἀλλ' ἐντολὴν παλαιὰν, "but an old commandment", in 2:7, to πνεύματι, "spirits", at 4:1. The πνεύματι at 4:1 are not of course to be identified with the πνεύματος at 3:24: the former are human, or even diabolic, but the latter is divine. The contrast is deliberate.[198]

Brown offers a simpler literary structure of 1 John as follows:[199]

I. *The Prologue (1:1-4).*
   I. Part One (1:5–3:10): *The Gospel that God is light, and we must walk in the light as Jesus walked.*
   II. Part Two (3:11–5:12): *The Gospel that we must love one another as God has loved us in Jesus Christ.*
   Conclusion (5:13-21): A statement of the author's purpose.

Brown defends this structure, which he says imitates that of John's Gospel, by arguing that the bipartite division for which he argues is best placed at 1 John 3:10; he says this is because 3:11 opens the second section by a change of subject, where "the Gospel which we have heard from the beginning" is defined as "we should love one another", so that although "the secessionists are never out of mind", the "intensity of direct address to the author's adherents becomes more pronounced".[200]

That may be so, but ἡ ἀγγελία ἣν ἠκούσατε ἀπ' ἀρχῆς, ἵνα ἀγαπῶμεν ἀλλήλους, "the message which you have heard from the beginning, that we must love one another", at 3:11 surely refers directly back to 2:10, ὁ ἀγαπῶν τὸν ἀδελφὸν αὐτοῦ ἐν τῷ φωτὶ μένει, "whoever loves the brother lives in the light". The thought is similar.

On the other hand, Schnackenburg's "strong caesura" at 3:24 introduces the new discussion at 4:1 onwards until 4:6, of πνεύματι who might lead the community astray into false Christology. Before then, the subject is obeying Jesus' commandments; after 4:1, the subject is those πνεύματι who do (or do not) confess that Ἰησοῦν Χριστὸν ἐν σαρκὶ ἐληλυθότα, "Jesus Christ has come in the flesh" (4:2b). The change of subject

---

[197] *Ibid.* Coombes' comment, that determining structure is helpful in following the line of argument in the text of 1 John, and that the presence of subunits shows John's grouping of ideas in small segments linking together to form a unit in which the ideas are developed repetitively, is cogent here: Malcolm Coombes, *1 John: The Epistle as a Relecture of the Gospel of John* (Preston, Vic.: Mosaic Press, 2013), 47.

[198] So Brown, *Epistles of John*, 486. Talbert sees a change of subject between 3:24a and 3:24b, seeing 3:24a as the last of three "signs" in 3:14-15, 3:18-22 and 3:24a: Charles Talbert, *Reading John: A Literary and Theological Commentary on the Fourth Gospel and the Johannine Epistles* (London: SPCK, 1992), 32–3. But this view takes insufficient account of the linking function of the verb μένει in 3:24a and 24b, which links the "abides" statements in 3:24a with the Spirit, our means of knowledge of them, in 3:24b.

[199] Brown, *Epistles of John*, 124.

[200] *Ibid*, 127.

from ethics, obedience to Jesus' commandments, to Christology is obvious. Therefore the most obvious bipartite division in 1 John, if there is one, may occur after 3:24.

In 4:7 the ἀγάπη, which ἐκ τοῦ θεοῦ ἐστιν, "is from God", is yoked indissolubly to the commandment ἀγαπῶμεν ἀλλήλους, "let us love one another", by the linking ὅτι, which is causal.[201] That sets the tone for the whole discourse until 5:13 where the Epilogue begins. All the way through from 4:7 to 4:21, the theme is that God has loved us by sending his Son, so we ought to love one another. Had not Jesus been the Christ, the true divine Son, the command to love one another would dissolve.

In 5:1-5 we see the proof of loving τὰ τέκνα τοῦ θεοῦ, "the children of God" (5:2a), that is, *each other*, as being loving God and obeying God's ἐντολὰς (5:2b). Then in 5:6-12 the Spirit is μαρτυροῦν, "testifying" (5:6b), along with the water – Jesus' baptism – and the blood – his death – to Jesus being God's Son.[202] And so (5:11) ἡ μαρτυρία is that God gave us eternal life, which is his Son.

Again, love of one another is yoked to God's love of us and to obeying his commandments. This is a return to the theme announced at 4:7 that we must love each other, because love is from God. The whole section from 4:7 to 5:12 shows this linkage. It is dependent on 4:1-6: we must believe only those spirits that confess that Jesus Christ is come in the flesh, because only by confessing this does the reader see the true reason for the command to love one another. Thus there is a strong argument that the true caesura in 1 John is not at 3:10, as Brown maintains, but at 3:24.

More satisfying is Painter's literary structure for 1 John, largely following Häring's of 1892, but also built on the later "tests" analysis of Law, Brooke and Schnackenburg.[203] Its scheme is as follows (simplified here for reasons of space):

I. *Prologue (1:1-5)*
II. *First presentation of the two tests (1:6–2:27)*
   1. *The ethical (love) test (1:6–2:17)*
   2. *The Christological test (2:18-27)*
III. *Second presentation of the two tests (2:28–4:6)*
IV. *Third Presentation of the two tests (4:7–5:12)*
V. *Conclusion (5:13-21)*

This analysis is more satisfying because, as Painter says, it emphasises the controversial nature of 1 John, in that the "tests" were necessary because the author believed that "counterfeit claims were abroad in the church", and the claims of the opponents had to be set out and tested, so the true could be affirmed and the false rejected.[204] While one can see that there is a strong caesura at 1 John 3:24, the structure which the epistle more truly yields on analysis is that of Häring as modified by Painter. It is one which presents each of the "tests", ethical and Christological, in turn, alternating between the

---

[201] Martin M Culy, *I, II, III John: A Handbook on the Greek Text* (Waco, Texas: Baylor University Press, 2004), 107.
[202] So Painter, *1, 2 and 3 John* 306.
[203] *Ibid*, 117–18.
[204] *Ibid*, 118.

ethical and the Christological, until the Epilogue is reached, which is more blessing and reassurance than a conclusion drawn from the preceding argument. In that way the author shows that the "tests" are interlinked to bring understanding that without right Christology, affirming that Jesus is the true Son of God who truly came in the flesh, the love of God in sending the Son cannot be rightly apprehended, and neither can the proper ground for loving each other.

Smalley presents a bipartite outline of 1 John, as follows:

I. Preface (1:1-4) *The Word of Life*
II. Live in the light (1:5–2:29)
God is light (1:5-7)
First condition for living in the light: renounce sin (1:8–2:2)
Second condition: be obedient (2:3-11)
Third condition: reject worldliness (2:12-17)
Fourth condition: keep the faith (2:18-29)
III. Live as children of God (3:1–5:13)
 (a) God as Father (3:1-3)
 (b) First condition for living as God's children: renounce sin (3:4-9)
 Second condition: be obedient (3:10-24)
 Third condition: reject worldliness (4:1-6)
 Fourth condition: be loving (4:7–5:4)
 Fifth condition: keep the faith (5:5-13)
IV. Conclusion (5:14-21) Christian confidence.[205]

What will be immediately noticed in Smalley's suggested structure is, firstly, that he places the division or caesura at 3:1, and secondly the resemblance between Smalley's "conditions" and Law, Brooke, Schnackenburg and Painter's "tests". As to the placement of the caesura, this depends on where one sees the major change of subject occurring. The argument for finding it at 4:1 has already been presented, as has the reason why it may not matter. As to Smalley's "conditions" and Painter's "tests", both terms emphasise John's object to uphold the author's Christology and ethics against the "heretical" views of the opponents and demonstrate their falsity.

Thomas criticises Brown and Smalley's suggested structures as "contrived"[206] and "forced",[207] suggesting instead a concentric or chiastic structure.[208] This proposal, while ingenious, has the defect that in seeing 3:11-18 as the centre of the chiasm, it takes insufficient account of the caesura at either 3:10, 3:24 or 4:1, as set out above.

As we have seen, if 1 John's unifying themes of faith in Jesus' coming in the flesh and mutual love are deliberately yoked together by the author in the structure of his letter, serving that connection, it is clear that the epistle teaches that an ethic of mutual love and forbearance is compelled by faith in Jesus as truly incarnate in human form.

---

[205] Smalley, *1, 2, 3 John*, xxxiii–xxxiv.
[206] John Christopher Thomas, "The Literary Structure of 1 John", *Nov T* 40:4 (1998): 369–81, 370.
[207] *Ibid*, 371.
[208] *Ibid*, 372.

Painter's "tests" outline demonstrates precisely this connection. And it is a connection which is developed against a background of present conflict with opponents with false "slogans" contradicting any such connection, aiming at picking off stragglers from the remaining Johannine community. That the remedy for this situation in which 1 John was written is faith in Jesus as God's true Son and mutual love, not hatred of the opponents, makes a peacemaking hermeneutic of 1 John more feasible than it would have been if hatred of the opponents themselves, rather than strong denunciation of their doctrines, were offered as the solution to the conflict.

Reception of 1 John in the Early Church

There remains a scholarly division regarding the time by which the Johannine writings, and John's Gospel in particular, were accepted by the Great Church[209] as orthodox, and the extent to which they were used by dissident groups ultimately recognised as heterodox. Bauer is the modern progenitor of the view that a tendency towards caution when approaching the Gospel of John was continuous in ecclesiastical Rome, the centre of orthodoxy.[210] Sanders thinks that John's Gospel appeared to have been used first by the Gnostics.[211]

Hill correctly observes that to speak of "orthodox Johannophobia", as if the consensus were that what became orthodox Christianity was wary of the entire Johannine corpus, including 1 John, may put the matter too simply, because any such reservations about the orthodoxy of John's Gospel may not have applied to 1 John.[212] This would be unsurprising if the view adopted in this study is correct, namely that 1 John was written to correct both an over-high Christology, derived from pressing too far the Christological implications of John's Gospel, and consequent ethical indifference in the secessionist group who had left the original Johannine community. The controversy as to reception of John's Gospel in the very early church is beyond our scope. But as will be shown, use of 1 John, and recognition of it as authoritative teaching, appears very early and indeed not long after its most likely time of writing, the last decade of the first century. The consequences of this for a non-violent interpretation of 1 John will be briefly examined later.

For present purposes, a brief survey of scholarship on this question over the last 150 years or so will suffice. Westcott noted that 1 John was spoken of as an ἐ πιστολὴ, καθολική "Catholic epistle", from the close of the second century CE onwards, citing Clement of Alexandria and Origen.[213] Law notes its quotation by these two Fathers, and

---

[209] This convenient phrase, legion in scholarly writings since Bauer, is used here to denote the church circles or groups who embraced what later became orthodox teaching – no value judgement is implied.

[210] Walter Bauer, *Orthodoxy and Heresy in Earliest Christianity* (London: SCM Press, 1972), 208.

[211] JN Sanders, *The Fourth Gospel in the Early Church: Its Origins and Influence on Christian Theology up to Irenaeus* (Cambridge: Cambridge University Press, 1942), 86.

[212] Charles E Hill, *The Johannine Corpus in the Early Church* (Oxford: Oxford University Press, 2004), 11.

[213] Westcott, *Epistles of St John*, xxviii.

by Cyprian, Tertullian and Irenaeus, and its earlier use, without citing it by attribution to John, in Polycarp's *Epistle to the Philippians* ("*Philippians*"), which "contains an almost verbal reproduction of 1 John 4".[214]

Brooke offers use by "the Presbyter" and by Papias (as related by Eusebius) of the phrase αὐτὴ ἡ ἀλήθεια as evidence that 1 John was both known and valued during the first quarter of the second century.[215] Schnackenburg too notes acknowledgement of 1 John by Origen and Eusebius, and its use by Tertullian, Cyprian and Clement of Alexandria, and its citation in the Muratorian Canon in the second half of the second century.[216] Brown notes use by Ignatius of Antioch of Johannine ideas, maintaining that to Ignatius, the Matthean-Lucan infant Christology and the Johannine pre-existence Christology is sequential rather than contradictory.[217] Brown argues that in the second century, Polycarp of Smyrna supplied "eloquent proof" as to the sympathies of church writers when choosing between the two communities that emerged from the schism of 1 John 2:19, noting, as Law does, the strong verbal resemblance to 1 John 4:2-3, without citation, of Polycarp's *Philippians*.[218]

Painter also sees the Epistles of Ignatius of Antioch (which he dates at circa 110-115 CE) as alluding to 1 John 2:18 and 3:2.[219] He too notes passages in Polycarp's *Philippians* (which he dates as not later than 140 CE), which he thinks are almost certainly dependent on 1 (and 2) John.[220] Marshall refers to "citations" of 1 John by Polycarp in *Philippians* and to "possible allusions" to it in Ignatius' *Letter to the Ephesians*.[221] Lieu sees the earliest citation of 1 and 2 John as being by Irenaeus, who attributes them to the Beloved Disciple and to John the son of Zebedee.[222]

Hartog offers a more detailed examination of Polycarp's use of 1 (and 2) John, noting that in *Philippians* 7, Polycarp's concern is with the "many" who do not confess, inter alia, that Jesus Christ is come in the flesh.[223] The similarity here to 1 John 4:2 is obvious. Hartog also notes the close verbal parallels between *Philippians* 7.1 and 1 John 4:2b-3a.[224] These are certainly present, as Hartog sets out.[225] *Philippians* 7.1 uses the phrase Ἰησοῦν χριστὸν ἐν σαρκί ἐληλυθέναι ἀντιχριστόςἐστιν,[226] and the almost identical statement in 1 John 4:3a is καὶ πᾶν πνεῦμα ὃ μὴ ὁμολογεῖ a τὸν b Ἰησοῦν ἐκ τοῦ θεοῦ οὐκ ἔστιν· καὶ τοῦτό ἐστιν τὸ τοῦ ἀντιχρίστου. Furthermore, as Hartog points

---

[214] Law, *Tests of Life*, 39. So also Brooke, *Johannine Epistles*, liii; Brown, *Epistles of John*, 106 n.248.
[215] Brooke, *Johannine Epistles*, liv.
[216] Schnackenburg, *Johannine Epistles*, 46–7.
[217] Brown, *Epistles of John*, 112–13.
[218] *Ibid*, 9, 113.
[219] Painter, *1, 2 and 3 John*, 40.
[220] *Ibid*, 41.
[221] Marshall, *Epistles of John*, 48.
[222] Lieu, I, II, and III John, 26.
[223] Paul A Hartog, "The Opponents of Polycarp, *Philippians* and 1 John" in *Trajectories through the New Testament and the Apostolic Fathers* (ed. A Gregory & C Tuckett; Oxford: Oxford University Press, 2005), 375–91, 377: see also *The Apostolic Fathers: Greek Texts and English Translations* (ed. & trans. Michael W Holmes; Grand Rapids: Baker Academic, 3rd ed., 2007), 289.
[224] Hartog, "The Opponents of Polycarp," 379–80.
[225] *Ibid*, 380.
[226] *Apostolic Fathers*, 288.

out,[227] in a "probable allusion", the phrase ἐκ τοῦ διαβόλου is found in *Philippians* 7.1,[228] and also in 1 John 3:8, although referring there to those who commit sin. These and other examples offered by Hartog suggest not merely verbal dependence of Polycarp on 1 John in *Philippians*, but also common opponents and tendencies being addressed by both authors.

Hill notes Irenaeus' reference to his association with the aged Polycarp and Polycarp's intercourse in turn with John and others who had "seen the Lord" (ἑωρακότων, cf. 1 John 1:1-2) as evidence of his authority, as reported by Eusebius in his *Historia Ecclesiastica*.[229] He notes that Irenaeus, as reported by Eusebius, refers to Polycarp receiving traditions from these persons, "the eyewitnesses of the word of life" παρὰ τῶν αντπτῶν τῆς ζωῆς τον λόγου, a reference to 1 John 1:1, τοῦ λόγου τῆς ζωῆς.[230] This suggests use of 1 John by Irenaeus to identify and combat similar tendencies to those against which 1 John was written. Thus in very early times we have two examples of 1 John being utilised in polemic against heresy by prominent figures in what became the Great Church. We may deduce from this that certainly 1 John – whether or not there were early reservations about John's Gospel – was seen early on as an ἀπιστολὴ καθόλικη in the Great Church. The implications of this for a non-violent hermeneutic of 1 John will be drawn together in our final chapter. But in short, if 1 John's commandment to its readership to love one another was an inevitable concomitant to right belief, and the Great Church accepted this teaching in very early times, then it was really accepting that the corrective to heresy is the belief that Jesus came in the flesh, in love for humankind, and that this divine love itself commands mutual love and concern, rather than hatred and violent killing, as 1 John 3:11-17 teaches.

Conclusion

1 John might seem the very last NT text to which to apply a peacemaking or non-violent hermeneutic. It is undoubtedly the record of a bitter theological battle between John and those who have left his community, divided from it by irreconcilable differences, over ethics but also over the nature of Jesus himself, and of his mission on earth. Was he God's true Son? Was he truly human no less than truly divine? What were the implications for ethics in the remaining Johannine community? How could it protect itself from further incursions by the dissidents?

As we have seen, the feasibility of applying a non-violent or peacemaking hermeneutic to 1 John can only be judged after asking prior questions of the text. To whom and why was it written? What is its literary structure? When and how was it

---

[227] Hartog, "The Opponents of Polycarp", 380.
[228] *Apostolic Fathers*, 288.
[229] Hill, *Johannine Corpus*, 353.
[230] *Ibid*.

received in the early church? These suggest that such a hermeneutic may be applied to 1 John. Whether it can be examined in the following chapters of this study.

There are strong indications that the slogans or "boasts" opposed in the ὁ λέγων and like formulae indicate still-raw conflict with theological opponents now departed from the Johannine community. They are "antichrists" and to be avoided, but hatred is condemned as being "like Cain" (3:12), leading to murder. Thus present conflict may present difficulty for any peacemaking hermeneutic of the epistle. But love, hatred's opposite, is counselled within the community at every turn, rather than a lust for revenge against opponents, who might otherwise have been seen as deserters and traitors to the remaining Johannine community. How this may yet permit a peacemaking hermeneutic is examined in the forthcoming chapters.

2

Ἱλασμός and Its Cognates in the Septuagint, the Intertestamental Literature and the Dead Sea Scrolls

Introduction

Peacemaking theology has made much of Jesus' death as both an uncovering and an ending of the notion of sacrificial placation of an angry God, or as a demonstration of God's love for humanity, as opposed to a propitiatory sacrifice to be appropriated by humankind to placate a wrathful God, to divert the divine anger that would otherwise fall upon them. The battleground on which these competing ideas have been contested is ἱλασμός in 1 John 2:2[1] and 4:10.[2] The debate is not new. Rather than making a futile attempt to resolve it, the contribution this and the next chapter seek to make is to ask whether 1 John, in its use of the word ἱλασμός and the ideas behind it, supports the conclusions for which some peacemaking theologians cite it.

This chapter first examines the seven uses of ἱλασμός in the LXX. It is beyond the scope of this study to analyse comprehensively the LXX uses of its cognates, ἱλάσκεσθαι, or the more common intensive, ἐξιλάσκεσθαι, for they are many, although a few will receive some brief attention. It will then look at some uses of ἱλασμός in the intertestamental literature, which will necessarily be selective as the field is so vast. Then, to illustrate further the Jewish background against which 1 John was written, we shall briefly examine some presentations of atonement ideas using the Hebrew word כִּפֶּר, "atone", derived from the root כָּפַר, *kaphar* ("cover") in the Dead Sea Scrolls. Finally some conclusions will be drawn concerning the Jewish background which may underlie the use of ἱλασμός in 1 John 2:2 and 4:10. The next chapter will then deal with the two uses of ἱλασμός in 1 John itself, making use of the conclusions reached in this chapter as to its Jewish background.

Ἱλασμός in the Septuagint

There are six occurrences of ἱλασμός in the LXX which correspond to the Hebrew Bible, translated in modern English versions. There is another in 1 Chronicles 28:20

---

[1] "And he is the atoning sacrifice for our sins, and not only for our, but also for the whole world's sins."
[2] "Love is in this, not that we loved God but that he loved us and sent his Son to be the atoning sacrifice for our sins."

which, although in the LXX, does not appear in the Hebrew or in modern English translations. It must be dealt with here, as in LXX form it would probably have been available to the author of 1 John.

As we shall see, it is not the case that ἱλασμός always, or even usually, conveys the idea of propitiation, although it often refers to sacrifice. We shall see that as used in the LXX, ἱλασμός translates a variety of Hebrew words, and the thought behind them varies widely. Unsurprisingly, ἱλασμός has no fixed meaning in the LXX.

Any attempt to give ἱλασμός a static or fixed meaning in the LXX is to fly in the face of James Barr's cogent warning that while it is often essential to undertake comparative etymological study to unlock the meaning of Hebrew words (and, one might add, Greek words), etymology should not be used to impose a meaning on known usage of Hebrew terms. As Barr warns, etymological associations which appear to be theologically attractive cannot be allowed to assume command of the whole task of interpretation without attending to the semantic context of the word in the passage under consideration.[3] Words are used differently in regions and over time by different language users. The following analysis must take these facts into account and identify different shades of meaning when using the same word. This approach has proved fruitful in examining the differing meanings of ἱλασμός in the LXX. The uses of this LXX term will be examined in the order of their appearances.

(i) Leviticus 25:9

The first LXX occurrence of ἱλασμός is in Leviticus 25:9b.[4] This unit, Leviticus 25:8-55, concerns all of the ritual and social obligations upon Israelites, to the Lord and to each other, in a Jubilee year. The Hebrew for ἱλασμοῦ in v.9b is הַכִּפֻּרִים in the plural.[5] Despite the common rendering of "atonement" for the term, "purgation" may be a more appropriate translation in this verse. It better conveys the original sense of "cleanse" lying behind it. In the OT, כִּפֶּר can be used synonymously and in parallel with "wipe" or "remove" (e.g. Isaiah 27:9a, "by this will Jacob's guilt be atoned for, יְכֻפַּר, and this will be the first fruit of the removal, הָסֵר of his sin") and with "blot out" (e.g. Jeremiah 18:23b: "do not forgive, תְּכַפֵּר their crimes or blot out, תֶּמְחִי their sins").[6] Noting these parallels, "wiping" or "removal" is closer to the sense conveyed by the term הַכִּפֻּרִים in Leviticus

---

[3] James Barr, *The Semantics of Biblical Language* (Oxford: Oxford University Press, 1961), 158–9.
[4] "On the day of purgation (ἱλασμοῦ) you shall make a proclamation with a trumpet throughout all your land." In this study the author's translations from the LXX and the Hebrew appear, but as before, in many cases, where those of the NRSV (*Holy Bible: New Revised Standard Version* (London: HarperCollins, 1998)) cannot be bettered, they are mirrored.
[5] The Hebrew OT text in this study is taken from *The Interlinear NIV Hebrew-English Old Testament* (ed. John R Kohlenberger III; Grand Rapids: Zondervan, 1987).
[6] Jacob Milgrom, *Leviticus 1–16* (New York: Doubleday, 1991), 1080. However, to the extent that Milgrom relies (partially) on Akkadian and other nearby Semitic languages' use of cognates of *kipper* to mean "wipe" or "obliterate", Feder cogently suggests that the variation in usages of Semitic cognates of *kipper* may be too wide to base a conclusion that this term *always* means "wipe" or "obliterate" in Hebrew: Yitzhaq Feder, "On *Kupperu, Kipper* and Etymological Sins that Cannot be Wiped Away", *VT* 60 (2010): 535–45, 537–8.

25:9b than "propitiate", a translation which implies appeasement or that "the principle of substitution is at work on the altar: animal life takes the place of human life".[7]

Textually, Wevers argues against ἐξιλασμόν as the LXX original in 25:9b, shortened in later texts to ἱλασμόν, maintaining that ἱλασμόν is indeed original here.[8] If ἱλασμόν is in the original, its meaning is far less specifically propitiatory than ἐξιλασμόν would carry. A mid-position, which preserves *both* propitiation and cleansing as ideas expressed by כִּפֶּר, is just as unsatisfactory, as the two notions are really contradictory: one implies cleansing *by* God after the required ritual, and the other implies propitiation offered *to* the deity.

Scholars differ over the many possible meanings of כִּפֶּר in the entire OT, and a full examination of this debate is outside our present scope. We will examine its meaning only in those LXX examples where ἱλασμός and occasionally where its cognates are used to translate כִּפֶּר, to cast light on use of ἱλασμός in its LXX context.

There is no doubt that elsewhere in Leviticus, and in Deuteronomy, in the rites of the scapegoat (Leviticus 16:10, 20-21) and the broken-necked heifer (Deuteronomy 21:1-9), the "*kipper*-carrier" (or bearer) is a ransom or substitute, onto which the impurities in the sanctuary are transferred. Thus it becomes lethal and must be driven out. But in the Masoretic Text in its final form these rites have a new purpose: the *expiation* of the people's sins.[9] This is clear from the fact that the driving out of the goat, the "*kipper*-bearer", although it bears the people's culpability, does not in Leviticus 16:10 or 20-21 *itself* purify them from sin. That is the exclusive function of the purification of the sanctum by cleansing sacrifice.[10] In Leviticus 16:10, the goat on which the lot fell "for Azazel" just refers to the goat which must be "sent away". The Hebrew לַעֲזָאזֵל in 16:10 means "as a goat of departure", which refers to that which must be *sent away* alive into the wilderness to purify the people from sin. In the LXX, לַעֲזָאזֵל is rendered by τήν ἀποπομπήν, which carries the sense of *carrying away evil*. The Hebrew does not have that specific connotation. We shall come later to the same term in 1 Enoch, where it refers to a demon.

Equally, in Leviticus 4 different types of unintentional sin – by the priest attributed to the people (4:3-12), by the whole congregation of Israel (4:13-21), by a ruler (4:22-26) or by one of the people (4:27-31) – are identified with differing sin offerings

---

[7] N Kiuchi, *The Purification Function in the Priestly Literature: Its Meaning and Function* (Sheffield: JSOT, 1987), 107. Kiuchi writes here of Leviticus 17:11, but it follows from his argument that הַכִּפֻּרִים in Leviticus 25:9b would be translated similarly.

[8] John William Wevers, *Notes on the Greek Text of Leviticus* (Atlanta, Georgia: Scholars Press, 1997), 405.

[9] Milgrom, *Leviticus 1–16*, 1082. Or as Gorman puts it, the Priestly (P) text here draws on the symbolic equation of the wilderness with chaos, so that the goat takes Israel's anti-moral acts outside the social structure they have endangered: FH Gorman, *The Ideology of Ritual: Space, Time and Status in the Priestly Theology* (Sheffield: Sheffield Academic Press, 1990), 98–9, cited in David Janzen, *The Social Meaning of Sacrifice in the Hebrew Bible* (Berlin/New York: Walter de Gruyter, 2004), 108.

[10] Roy Gane, *Cult and Character: Purification Offerings, Day of Atonement, and Theodicy* (Winona Lake, Indiana: Eisenbrauns, 2005), 262–3. Gane disagrees with Milgrom's view that purification offerings purge only the holy place itself (Jacob Milgrom, "A Prolegomenon to Leviticus 17:11", *JBL* 90 (1971): 150–1), holding that they also purify the offeror who has sinned or is ritually impure: Gane, *Cult and Character*, 127, 129. But either way, what is offered effects *cleansing* rather than propitiation.

prescribed in each case. In each case, except the first, the priest makes atonement on behalf of others by cleansing the horns of the altar with the blood of a bull in the second case and with that of a goat in the last two. In each case, that which is offered "as a sin offering", 4:14, לְחַטָּאת, *cleanses* not the sinner but the holy place.[11] This is shown by the fact that the noun used for "sin offering" here is formed from the *Piel* of the verb חָטָא, sin. In Biblical Hebrew, the *Piel* stem may connote the undoing or elimination of the very act signified by the *Qal* stem of the same verb.[12] Again, expiation, not propitiation, is the idea conveyed.

In its ritual usage the subject of כָּפֶר is usually the priest, and the object is something contaminated, but by contrast, outside its ritual usage the subject of כָּפֶר is usually God, and its direct object is sin: for example, Isaiah 6:7b,[13] 22:14b,[14] Jeremiah 18:23b,[15] Ezekiel 16:63,[16] Psalms 66:5a,[17] 78:38a,[18] 79:9b.[19] But this is consistent with the ritual usage of this word group. Even there, ritual impurity is ultimately caused by sin, and *God* grants purification on performance of the rite.[20]

It is often assumed that reference to blood from a sacrificed animal in OT purification rites implies substitutionary sacrifice, and that part of the meaning of כָּפֶר is to placate an angry God or to pay a ransom.[21] But in Leviticus 16:18-19,[22] using in its LXX version a ἱλασμός derivative, *expiation* in the sense of *cleansing*, is the idea conveyed. Again, וְכִפֶּר, "and he shall atone" (LXX ἐξιλάσασθαι) (v.18) is synonymous with וְטִהֲרוֹ, "and he shall cleanse" (LXX ἀκαθαρσιῶν) in v.19.

Here, expiation or forgiveness is not just an effect of the priest's actions. These are a prerequisite, as is contrition, but *God* grants expiation or purification from sin.[23] The priest is the subject of the action, the holy place the direct object, but the people are the indirect object, *for* whose sin the rite is performed, as is clear from Leviticus 16:33, "he shall purify (וְכִפֶּר) the sanctuary and the tent of meeting and the altar, and shall perform expiatory rites with respect to the sins of the people".[24]

---

[11] Milgrom, *Leviticus 1-16*, 255.
[12] *Ibid*; Baruch A Levine, *Leviticus* (Philadelphia: The Jewish Publication Society, 1989), 20.
[13] "Now that this [a burning coal] has touched your lips, your guilt has gone, and your sin is blotted out."
[14] "Surely this sin will not be forgiven for you until you die."
[15] "Do not forgive their iniquity, do not blot out their sin from your sight."
[16] "In order that you may remember and be confounded, and never open your mouth again because of our shame, when I forgive you all that you have done, says the Lord."
[17] "You atoned for our transgressions with goodness."
[18] "Yet he, being compassionate, forgave their iniquity, and did not destroy them."
[19] "And forgive our sins, for your name's sake."
[20] Milgrom, *Leviticus 1-16*, 1083-4.
[21] Cf. R Laird Harris, "The Meaning of '*Kipper*', Atone", *JETS* 4:1 (1961), 3; Silvain Romerowski, "Old Testament Sacrifices and Reconciliation", *Euro J Th* 16:1 (2007), 13-24, 16.
[22] "Then he shall go to the altar before the Lord and make purgation on its [the assembly's] behalf, and shall take some of the bull's blood and that of the goat, and put it on the horns of the altar. He shall sprinkle some of the blood with his finger seven times on it, and shall cleanse and hallow it from the uncleanness of Israel's people."
[23] Baruch A Levine, *In the Presence of the Lord* (Leiden: EJ Brill, 1974), 65-6.
[24] *Ibid*, 65.

Notably, here an angry God is *not* the direct or indirect object of the verb יְכַפֵּר. God grants the result, expiation or cleansing of sin, freely, *after* the action has been performed. The point here is that, as the Holiness Code in Leviticus 19 shows, holiness is maintained by obedience to the Commandments, so offerings must be made to *cleanse* the holy place, defiled by human sin, that is disobedience of the Commandments.[25] Divine forgiveness then follows. Rather than propitiation of divine anger, this divine forgiveness through *cleansing* sacrifice is what is connoted by ἱλασμός in Leviticus 25:9b. If propitiation of an angry God were the meaning intended, one might expect God to be the direct, or at least the indirect, object.[26]

(ii) Numbers 5:8

Numbers 5:8[27] in the LXX show ἱλασμός being used in a somewhat different context. Numbers 5:5-8 contain legal instruction regarding the procedure to be followed when a man (or woman) wrongs another and so (importantly) breaks faith with the Lord (5:6). In 5:8 we find τοῦ κριοῦ τοῦ ἱλασμοῦ used to render the Hebrew אֵיל הַכִּפֻּרִים, "the ram of the expiation rites", a phrase which includes כַּפֵּר, referring the offering of the ram in sacrifice by the wrongdoer to expiate their wrong.

This term אֵיל הַכִּפֻּרִים, "the ram of the expiation rites", refers to the ritual referred to in Leviticus 5 as אָשָׁם, "guilt" (or reparation) offering: the procedure is set out in Leviticus 7:1-10.[28] In 5:8a, it is that where the injured person has no next of kin, what is offered "as a guilt offering", לַחֲטָאת, is made to the priest.[29] But the actual "atoning process" is set out in Leviticus 6:1-7 in four steps: first, the wrongdoer must feel guilt (6:4); second, the wrong done must be confessed (6:7a); third, the principal sum representing the value of the wrong plus twenty percent interest must be paid to the injured party (6:5b) and fourth, a ram is presented to the Lord as reparation for sacrilege.[30] So *shalom* is restored between perpetrator and victim.[31]

What this demonstrates is that this process, including אֵיל הַכִּפֻּרִים, the ram offered in the guilt offering to the Lord, has a *relational* function. Here we see the expiation

---

[25] Daniel P Wright, "Holiness in Leviticus and Beyond", *Int* 50:4 (1999), 351–64, 353, 356, 359; similarly Levine, *Leviticus*, 102–3.

[26] It is acknowledged by Glenn N Davies and Michael R Stead in their magisterial essay, "Atonement and Redemption" in *Christ Died for Our Sins: Essays on the Atonement* (ed. Michael R Stead; Canberra: Barton Books, 2013), 35–58, 43–5, that the "semantic map" of Atonement in the Pentateuch is concerned with the forgiveness of sin, cleansing and removal of guilt, consecration and the averting of plague or wrath, rather than redemption, although the theme of the essay is the mixing of atonement and redemption metaphors elsewhere in the OT, a subject beyond the scope of this study.

[27] "If the injured person has no next of kin to whom restitution can be made for the wrong, the restitution for wrong shall go to the Lord for the priest, as well as the ram of atonement (ἱλασμοῦ) with which atonement is made for the guilty man."

[28] Baruch A Levine, *Numbers 1–20* (New York: Doubleday, 1993), 190.

[29] *Rashbam's Commentary on Leviticus and Numbers* (ed. & trans. Martin I Lockshin; Providence: Brown Judaic Studies, 2001), 168.

[30] John H Hayes, "Atonement in the Book of Leviticus", *Int* 52:1 (1998), 5–15, 11.

[31] *Ibid.*

process employed, not to placate an angry God, but to reconcile humanity with God and with each other. It follows from the requirements of Leviticus 5:1-7 that a sinner cannot receive expiation of sin without repentance.[32] The ram of atonement is the guilt offering required in Leviticus 5:25.[33]

Returning to Numbers 5:5-10, it is notable that this unit repeats Leviticus 5:20-26. But unlike the latter passage, the former contains no explicit reference to a false oath to the deity (cf. Leviticus 5:22). This indicates that in Numbers 5:5-10 we see the transformation of the notion of a guilt (or reparation) offering, discussed above, from the sacral to the moral-legal sphere: the object of the obligation prompted by the incurring of guilt is transferred primarily from the deity to the injured person.[34] The defrauding of a fellow is a sin against God.[35]

The point in Numbers 5:8 is that אֵיל הַכִּפֻּרִים, the ram offered in the guilt offering, is offered to cleanse the sin of the wrongdoer against both the deity *and* their neighbour. This offering expiates the wrong, so as to reconcile the wrongdoer with God and their neighbour. Thus the atonement process here, and thus ἱλασμός as used in translation in the LXX in Numbers 5:8, while it certainly bears a *sacrificial* meaning, does not connote *propitiation* of divine anger, but rather expiation of sin by the deity, after performance of the cleansing ritual and repentance by the wrongdoer.

(iii) 1 Chronicles 28:20c

First Chronicles 28:20c in the LXX, which does not appear in the Hebrew text, reads:

καὶ ἰδοὺ τὸ παράδειγμα τοῦ ναοῦ καὶ τοῦ οἴκου αὐτοῦ, καὶ ζακχω αὐτοῦ, καὶ τὰ ὑπερῷα καὶ τὰς ἀποθήλας τὰς ἐσωτέρας, καὶ τὸν οἶκον τοῦ ἱλασμοῦ, καὶ τὸ παράδειγμα οἴκου Κυρίου.[36]

This follows 28:20a-b, which does appear in the Hebrew. First Chronicles 28:20 is part of David's public speech in the assembly at Jerusalem, directed to his son Solomon, where he lays out for him the plan of the Temple for the Ark of the Covenant (28:2). The Temple is the unifying point for all Israel.[37] David's plan for it also contains items only attributed elsewhere to the Tabernacle. So it reinforces the Temple's role as the carrier and embodiment of Israel's most sacred institutions.[38] The point here is that it provides for Israel a place of God's continued *presence*.

---

[32] Gane, *Cult and Character*, 202–3.
[33] Philip J Budd, *Numbers* (Waco, Texas: Word Books, 1984), 58.
[34] Israel Knohl, "The Guilt Offering of the Holiness School (Num. V 5–8)", *VT* 54:4 (2004), 516–26, 521.
[35] *Ibid*, 522; Jacob Milgrom, *Numbers* (Philadelphia: Jewish Publication Society, 1990), 35–6; similarly Levine, *Numbers 1–20*, 190–1.
[36] "And look, the plan of the temple, indeed his house, and its treasury and the upper chambers, and the inner store rooms and the mercy seat, and the plan of the house of the Lord."
[37] Roddy Braun, *1 Chronicles* (Waco, Texas: Word Books, 1986), 276.
[38] Gary N Knoppers, *1 Chronicles 10–29* (New York: Doubleday, 2009), 941–2.

The phrase τόν οἶκον τοῦ ἱλασμοῦ in 1 Chronicles 28:20c, usually translated "the place of propitiation", may also be translated "the house of the mercy seat".[39] The "mercy seat" or "atonement cover", כַּפֹּרֶת, ἱλαστοριον in the LXX, occurs at Exodus 25:17, part of the Lord's instructions to Moses regarding the building of the Ark of the Covenant. The instruction here is to build a mercy seat of pure gold, flanked by cherubim (25:18), to be placed atop the Ark (25:21) containing "the Covenant which I shall give you".

One may also translate כַּפֹּרֶת as "place of clearing (or cleansing)"; each year at *Yom Kippur* it receives a sin offering whereby the people and the Tabernacle are "cleared". Yahweh's continued presence is assured (Leviticus 16:14-15); Yahweh's spirit can only abide in a place of the utmost ritual cleanliness atop the כַּפֹּרֶת.[40]

Thus the thought in 1 Chronicles 28:20c may be seen to be in harmony with that in 28:20b, οὐκ ἀνήσει σε, καὶ οὐ μή ἐγκαταλίπῃ, "he [the Lord] will not forsake nor fail you". Divine assurance lies at the heart of David's promise to his son Solomon. The assurance that "he will not forsake nor fail you" is Deuteronomic: see Deuteronomy 4:31; 31:3; also Joshua 1:5.[41] First Chronicles 28:20 contains another Deuteronomic formulae: "be strong and of good courage" (Deuteronomy 31:7, 23). All of these are concentrated in Deuteronomy 31:1-8, which also contains "God is with you", also found in 1 Chronicles 28:20.[42]

Beneath the ideas conveyed in 1 Chronicles 28:20c by the mercy seat, כַּפֹּרֶת, lies the thought of God's reassurance and constancy. The mercy seat is seen, not as connoting a place of propitiation of an angry deity, but as the symbol and embodiment of a merciful God who forgives sinners and is with them always. The point of David's instructions to Solomon is that the Temple, especially the mercy seat in the Holy of Holies covering God's Covenant with the people, stands as a symbol that God will be with them always.

(iv) Psalm 130:4

In the LXX Psalm 130(129):4,[43] ἱλασμός appears in an entirely different context. It translates הַסְּלִיחָה, literally "the forgiveness", rather than כִּפֶּר. The ordinary meaning of the root סָלַח is "forgive".[44] The Hebrew conception in Psalm 130:4 is of *removal* of sin from God's sight by forgiveness, promoting reverence for the deity by removal

---

[39] Edward Lewis Curtis and Albert Alonzo Madsen, *The Book of Chronicles* (Edinburgh: T&T Clark, 1910), 300.
[40] William HC Propp, *Exodus 19–40* (New York: Doubleday, 2006), 385–6; similarly U Cassuto, *A Commentary on the Book of Exodus* (trans. Israel Abrahams; Jerusalem: The Magnes Press, The Hebrew University, 1967), 332; John C Durham, *Exodus* (Nashville: Thomas Nelson, 1987), 359–60.
[41] Ralph W Klein, 1 *Chronicles* (Minneapolis: Fortress Press, 2006), 528.
[42] Sara Japhet, *I and II Chronicles* (London: SCM Press, 1993), 485.
[43] A closer translation of 130(129): 4 in the LXX is "for with you there is forgiveness (ἱλασμός), so your *name* may be revered" because of the appearance of ὀνόματος, "name", of which there is no direct equivalent in the Hebrew, which simply reads תִּוָּרֵא, lit. "you are feared": but see below.
[44] Cf. Exodus 34:9, "This is a stiff-necked people: forgive (וְסָלַחְתָּ) (lit. 'and you forgive'), our iniquity and our sin, and take us for your inheritance"; Leviticus 4:26, "and he shall be forgiven (וְנִסְלַח)".

of human sins after penitence.[45] Forgiveness is for God alone.[46] Fear of God is not terror, but reverence for a deity who is all-powerful *and* compassionate.[47]

Psalm 130 is a penitential Psalm, focusing not on retribution against Israel's enemies but on the iniquities of Israel itself.[48] Verse 4 stands out in its context because it marks a caesura which is also a turning point in the thought of the psalm. Verses 1-3 sound a note of almost-despairing supplication:

> Out of the depths have I cried unto thee, O Lord; Lord, hear my voice. Let thine ears be attentive to the voice of my supplications. If thou, Lord, shouldest mark iniquities, O Lord, who shall stand?[49]

There is a change of mood with the words of assurance: "But there is forgiveness with thee, that thou mayest be feared." The new thought in v.4 is that the God from whom we are alienated is the God to whom we may appeal, as there is no other source of forgiveness.[50] Here ἱλασμός denotes something very different from ritual cleansing from sin by sacrifice. In Psalm 130:4, God is the *subject* of the action, humankind the *object*. Forgiveness, ἱλασμός is not something extracted from a wrathful God by propitiation, not in view at all. It is a free divine gift to the penitent.

The same root, סָלַח (in the form וְסָלַחְתָּ, "now you forgive"), appears in Psalm 25:11.[51] Here the LXX (Psalm 24) renders it as ἱλάσῃ, a ἱλασμός cognate. But in Psalm 65:3, כִּפֶּר in the phrase, תְּכַפְּרֵם (lit. "you forgave [atoned for] them") appears, with the same idea, forgiveness, being conveyed.[52] Here the LXX (Psalm 64) again renders it as ἱλάσῃ. This strongly suggests that the same idea as that underlying וְסָלַחְתָּ in Psalm 25:11, forgiveness, rather than propitiation, is being conveyed by תְּכַפְּרֵם in Psalm 65:3. Similarly, no propitiatory connotations underlie הַסְּלִיחָה, translated by ἱλασμός in Psalm 130(129):4.

(v) Ezekiel 44:27

In Ezekiel 44:27[53] in the LXX we find ἱλασμός used to mean "sin offering". The LXX reads προσοίσουσιν ἱλασμόν. But there is *no* equivalent of ἱλασμόν in the Hebrew, which simply reads יַקְרִיב, literally "he must offer", from the root קרב, "offer", "approach", "bring near". This word often refers to humankind's approach to the presence of God: in Psalm 65:4a[54] we find וּתְקָרֵב used in the sense of God bringing people into God's presence.

---

[45] Charles Augustus Briggs, *A Critical and Exegetical Commentary on the Book of Psalms Vol II* (Edinburgh: T&T Clark, 1925), 465; similarly *Tehillim Vol 2* (trans. Rabbi Avrohom Chaim Feuer in association with Rabbi Nosson Scherman, commentary by Rabbi Avrohom Chaim Feuer; Brooklyn, NY: Mesorah Publications), 1565.
[46] Ibid.
[47] Robert Alter, *The Book of Psalms* (New York: W. W. Norton, 2007), 455.
[48] Ibid.
[49] The KJV wording of this famous and much-loved psalm cannot be bettered!
[50] Walter Brueggemann, *Old Testament Theology* (Nashville: Abingdon Press, 2008), 318.
[51] "Now you forgive my iniquity, O Lord, for it is great."
[52] "When works of iniquity overwhelm us, you forgave our transgressions."
[53] "In that day when he shall go into the holy place, to the inner court, to minister in the holy place, he shall offer his sin offering (ἱλασμον), says the Lord God" is a fair translation of the LXX.
[54] "They are happy whom you choose (וּתְקָרֵב, lit. 'and you bring near') to live in your courts."

In Ezekiel 44:27, קרב is used in a sense analogous to the offering by the high priest after inadvertent sin and by others after ceremonial uncleanliness (Leviticus 4:3; 12:6-8; 14:12-19; 15:15; Numbers 6:11-14).[55] These instructions are intended to be equivalent to the Torah.[56] The context of Ezekiel 44:27 in this unit (44:15-31) is the guarding of boundaries in the Temple (44:15-27) and among the people by the Levitical priests, the sons of Zadok (44:15).[57]

Ezekiel 44:11 lays down a new law that the Levitical priest shall offer and slay these sacrifices presented by the people: beforehand they used to offer them themselves.[58] But 44:25 prescribes that the Levitical priests (44:15) *generally* may not defile themselves by contact with a corpse. However an exception is made for deceased parents, children, sons or unmarried daughters. The need for a priest to count seven days after he has become clean (44:26) increases the ritual demands on an unclean priest, compared to the instructions to a lay person in Numbers 6:11-14.[59]

Traditionally these verses have been read as permitting a *lay* person to touch a corpse, perhaps a loved one, provided that a cleansing offering is then performed.[60] But it is more likely that the lay regulation of Numbers 19:11-19 is indeed referred to, but with extra demands befitting the priestly status of the offeror, because he, a priest, has touched a relative's corpse, as permitted by 44:26.[61] In part, the association of this ritual by the priest with that imposed on lay people may be so that the priest may teach them the difference between the holy and the common.[62]

Either way, it is clear that Ezekiel 44:25-27 does not *forbid* a priest touching the corpse of a relative, as distinct from a non-family member. A priest who has touched such a corpse therefore does not *sin* by violating the law in 44:25: it falls within the permission contained in the exception for relatives. Rather, he becomes ritually *unclean* and must count seven days after he becomes clean (44:26) and then make his offering in the inner court of the holy place (44:27) before resuming his duties.

The Hebrew contains no equivalent of ἱλασμός at all: what is offered does not *propitiate* the deity for human sin but effects *purification*.[63] The offering is made so that, in the eyes of God, the offeror is cleansed and fit to resume priestly duties. It may be that the offerings in Ezekiel 40-48 function to demonstrate the worshipper's complete devotion to God, so that they can make atonement, that is, be cleansed from

---

[55] GA Cooke, *A Critical and Exegetical Commentary on the Book of Ezekiel* (Edinburgh: T&T Clark, 1936), 487.
[56] Daniel I Block, *The Book of Ezekiel Chapters 25-48* (Grand Rapids: Eerdmans, 1998), 644.
[57] Nancy R Bowen, *Ezekiel* (Nashville: Abingdon Press, 2010), 252.
[58] Cooke, *Ezekiel*, 481.
[59] Walther Zimmerli, *Ezekiel 2* (trans. James D Martin; Philadelphia: Fortress Press, 1983), 461; Leslie C Allen, *Ezekiel 20-48* (Dallas: Word Books, 1990), 264.
[60] William Greenhill, *Ezekiel* (Edinburgh: Banner of Truth Trust, first published 1645-1667, 1863 ed., repr. 1994), 804.
[61] Allen, *Ezekiel 20-48*, 264; contra Rabbi Dr S Fisch, *Ezekiel* (London & Bournemouth: Socino Press, 1950), 308-9, reflecting the traditional rabbinical interpretation of Rashi and others, that 44:27 has no connection with 44:26 and relates to the offering of a tenth of an ephah brought by all priests at their consecration when they officiated for the first time.
[62] Robert Jenson, *Ezekiel* (Grand Rapids: Brazos Press, 2009), 318.
[63] Darrin W Snyder Belousek, *Atonement, Justice and Peace* (Grand Rapids, Mi.: Eerdmans, 2012), 248.

ceremonial defilement.[64] But these offerings are not propitiations of a wrathful deity, by substitution of an animal victim for a human one.

(vi) Daniel 9

In Daniel 9:9[65] in the LXX we find ἱλασμός used in a non-sacrificial way, translating the Hebrew וְהַסְּלִחוֹת, "and the forgivenesses", from סָלַח, "forgive". Here 9:9a is prompted by 9:9b, "for we have rebelled against him".[66] God allows us to live, though we have rebelled.[67]

The context in Daniel 9:4-19 is Daniel's great prayer to the Lord, seeking to atone for his sins and those of Israel itself, for freedom in return. The reference in 9:2 to Jeremiah is to the prophecy in Jeremiah 25:11-12 and 29:10 of seventy years of service by the Israelites to the King of Babylon, followed by return to Israel and punishment of Babylon. Daniel makes this prayer at a time when Darius, a Mede, has become king also of the Chaldeans (9:1). He, one might anticipate, may be God's instrument to right Israel's wrong, in accordance with Jeremiah's prophecy.[68]

The theology of Daniel's prayer seems strongly Deuteronomic: Israel is punished for its sin and appeals to God for mercy, which God will grant, although it must be said that the primary focus in Daniel's visions is the sin of the Gentile king.[69]

In Daniel 9:9, therefore, ἱλασμός as a translation of the Hebrew וְהַסְּלִחוֹת depicts God as merciful and forgiving. In no sense does God require propitiation or a turning away of divine anger otherwise falling on Israel. Daniel makes his prayer in light of prophecy promising freedom after exile as punishment. The term of imprisonment has been served, and God has already promised release. Daniel simply asks the Lord to keep a promise, while appropriately acknowledging his and Israel's sin, and that it deserved the penalty of exile. In no sense does ἱλασμός here convey even a faint echo of propitiation. The idea is of a free gift by a forgiving God to a penitent people – after paying the penalty of exile.

(vii) Amos 8:14

In Amos 8:14[70] in the LXX, ἱλασμός translates בְּאַשְׁמַת, "by the guilt (or shame) of" Samaria.[71] The Hebrew comes from the root אָשָׁם, "guilt". The idea here is false Gods: the two false deities mentioned here are, as is often the case, associated with places,

---

[64] So Jerry M Hullinger, "The Function of the Millennial Sacrifices in Ezekiel's Temple, Part 1", *B Sac* 167: 40–57, 55.
[65] "Compassion and forgiveness belong to the Lord our God, for we have rebelled against him."
[66] James A Montgomery, *A Critical and Exegetical Commentary on the Book of Daniel* (Edinburgh: T&T Clark, 1927), 365.
[67] Rabbi Hersh Goldwurm, *Daniel* (Brooklyn, NY: Mesorah Publications Ltd, 1998), 248.
[68] See generally Iain M Duguid, *Daniel* (Phillipsburg, NJ: P & R Publishing, 1998), 149–50.
[69] John J Collins, *Daniel* (Minneapolis: Fortress Press, 1993), 359–60.
[70] "Those who swear by the guilt of Samaria, and 'by the life of your God' from Dan, and 'by the life of your pantheon' to Beersheba, they shall fall and never rise again": for this translation, closer to the Hebrew than most, see Francis L Andersen and David Noel Freedman, *Amos* (New York: Doubleday, 1989), 826.
[71] This apparently refers to the fall of Samaria to the Assyrians, related in 2 Kings 17:5-6: this ended the rule of King Hoshea of Samaria, who did evil in the sight of the Lord (17:1-2).

Beersheba and Samaria, with both gods found together at Dan.[72] In the case of Samaria, the reference may be to worship at the Samarian sanctuary in Bethel with its image of a calf.[73] Hosea 8:6 speaks of "the calf of Samaria", עֶגְלֵךְ שֹׁמְרוֹן, and the golden calf is called "your sin", חַטַּאתְכֶם, in Deuteronomy 9:21.[74]

Amos 8:7[75] and 8:14 work to form a larger inclusion.[76] The two participles, הַשֹּׁאֲפִים, "those who trample", in 8:4 and הַנִּשְׁבָּעִים, "those who swear", in 8:14, match each other.[77] The reference in 8:7 is to the evil actions in 8:4-6: trampling down the poor and bringing them to ruin, offering wheat for sale on the Sabbath, currency speculation, false weights and measures, buying the poor for silver and the needy for footwear, and selling grain refuse. This last may have been aimed at powerful corn merchants.[78] This inclusion shows that it is for the true God to swear not to forget such deeds, not for those unfaithful to him to swear by false deities. The evil-doers in 8:4-6, as well as the false-swearers (8:14), will never rise again.[79]

In Amos 8:14, ἱλασμός is often translated "propitiation", but the context makes it clear that this is not the meaning conveyed. It may be that there is here introduced in the LXX an ironic reference to the (ineffective) "sin-offering", ἱλασμός of Samaria.[80] But this idea is not present in the Hebrew, where the thought is simply "guilt", אָשָׁם. The whole unit, Amos 8, is a prediction of divine punishment for evil-doing of all kinds. The point in 8:14 is that divine punishment will inevitably fall on evil-doers. The thought is not propitiatory sacrifice, deflecting divine anger, but the inexorability of divine punishment for evil deeds.

Cognates of ἱλασμός in the Septuagint

There is space here for only five representative examples. It is convenient to examine those offered by Law in his analysis of the meaning of ἱλασμός in 1 John 2:2 and 4:10: his work is early, but still germane. Law notes that כֹּפֶר, "ransom" or "price of a life" and its derivatives, from the root כָּפַר, "cover", are translated by the LXX in Psalms 65:3, 78:38 and 79:9 as ἱλάσκεσθαι, but more frequently in the LXX by the intensive ἐξιλάσκεσθαι, whereas ἱλασμός is the regular translation of הַכִּפֻּרִים, lit. "the atonements" (always used in the plural) in the LXX.[81]

Law's examples of the use of ἱλασμός-derived words in the LXX are worthy of examination, as they convey a variety of meanings, although they all translate

---

[72] Ibid, 828.
[73] Shalom M Paul, Amos (Minneapolis: Fortress Press, 1991), 270.
[74] Ibid.
[75] "The Lord has sworn by the pride of Jacob: I will surely not forget their deeds."
[76] Andersen and Freedman, Amos, 829.
[77] Ibid.
[78] AG Auld, Amos (Sheffield: Sheffield Academic Press, 1995), 86.
[79] Andersen and Freedman, Amos, 829.
[80] W Edward Glenny, Finding Meaning in the Text: Translation Techniques and Theology in the Septuagint of Amos (Leiden/Boston: Brill, 2009), 173–4.
[81] Robert Law, The Tests of Life: A Study of the First Epistle of St John (Edinburgh: T&T Clark, 1909), 160.

כִּפֶּר phrases. His first is Exodus 32:30.[82] Here the LXX uses ἐξιλάσκεσθαι for the Hebrew אֲכַפְּרָה. Moses proposes to "make atonement" by intercession. Moses is the subject of the action, and the Lord the object. This follows the people's faithless worship of the golden calf. But a plea for forgiveness (32:32) for profound violation of divine law,[83] rather than propitiation of divine anger, is the sense conveyed.

Law's second example is Ezekiel 16:63.[84] Here in the LXX ἐξιλάσκεσθαι is used for the Hebrew בְּכַפְּרִי. Here the Lord is the *subject*, the actor in the act of atonement (or forgiveness), and sinful humanity its object. No sacrifice is in view. Divine wrath is *not* present. Rather, the Lord makes an "everlasting covenant" (16:60) with the people, forgiving them for breaking a previous one (16:59). The idea conveyed by בְּכַפְּרִי in the Hebrew is that the Lord will *cover* their sin.[85]

Law's third example is Psalm 65:3.[86] Here the LXX has the imperative ἱλάσῃ for the Hebrew תְּכַפְּרֵם. Here again the Lord is the actor, the subject of the act of atonement. The Lord is praised for forgiving the people when "deeds of evil" overcome them: this is the very reverse of divine wrath. Again the Hebrew תְּכַפְּרֵם conveys the idea of *covering* sin.[87]

Law's fourth example is Leviticus 4:20.[88] Here the LXX uses ἐξιλάσωμαι for the Hebrew וְכִפֶּר. Here the priest is the subject in the ritual act of sacrifice of a bull to the Lord, by whom the people will be forgiven, and the people themselves are the direct object, and the Lord the indirect object. Purgation[89] or expiation[90] of the people's sin is the idea conveyed.

Law's fifth example, Leviticus 12:7,[91] is similar. The LXX renders the Hebrew וְכִפֶּר by ἐξιλάσεται. Again the priest is the actor in a ritual sacrifice to the Lord, this time of a lamb, to cleanse a woman, who has recently given birth, of her flow of blood. Here the idea is very clearly cleansing[92] or expiation,[93] not propitiation for sin. The Lord is the indirect object of the action, and the woman the direct object.

In these examples there is a wide variety of senses in which other ἱλασμός cognates are used to translate the Hebrew כִּפֶּר, with God as the subject, as well as the object of the act of atonement. Such events are *not* portrayed in the LXX as acts of propitiation of God for human sin, but as acts of cleansing, or of divine generosity in which God forgives a people's sin without any prior propitiation by them.

---

[82] *Ibid*, 161 n.1: "You have committed a great sin. But I will now go up to the Lord. Possibly I can make atonement for your sin." In each of Law's examples, his LXX translation is used for convenience.

[83] Brueggemann, *Old Testament Theology*, 59.

[84] Law, *The Tests of Life*, 161 n.1: "In order that you may remember and be refuted, and never speak again because of your shame, when I forgive all you have done, says the Lord."

[85] Bowen, *Ezekiel*, 90.

[86] Law, *The Tests of Life*, 161 n.1: "When deeds of evil overcome us, forgive us our sins."

[87] Briggs, *Psalms*, 81.

[88] Law, *Tests of Life*, 161 n.2: "He shall do to the bull just what is done to the bull of sin offering: He shall do likewise with this. The priest shall make atonement for them, and they will be forgiven."

[89] Milgrom, *Leviticus 1–16*, 245.

[90] Levine, *Leviticus*, 23; Hartley, *Leviticus*, 62.

[91] Law, *Tests of Life*, 161, n.3: "He shall offer it before the Lord, and make atonement for her: then she will be cleansed from her blood flow. This is the ritual for the one who bears a male or female child."

[92] Milgrom, *Leviticus 1–16*, 760; Hartley, *Leviticus*, 169.

[93] Levine, *Leviticus*, 74.

Conclusions on Usage of ἱλασμός and Its Cognates in the LXX

Three principal points emerge from our examination of the use of ἱλασμός and its cognates in the LXX. First, where God is the object of the action depicted by the Hebrew כִּפֶּר translated by ἱλασμός, it is as an *indirect* object, not a direct one. Second, ἱλασμός often connotes divine forgiveness, not sacrifice, and here God is the *subject* of the action. Sometimes when it is used in this sense, ἱλασμός translates כִּפֶּר, and sometimes it translates סָלַח, "forgive", a root without sacrificial associations. Third, where cognates of ἱλασμός appear in the LXX, ideas other than sacrifice, such as intercession, are often translated by it: God is there the direct object of the action, which is however not sacrificial.

In summary, what we find in the varying uses of ἱλασμός in the LXX is a variety of Hebrew roots translated, some sacrificial in meaning and some not, such as forgiveness. God may be either the subject or the indirect object of the action, depending on what it is. None may be precisely identified as depicting divine propitiation. Where sacrifice is conveyed, cleansing rather than propitiation is the aim of the action or ritual depicted, because its direct object is a person or thing, rather than the deity. Where ἱλασμός cognates appear in the LXX, in the examples we have noted, כִּפֶּר is translated, but again the sense in which the Hebrew original is used may or may not be sacrificial. God may be the subject or the indirect object.

If propitiation of divine wrath were the main sense in which ἱλασμός is used in the LXX, one would expect God usually to be the direct, rather than the indirect object of the action – and certainly not the *subject*. The LXX is an unreliable indication that where in 1 John ἱλασμός is used, it has a propitiatory meaning. If the LXX is a reliable guide to John's use of ἱλασμός in 1 John – a question for the next chapter – it suggests that expiation or cleansing from sin is the meaning intended there.

Atonement and Forgiveness in Some Intertestamental Pseudepigrapha

In this and the following section, the purpose is not to isolate and to analyse the use of ἱλασμός in the texts examined, as in our study of this term in the LXX. The LXX was the translation of the Hebrew Bible available to Greek-speaking Jews in the first century CE. Its likely influence on the use and meaning of Greek LXX terms, such as ἱλασμός, in the NT, including 1 John, has been well recognised and argued over, as we have seen. However the influence of the pseudepigrapha and the Qumran material on the NT, while much discussed, is more problematical. In the absence of textual similarities, such as those between 1 Enoch 1:9 and Jude 14-15,[94] and between 1 Enoch 9:1 and 1

---

[94] RH Charlesworth, *The Old Testament Pseudepigrapha and the New Testament* (Cambridge: Cambridge University Press, 1985), 73.

Peter 1:11,[95] proof positive that the author of 1 John had access to, and utilised, this material is impossible. All that can be done for present purposes is to note significant parallel attitudes to atonement and forgiveness between some pseudepigraphica and 1 John and to postulate a possible connection.

Only the pseudepigraphic 1 Enoch, Jubilees and Testament of Abraham will be examined, as most scholars consider they are pre-Christian. English translations are used in the absence of a complete Greek or Hebrew original. However 4 Ezra, which might have yielded insights about the development of atonement ideas in first century Judaism, has not been studied here because it most likely dates from after the destruction of the Temple in 70 CE, and therefore may postdate 1 John, or may be contemporaneous with it; no direct influence from 4 Ezra on 1 John is likely.[96]

(i) 1 Enoch

Apart from Aramaic fragments and an incomplete Greek manuscript found at Qumran, 1 Enoch survives only in Ethiopic translation.[97] Nickelsburg and Vanderkam consider that the original was probably written in Aramaic rather than Hebrew.[98] But caution may be required in drawing conclusions from the Ethiopic version of 1 Enoch as to the development of the Aramaic original, as the Ethiopic text may represent a considerable recasting of the Aramaic.[99] It is a composite work, and the likely dates of composition of its parts vary widely. Overall, its sections demonstrate developing stages in the Enochic tradition, expressing a common world view that the present age is evil and unjust and in need of divine judgment and renewal.[100] The authority of these sections rests on the claim that they transmit divine revelation given to the very early patriarch Enoch (Genesis 5:21-24).[101]

As noted above, the idea of לַעֲזָאזֵל, "as a goat of departure", in Leviticus 16:10 is taken up in 1 Enoch where the notion is extended to refer to a demon. In 1 Enoch 10:4-6, in the *Book of Watchers* (1 Enoch 1-36), generally dated to circa 200 BCE or earlier,[102] we find:

> 4 And again the Lord said to Raphael: "bind Azazel hand and foot, and cast him into the darkness: and make an opening in the desert, which is in Dudael, and cast him therein. 5 And place upon him rugged and jagged rocks, and cover

---

[95] Peter H Davis, "The Use of the Pseudepigrapha in the Catholic Epistles" in *The Pseudepigrapha and Early Biblical Interpretation* (ed. JH Charlesworth and Craig A Evans; Sheffield: Sheffield Academic Press, 1993), 228–45, 237.
[96] Charlesworth, *The Old Testament Pseudepigrapha and the New Testament*, 42.
[97] George WE Nickelsburg and James C Vanderkam, *1 Enoch 2* (Minneapolis: Fortress Press, 2012), 30–1.
[98] *Ibid*, 31–2.
[99] Michael A Knibb, "Interpreting the Book of Enoch: Reflections on a Recently Published Commentary", *JSJ* (2002) 33:4: 437–50, 440.
[100] George WE Nickelsburg and James C Vanderkam, *1 Enoch* (Minneapolis: Fortress Press, 2004), 1.
[101] *Ibid*.
[102] John S Bergsma, "The Relationship between Jubilees and the Early Enoch Books", 36–51 in *Enoch and the Mosaic Torah: The Evidence of Jubilees* (ed. Gabriele Boccaccini and Giovanni Ibba; Grand Rapids, Michigan/Cambridge, UK, 2009), 39.

him with darkness, and let him abide there forever, and cover his face that he might not see light. 6 And on the day of the great judgment he shall be cast into the fire".[103]

Why does Azazel deserve this fate? Azazel is identified in 1 Enoch 8:1 as the one who "taught men to make swords of iron and weapons and shields and breastplates and every instrument of war".[104] In 1 Enoch 9:6 Azazel is the one who "taught all iniquity upon the earth, and has revealed the eternal mysteries which are in heaven, which the sons of men were striving to learn".[105]

In 1 Enoch 8, 9 and 10 the idea of לַעֲזָאזֵל, "as a goat of departure", from Leviticus 16:10 is taken up and made to stand for the one who introduced violence to the earth. Azazel's fate therefore may stand in 1 Enoch for the ultimate expulsion of violence from the earth. Seen through the eyes of 1 Enoch, the atonement ritual in Leviticus 16:10 represents, not propitiation of an angry deity, but the purging or cleansing of violence from the earth. Whether such Enochic notions influenced the author of 1 John in his use of ἱλασμός in 2:2 and 4:10 is entirely speculative.

In the section of the apocalyptic *Book of Parables* in 1 Enoch 37-41, attested only in Ethiopic translation,[106] we find Enoch's revelation of the coming of the "Chosen One" and of "light" to the "righteous" and of the "dwelling place of the sinners".[107] First Enoch 40:6 refers to Michael the archangel, who "is merciful and long suffering".[108] This may allude to Exodus 34:6, where God is merciful, and gracious, slow to anger, and abounding in love and faithfulness.[109]

In 1 Enoch 40:9 Raphael is the "healer", in Aramaic from the Hebrew רָפָא, "to heal".[110] This casts further light on the command to Raphael in 1 Enoch 10:4, which we have already noticed, to "bind Azazel hand and foot, and cast him into the desert". As we have seen, this reflects and builds upon the ritual driving out of the scapegoat into the desert at *Yom Kippur* in Leviticus 16:10. Because in 1 Enoch 8:1, Azazel is the one who brought the means of war to humankind, the healing which Raphael is commanded to undertake may constitute the final removal of the means of violence from humankind by driving out Azazel.

In 1 Enoch 41:2 the dwelling place of the "sinners" is spoken of as the abode of those who "deny the name of the Lord".[111] Notably, 1 Enoch's theology does not define sinners by their evil deeds, but by their *allegiances.* This is consistent with the character of Michael (40:6; see above), representing those of the deity, depicted as "merciful and long suffering". Here final rebellion, not sin itself, causes banishment.

---

[103] *The Book of Enoch* (trans. RH Charles; London: SPCK, 1917), 37. A more modern translation of this section is Nickelsburg & Vanderkam, *1 Enoch* 2, but it does not differ substantially from that of Charles in these verses.
[104] *Ibid*, 25.
[105] *Ibid*, 26.
[106] Nickelsberg & Vanderkam, *1 Enoch 2*, 4.
[107] Nickelsberg & Vanderkam, *1 Enoch*, 50.
[108] Nickelsburg & Vanderkam, *1 Enoch 2*, 134.
[109] *Ibid.*
[110] *Ibid.*
[111] *Ibid*, 136.

Because the *Book of Parables* may date from as late as the first century CE,[112] although perhaps from nearer the turn of the Common Era,[113] or even from about 40 BCE,[114] its influence on 1 John is likewise somewhat problematical. It most likely was written before 1 John, so the most one can say is that its ideas concerning God's forgiving nature *may* lie behind the use of ἱλασμός in 1 John 2:2 and 4:10.

In the *Second Parable* in 1 Enoch 46, we find in 46:2 the "angel of peace", who predicts the "Son of Man", who will "overturn the kings from their thrones" (46:5) and "turn aside" the "faces of the strong" (46:6).[115] The reference is to Daniel 7:9: the phrase, the "ancient of days", is repeated in 1 Enoch 46:13.[116]

In 1 Enoch 45:6 the "chosen one" is spoken of as one who has "satisfied my righteous ones with peace", "peace" being in Aramaic from the Hebrew שָׁלוֹם, a keyword denoting God's eschatological gift of wholeness and well-being.[117] Here the theology of 1 Enoch depicts the "Son of Man" of Daniel 7:13 as one bringing primarily peace and reconciliation, rather than retribution by separation, a fate reserved for those who "deny the name of the Lord" (41:2).

Certainly in 1 John there is no reference to Jesus as the "Son of Man", a descriptor often applied by Jesus to himself in the synoptic Gospels, although it is used elsewhere in the Johannine literature, in the Fourth Gospel in 1:51, 3:13, 3:14, 6:27, 6:53, 6:62, 8:28, 12:23, 12:34 (twice) and 13:31, and in Revelation 1:13 and 14:14. Again, the most that can be said is that the idea of the deity as the bringer of peace in 1 Enoch *may* underlie, though negatively, the reference in 1 John 3:15 to those who hate a brother as "murderers" who "do not have eternal life abiding in them".

These ideas from 1 Enoch represent part of the intellectual background of first-century Judaism against which 1 John was written. Its author was probably Jewish and may have been aware of these ideas in 1 Enoch, written in its entirety at different times, but on most estimates well before 1 John. The author's horror of violence and murder, the polar opposite of love in 1 John 3:15, may possibly reflect adoption of some of the ideas in 1 Enoch which we have surveyed – nobody can be sure.

(ii) Jubilees

The pseudepigraphic Jubilees also survives in full only in Ethiopic translation, although Hebrew, Greek, Latin and Syriac fragments have been found.[118] It is a rewriting of the OT

---

[112] Martin McNamara MSC, *Intertestmental Literature* (Wilmington, Delaware: Michael Glazier Inc., 1983), 68.
[113] Nickelsburg and Vanderkam, *1 Enoch 2*, 61–2.
[114] RH Charlesworth, "Can We Determine the Composition Date of the Parables of Enoch?" 450–68 in *Enoch and the Messiah Son of Man* (ed. Gabriele Boccaccini; Grand Rapids, Michigan/ Cambridge, UK, 2007), 467.
[115] *Ibid*, 153.
[116] *Ibid*, 157.
[117] *Ibid*, 146, 151.
[118] JH Charlesworth, *The Pseudepigrapha and Modern Research* (Missoula, Montana: Scholars Press, 1976), 143; James C Vanderkam, "The Manuscript Traditions of Jubilees", 3–21 in *Enoch and the Mosaic Torah: The Evidence of Jubilees* (ed. Gabriele Boccaccini and Giovanni Ibba; Grand Rapids/ Cambridge, UK, 2009), 3.

books of Genesis and Exodus, with many variations.[119] It has been estimated to have been composed before 152 BCE.[120] By his prologue and first chapter, the author introduces his narrative and places his story at Sinai in the events depicted in Exodus 24 when Moses climbs Mount Sinai the day after the revelation upon it (Exodus 24:4),[121] claiming thereby that what he writes is a God-given revelation to Moses at Sinai.[122] Its title derives from its arrangement of its account in forty-nine periods, each forty-nine years long: it is a jubilee of jubilees.[123] For reasons of space, we shall examine only two passages in Jubilees which relate to the theme of atonement or covering of sin, because these particularly highlight possible connections between the thought of Jubilees and that of 1 John.

In Jubilees 7:27-29, 30-33, Noah's injunctions to his sons (7:20), we find in v.28 the threat of destruction for those who shed human blood or eat the blood of any flesh. The allusion is to Genesis 9:4-6. But the earth is impure as a result of such bloodshed, which must be "covered" by the slaughter of beasts or cattle, as a "good work" (v.30). This notion of the impurity of the earth as a result of bloodshed is more clearly alluded to in Jubilees 21:19-20.[124] The theology in these passages may be seen as congruent with that which we have seen in Leviticus 16:33, "he shall purify [וְכִפֶּר] the sanctuary and the tent of meeting and the altar, and shall perform expiatory rites [with blood] with respect to the sins of the people". It may be argued that Jubilees here endorses the notion that while sin normally entails death, it may be "covered" or expiated by rites of cleansing by blood, on the performance of which the deity grants deliverance from sin – always supposing appropriate penitence.

At Jubilees 34:12-19 we find the episode of the faked "death" of Joseph rewritten so as to associate it with the origin of the Day of Atonement, upon which (34:18) the children of Israel should "make atonement for themselves thereon with a young goat".[125] This is a significant reworking of Leviticus 16, where it is placed in the Mosaic legislation.[126] The biblical subject of this rewriting is the sins of Jacob's children and their slaughter of a goat, dipping Joseph's robe in its blood (Genesis 37:31-35), which leads Jubilees' author to associate this event with the prescriptions for *Yom Kippur* in Leviticus 16 and to claim a patriarchal origin for them.[127]

---

[119] Michael Segal, "The Composition of Jubilees", 22–35 in *Enoch and the Mosaic Torah: The Evidence of Jubilees* (ed. Gabriele Boccaccini and Giovanni Ibba; Grand Rapids, Michigan/Cambridge, UK, 2009), 22; James C Vanderkam, "Biblical Interpretation in 1 Enoch and Jubilees" in *The Pseudepigrapha and Early Biblical Interpretation* (ed. JH Charlesworth and Craig A Evans; Sheffield: Sheffield Academic Press, 1993), 96–125, 97–8.

[120] Charlesworth, *The Old Testament Pseudepigrapha and the New Testament*, 41; similarly Gene L Davenport, *The Eschatology of the Book of Jubilees* Leiden: EJ Brill, 1971), 13(late third or early second century BCE).

[121] James C Vanderkam, "The Scriptural Setting of the Book of Jubilees", *DSD* 13:1 (2006), 61–72, 61.

[122] Vanderkam, "Biblical Interpretation in 1 Enoch and Jubilees", 117.

[123] McNamara, *Intertestmental Literature*, 118.

[124] See generally Lutz Doering, "Purity and Impurity in the Book of Jubilees" in *Enoch and the Mosaic Torah: The Evidence of Jubilees* (ed. Gabriele Boccaccini and Giovanni Ibba; Grand Rapids, Michigan/Cambridge, UK, 2009), 261–75, 269.

[125] *The Book of Jubilees or the Little Genesis* (ed. RH Charles; London, SPCK, 1917), 171.

[126] Vanderkam, "Biblical Interpretation in 1 Enoch and Jubilees", 122.

[127] *Ibid.*

What is the importance of Jubilees' rewriting of the origin of the Day of Atonement for our purposes? In Genesis 37:31-35, the intent of Joseph's brothers in slaughtering a goat and dipping Joseph's robe in it is to deceive their father Jacob/Israel into believing that Joseph had been taken by a wild beast, to conceal their abandonment of him in a pit (37:24) thus enabling his sale by Midianites to Ishmaelites (37:28). As a result of his sale, Reuben, one of the brothers, found Joseph missing when he returned to the pit (37:29), hence the brothers' action in dipping Joseph's robe in the slaughtered goat's blood. In this deceit they were successful (Genesis 37:33). The purpose of their action in killing the goat was not therefore to atone for sin at all, but to conceal and thereby to reinforce it. Ironically, however, even if Reuben and the other brothers were half successful in their deceit, it delivered Joseph.[128] From what? From the brothers' jealousy and the danger to him from it. So in one sense, the slaughter of the goat effected deliverance, but not from sin. In another, it simply allowed the brothers to explain deceitfully to their father the loss of his son Joseph.

It may be argued that here the author of Jubilees intentionally turns the sordid story of the brothers' deceit of their father in Genesis 37:31-35 on its head, by making the slaughter of the goat a prefiguring of the rite of the Day of Atonement. His purpose may have been to take the brothers' deceit as emblematic of human sin, and to represent the slaughter of the goat, not merely as enabling the commission of sin, but as prefiguring deliverance by cleansing from it on the Day of Atonement. If this proposal is correct, it does not involve propitiation of an angry deity. Rather, it prefigures performance of a rite of cleansing from sin, effected by the deity after the blood of the slaughtered goat is applied to the holy places, as in Leviticus 16.

Again it is impossible to say more than that because Jubilees predates 1 John and is part of the first-century Jewish intellectual background against which 1 John's author wrote, the ideas we have isolated in Jubilees *may* have influenced his use of ἱλασμός on two occasions in 1 John. We have seen that atonement is central to Jubilees' rewriting of the origin of the Day of Atonement and may convey the idea of cleansing from human sin by the blood of the goat, rather than propitiation of a wrathful God. It is possible that this rewriting influenced 1 John's author in his use of ἱλασμός in 2:2 and 4:10, but no one can be sure.

Atonement and Forgiveness in the Dead Sea Scrolls

Some significant uses of כִּפֶּר which are not propitiatory in their meanings are found in the Qumran material in the Dead Sea Scrolls.

In the Cave IV fragments related to the *Rule of the Community* (4Q255-264), in Fragment 2 we find, at line 8, בכפרי used in the statement אז ירצה בכפרי גיהות לפגי אל, "then he will be accepted by an agreeable atonement before God".[129] This is the climax

---

[128] Derek Kidner, *Genesis* (London: Tyndale Press, 1968), 182.
[129] *The Dead Sea Scrolls: Hebrew, Aramaic Texts with English Translations*, Vol 1, Rule of the Community and Related Documents (ed. James A Charlesworth et al.; Tubingen: JCB Mohr/Louisville: Westminster John Knox Press, 1994), 5; see also *The Dead Sea Scrolls Study Edition* Vol 1, 510–11.

to a passage from lines 1 to 7 proclaiming that by God's "Holy Spirit" the community aspirant is "cleansed from his iniquity". Thus "by an upright and humble spirit his sin can be atoned". And "it is by humbling himself to all God's statutes that his flesh can be cleansed by the sprinkling of any waters of purification" and "by sanctifying himself with the waters of purity". Cleansing is achieved "by walking perfectly in all God's way, as he commanded that he may not turn aside to the right or to the left and ... not transgress a single one of all his commands".[130] Then comes the reassurance quoted above that "he will be accepted ... ". In no sense is atonement here connected with propitiation. Rather, it connotes forgiveness or reconciliation as the fruit of repentance for sin and righteous conduct thereafter and associates water purification with atonement for sin.[131]

In the *Temple Scroll* we find a redaction of the goat sacrificial rite in Leviticus 16. At 11QT 26:5-7 there is reference, combining Leviticus 16:9 and 16, to the requirement that the priest (replacing the Bible's reference to Aaron himself) receive the blood of the goat in the golden basin in his hand and do with it what he did with the blood of the bull, that is, make atonement with it for the people of the congregation.[132] But interestingly the rest of the passage further adapts Leviticus 16:15-16, *omitting* the Biblical instruction to sprinkle the blood on and before the ark cover. This, as Schiffman postulates, is because "the author of our scroll views the meaning of the Hebrew root כפר in ritual context as a technical term for the sprinkling of blood, in accord with usage later found in rabbinic literature".[133] That is, the primary meaning of the Hebrew root here is *cleansing* or *covering* rather than propitiation.

Furthermore, in the *Manual of Discipline*, deliverance from sin is described as *cleansing*: human purity is brought about by "atonement", כפרים (1QS iii.4; xi.14).[134] Nevertheless this is not by the flesh of offerings or animal sacrifices (1QS ix.4).[135] Insofar as humans contribute to atonement, they do so by turning away from evil conduct (1QS ix.13)[136] and by meekness and submission to divine command (1QS iii.7-8).[137] Then cleansing follows from "sprinkling with the waters of purification" and by "sanctification with running water" (1QS iii.4, 9, 13).[138] But finally it is God who

---

[130] *The Dead Sea Scrolls: Hebrew, Aramaic Texts with English Translations*, 5; see also *The Dead Sea Scrolls Study Edition* Vol 1, 510–11.

[131] As to the connection between water purification and atonement for sin in the *Rule of the Community*, see generally Hannah K Harrington, "Purification in the Fourth Gospel in light of Qumran" in *John, Qumran and the Dead Sea Scrolls: Sixty Years of Discovery and Debate* (ed. Mary L Coloe and Tom Thatcher; Atlanta: Society of Biblical Literature, 2011), 117–39, 125–30.

[132] Lawrence H Schiffman, "The Case of the Day of Atonement Ritual" in *Biblical Perspectives: Early Use and Interpretation of the Bible in Light of the Dead Sea Scrolls* (ed. Michael E Stone and Esther G Chazon: Leiden/Boston/Cologne: Brill, 1997), 181–8, 187; see also *The Dead Sea Scrolls Study Edition* Vol 2, 1248–9.

[133] *Ibid*, 187.

[134] *The Dead Sea Scrolls Study Edition* Vol 1, 75.

[135] *Ibid*, 90–1; see also Helmer Ringren, *The Faith of Qumran: Theology of the Dead Sea Scrolls* (trans. Emilie T Sander; Philadelphia: Fortress Press, 1963), 124.

[136] *The Dead Sea Scrolls Study Edition* Vol 1, 92–3.

[137] *Ibid*, 74–5.

[138] *Ibid*; see also Ringren, *The Faith of Qumran*, 124.

reconciles or purifies (1QS xi.14).¹³⁹ Here again, כפרים connotes, not propitiation but *cleansing* from sin – an idea we shall meet again in 1 John 1:7.

Also in the *Manual of Discipline*, sacrifices are not rejected outright, but fulfilment of the program of the Community atones for guilt and transgression "better than [or 'without'] flesh of burnt offerings and fat of sacrifices". Thus "offerings of the lips is accounted as a sweet fragrance of righteousness and blamelessness of conduct as an acceptable freewill offering" (1QS ix.4-5).¹⁴⁰ This enumeration of the times of prayer speaks of an "offering of the lips" in a context where it clearly relates to praise and prayer (1QS ix.26-x.5).¹⁴¹ The term כִּפֶּר is used to refer to the result of the Community's activity: for example, the righteous life led within the Community is said to bring "atonement to the land" (1QS viii.6; ix.4).¹⁴²

It is hard to prove that the Qumran school influenced the author of 1 John. Certainly its material was composed at about the same time. The intellectual climate of first-century Judaism, insofar as it inherited and reworked the OT idea of atonement by taking from it the elements of human repentance and divine forgiveness, rather than propitiation, *may* underlie the thought in 1 John 2:2 and 4:10 in the author's use of the term ἱλασμός. One can only say that such a connection is possible.

Conclusion

In summary, we have seen that in the varying uses of ἱλασμός in the LXX a variety of Hebrew roots are translated, some sacrificial in meaning and others not so, such as forgiveness. God may be either the subject or the indirect object of the action, depending on what it is. None depicts divine propitiation. Where sacrifice is conveyed, cleansing rather than propitiation is the aim of the action or ritual depicted, because its direct object is a person or thing, rather than the deity. It is unlikely that ἱλασμός in the LXX ever means "propitiation" for three reasons.

Firstly, if ἱλασμός were to be understood in the LXX as always, or predominantly, propitiatory in meaning, one would expect the deity to be solely or predominantly the direct or indirect object of the action. This is not always or even usually the case. A sense of forgiveness, without any implication of sacrifice, let alone propitiation, attends the use of ἱλασμός in Psalm 130:4 and Daniel 9:9, and God is the subject, not the object of the action. Secondly, in the other occurrences of ἱλασμός in the LXX, Leviticus 25:8, Numbers 5:8, 1 Chronicles 28:20c, Ezekiel 44:27 and Amos 8:14, a sense of "covering", "cleansing" or "expiation" is more contextually apposite than "propitiation". Thirdly, ἱλασμός in the LXX does not always translate כִּפֶּר relating to sin: cf. Psalms 130:4, Ezekiel 44:27 and Daniel 9:9.

This is not the case with the five examples of ἱλασμός cognates in the LXX which we have examined. All translate the Hebrew כָּפַר. But in each case the more appropriate

---

¹³⁹ *Ibid*; see also *The Dead Sea Scrolls Study Edition* Vol 1, 92–3.
¹⁴⁰ *Ibid*, 90–1; see also Ringren, *The Faith of Qumran*, 214–15.
¹⁴¹ *The Dead Sea Scrolls Study Edition* Vol 1, 92–3, 94–5; see also Ringren, *The Faith of Qumran*, 214–15.
¹⁴² *Ibid*; see also *The Dead Sea Scrolls Study Edition* Vol 1, 88–9, 90–1.

sense of this term in the context is "cover", "cleanse" or "expiate" rather than "propitiate". In no case are they used with the deity as the direct object.

The LXX was the version of the Hebrew Bible available to and used by Greek-speaking Jews in the first century CE. The author of 1 John was most likely such a person. It is likely in these circumstances that the uses of ἱλασμός and its cognates in the LXX were known to him. Whether they influenced him in his own twofold use of this term in 1 John 2:2 and 4:10 must be examined in our next chapter.

In the examples of the definitely pre-Christian pseudepigrapha we have examined, firstly, in 1 Enoch, the atonement ritual in Leviticus 16:10 may represent, not propitiation of an angry deity, but the purging or cleansing of violence from the earth. Secondly, in 1 Enoch we find a reference to Michael, one of the archangels, who "is merciful and long suffering". This may be a reference to Exodus 34:6, where God is merciful and gracious, slow to anger, and abounding in love and faithfulness: hardly the characteristics of a deity who demands propitiation. Thirdly, in 1 Enoch the dwelling place of the "sinners" is spoken of as the abode of those who "deny the name of the Lord". Here 1 Enoch's theology does not define sinners by their evil deeds, but by their *allegiances*. It may be argued that this is consistent with the characteristics of Michael, representing those of the deity, depicted as "merciful and long suffering", because final rebellion, not sin itself, causes banishment. Fourthly, in 1 Enoch in the *Second Parable*, we find the "angel of peace", who predicts the "Son of Man", who will "overturn the kings from their thrones" and "turn aside" the "faces of the strong". The reference is to Daniel 7:9. In 1 Enoch the "chosen one" has been spoken of as one who has "satisfied my righteous ones with peace", "peace" being a keyword denoting God's eschatological gift of wholeness and well-being. It may be argued that here the theology of 1 Enoch depicts the "Son of Man" of Daniel 7:13 as one bringing primarily peace and reconciliation, rather than retribution by separation, a fate reserved for those who "deny the name of the Lord" (41:2). The idea of the deity as the bringer of peace in 1 Enoch *may* underlie, though negatively, the reference in 1 John 3:15 to those who hate a brother as "murderers" who "do not have eternal life abiding in them". Generally, these ideas from 1 Enoch represent part of the intellectual background of first-century Judaism against which 1 John was written. The most that can be said is that they predate 1 John and *may* possibly have influenced its composition.

In Jubilees, in Noah's injunctions to his sons, we firstly find the threat of destruction for those who shed human blood or eat the blood of any flesh. The allusion is to Genesis 9:4-6. But the earth is not pure as a result of such bloodshed, which must be "covered" by the slaughter of beasts or cattle, as a "good work". The theology in these passages is congruent with that in Leviticus 16:33, "he shall purify the sanctuary and the tent of meeting and the altar, and shall perform expiatory rites [with blood] with respect to the sins of the people". Jubilees here appears to endorse the notion that while sin normally entails death, it may be "covered" or expiated by rites of cleansing by blood, on performance of which God grants deliverance from sin – presupposing appropriate penitence. Secondly, at Jubilees 34:12-19 we find the episode of the death of Joseph rewritten to associate it with the origin of the Day of Atonement, upon which the children of Israel should "make atonement for themselves thereon with a young goat", a significant reworking of Leviticus 16, where it is placed in the Mosaic legislation. The biblical subject of this rewriting is the sins of Jacob's children and their slaughter of a goat, dipping Joseph's robe in its blood (Genesis 37:31-35), which leads the author to associate this event with the prescriptions for *Yom Kippur* in Leviticus 16, to claim a patriarchal origin for them.

Here the author of Jubilees turns the story of the brothers' deceit of their father in Genesis 37:31-35 on its head by making the slaughter of the goat a prefiguring of the rite of the Day of Atonement. His purpose may have been to take the brothers' deceit as emblematic of human sin and as prefiguring deliverance by cleansing from it on the Day of Atonement. If so, this Jubilees rewriting does not involve propitiation of an angry deity. Rather, it prefigures performance of a rite of cleansing from sin, effected by the deity after the blood of the slaughtered goat is applied to the holy places, as in Leviticus 16.

Again, it is impossible to say more than that because Jubilees predates 1 John, as part of the first-century Jewish background again which 1 John's author wrote, the ideas examined above in Jubilees may have influenced his use of ἱλασμός twice in 1 John.

In the Qumran material, firstly, in the *Rule of the Community*, atonement is not connected with propitiation. It connotes forgiveness or reconciliation as the fruit of repentance for sin and righteous conduct thereafter. Secondly, in the *Temple Scroll* we find a redaction of the goat sacrificial rite in Leviticus 16, combining Leviticus 16:9 and 16, referring to the requirement that the priest receive the blood of the goat in the golden basin in his hand and do with it what he did with the blood of the bull, that is, make atonement with it on behalf of the people of the congregation. The remainder of the scroll passage adapts further Leviticus 16:15-16 but omits the biblical instruction to sprinkle the blood on and before the ark cover. The primary meaning of כִּפֶּר here is *cleansing* rather than propitiation. Thirdly, in the *Manual of Discipline*, deliverance from sin is described as *cleansing*: humans' purity is brought about by "atonement", but not by the flesh of offerings or animal sacrifices. Insofar as humans contribute to atonement, they do so by turning away from evil conduct, and meekness and submission to divine command. Then cleansing follows "sprinkling with the waters of purification" and "sanctification with running water". But *God* reconciles or purifies. Here again כִּפֶּר connotes, not propitiation but *cleansing* from sin. Fourthly, also in the *Manual of Discipline*, while sacrifices are not rejected outright, fulfilment of the program of the Community atones for guilt and transgression "better than [or 'without'] flesh of burnt offerings and fat of sacrifices". So "offerings of the lips are accounted as a sweet fragrance of righteousness and blamelessness of conduct as an acceptable freewill offering". This enumeration of the times of prayer speaks of an "offering of the lips" in a context clearly relating to praise and prayer. Here כִּפֶּר refers to the result of the Community's activity: for example, the righteous life led within the Community brings "atonement to the land".

We cannot prove that the Qumran school influenced the author of 1 John. One can say that the intellectual climate of first-century Judaism, as it inherited and reworked the OT concept of atonement by taking from it the elements of human repentance and divine forgiveness, rather than propitiation, *may* underlie the thought in 1 John 2:2 and 4:10 in the author's use of the term ἱλασμός. While there is likely influence from the LXX uses of ἱλασμός on the author of 1 John in his two uses of it, any contribution to his thought from the intertestamental pseudepigrapha and the Qumran material is speculative, and a possibility at best. But in that the Qumran documents do not seem to use כָּפַר in a sense that connotes propitiation of divine wrath; they do suggest that at least in that part of the thought-world of first-century Judaism potentially available to the author of 1 John, the "covering" of sin was not thought to require a sacrifice to an angry deity. Using our findings here in the next chapter, we shall attempt a resolution of the meaning and function of ἱλασμός as used in 1 John 2:2 and 4:10. We shall then examine the implications for peacemaking theology.

3

Ἱλασμός in 1 John

Introduction

What work does Jesus' death do for us? What was the role of God the Father in it? Peacemaking theology must face these issues, for they are crucial to our picture of God. If God is a wrathful deity requiring punishment for sin, even if visited on God's own Son by his vicarious death, that same deity requires infliction of violence on the Son, a idea repugnant to peacemaking, non-violent theology. In 1 John 2:2 and 4:10 the word ἱλασμός occurs, and many think its use provides clear and unequivocal answers to these questions. Others are not so sure. This chapter draws together and evaluates various exegeses of ἱλασμός in these two verses. Only representative contributors have been selected; otherwise the task would be never ending.[1]

This is of course a well-ploughed field, as is that tilled in Chapter 2. The contribution this chapter makes is to review and evaluate influential scholarly views, followed by a fresh exegesis of the occurrences of ἱλασμός in 1 John 2:2 and 4:10 in their respective contexts, and finally some conclusions on atonement models in peacemaking, non-violent theology.

Extending this selection to include earlier exegetes from the nineteenth and early twentieth centuries – but omitting, for reasons of space, still earlier writers such as Anselm and Calvin – hopefully produces a genuinely diachronic study, tracing views on ἱλασμός in 1 John over a longer time. After this survey of scholarship and an appraisal of it, exegesis of John's use of ἱλασμός in 1 John 2:2 and 4:10 in their respective contexts will follow, using the insights in this and the previous chapter.

Before beginning our survey, however, we should note that the LXX was available to, and used by, Greek-speaking first-century Christians, including the Johannine community, and the Johannine literature contains specific LXX citations: see, for example, John 1:15 (Isaiah 40:3) and Revelation 11:15, 18 (Psalm 2:1-2) and, less clearly, Revelation 2:26-27, 12:5, 19:15 (Psalm 2:8-9).[2] This suggests that the author of 1 John may have had LXX uses of ἱλασμός in mind when he used the term.

---

[1] See the remarks of Christopher Rowland and Jonathan Roberts, "Introduction," *JSNT* 33:2 (2010), 131–6, 131, to a number of that journal devoted to *Wirkungsgeschichte*, reception history, regarding the "gargantuan volume of secondary literature" on NT interpretation of recent days; they there write that an ability to digest and discuss the secondary literature on the NT has become the basis of a scholarly contribution. This study seeks to avoid that pitfall by interacting directly with the original texts of both the OT and NT and other primary sources.

[2] Timothy Michael Law, *When God Spoke Greek: The Septuagint and the Making of the Christian Bible* (Oxford/New York: Oxford University Press, 2013), 102, 114.

The central atonement debate over ἱλασμός in 1 John 2:2 and 4:10 is whether Jesus' death is offered as propitiation to God by vicarious punishment for our sin, or whether God sends the Son to cleanse, expiate or expunge our sin, although some writers, in offering other views, seek to avoid either camp. Broadly, peacemaking theology advocates an expiatory view or *assumes* it is the correct model.[3]

The following assurance appears in 1 John 2:1-2:

> Τεκνία μου, ταῦτα γράφω ὑμῖν ἵνα μὴ ἁμάρτητε. καὶ ἐάν τις ἁμάρτῃ, παράκλητον ἔχομεν πρὸς τὸν πατέρα Ἰησοῦν Χριστὸν δίκαιον, καὶ αὐτὸς ἱλασμός ἐστιν περὶ τῶν ἁμαρτιῶν ἡμῶν, οὐ περὶ τῶν ἡμετέρων δὲ μόνον ἀλλὰ καὶ περὶ ὅλου τοῦ κόσμου.

This may be translated:

> 1 My little children, I am writing these things to you so you will not sin. But if anyone sins, we have an advocate with the Father, Jesus Christ the righteous one; 2 and he is an atoning sacrifice for our sins, not for ours only but also for those of the whole world.[4]

In 1 John 4:10 we read:

> ἐν τούτῳ ἐστὶν ἡ ἀγάπη, οὐχ ὅτι ἡμεῖς ἠγαπήκαμεν τὸν θεόν, ἀλλ' ὅτι αὐτὸς ἠγάπησεν ἡμᾶς καὶ ἀπέστειλεν τὸν υἱὸν αὐτοῦ ἱλασμὸν περὶ τῶν ἁμαρτιῶν ἡμῶν.

This may be translated:

> In this is love, not that we loved God, but he loved us and sent his Son as an atoning sacrifice for our sins.

As Painter says, because in 1 John the work of the Son in a world where death reigns is to give life (2:2; 3:5; 4:9, 10, 14), this involves dealing with sin.[5] How is this accomplished? Jesus as ἱλασμός, an "atoning sacrifice",[6] is presented as the solution at 2:2 and 4:10. We must review how scholars have understood this term. They have been gathered in three broad groups: "expiation", "propitiation" and "other views".

Like all such simple categories, these are not watertight. The proper interpretation of ἱλασμός in 1 John 2:2 and 4:10 is an old dispute. Positions have been taken, walls have been erected and stalemate has for some time prevailed. A review of this scholarship, divided into those who support an expiatory, or alternatively a propitiatory translation of ἱλασμός, with some discussion of other less easily classified views, and some testing

---

[3] See Chapter 1.
[4] Again the translations in this chapter are the author's, although on occasions, where that of the *NRSV* cannot be bettered, it is mirrored.
[5] Painter, *1, 2 and 3 John*, 97.
[6] So the *NRSV*. This neutral translation of ἱλασμός has been adopted at this early point, because to render it as either "propitiation" or "expiation" at this stage begs the very question this chapter asks.

of these various views, is set out. There then follows an exegesis of 1 John 2:2 and 4:10 in their respective literary contexts.

Scholarship Review

(i) Expiation

Brooke Foss Westcott translates ἱλασμός as "propitiation" in 2:2, but he does not in fact adopt that view in preference to "expiation", as we shall see. He notes that the present tense is used – Jesus *is* the ἱλασμός for our sins – so Jesus' advocacy is "the act of a Saviour still living".[7] Jesus *is* the propitiation, not the propitiator. The propitiation is not simply a past event.[8]

Westcott notes that in 1 John 1:7b, καὶ τὸ αἷμα ἀ Ἰησοῦ τοῦ υἱοῦ αὐτοῦ καθαρίζει ἡμᾶς ἀπὸ πάσης ἁμαρτίας, the verb καθαρίζει denotes purification, and the idea is preparation for divine service and fellowship.[9] To Jews, blood is spoken of directly in the OT as life itself, נֶפֶשׁ – cf. Genesis 9:4, "you shall not eat flesh with its life, that is, its blood", and Deuteronomy 12:23, "only be sure that you do not eat the blood, for the blood is the life, and you shall not eat the life with the meat".[10] Also, נֶפֶשׁ occurs in Leviticus 17:11a-b, "for the life of the flesh is in the blood, and I have given it to you for making atonement for your lives on the altar". Thus "its atoning value lies not in its material substance but in the life of which it is the vehicle".[11] So for Westcott, the sacrifice of a victim had double significance, the death of the victim and the liberation of "the principle of life" through the shedding of its blood. In OT sacrifices the killing of the animal was often the work of the offeror, but the sprinkling of its blood on the altar was the exclusive work of the priest. Jesus himself, however, by being offered and offering himself, fulfils both offices.[12]

Westcott correctly identifies that Jesus fulfils both offices in 1 John 2:2. This is also the case in 1:7b, καὶ τὸ αἷμα ἀ Ἰησοῦ τοῦ υἱοῦ αὐτοῦ καθαρίζει ἡμᾶς ἀπὸ πάσης ἁμαρτίας, "the blood of Jesus the Son cleanses us from all sin"; cf. Hebrews 7:27, "unlike the other high priests, he has no need to offer daily sacrifices, first for his own sin and then for the people's: he did this once for all when he offered himself".

To Westcott, propitiation is again intended in 1 John 4:10, but the idea is introduced here to prepare us for fellowship with God[13]: thus the emphasis in 1 John's use of ἱλασμός, at 4:10 is on divine love, rather than blood sacrifice.

Westcott analyses the use of ἱλασμός and its cognates in the LXX. From a large number of LXX uses of ἱλασμός, and words derived from it, Westcott shows that they bear such widely disparate meanings as "propitiation", "mercifulness", "expiate", "atone"

---

[7] Westcott, *The Epistles of St John*, 43.
[8] *Ibid*, 44–5.
[9] *Ibid*, 22.
[10] *Ibid*, 34.
[11] *Ibid*.
[12] *Ibid*, 35.
[13] *Ibid*, 150.

and "cleanse".[14] He contrasts these variegated meanings with the classical and Hellenistic usage of ἱλασμός, in which the person propitiated normally takes the accusative case. If that were the sense in the LXX, he argues, God would be the direct object of the action. Crucially, Westcott concludes of the *scriptural* usages of ἱλάσκεσθαι, the cognate verb to ἱλασμός, that

> they show that the scriptural conception of ἱλάσκεσθαι is not that of appeasing one who is angry, with a personal feeling against the offender; but of altering the character of that which from without occasions a necessary alienation, and interposes an inevitable obstacle to fellowship. Such phrases as "propitiating God" and God "being reconciled" are foreign to the language of the NT.[15]

Here it seems clear that despite his use of "propitiation", Westcott does not support any idea of placating divine wrath against humanity by Jesus' substitutionary death.

Generally Westcott's conclusions are supported by our survey of the many uses of ἱλασμός and some uses of its cognates, and of the variety of Hebrew words it translates in the LXX. In none of the uses examined does it mean "propitiation", as opposed to "expiation" or "cleansing" or "forgiveness". Of course that fact does not dictate its meaning in 1 John 2:2 or 4:10, but it certainly does not *support* a propitiatory meaning for ἱλασμός, there.

Heinrich Holtzmann remarks of 1 John 2:2:

> Now, beside the quality of being righteous, a second quality of Christ has to be mentioned, without which he cannot be the παράκλητος: he is the expiation [Versöhnung] ... But that generally used expression [propitiation] is missing in 1 John. Ἱλασμός is more to be understood as resulting in an actual taking away of sins, in so far as the once-shed blood of redemption (1:7-9) will continue its cleansing power until the aim is achieved.[16]

Holtzmann distinguishes the notions of propitiation and expiation, using the thought in 1 John 1:7-9 that Jesus' blood has "cleansing power". Of 1 John 4:10 he says:

> This is the nature of love, not that we have loved God, but that he has loved us and has sent his Son as the expiation [Versöhnung] for our sins. Hence the death of the Son seems a free, unconditional sacrifice of love, given to a world which is estranged from God, whereas on the human side, we can only speak of giving back love in return.[17]

---

[14] *Ibid*, 85–7.
[15] *Ibid*, 87.
[16] HJ Holtzmann, *Briefe und Offenbarung des Johannes* (Freiburg IB und Leipzig: JCB Mohr (Paul Siebeck), 1893), 243 (author's translation).
[17] 16 *Ibid*, 258 (author's translation). *Versöhnung* can signify "propitiation" as well as "expiation", but it is best given the latter translation in this context and in Holtzmann's discussion of 2:2.

Here Holtzmann characterises God's sending of the Son, not as an offering to be appropriated by humanity to placate God's anger towards them, but rather as a loving, unconditional gift. This view is supported by our analysis of LXX use of Ἱλασμός and some of its cognates, and of the Hebrew words it translates.

Robert Law views 1 John as containing a number of "tests" whereby believers may satisfy themselves of being "begotten of God" under three main headings: doing righteousness, loving one another and "believing that Jesus is the Christ, come in the flesh to be the Saviour of the World".[18] In 1 John, "reference to the death of Calvary as a substitutionary ransom is excluded by the context, in which it is held up specifically as our pattern, binding on us the obligation to lay down our lives in like matter for the brethren", referring to 1 John 3:16.[19]

We have seen in the previous chapter, from our own analysis of Law's examples of ἱλασμός cognates in the LXX, that substitutionary propitiation is in each case not the meaning conveyed.

Law so concludes in relation to 1 John 2:2 and 4:10:

Two great truths emerge. First, propitiation has its ultimate source in God. Paganism conceives of propitiation as a means of changing the disposition of the deity, of mollifying his displeasure and rendering him literally "propitious". In the Old Testament the conception rises to a higher plane; the expiation of sin begins to supersede the idea of the appeasing sacrifice, and language is chosen as if to guard against the supposition that a feeling of personal irritation, pique, or resentment, such as mingles almost invariably with human wrath, mars the purity of the Divine indignation against sin. And this ascent from pagan anthropomorphism reaches the climax of all ethical religion in St John's conception of the Divine atonement for human guilt: "Herein is love, not that we loved God, but that God loved us, and sent His Son as a propitiation for our sins" (4:10).[20]

Therefore:

The action of which, in some sense, God himself is the object, has God himself as its origin. Propitiation is no device for inducing a reluctant deity to forgive; it is the way in which the Father in Heaven restores His sinning children to Himself.[21]

Granted, as seen in Chapter 2, that the LXX uses ἱλασμός, among its varying meanings, in a sacrificial sense, but it does not use it to connote propitiation. It does not use this word to connote a sacrifice to an angry deity to deflect wrath from the offeror to the victim. On more than one occasion this word is used to signify the action of a loving Father in forgiving sinners, by an unasked and unmerited gift. Law's conclusions are cogent.

---

[18] Law, *The Tests of Life*, 6.
[19] *Ibid*, 159.
[20] *Ibid*, 162.
[21] *Ibid*.

Alan Brooke also contends that in 1 John 2:2 Jesus in his death is both high priest, qualified to offer sacrifice, and is also the propitiation which he himself offers.[22] Ἱλασμός in 1 John 2:2 picks up the OT belief that sin must be "covered" to restore relations between God and humanity. It conveys the idea that now, after Jesus' death, "the ceremonial has given way to the spiritual". Through Jesus' free and voluntary death, the removal of sin, which keeps humans from God, is made possible.[23]

As to 1 John 4:10, Brooke writes that "God could not give himself while men's sins formed a barrier between them and Him" and that "true love must sweep away the hindrances to the fulfilment of the law of its being".[24] Again, despite Brooke's use of "propitiation", his exegesis is closer to an expiatory sense of ἱλασμός. In this connection, Brooke notes that while the Vulgate has *propitiatio*, Augustine's *Tractates* on the Epistles, using an Old Latin text not identical with the Vulgate, has *litator*. Another Old Latin text has *expiator* as a translation for the noun.[25] Brooke favours this last sense as the proper translation of ἱλασμός in 1 John 2:2 and 4:10. This variation in Latin terms to translate ἱλασμός in 1 John suggests that in early times there was in the Church a live debate about its meaning. Our analysis of LXX uses of ἱλασμός and its cognates in Chapter 2 supports Brooke's view.

Charles Dodd contends that although 1 John 1:7, in its reference to the blood of Jesus, suggests animal sacrifices, the term ἱλασμός in 2:2 does not *itself* signify blood sacrifice, and is wide enough to refer to the whole work of Jesus – his incarnation, his earthly ministry, his resurrection and ascension, and his death.[26] This perspective is critical to the debate over the meaning of ἱλασμός in 1 John. Dodd's statement here is cogent: our exegesis of ἱλασμός in 1 John 4:10 will show that the love enjoined to Christians should be in imitation of the love Jesus showed to others, not only in his self-sacrificial death but over his whole life.

Dodd recognises Jesus *himself* as the ἱλασμός in 2:2. He offers "expiation" as the proper translation, noting that in antiquity it was believed that performance of rituals was seen as a "powerful disinfectant". Thus, this sense of ἱλασμός is what is meant in 2:2: "The entire work of Jesus is an act of expiation, and God is the author of it."[27]

Rather than referring generally to the "powerful disinfectant" effected by ritual in antiquity, more may be achieved by analysing the most obvious influence to hand for 1 John's author, the LXX, in its use of ἱλασμός as examined in our last chapter, as Dodd indeed does. We have seen there in our analysis of the use of ἱλασμός and its cognates, particularly in Leviticus, that this word very often conveys the idea of *cleansing* by the blood of sacrifice.

In an analysis of the cognates of ἱλάσκεσθαι in the LXX in a much-discussed article, Dodd notes that the "stock rendering" in the LXX of כִּפֶּר, usually "to atone", "make

---

[22] Brooke, *Johannine Epistles*, 28.
[23] Ibid, 28–9.
[24] Ibid, 119.
[25] Ibid.
[26] Dodd, *Johannine Epistles*, 26–7; similarly Houlden, *Johannine Epistles*, 62.
[27] Ibid, 27.

atonement", is ἱλάσκεσθαι and its various derivatives. He notes that in classical and *Koine* Greek, these words regularly mean "placate" or "propitiate", with a person as the object.[28] However he offers an example from Plato where ἐξιλάσκεσθαι has the secondary meaning "expiate" and therefore describes this ἱλάσκεσθαι derivative as "ambiguous".[29] If 1 John is influenced by pagan sacrificial views – which is contestable – it may argue *against* such views by presenting a model of atonement based on divine love, rejecting placation of a wrathful deity as a reason for Jesus' willing death.

Dodd notes an example in the LXX where כָּפֶר is translated by words not derived from ἱλάσκεσθαι (Daniel 9:24). He notes another where two *kpr* derivatives are respectively translated by an ἱλάσκεσθαι derivative and by a word not so derived (Exodus 30:10). He notes two others where כָּפֶר is not rendered by an ἱλάσκεσθαι derivative (Exodus 39:33, 36). He notes another where כָּפֶר is again not rendered by an ἱλάσκεσθαι derivative, but by ἀθῳοῦν, which means to declare or pronounce ἀθῷς, free from guilt or sin.[30] Therefore, he says, where the LXX does not render *kpr* and its derivatives by ἱλάσκεσθαι related words, it uses words meaning "sanctify", "purify", "purge away" or "forgive" in relation to sin.[31]

This is cogent. Dodd shows that not only do ἱλασμός and its cognates not always translate כָּפֶר, but that כָּפֶר is not always translated b ἱλασμός and its cognates. It cuts away support for the proposition that ἱλασμός and its cognates usually carry a propitiatory meaning in the LXX. Our survey in Chapter 2 indicates that they do not.

Dodd then examines words *other* than כָּפֶר which *are* rendered in the LXX by ἱλάσκεσθαι and its cognates. He notes that where this occurs, they render either words with a human subject, meaning "to cleanse from sin or defilement", or "to expiate", or with a divine subject, meaning "to be gracious", "to have mercy" or "to forgive".[32] He contends that there was a development away from the use of ἱλάσκεσθαι and its derivatives in their usual pagan sense of "propitiate". He argues that on many occasions in the LXX, though in *no* pagan writer, the words when used with a divine subject refer to an act of cancelling sin, an act of forgiveness, "an entirely new usage with no pagan parallels".[33]

Dodd then examines the numerous examples where כָּפֶר *is* translated in the LXX by ἱλάσκεσθαι cognates.[34] He argues that the general use of such cognates to translate כָּפֶר related words in the LXX supports his conclusion, reached after examination of the use of ἱλάσκεσθαι derivatives to translate other Hebrew words and of their synonyms to translate other Hebrew words. Dodd's conclusion is that "the LXX translators did not see כפד (when used as a religious term) as conveying the sense

---

[28] CH Dodd, HILASKESTHAI, Its Cognates, Derivatives and Synonyms, in the Septuagint," *JTS* 32 (1931): 352–60, 352. This article is reproduced without substantial amendment as Chapter V, "Atonement" in CH Dodd, *The Bible and the Greeks* (London: Hodder & Stoughton, 1935), 82–95.

[29] Dodd, HILASKESTHAI, Its Cognates, Derivatives and Synonyms, in the Septuagint," 352.

[30] *Ibid*, 352–3. Dodd refers to many variations in different texts of the LXX, but there is no space to discuss that subject here. It does not significantly affect the thrust of his argument.

[31] *Ibid*, 353.
[32] *Ibid*, 353–6.
[33] *Ibid*, 356.
[34] *Ibid*, 356–9.

of propitiating the Deity, but of performing an act whereby guilt or defilement is removed".[35] Our analysis in Chapter 2 supports his opinion.

Dodd concedes that the Johannine Epistles are probably less influenced by the LXX than any other NT writing and that this may itself support usage by the Johannine author of the "non-biblical, propitiatory" sense ὁ ἱλασμός. Nevertheless, he says, we may see the use of an ἱλάσκεσθαι derivative in 2:2 as equivalent to the verb καθαρίζειν, "to cleanse", in 1:7, so that "Christ is a 'sin-offering', a divinely supplied means of cancelling guilt and purifying the sinner".[36] In the end, Dodd picks up what he regards as the most common sense of ἱλάσκεσθαι derivatives where they are used in the LXX with a divine subject and applies that as the most likely meaning of ἱλασμός in 1 John 2:2, because it appears to accord with 1:7. Its many and varied meanings in the LXX negative the suggestion that its LXX background supports, much less compels, a propitiatory meaning in 1 John.

Rudolf Schnackenburg[37] says ἱλασμός in 1 John 2:2 is either a "substitute of an abstract for a concrete" expression or a "neologism for sin offering", which "clearly betrays its Old Testament roots", referring to ἱλάσκομαι περί in the LXX.[38] We have seen in Chapter 2 that a wide variety of meanings is conveyed in the LXX by ἱλασμός and its cognates. Schnackenburg refers to two of the examples of LXX use of ἱλασμός noted above: Ezekiel 44:27 and Numbers 5:8.[39] But he thinks the author of 1 John does not derive his ideas about sacrifice only from the OT itself, pointing to the theology of later Judaism relating to the blood of martyrs as *purification*, most notably the apocryphal 4 Maccabees 6:28f.[40]

Some brief analysis of this last citation is required to evaluate Schnackenburg's view. In 4 Maccabees 6 we find the story of old Eleazar's heroic martyrdom by burning at the hands of the tyrant Antiochus, when he refused to obey the tyrant's command to eat defiling food. In 6:29 we read of Eleazar crying out to the Lord, asking him to spare his people, καθάρσιον αὐτῶν ποίησον τὸ ἐμόναῖαμ, καὶ ἀντίψυχον αὐτῶν λβαὲ τὴν ἐμὴν ψυχήν, "may my blood be made cleansing for them, and take my life instead of theirs".[41]

It is feasible that the author of 1 John had this verse in mind in 1:7b, καὶ τὸ αἷμα Ἰησοῦ τοῦ υἱοῦ αὐτοῦ καθαρίζει ἡμᾶς ἀπὸ πάσης ἁμαρτίας, "the blood of Jesus his Son cleanses us from all sin", and by extension in 2:2. If so, this supports the view that a

---

[35] *Ibid*, 359.
[36] *Ibid*, 360.
[37] Schnackenburg's commentary was not translated into English before Raymond Brown's magisterial work was published, but its German edition was published in 1975 and had considerable influence on the subsequent work of Brown, and that of Painter, which will be examined shortly.
[38] Schnackenburg, *Johannine Epistles*, 88.
[39] *Ibid*, 88 n.77.
[40] *Ibid*.
[41] Talbert employs 4 Maccabees 6:29, among other citations, to suggest that Ἰλασμός in 1 John 2:2 carries a primarily propitiatory meaning: Talbert, *Reading John*, 22. But the analogy is strained: Eleazar is pleading with God for his people's lives, knowing that his own death is imminent, but he is a martyr-to-be, not, as Jesus is, one who has already suffered earthly death, but who was with the Father from the beginning (1 John 1:1).

model of atonement different from one of propitiation is expressed in 1 John 2:2, that is *sacrificial cleansing*.

Schnackenburg writes that 4:10b "takes up the idea of sending", pointing out that Jesus was sent by the Father to atone for sin.[42] So here Jesus as ἱλασμός is seen as loving gift. It appears incongruous that a God of such love would visit anger directed at humankind on God's own Son, which is what a theory of Jesus' death as propitiatory sacrifice requires. Here Dodd's conception of the *whole* of Jesus' life and work as an expiation of human sin may profitably contribute. Schnackenburg's view is not inconsistent with it. Indeed in an excursus on "Love as the Nature of God", Schnackenburg writes that "only in the giving of the Son as an atoning sacrifice for sin is the transcendent love of the Father for the human race revealed" (1 John 4:10). He quotes Dodd: "God's love is no longer parallel to his wrath or parallel to his righteousness … he *is* love."[43]

Raymond Brown, in discussing ἱλασμός in 1 John 2:2, notes that in the LXX version, in Zechariah 7:2 and Malachi 1:9, ἱλάσκεσθαι "is used with God as an object to express the pagan idea of placating God, an idea of which the author disapproves". But he argues that the dominant uses of ἱλασμός related words in the LXX "normally do not have God as an object".[44] He suggests that in the LXX, ἱλάσκεσθαι and ἐξιλάσκεσθαι related words also "normally do not have God as an object". Rather, they either have God as the subject, so that the word means "forgiving" or that there is a human subject, a priest, who "cleanses something from sin and impurity, thus making it pleasing to God".[45] This is in keeping with the findings in Chapter 2 of this study.

Brown notes that most often in the LXX these words, ἱλάσκεσθαι and ἐξιλάσκεσθαι, render a Hebrew word from the root כָּפַר, one meaning of which is "cover over".[46] Therefore, on the strength of Hebrew background and LXX usage, there has been a "growing tendency" to translate ἱλασμός, ἱλάσκεσθαι and ἱλαστήριον in the NT "in terms of 'expiate, expiation'", aimed at removing sin by Jesus' cleansing action and so reconciling humankind to God.[47]

If, as Brown says, ἱλασμός and its derivatives in the LXX do not usually have God as the object – even if they do in the specific examples he gives, Zechariah 7:2 and Malachi 1:9 – one might conclude that because sin is the object and God is the subject of the action in 1 John 2:2, ἱλασμός is better translated here as "expiation", not "propitiation". This is supported by 1 John 1:7 and its use of the verb καθαρίζειν to characterise the role of Jesus' blood in dealing with sin. Brown's view gains is supported by our survey of ἱλασμός and its derivatives in the LXX in Chapter 2. A wide variety of senses is comprehended by these words, depending on their context.

In Brown's analysis of 1 John 2:2, he notes views in favour of either "expiation" or "propitiation" in this verse but attempts a resolution by referring to the background

---

[42] Schnackenburg, *The Johannine Epistles*, 209.
[43] *Ibid*, 210.
[44] Brown, *Epistles of John*, 219.
[45] *Ibid*.
[46] *Ibid*.
[47] *Ibid*.

of Hebrews 9-10 (10:19 in particular). He says, "There is no doubt that the sacrifice of Christ on the once-for-all Christian day of atonement described in Hebrews is more an expiation than a propitiation."[48] He says the similarity in wording in 1 John 2:2 (and 1:7) provides "good reason to think that 1 John reflects this background".[49]

Brown also makes a comparison with the Abraham and Isaac story.[50] He says it shows that the author is thinking of Jesus' death, as well as the Incarnation, as in 1 John 3:16.[51] Here we see a view similar to Dodd's that Jesus' *whole* life and death are an expiation of sin. To Brown, this verse shows that the author is advancing Jesus as the saviour of a *people*, not just individuals.[52] This fits with the idea conveyed by περὶ ὅλου τοῦ κόσμου in 1 John 2:2b that God's love is universal and not conditional on performance of an act of propitiatory sacrifice by the Son.

John Painter concludes, following Law, that John's Gospel and Epistle were either written by the same author or that the Epistle was written by an author steeped in the knowledge of the Gospel.[53]

As to 1 John 2:2, Painter writes that there are only six occurrences of ἱλασμός in the LXX. He argues that its use, and that of related terms in the LXX, suggests that where used in relation to sin, its sense is expiation.[54] In 1 John 2:2 it also carries the sense of "expiation", and especially "where God himself is the agent of the action, as he is in 1 John 4:10".[55] In Leviticus 25:9, Numbers 5:8, Psalm 130:4, Ezekiel 4:27, Daniel 9:9 and Amos 8:14 in the LXX, ἱλασμός is used in a variety of senses, some not sacrificial at all, and some connoting sacrifice but not necessarily propitiation. These LXX examples show the exact word we are considering in 1 John 2:2, ἱλασμός, used to translate a variety of Hebrew words which are *not* always derived from the Hebrew root כָּפַר, "cover", כִּפֶּר in particular. They show that there is no precision in the LXX use of ἱλασμός, as one would expect when the Hebrew ideas it renders are disparate and when this one Greek word may overlie several Hebrew words. In particular, ἱλασμός in the LXX has no necessary connection with propitiation of God for sin.

---

[48] *Ibid*, 220-1.
[49] *Ibid*, 221.
[50] Brown, *The Epistles of John*, 551.
[51] *Ibid*, 552.
[52] *Ibid*, 553.
[53] Painter, *1, 2 and 3 John*, 3.
[54] *Ibid*, 147-7.
[55] *Ibid*, 159, and also 147. Similarly Grayston, *Johannine Epistles*, 59-60; Neil Alexander, *The Epistles of John* (London: SCM Press, 1962), 54-5; D Moody Smith, *First, Second and Third John* (Louisville: John Knox Press, 1991), 51-2, 107; Johnson, *1, 2 and 3 John*, 35, 104; Rhea Jones, *1, 2 and 3 John*, 48-9, 184; Rensberger, *1 John, 2 John, 3 John*, 55-6, 118; Martin M Culy, *I, II, III John: A Handbook on the Greek Text* (Waco, Texas: Baylor University Press, 2004), 23, 109; Scott M Lewis, *The Gospel According to John and the Johannine Letters* (Collegeville, Minnesota: Liturgical Press, 2005), 113; Michèle Morgen, *Les épîtres de Jean* (Paris: Les Editions du Cerf, 2005), 71; François Vouga, *Die Johannesbriefe* (Tübingen: JCB Mohr (Paul Siebeck), 1990), 32 ("Versöhnung"); Belousek, *Atonement, Justice and Peace*, 248-9; Olsson, *A Commentary on the Letters of John*, 300-3 ("reconciliation" or "forgiveness"). For a mid position acknowledging Morris and Hill's criticisms of Dodd but ultimately supporting "expiation", see TGD Thornton, "Propitiation or Expiation," *Exp Tim* 80 (1968-9): 53-5; similarly Norman H Young, "CH Dodd, HILASKESTHAI and His Critics," *Ev Q* 48:2 (1976), 67-78.

As with Law's examples of ἱλασμός derivatives in the LXX, which *do* translate כָּפַר in the Hebrew, Painter's examples offer support for his view that ἱλασμός in the LXX conveys expiation, not propitiation, and that likewise in 1 John 2:2 and 4:10, ἱλασμός should not be translated as "propitiation", but rather "expiation".

Georg Strecker sees 1 John 2:2 as not only an "explication" of 2:1b, but as giving a reason for the statements in 2:1.[56] The author uses "primitive Christian concepts" here, and ἱλασμός can be translated either as "expiation" or "propitiatory sacrifice", noting also its use at 4:10.[57] To Strecker the idea of the ἱλαστήιου in Romans 3:25 is related, as is the ἱλάσκεσθαι of the "faithful high priest" who "atones" for the sins of the people in Hebrews 2:17.[58]

For Strecker, 1 John 2:2 employs the idea of atonement, introduced by 1:7, which refers to αἷμα Ἰησοῦ, in that

> the advocacy that the exalted Christ exercises for the community before the Father is based on the atonement for sins accomplished by Jesus Christ's redeeming sacrifice. Christ's standing before God as δίκαιος and acting as advocate for the community is founded upon his atoning death. Because he, who is sinless, has made atonement on the cross, he can stand before God's throne in the present as the trustworthy Paraclete and perform effective intercession for those who are his own.[59]

So, as to how Jesus is ἱλασμός in 2:2, Strecker notes Henri Clavier's opinion that these words describe the event of *reconciliation*, identified with the Son.[60] For Strecker, based on LXX examples in Ezekiel 44:27 and Numbers 5:8, the idea of Jesus' propitiatory sacrifice "ought not be excluded".[61] By so saying, however, it is clear from Strecker's exegesis of 1 John 2:2 in light of 1:7 that he does not necessarily put forward *positively* any explicit notion of the Father being placated or appeased by Jesus' death.

Evaluating this view, as we saw in the preceding chapter, Ezekiel 44:27 and Numbers 5:8 do indeed convey the idea of sacrifice for the primary purpose of cleansing, but not necessarily propitiation. And in Psalm 130:4 and Daniel 9:9, ἱλασμός does not convey the idea of sacrifice at all, but rather divine forgiveness and reconciliation. Strecker's is a careful view, but in the LXX, Ἱλασμός does not primarily convey the idea of propitiation. As to its use in 1 John 2:2 and 4:10, its context might indicate whether ἱλασμός means "propitiation" or "expiation". Where 1 John 1:7 refers to αἷμα Ἰησοῦ, it is not necessarily introducing the idea of propitiation but is depicting Jesus' suffering and death as a *cleansing*, suggested by καθαρίζει. Similarly Jesus' standing as a παρά with the Father in 1 John 2:1 is a means of reconciliation, not because he is the propitiation

---

[56] Strecker, *Johannine Letters*, 39.
[57] Ibid.
[58] Ibid.
[59] Ibid, 39–40.
[60] Henri Clavier, "Notes sur un Mot-clef du Johannisme et de la Sote/riologie Biblique: Ἱλασμός," *Nov T* 10 (1968): 287–304.
[61] Ibid, 39 n.17.

for human sin, but rather because he is the one who removes or cleanses it – the idea introduced at 1:7.

In his analysis of 1 John 4:10, Strecker approaches this view. He describes ἱλασμός as "a synonym for the soteriological action of Jesus Christ", and, while noting that its meaning can frequently "approach" atoning sacrifice (as we have seen from some of our examples of its use in the LXX), he says:

> In general, it refers to *God's* act of forgiving. Accordingly, Jesus Christ is represented here not as a means or result of the divine forgiveness of sins. Instead, the sending of the Son, an action proceeding from the Father, is the act which creates reconciliation between God and humanity.[62]

In Psalm 130:4 and Daniel 9:9, ἱλασμός is used in the LXX to refer to divine forgiveness or reconciliation, rather than sacrifice. These same ideas may be conveyed in 1 John 4:10.

Marianne Thompson suggests that the context of the author's use of ἱλασμός in 1 John 2:2 suggests that "expiation" rather than "propitiation" is the preferable translation. She does so on the basis that in 4:10 God's action is directed "toward our sins and toward us". Thus one should read 2:2 as also taking sin as its object, so that cleansing or removal of sin by God is the sense conveyed.[63] She writes of 4:10 that "God not only gives us the command to love but modelled for us what true love is".[64] That idea will be taken up later.

(ii) Propitiation

Roger Nicole sounds a significant counter-blast to Dodd's views. In an influential article among later writers unconvinced by Dodd's "expiation" view of ἱλασμός in 1 John 2:2 and 4:10, he argues five main points. First, he notes the unpopularity of the idea of propitiation with those who, he says, uphold what he terms a "purely subjective" notion of the atonement, noting that Dodd argues for "expiation" as the proper translation of ἱλασμός in 1 John 2:2 and 4:10.[65] To Nicole, the typical attack on "propitiation" presents it in the crudest pagan terms and attacks it as being unsupported in scripture.[66] For Nicole, the biblical concept of propitiation is on "a far higher plane" than the pagan one, and "the giver of the propitiatory gift is God himself in his gracious mercy".[67]

Next, Nicole argues that Dodd's examples provide incomplete evidence, or evidence incompletely used.[68] Correctly, he notes that Dodd incompletely lists words of the

---

[62] *Ibid*, 153 (emphasis added).
[63] Marianne Meye Thompson, *1–3 John* (Downers Grove, Illinois: InterVarsity Press, 1992), 50, Note on 2:2.
[64] *Ibid*, 123.
[65] Roger R Nicole, "CH Dodd and the Doctrine of Propitiation," *Tyn Bul* 17.2 (1955): 117–57, 121–5.
[66] *Ibid*, 122.
[67] *Ibid*, 150.
[68] *Ibid*, 127–35.

כִּפֶּר group translated in the LXX by words other than the ἱλάσκεσθαι class.⁶⁹ But this does not prove the converse, that words of the ἱλάσκεσθαι class *necessarily* connote propitiation where they translate words in the כִּפֶּר group in the LXX. Nicole pays too little attention to the distinction between uses of words of the ἱλάσκεσθαι class in the LXX where God is the *object*, direct or indirect, of the action, and those where God is the *subject* of the action.

Nicole also correctly observes that Dodd's omission of any reference to the books of the Maccabees is serious.⁷⁰ Then he gives examples of conclusions by Dodd which, he says, go beyond the evidence adduced.⁷¹ This criticism also has some weight, as does his reference to questionable assumptions by Dodd.⁷² Then he refers to what he says is lack of caution by Dodd in dealing with debatable issues.⁷³ Certainly Dodd displays a certain dogmatism in referring to some other scholars on occasions as "wrong", without sufficient argument.

But to Nicole, one must refute all Dodd's findings, because they are independent of each other. He argues that if the LXX and NT writers shared Dodd's distaste for propitiation, they would not have used the word ἱλάσκεσθαι to mean "forgive" or "expiate" when "the usual connotation of this word was overwhelmingly 'propitiation'".⁷⁴ For Nicole, Dodd must "explain away" all propitiatory uses of this word to connote the wrath of God. Dodd's "expiatory" interpretation begs the question of who it is that requires expiation and why.⁷⁵

No one would now contend that Dodd provides a complete solution to this debate, however influential his views have been. But Nicole is incorrect to describe the ideas conveyed by the ἱλάσκεσθαι group as "overwhelmingly" propitiatory. Many are not, as we have seen. As but one example, which we have noticed in reviewing Law's work, in Ezekiel 16:63 in the LXX, ἐξιλάσεσθαι is used for בְּכַפְּרִי, a כִּפֶּר phrase. Here the Lord is the *subject*, the actor in the act of atonement, and sinful humanity is its object – no sacrifice is in view. Divine wrath is *not* present. Rather, the Lord here makes an "everlasting covenant" (16:60) with the people, forgiving them for breaking a previous one (16:59).

Leon Morris also strongly criticises Dodd's view that the ἱλάσκομαι word group has a non-propitiatory secondary meaning of "expiate" in pagan usage, arguing that in Dodd's Plato example, the context is the need to pay for injury, carrying the idea of soothing anger.⁷⁶ As to its use in the LXX, Morris agrees with Dodd's conclusion that it does not convey the idea of a capricious deity who must be bribed into a good mood by his worshippers.⁷⁷ He argues that the wrath of God is ever present in the OT.⁷⁸ Morris

---

⁶⁹ *Ibid*, 127.
⁷⁰ *Ibid*, 131–2.
⁷¹ *Ibid*, 135–46.
⁷² *Ibid*, 146–7.
⁷³ *Ibid*, 147–9.
⁷⁴ *Ibid*, 140.
⁷⁵ *Ibid*, 149–50.
⁷⁶ Leon Morris, *The Apostolic Preaching of the Cross* (Leicester: IVP 3rd ed., 1965, repr. 1976), 146.
⁷⁷ *Ibid*, 148.
⁷⁸ *Ibid*, 148–54.

is critical of Dodd's conclusion that the LXX translators did not see כִּפֶּר as conveying the idea of propitiation of the Deity, but rather of an act removing guilt or defilement.[79]

Morris acknowledges that Dodd is correct to say that the ἱλάσκομαι word group is used in the LXX in a wide variety of senses, many not conveying the idea of propitiation. He suggests the categories may be even wider than Dodd perceives. But he argues that as the senses in which the LXX uses the ἱλάσκομαι word group are so wide, it is "meaningless" to conclude that it "generally" conveys, not propitiation of the Deity, but rather an act removing guilt or defilement.[80] He considers that it is incorrect to say, as Dodd does, that because the ἱλάσκομαι word group translates one Hebrew word or idea and on occasions another, the two Hebrew words or ideas must necessarily be similar. For Morris, the important thing is not to look at the Hebrew word the LXX translates, but the general idea it seeks to render.[81]

One can see why Morris argues this way from his examples of use of the ἱλάσκομαι word group in the LXX, namely Exodus 32:14, Lamentations 3:42, Daniel 9:19, 2 Kings 24:3f., Psalm 77(78):38, Psalm 78(79):9, Psalm 24(25):11, Psalm 64(65):4, Esther 13:17 and 2 Kings 5:18. He concedes that in each case forgiveness is conveyed but asserts that it carries the idea of turning away divine wrath, so that a propitiatory meaning is justified.[82]

The defect in this argument is that each of these usages conveys the idea of the Lord *freely* turning away his wrath, without any propitiation offered by a sinful people. Far from supporting a propitiatory meaning for the ἱλάσκομαι word group where used, Morris' examples in fact support Dodd. They depict the LXX conveying by this word group the idea of a God who is both wrathful and merciful, and who may be petitioned to turn away wrath freely, without blood sacrifice being offered.

Morris argues also from the many cultic LXX usages of ἱλαστήριον for "place of atonement" or "means of atonement" that its association with propitiation is clear.[83] This is contestable. We have seen in Chapter 2 that the expression τὸν οἶκον τοῦ in 1 Chronicles 28:20c in the LXX, which does not appear in the Hebrew, and which can be translated "the place of propitiation", can also be translated "the house of the mercy seat".[84] As but one example, as noted in Chapter 2, ἱλαστήριον occurs in Exodus 25:17, where the Lord's instructions concerning the building of the Ark of the Covenant include a mercy seat, כַּפֹּרֶת of gold to be placed atop the Ark (25:21): כַּפֹּרֶת may also be translated "place of clearing (or cleansing)", because yearly at *Yom Kippur* it receives the sin offering by which the people and the Tabernacle are "cleared". Thus Yahweh's continued presence is assured (Leviticus 16:14-15), as Yahweh's spirit can only abide in a place of utmost cleanliness atop the כַּפֹּרֶת.[85] The idea conveyed by the use of

---

[79] Ibid, 155.
[80] Ibid, 155-6.
[81] Ibid, 156.
[82] Ibid, 157-8.
[83] Ibid, 159.
[84] Curtis and Madsen, *The Book of Chronicles*, 300.
[85] Propp, *Exodus 19–40*, 385–6; similarly Cassuto, *A Commentary on the Book of Exodus*, 332, Durham, *Exodus*, 359–60.

ἱλαστήριον in Exodus 25:17 (and in the use of τὸν οἶκον τοῦ ἱλασμοῦ in 1 Chronicles 28:20c in the LXX) is not propitiation of divine wrath, but cleansing of a holy place by ritual sin offering, to ensure Yahweh's continued presence.

Morris contends that ἐξιλάσκομαι, while not used in the NT, should be considered in that context because of its close association with ἱλάσκομαι. He says it is the usual expression for "make atonement", in association with the sacrificial system. To him, the fact that ἐξιλάσκομαι renders כִּפֶּר eighty-three times and another Hebrew root only eleven times shows that in the LXX ἐξιλάσκομαι and כִּפֶּר are "nearly synonymous".[86]

There are two objections to this argument. Firstly, since ἱλάσκομαι and its derivatives are on a number of occasions used to translate Hebrew words other than כִּפֶּר, this might indicate that the two word groups are not "nearly synonymous". It might show simply that they are used on many, but by no means all occasions to translate a particular Hebrew word group. To assert a stronger association runs into the same pitfall as Dodd's argument that because different Hebrew word groups are translated by ἱλάσκομαι related words, the Hebrew word groups must be closely related, if not identical in meaning.

Secondly, precisely because ἐξιλάσκομαι is not used in the NT, its LXX use is anything but a sure guide to the use of words such as ἱλασμός in the NT (used only in 1 John 2:2 and 4:10) where reference to a sacrificial or propitiatory idea is not *otherwise* clear in the context. Put another way, ἐξιλάσκομαι and ἱλάσκομαι and its derivatives may be grammatically related, but to assert, without further argument, that the two word groups are "closely associated" falls into the same error as Morris stigmatises in Dodd's analysis, of assuming a similarity in meaning without examining the context in which these two words occur.

Morris gives examples of the non-cultic use of כִּפֶּר in the LXX, namely Exodus 30:12-16, Numbers 31:50, Genesis 32:20, Isaiah 47:11, Exodus 32:30, 2 Samuel 21:1-14, Numbers 35:33, Deuteronomy 32:41-43, Deuteronomy 21:1-9, Proverbs 16:6, Isaiah 27:9, Ezekiel 16:63, Psalms 78:38, Daniel 9:24, Jeremiah 18:23, Numbers 25:3-9, 11-13, 2 Chronicles 30:18 and Isaiah 6:7. He argues that in each case כִּפֶּר is used in close association with בֹּפֶר, "ransom", which has clear sacrificial associations, and that כִּפֶּר may be more original than בֹּפֶר, and that the latter may be a denominative from the former.[87]

But there is no mention of divine wrath being turned away by sacrifice in most of these examples. To suggest that because כִּפֶּר may be a denominative from בֹּפֶר, the meaning of the latter may control the meaning of the former is a weak reed on which to found the notion that in *all* of these examples, propitiation of wrath is the idea conveyed. Granted that in Morris' first example, Exodus 30:12-16, this *may* be so. But in Numbers 31:50 what is spoken of is a gift, not a sacrifice. In Genesis 32:20 there is simply appeasement of *human* anger. Isaiah 47:11 speaks of punishment for sin, not propitiation. In Exodus 32:30 Moses entreats the Lord to forgive the people's

---

[86] *Ibid*, 160.
[87] *Ibid*, 161–6.

sin. In 2 Samuel 21:1-14 David recompenses the Gibeonites for Saul's vengeance upon them. In Numbers 35:33 pollution of the land by the blood of the victim requires the death of the murderer, which is not so much propitiatory as a form of primitive justice. In Deuteronomy 32:41-43 the Lord vindicates his servants over their adversaries. In Deuteronomy 21:1-9, land where a corpse is found is cleansed by the sacrifice of a broken-necked heifer. In Isaiah 27:9 the guilt of Jacob is expiated and his sin is removed by the Lord, who crushes sacrificial altars. In Daniel 9:24, of which Morris admits "its precise meaning is not easy to determine",[88] the idea is repentance for iniquity, rather than propitiation for it. Only in Numbers 25:3-9 and 11-13 is there unequivocal reference to divine wrath being turned away, by impaling the chiefs of the people and the two Midianite men to avert plague, resulting in the Lord's revelation to Moses of a new covenant.

However in Proverbs 16:6 we find simply a reference to iniquity being "atoned for" by "loyalty and fidelity". There is no hint of sacrificial propitiation. Likewise in Ezekiel 16:63 the Lord commands his people never to open their mouths because of their shame, when he forgives them all they had done. Free forgiveness, not sacrificial propitiation, is the idea conveyed. In Psalm 78:38, God, "the compassionate, forgave their iniquity and did not annihilate them". Again, loving forgiveness, without any act of propitiation is conveyed. In Jeremiah 18:23 we find a prayer by the prophet that the Lord will *not* forgive the iniquity of those who plot to kill him. Divine wrath is invoked, but there is no sense of denial of a propitiatory offering by the plotters. In 2 Chronicles 30:18 there occurs a prayer by Hezekiah for a number of the people who ate the Passover despite not being ritually cleansed, proclaiming (30:18-19) that "the good Lord pardons all who set their hearts to see God". The prayer is granted (30:20). The idea here is of free forgiveness, despite lawlessness. In Isaiah 6:7 the seraph in Isaiah's vision touches his mouth with a live coal (6:6), saying "your guilt has departed and your sin is blotted out". Far from sacrifice or propitiation, the idea here is that divine wrath is freely turned aside by divine action through the seraph, an agent of God. Thus in a significant number of Morris' examples of non-cultic use of כָּפֶר, there is no hint of propitiation or even sacrifice, although this last element is present in a number of cases.

Morris' examples of the purely *cultic* use of כָּפֶר *may* demonstrate a *sacrificial* usage, as one might expect: the OT cultus was partly based on sacrifice, but ritual cleansing rather than propitiation was its primary purpose. This does not prove Morris' point, because almost *ex hypothesi*, cultic examples are likely to demonstrate a sacrificial, but not necessarily a *propitiatory* usage.

Morris says Westcott and Dodd "go too far" in arguing that when the LXX translators used "propitiation", they did not mean "propitiation".[89] This is *not* what they said. They wrote that when we find כָּפֶר translated by the ἱλάσκομαι word group in the LXX, propitiation is not *necessarily* conveyed. As we have seen from Morris' examples of non-cultic use of כָּפֶר, he arguably goes too far in suggesting that they always, or even usually, convey ideas of propitiation of divine anger.

---

[88] *Ibid*, 165.
[89] *Ibid*, 173.

Morris concludes that in 1 John 2:2 and 4:10, ἱλασμός is to be read with a propitiatory meaning, if his analysis of this word group in the LXX is sound.⁹⁰ With due respect, it is not. As we have seen from his examples, כָּפַר words translated by the ἱλάσκομαι word group in the LXX mostly do not carry a propitiatory meaning or even one of sacrifice.

Morris contends that the reference in 1 John 2:1 to our need for an advocate with God means that "we are in no good case" and that "our misdeeds prevail against us, we are about to feel the hostility of God to all that is sinful". Thus "under these circumstances we may well speak of Christ turning away the wrath of God".⁹¹ That is all inferred by Morris from 2:1.

What 1 John 2:1 says is that if we sin, we have an advocate with the Father, Jesus Christ himself. First John 2:1 only implies the wrath of God if ἱλασμός in 2:2 is to be read as "propitiation". This translation, on Morris' argument, depends on the soundness of his analysis of the ideas conveyed by the word group containing ἱλασμός in the LXX. As we have seen, this analysis has considerable defects arising from the text of the LXX.

Furthermore, there is no reference in the text of 1 John itself, in the verses surrounding 1 John 2:2 and 4:10, or for that matter in the whole letter, to John's readers facing divine wrath, ὀργή. However, it must be conceded, ὀργή occurs elsewhere in the Johannine literature in John 3:36 and of course in Revelation 6:16, 6:17, 11:18, 14:10, 16:19 and 19:15. But even there, it occurs in somewhat different contexts, involving punishment *simpliciter* rather than propitiation. The other koinē Greek word for "wrath", θυμός, with a sense closer to "fury", is only used in Revelation: see 12:12; 14:8, 10, 19; 15:1, 7; 16:19; 18:3; 19:15. The idea conveyed is not always divine wrath: Revelation 12:12 refers to the Devil's wrath, and 14:8 and 18:3 speak of the wrath of Babylon's fornication, and where the concept conveyed *is* divine wrath (see 14:10 and 19, 15:1 and 7, 16:19 and 19:15); again the idea is divinely imposed punishment, not propitiation.

Nor do the verses surrounding 1 John 2:2 and 2:10 refer to the necessity for the reader to appropriate Jesus' sacrificial death to propitiate the Father for their sin, before Jesus' ἱλασμός is available to them. No one should seek to "write out" of the NT the theme of divine wrath, often prominent in it; the point here is that this idea should not dominate the meaning of ἱλασμός in 1 John when it is nowhere mentioned in the epistle. The defect in Morris' argument is that it is crucially dependent on the propitiatory interpretation of the LXX references to the ἱλασμός word group which he marshals, which cannot be sustained.

David Hill is another formidable exponent of the "propitiatory" view of ἱλασμός in 1 John 2:2 and 4:10. As with Morris' objections to Dodd's work, his argument is careful

---

[90] *Ibid*, 206.
[91] *Ibid*, 206–7. Similarly Derek Kidner, "Sacrifice: Metaphors and Meaning", *Tyn Bul* 33 (1982): 119–36, 120; E Earl Ellis, *The World of St John: The Gospel and Epistles* (Grand Rapids: Eerdmans, 1984), 86; John RW Stott, *The Letters of John* (Downers Grove, IL: IVP Academic, 2nd ed., 1988), 89–92; Gary M Burge, *The Letters of John* (Grand Rapids: Zondervan, 1996), 86; Peter Adam, "The Atoning Saviour" in *Christ Died for Our Sins: Essays on the Atonement*, 15–34, 19; Clark, *First John*, 45; Campbell, *1, 2 & 3 John*, 48–54; Akin, *1, 2, 3 John*, 82–6; O'Donnell, *1–3 John*, 36–7.

and detailed. Hill's central criticism of Dodd's work is that Dodd "limited his discussion of ἱλάσκεσθαι and related words in the LXX to matters of grammar and translation equivalence", which Hill thinks "partly explains its inadequacy".[92] This criticism has some merit, but it does not necessarily entail the consequence that Dodd's views on the use of ἱλασμός in 1 John 2:2 and 4:10 are misconceived.

Hill's view, contra Dodd, is that the terms "propitiation" and "expiation" are so closely related that they are often seen as interchangeable, in part because there is no difference between the actions taken to bring either result.[93] That opinion is contestable, at least in relation to the use of ἱλασμός and its derivatives in the LXX, because they do not always, or even usually, refer to propitiatory sacrifice for sin. As we have seen, there is no precision in the use of these words in the LXX, in either meaning or context.

Hill rightly observes that notions of divine wrath are anything but absent in the LXX.[94] But as we have seen from Law's examples, the undoubted fact that divine wrath is present in the LXX does not necessarily prove that in LXX occurrences of ἱλάσκεσθαι and its cognates, the context clearly refers to the anger of God.[95] Hill indeed concedes that the meanings of Greek words *other* than ἱλάσκομαι which translate כִּפֶּר vary greatly, from "sanctify" to "cancel", so they cannot give a precise indication of the meaning of the ἱλάσκομαι group.[96]

Hill's contention is that in almost all cases where ἱλάσκομαι and related words do *not* render כִּפֶּר and its derivatives, they render words which either have a human subject, and refer to cleansing from defilement or expiation of sin, or have a divine subject and refer to grace, mercy or forgiveness.[97] Hill is forced to resort to the argument that the *meaning* of the Hebrew term translated is a less-reliable guide to the LXX word used than its *context*, and therefore the *idea* sought to be conveyed by the LXX translators.[98] One would have thought that both etymology and context are equally important here. Be that as it may, Hill gives many examples where he maintains that in context, words other than כִּפֶּר could easily have been rendered otherwise than by ἱλασμός derivatives.

The difficulty for this argument is that the LXX translators *do* in fact use ἱλασμός derivatives to translate disparate Hebrew words not in the כִּפֶּר group and not conveying the idea of sacrifice. This suggests, contra Hill and supporting Dodd, that ἱλασμός and its derivatives as used in the LXX have no necessary frame of reference to propitiatory sacrifice.

Hill deploys his findings concerning the LXX use of ἱλασμός and its derivatives to show that in 1 John 2:2 and 4:10, because in the LXX the word group refers not to "expiation" but "atonement", "forgiveness" or "propitiation", only the first and third

---

[92] D Hill, *Greek Words and Hebrew Meanings* (Cambridge: Cambridge University Press, 1967), 24.
[93] *Ibid*, 23.
[94] *Ibid*, 25.
[95] *Ibid*.
[96] *Ibid*, 25–6.
[97] *Ibid*.
[98] *Ibid*, 26–7.

of these meanings are correct in 1 John 2:2 and 4:10.[99] The first objection to this argument is that as we saw at the outset, Hill maintains that the terms "propitiation" and "expiation" are so closely related that they are often seen as interchangeable. This is in part because there is no difference between the actions taken to bring either result.[100] For reasons already given, this is not so.

The second, more potent objection to Hill's view here is that as we have seen from Law's examples, ἱλασμός derivatives are often used in the LXX to translate כָּפַר words with the Lord as the *subject*, as well as the object of acts of atonement. In these examples, such acts are not always portrayed in the LXX as acts of propitiation of the Lord for human sin and are often pictured as acts of divine generosity, in which the Lord forgives humans' sin without any act of propitiation by them.

Following Morris,[101] Hill is forced to maintain a "paradox" that if acceptance of the personal breach with God created by sin requires a propitiatory interpretation of 1 John 2:2 and 4:10, then the means of turning aside the consequences of sin comes from God's love.[102] To this one may retort that if the idea of expiation rather than propitiation is conveyed by ἱλασμός in 2:2 and 4:10, there is no paradox. If that be so, then God has not propitiated God's wrath by sending the Son. Instead, God sent the Son to act as the expiator of sin, to cleanse us (1:7) from the sin we inevitably commit, despite our self-deceptions (1:8). On this view, Jesus does not propitiate the Father but acts in loving concert with the Father in delivering us from sin.

As we have noted, there is no reference in 1 John 2:2 and 4:10, or for that matter in the whole letter, to John's readers facing divine wrath or to the necessity for them to appropriate Jesus' sacrificial death to propitiate the Father for their sin, before Jesus' ἱλασμός is available to them. Hill's thesis, like that of Morris, is crucially dependent on a propitiatory interpretation of the LXX references to the ἱλασμός word group which he marshals, which is unsustainable.

Howard Marshall writes of 1 John 2:2 that ἱλασμός in extra-biblical Greek writing refers to an offering made by a person to placate the anger of a deity, whereas Westcott and Dodd argue that in the OT the object of the action is the sin itself, so that in the Bible the term refers to "expiation", a means of cancelling sin.[103] Marshall's answer to this is that of Morris and Hill. It is that in the OT, the idea of placating God or some other injured person is often present when the ἱλασμός word group is used. Therefore in the NT, and in particular 1 John 2:2, there is "no real doubt" that the meaning of ἱλασμός is "propitiation", so that "Jesus propitiates God with respect to our sins".[104]

This is a very frank presentation of the propitiatory view of atonement in 2:2. It has the difficulty, firstly, that use of ἱλασμός and its cognates in the LXX is anything

---

[99] *Ibid*, 37.
[100] *Ibid*, 23.
[101] Morris, *Apostolic Preaching of the Cross*, 178–9.
[102] Hill, *Greek Words and Hebrew Meanings*, 37–8.
[103] Marshall, *Epistles of John*, 117.
[104] *Ibid*, 118. Similarly FF Bruce, *The Epistles of John* (London: Pickering & Inglis, 1970), 50.

but uniform in its portrayal of the idea of sacrifice, which itself is not necessarily propitiatory. Sometimes this idea is present; sometimes it is not. Indeed Marshall, ever the careful and fair scholar, concedes as much. He gives many examples and notes that "the fact would seem to be that the word group can have different nuances in different contexts".[105] It follows that usage in the LXX of ἱλασμός is not an entirely authoritative guide to its meaning in 1 John 2:2.

Secondly, Marshall's argument presents an unwarranted separation between the mind and action of the Father and that of the Son. This is a view rightly castigated early on by Charles Gore as having the consequence that "contrary to all the teachings of the New Testament, the mind of Christ has been distinguished from the mind of the Father as mercy from justice".[106]

The same difficulties attend Marshall's view of 1 John 4:10. He rightly says of humanity that here God "pardons their sins against himself at his own cost". But he goes on to quote James Denney: "So far from finding any kind of contrast between love and propitiation, the apostle can convey no idea of love except by pointing to the propitiation."[107] This view does not engage with the difficulty that the LXX's use of ἱλασμός and its cognates is anything but consistent in its presentation of the idea of propitiation, as compared with others, such as forgiveness and reconciliation, without any prior propitiation.

Stephen Smalley's view of ἱλασμός in 1 John 2:2 is not dissimilar from that of Morris, Hill, Marshall and Bruce, though with some variations, as we shall see. He provides a full and fair summary of the scholarly debate centring on a comparison of the use of the word in 2:2 and in the LXX. He maintains that the opinions that ἱλασμός in 1 John means that God is either the subject or alternatively the object of the action, and therefore that either expiation or propitiation of sin is the idea conveyed, ought not to be regarded as mutually exclusive ideas.[108]

Smalley's argument here rests first on the contributions of Dodd and those who follow him, arguing that כָּפַר in the OT has the root meaning of "cover". He notes that they argue that this idea, referring to sin, is best translated by "expiation" rather than "propitiation" and that one may find LXX examples of this where כִּפֶּר words are translated by ἱλασμός and its cognates to convey the idea of "expiation" of sin (cf. Psalm 130:4; Daniel 9:9).[109] Smalley then notes the work of Hill and those who follow him (Marshall, for example) who posit that ἱλασμός and its cognates in the LXX are often seen more "objectively", depicting God as the recipient of propitiatory sacrifice for sin (cf. Ezekiel 44:27; 2 Maccabees 3:33).[110]

Smalley suggests that because ἱλασμός and its cognates may carry *either* an expiatory *or* propitiatory meaning in the LXX, then possibly in 1 John 2:2 *both* senses may be conveyed. This is because even in the OT, God is both the initiator (by the

---

[105] *Ibid*, 118 n.29.
[106] Charles Gore, *The Epistles of St John* (London: John Murray, 1920) 88.
[107] *Ibid*, 215, quoting James Denney, *The Death of Christ* (London: 1951) 152.
[108] Smalley, *1, 2, 3 John*, 39.
[109] *Ibid*.
[110] *Ibid*.

law's prescriptions) and the recipient of sin offerings, and the same pattern may exist in 1 John 2:2.[111] To Smalley, in 2:1 Jesus is the heavenly intercessor (παράκλητον) and can do so because *he* (αὐτὸς) is righteous (δίκαιον) – he is the offering, and God is the *object*, but God is also the *subject* of the action, as the ultimate source of forgiveness and purification of the sinner (4:9).[112]

To Smalley's argument that by God's prescriptions in the Jewish law, God is the subject, the provider of propitiatory sacrifice, one may retort that in the OT the *point* of blood sacrifice is that humankind offers to God what would otherwise be to its benefit – otherwise how is it a "sacrifice" at all? In 1 John 2:2, God indeed is the provider of the sacrifice – as we learn in 4:9 where we read that τὸν υἱὸν αὐτοῦ τὸν μονογενῆ ἀπέσταλκεν ὁ θεός. In no sense does humanity itself provide the sacrifice of God's own Son. To those adhering to penal substitution, one may reply that even in the OT, as we have seen from our survey of ἱλασμός and its cognates in the LXX, particularly Leviticus, blood sacrifice does not necessarily connote propitiation of the deity, but rather a *cleansing* of sin by the blood of a victim.

As to ἱλασμός in 1 John 4:10, Smalley too argues that there Jesus is not *the* sacrifice for our sin, to the exclusion of all other sacrifices, but "generically a *sacrifice* for all sin". He compares this verse to Romans 8:32, which he says refers to Genesis 22:1-14, relating Abraham's intended sacrifice of his only son.[113] The defect in this argument is that it is clear that in the OT, sacrifices for sin are different in *kind* from that depicted in 1 John 4:10. As we have just seen, in no sense in 2:2 or 4:10 does humanity itself provide the sacrifice of God's own Son – God alone does so. It is quite otherwise with Abraham. Although God does indeed provide a ram as an alternative sacrifice (Genesis 22:13), the central point of the OT story is Abraham's faith (cf. Romans 4:3), in being willing to offer the supreme sacrifice of his own son when tested by God. God's action in 1 John 2:2 and 4:10 is quite different. Granted, God in supreme love for humankind (4:9) sends the Son as ἱλασμός for our sin, but God does not sacrifice the Son to someone else, as Abraham was prepared to do.

(iii) Other Views

Judith Lieu brings a different perspective to the debate over ἱλασμός in 1 John 2:2 and 4:10. As to 2:2, she sees in 2:1 the tradition of a παράκλητος, a just one, persecuted even unto death. She cites Wisdom 2:18, where the fate of the just one whose opponents think they can act with impunity is described: "If the just one is a son of God, he will help him and rescue him from the hands of his opponents."[114]

---

[111] *Ibid*, 39–40. Similarly Colin G Kruse, *The Letters of John* (Grand Rapids: Eerdmans/Leicester: Apollos, 2000), 75–6; Robert W Yarbrough, *1–3 John* (Grand Rapids: Baker Publishing Group, 2008), 77–8, 239–40; Andreas J Kostenberger, *A Theology of John's Gospel and Letters* (Grand Rapids, Michigan: Zondervan, 2009), 536–7; Schuchard, *1–3 John*, 147; Jobes, *1, 2, & 3 John*, 79.

[112] Smalley, *1, 2, 3 John*, 40.

[113] *Ibid*, 244.

[114] Lieu, *I, II and III John*, 63. The theology in 1 John 2:1, where it speaks of Jesus Christ δίκαιον may have resonances with James 5:6, where the accusation is made that James' addressees had murdered τὸν δίκαιον, i.e. Jesus Christ, οὐκ ἀντιτάσσεται ὑμῖν. The idea in both verses is that Jesus was faithful, δίκαιος even unto death. I am indebted for this fruitful suggestion to discussion with Professor John Painter.

To Lieu, "against this background", 1 John suggests that Jesus' ability to intercede with the Father springs not from his divine status as God's own Son, but from being the one who remained faithful to God, even unto death.[115] She notes contemporary Jewish sources ascribing an intercessory role to those who die for their faith. She cites 2 Maccabees 7:37-38 where the seven die for God's law in the persecution of Antiochus Epiphanes, praying that God might be merciful to a suffering land, and 4 Maccabees 17:21-22 where because of the martyrs "the homeland is purified, for they became, as it were, a ransom (*antipsychon*) for the sin of the nation, and through the blood of these devout ones and through the atoning sacrifice (*hilastērion*) of their death, the divine Providence saved the oppressed nation".[116]

In such references to the undeserved death of God's faithful ones, according to Lieu, "the traditional language of sacrifice was being recast without any detailed reflection on why and how their deaths might be efficacious".[117] So in 1 John 2:2, the word ἱλασμός, used only once again in the NT in 4:10, in "its form as a noun emphasizes action rather than agent or means", so that "he is forgiveness" is the sense conveyed.[118] She notes that in the LXX a cultic sense is not necessarily conveyed by the term. She acknowledges that in Leviticus 25:9 it refers to the Day of Atonement but points out that in Nehemiah 9:17, Psalm 130:4 and Daniel 9:9, it refers simply to divine forgiveness.[119] Therefore, "the context here in 1 John supports a neutral translation rather than a cultic one; there is no reference here to Jesus' blood or death and no hint of a sacrificial framework".[120]

This viewpoint on ἱλασμός in 1 John 2:2 really places Lieu closer to the "expiation" rather than the "propitiation" camp. Granted that there is no precise indication in the LXX to support an accurate description by way of either "expiation" or "propitiation" of the action portrayed in 2:2, expiation is preferable, because it connotes cleansing of sin. First John 1:7 has already spoken of cleansing of sin by the blood of Jesus, God's Son. There is no hint there either of cultic sacrifice, except for the bare mention of Jesus' blood. This might more properly be read simply as a reference to his blood itself, rather than the precise mechanism by which it effects an ἱλασμός for human sin. Might ἱλασμός in 2:2 itself be a reference simply to the *fact* of divine forgiveness wrought through Jesus' blood, rather than to its precise mechanism, which we cannot know?

Similarly, as to ἱλασμός in 1 John 4:10, Lieu argues that "no specific understanding of how sins are forgiven is implied".[121] She suggests that in 2:2 the emphasis is on the present, on how God deals with sin *now*, whereas in 4:10 it is on what God in Christ did in the past.[122] To Lieu, the formula in 4:10 provides not precise detail of *how* God's love benefits believers, but rather the reason *why* that love is the foundation of our response.[123]

---

[115] *Ibid.*
[116] *Ibid.*
[117] *Ibid*, 64.
[118] *Ibid.*
[119] *Ibid.* See also Lieu, *Theology of the Johannine Epistles*, 63-4.
[120] Lieu, *I, II and III John*, 64.
[121] *Ibid*, 183.
[122] *Ibid.*
[123] *Ibid*, 183-4.

The context in 1 John 4:10 indeed suggests that John is speaking primarily of what God's love *effects*, so that our response (4:11) ought to be that we love one another. In 4:10 we do not find a precise theology of *how* atonement occurs, but rather rejoicing in God's love for us in sending the Son as a means of forgiveness of human sin, so in light of such a costly action, God's people should reflect that supreme love in their own community.

Pheme Perkins deals with ἱλασμός in 1 John 2:2 somewhat differently, but still in basic accord with Lieu's approach. She steers clear of the propitiation/expiation debate and says that 2:1-2 is anti-gnostic polemic: it affirms that rather than victory over sin being won by the individual spirit, it is attained by Jesus' prayers, in that "his intercession and atoning death make forgiveness a permanent reality within the community".[124] Of 1 John 4:10 she says that "1 Jn thus expresses a fundamental insight of the covenant theology of the Old Testament as it has been handed on in Christianity: that God takes the initiative in reconciling a sinful humanity to himself".[125] Perkins' view is helpful. Rather than defining the precise mechanism of atonement, the point of 1 John 2:2 (and 4:10) is that in love, the Father sent the Son to reconcile us to God by cleansing us from sin, through the death of the Son. This too really places Perkins closer to the expiation point of view.

Urban von Wahlde argues concerning ἱλασμός in 1 John 2:2 and 4:10 that the "more satisfying background" to its use is that of the rite of the Day of Atonement, referred to in Leviticus 25:9, which Leviticus 16 says was performed by a high priest sacrificing a bull and a goat. In Leviticus 16:16 in the LXX, using an ἱλασμός derivative, the Holy Place is cleansed by the outpouring of blood. Therefore, reading 1 John 1:7 with 2:2, both ἱλασμός and "blood" are associated with the Day of Atonement, so that a *cleansing* of the sin of the whole world (2:2) which still exists (1:8) by the blood of Jesus (1:7) is what the author portrays.[126]

This view, far from "explaining away" the apparently propitiatory sense in which ἱλασμός and its derivatives are used in the LXX, harnesses one of these apparently propitiatory uses and demonstrates that it may still bear a non-propitiatory, "cleansing" sense in 1 John. But did not the Johannine author also intend in 1:7 and 2:2 to draw in the sacrifice of a bull and a goat in Leviticus 16 as depicting the meaning of Jesus' sacrifice? Not so: the author's use of ἱλασμός in 1 John 2:2 and 4:10 refers more obviously to the actual cleansing by blood (cf. 1 John 1:7) in Leviticus 16:16, not the precise mechanism whereby it was accomplished.

A cautionary note must, however, be sounded here. If an analysis of past use of language proceeds as if such examination can *by itself* prove meaning in another context – and it is by no means clear that Von Wahlde falls into this trap – is in error. At most, the past range of meanings can be shown by such analysis. New meanings *do*

---

[124] Perkins, *Johannine Epistles*, 22.
[125] *Ibid*, 55.
[126] Urban C Von Wahlde, *The Gospel and Letters of John: Vol 3, Commentary on the Three Johannine Letters* (Grand Rapids, Michigan: Eerdmans, 2010), 44.

emerge in current use of language. Past usage, however, may reveal clues which may be helpful about the ways in which contextual elements reveal shades of meaning. In the end, analysis of past use can only show possibilities: the meaning of ἱλασμός in 1 John depends on its own particular context.

Conclusions from Scholarship Review

After a fairly extensive, but necessarily selective overview of scholarship on the use of ἱλασμός in 1 John 2:2 and 4:10, and of the way in which scholars have appealed to LXX use of the term and its cognates, we can see that much the same evidence has been interpreted in different ways. Some maintain that it supports a propitiatory interpretation for this term. Others opt for an expiatory one. Still others suggest that this evidence is so varied that no definite conclusion can be drawn. In the preceding chapter we examined LXX uses of ἱλασμός and concluded that no pattern of predominant or even frequent propitiatory usage of this term can be discerned, nor can such a use of ἱλασμός cognates be found. The LXX usage of ἱλασμός and its cognates is varied, with God as both the subject and the indirect object of the action. Non-sacrificial meanings such as forgiveness appear as often as notions of sacrifice. Even then, cleansing or expiation of sin by God, after humankind has taken the appropriate actions, rather than propitiation, is the dominant idea.

True it is that 1 John is remarkable among NT texts for its relative *lack* of allusion to the OT. First John 3:12, with its reference to Cain, is the only one. And yet a number of its key theological motifs are inexplicable, as we have seen, without reference to OT theological and ethical principles. First, Cain and Abel imagery affects more than this one verse.[127] It is apparent beneath 3:15, in the clause "he who hates a brother is a murderer", and indeed beneath the whole section from 3:11 to 3:17. Second, the author had available to him the LXX and the interpretative tradition built upon it in Second Temple Judaism, as shown in the intertestamental pseudepigrapha and the Qumran writings traced in the preceding chapter. We should not read 1 John in a vacuum, apart from, and without referring to, that background.

More guidance can be derived from the immediate literary contexts in which ἱλασμός occurs in 1 John 2:2 and 4:10 than from the LXX evidence. Context *always* influences the meaning of a word, and words *require* context so their precise meaning can be determined. This does not mean that the LXX evidence affords no help. However it provides the biblical background, of which the author was undoubtedly aware, against which the term ἱλασμός is used in 1 John. But the LXX background of usage of ἱλασμός does not by itself dictate its literal meaning, still less the theology it expresses in 1 John. To unlock this, we must embark on our own exegesis of 1 John 2:2 and 4:10 in their respective literary contexts.

---

[127] So Brown, *Epistles of John*, 442.

Exegesis of 1 John 2:2 and 4:10

(i) 1 John 2:2

This verse must be examined as part of a larger unit. Most scholars see 1 John 1:5–2:2 as a unit in itself or part of a larger one.[128] Brown, Marshall and Lieu consider that the section, 1:5–2:2, constitutes a unit by itself.[129] This is convincing. These verses are united by the three secessionist boasts (or claims) concerning sin, "if we say", ἐὰν εἴπωμεν, in 1:6, 1:8 and 1:10.[130] Each is followed symmetrically by a condemnatory statement in the same verse, 1:6, 1:8 and 1:10, and in the next verse, 1:7, 1:9 and 2:1, by a corrective statement of a positive consequence for us if we do *not* say what is stigmatised, but rather the reverse.[131]

The introduction to the unit is in 1:5. The preliminary statement that ἡ ἀγγελία, "the message", which we have heard from Jesus himself, that God is light and that in God there is no darkness, is introduced as a prelude to a discourse on sin in 1:6-2:1. That God is light formulates a basic truth upon which the first ethical remark in 1 John 1-6-7, to which we shall come in a moment, is based.[132] Symmetrically, its conclusion is in 2:2, where the discourse on sin at 1:6–2:1 is climaxed by the crowning statement that Jesus himself, from whom ἡ ἀγγελία, "the message", has come, is the ἱλασμός for our sins. So 1:5–2:2 form a single, symmetrical unit. The last statement that Jesus is the ἱλασμός for our sins is intimately connected to, and is the remedy for, the preceding secessionist "boasts". We shall see that this statement is especially connected to that in 1:7, that the blood of Jesus, God's son, cleanses us from all sin. By examining this context in 1 John 1:5–2:2 we may uncover what Jesus being ἱλασμός for our sins in 2:2 truly signifies.

In 1 John 1:5, ἀκηκόαμεν, "we have heard", echoes the same word in 1:1, and ἀπ' αὐτοῦ, "from him", refers back to τοῦ υἱοῦ αὐτοῦ Ἰησοῦ Χριστοῦ, "with his Son Jesus Christ" in 1:3. Both emphasize the dominical source of ἡ ἀγγελία, "the message", in 1:5. The statement, ὁ θεὸς φῶς ἐστιν καὶ σκοτία ἐν αὐτῷ οὐκ ἔστιν οὐδεμία, "God is light

---

[128] So Westcott, *Epistles of St John*, xlvi (1:5–2:17); Law, *Tests of Life*, 7 (1:5–2:28); Bultmann, *Johannine Epistles*, 15 (1:5–2:2); Schnackenburg, *Johannine Epistles*, 76 (1:6–2:2); Dodd, *Johannine Epistles*, 16 (1:5–2:28); Strecker, *Johannine Letters*, 23 (1:5–2:17); Smalley, *1, 2, 3 John*, 17 (1:5–2:29); Painter, *1, 2, and 3 John*, 141 (1:6–2:27).

[129] Brown, *Epistles of St John*, 128; Marshall, *Epistles of John*, 26; Lieu, *I, II and III John*, 48. Matthew Jensen argues that 1 John 1:5 forms a conclusion to 1:1-4, contending that the theme of sin that so dominates 1:6-2:2 is absent from 1:1-5, and the first ἐὰν εἴπωμεν statement of 1:6-7 requires *both* premises of 1:1-5, fellowship with God, and God as light without darkness:Matthew Jensen, "The Structure and Argument of 1 John," *JSNT* 35:1 (2012), 54–73, 63. The problem with this proposal is that in 1:6, κοινωνίαν ἔχομεν μετ' αὐτοῦ is a clear reference back to ὁ θεὸς in 1:5. Jensen concedes this, but if ὁ θεὸς in 1:5 is referred to as being the one in whom there is no σκοτία, "darkness", surely that affirmation is to be contrasted with 1:6, in which human "walking in darkness" is identified with sin.

[130] So Brown, *Epistles of St John*, 128.

[131] Painter, *1, 2, and 3 John*, 142.

[132] Jan Van der Watt, "On Ethics in 1 John" in *Communities in Dispute: Current Scholarship on the Johannine Epistles* (ed. R Alan Culpepper and Paul N Anderson; Atlanta: SBL Press, 2014), 197–222, 198.

and there is no darkness in him at all" in 1:5 may seem tautologous. But σκοτία is a prelude to the statement in 1:6, where it is repeated.

In 1:6 we find the first boast or claim of the secessionists, ἐὰν εἴπωμεν ὅτι κοινωνίαν ἔχομεν μετ' αὐτοῦ, "if we say we have fellowship with him", followed by the first rejoinder, ἐν τῷ σκότει περιπατῶμεν, ψευδόμεθα καὶ οὐ ποιοῦμεν τὴν ἀλήθειαν, "we walk in darkness, we tell lies and do not do what is true". The term "fellowship", κοινωνία, harks back to the "little prologue" in 1:3 where it refers to ἡ κοινωνία δὲ ἡ ἡμετέρα μετὰ τοῦ πατρὸς καὶ μετὰ τοῦ υἱοῦ αὐτοῦ Ἰησοῦ Χριστοῦ, "our fellowship is with the Father and with his son Jesus Christ". This contrasts the false claim to fellowship by the secessionists with the true fellowship with the Father and with one another. Walking in darkness, ἐν τῷ σκότει in 1:6 is associated with lying and failure to do what is true, literally "the truth", τὴν ἀλήθειαν, which is to be attained by adherence to ἡ ἀγγελία (1:5). Later John explains that to walk in darkness is to be like Cain and to walk in the light is to love one's brother (1 John 2:9:10), and that the God who is light is revealed by the God who is love (1 John 1:5, 4:7-12 and 4:8). Darkness is associated with hatred, and light with love.

First John 1:6 sets up the contrasting, corrective statement in 1:7a that if we walk "in the light", ἐν τῷ φωτὶ, we *will* have κοινωνία with each other. This is immediately followed by the consequential statement in 1:7b which is the hinge of the whole unit, τὸ αἷμα Ἰησοῦ τοῦ υἱοῦ αὐτοῦ καθαρίζει ἡμᾶς ἀπὸ πάσης ἁμαρτίας, "the blood of Jesus his Son cleanses us from all sin". As Brown notes, the Jewish outlook on cleansing from sin is well summarised in the words of Leviticus 17:11, where blood is given to the people "so you may make atonement with it upon the altar for your souls": Brown considers that John had in mind in 1:7 a particular OT sacrifice, that on the Day of Atonement, when he described the shedding of Jesus' blood.[133] This is convincing, because 1:7 states a remedy for human sin by bloodshedding, which is the precise point of the Day of Atonement sacrifice referred to in Leviticus 25:9, analysed in our examination of the use of ἱλασμός in the LXX. If, as argued above, ἱλασμός is better translated in Leviticus 25:9 (LXX) as "purgation", then the author of 1 John conveys in his use of καθαρίζειν in 1 John 1:7 not the idea of propitiation, but of expiation or removal of sin. This bears on the author's use of ἱλασμός in 2:2.

In 1:8 the second negative statement occurs: first the boast or claim, ἐὰν εἴπωμεν ὅτι ἁμαρτίαν οὐκ ἔχομεν, then the rejoinder, ἑαυτοὺς πλανῶμεν καὶ ἡ ἀλήθεια οὐκ ἔστιν ἐν ἡμῖν. The word ἀλήθεια recalls the first rejoinder in 1:6, and ultimately ἡ ἀγγελία, the "message" in 1:5, introduced by the "little prologue", 1:1-4. Denial of sin in oneself contradicts ἡ ἀγγελία and ultimately Ὃ ἦν ἀπ' ἀρχῆς in 1:1.

In 1:9a comes the corrective, ἐὰν ὁμολογῶμεν τὰς ἁμαρτίας ἡμῶν, πιστός ἐστιν καὶ δίκαιος ἵνα ἀφῇ ἡμῖν τὰς ἁμαρτίας, "if we confess our sins, the faithful and just one will forgive our sins". The thought here is similar to the rejoinder in 1:7: if we confess our sins, we recognise the truth of the message, ἡ ἀγγελία, about ourselves. If that were all, the action would be purely between the Father and sinful humanity.

---

[133] Brown, *The Epistles of John*, 203.

However the next statement in 1:9b, καὶ καθαρίσῃ ἡμᾶς ἀπὸ πάσης ἀδικίας, "and cleanses us from all [our] unrighteousness", repeats the thought in 1:7 of purgation or expiation by *cleansing* from unrighteousness, which is a *state* or *quality* of sinfulness, not a particular evil deed. This harks back again to the idea in Leviticus 25:9 in the LXX of ἱλασμός for sin by cleansing sacrifice. First John 1:9b depicts what may be described theologically as an action by the Father and the Son in concert, earlier depicted in 1:7. In 1:9b, the *Son's* blood cleanses us from unrighteousness, καθαρίσῃ ἡμᾶς ἀπὸ πάσης ἀδικίας. Therefore it is the *Father* who gives the Son, whose blood cleanses us from all sin in 1:7.

In 1 John 1:10 we find the third boast or claim of the secessionists, ἐὰν εἴπωμεν ὅτι οὐχ ἡμαρτήκαμεν, "if we say that we have not sinned", followed by the first rejoinder, ψεύστην ποιοῦμεν αὐτόν, "we make him into a liar". Here ψεύστην echoes ψευδόμεθα in 1:6, and ποιοῦμεν harks back to the same word in 1:6. In 1:6 it is we who lie. In 1:10 it is really our lie, by denying sin, that portrays the divine ἀγγελία in 1:5 as false. The consequence is in the second pejorative statement in 1:10, ὁ λόγος αὐτοῦ οὐκ ἔστιν ἐν ἡμῖν, "his word is not in us". "His word", ὁ λόγος αὐτοῦ, again refers to the divine ἀγγελία in 1:5: the idea is that we have not understood the divine message.

One corrective appears in 2:1a, Τεκνία μου, ταῦτα γράφω ὑμῖν ἵνα μὴ ἁμάρτητε, "my little ones, I write these things to you, so you may not sin" (cf. 1:7, 1:9). However the writer does not expect that his words will be a "cure-all" for sinful humanity. He qualifies his optimism by a second corrective statement in 2:1b of the remedy for sin: καὶ ἐάν τις ἁμάρτῃ, παράκλητον ἔχομεν πρὸς τὸν πατέρα Ἰησοῦν Χριστὸν δίκαιον, "but if anyone sins, we have an intercessor with the Father, Jesus Christ the righteous one". The aorist ἁμάρτῃ in 2:1, in contrast to the present form of the verb in 1:8 and the perfect in 1:10, suggests that individual acts in the definite past, rather than a process, are referred to in 2:1.[134] The theology is that *even though* we have sinned, παράκλητον ἔχομεν πρὸς τὸν πατέρα. Van der Watt puts it nicely: "The statement that a child of God 'cannot sin' should be understood ... as 'will not' or 'does not want to' or 'does not think of'", but "the strong social conventions [in the ancient world] did not succeed in eliminating disobedience in practice", so that a disobedient child needed "education".[135] Here the "education" is in avoidance of sin, and failing that, the knowledge imparted in 2.1 that if we do sin, we have a παράκλητος with the Father.

As Vouga says, the action of the παράκλητος in 2:1 is to effect a godly reversal (Entsündigung) of the effects of human sin.[136] The preposition πρός in 2:1 need not

---

[134] Lieu, *I, II, & III John*, 61; Culy, *I, II, III John: A Handbook on the Greek Text*, 21, Dodd, "*The Johannine Epistles*, 78–9. One is aware that on occasions too much has been made of the aorist as depicting "punctilliar" or "snapshot" action, as opposed to past continuous action: see Frank Stagg, "The Abused Aorist," *JBL* 91 (1972): 222–31. But as Stagg himself concedes (at 224) in relation to this very verse, Dodd "cautions against reading too much subtlety into tenses", and indeed that is so. Dodd here only relies partially on a "distinction of tenses in Greek" as a possible solution to this apparent contradiction. He finds a way through by suggesting that there is no logical contradiction between the *aim* of refraining from sin and the *remedy* if it is not achieved: this is convincing.

[135] JG van der Watt, "Ethics in First John: A Literary and Socioscientific Perspective," *CBQ* 61:3 (1999), 491–511, 497.

[136] Vouga, *Die Johannesbriefe*, 32.

imply that God is the recipient of Jesus' advocacy by his propitiatory death: it can be translated "with", in the sense of "in company with" the Father.[137] The statement in 2:1 that Jesus Christ, God's Son, is a παράκλητος for us refers back to the κοινωνία we have with God and with God's Son, Jesus Christ, in 1:3. First John's use of "paraclete", παράκλητος, in 1 John 2:1 is linked to its use in John 14:16 to show that as Jesus has lived among us as a manifestation of divine love, so, as Burridge says, ἄλλον παράκλητον, "another advocate" (John 14:16), will continue to offer that love.[138] The discourse in 1 John 1:5–2:2 focuses on sin and its remedy, and 2:1, as the climax of the unit approaches, links the remedy for sin, Jesus' intercession for us, with our communion with the Father and the Son. But this advocacy does not avail us, and we do not receive God's cleansing, unless we confess our sin (1:9). Similarly, the phrase Ἰησοῦν Χριστὸν δίκαιον takes us back to 1:9b. The thought is that Jesus the righteous one pleads for us with the Father and expiates our unrighteousness.

In symmetry with the introduction to the passage in 1:5, the climax to it, how sin is dealt with, is stated in 2:2a: καὶ αὐτὸς ἱλασμός ἐστιν περὶ τῶν ἁμαρτιῶν ἡμῶν, "and he is the expiation of our sins". Here ἱλασμός provides a climax to, and a summary of, the theology of the whole passage – especially the hinge in 1:7b, τὸ αἷμα Ἰησοῦ τοῦ υἱοῦ αὐτοῦ καθαρίζει ἡμᾶς ἀπὸ πάσης ἁμαρτίας. *God's* action, not ours, provides τὸ αἷμα Ἰησοῦ τοῦ υἱοῦ αὐτοῦ. God is the subject, not the object. By giving the Son, God has *expiated* our sins – Jesus has not *propitiated* the Father.[139]

To return to Leviticus 25:9b, we have seen in Chapter 2 that "wipe" or "remove" is a more convincing translation there of כִּפֻּרִים, ἱλασμός in the LXX than "propitiation".[140] The idea in Leviticus 25:9b is divine *cleansing*, removal or expiation of sin after the appropriate cultic sacrifice is performed. As we have seen, expiation or forgiveness is not there seen as a physical effect of the priest's actions: it is a prerequisite, as is contrition, and it is *God* that grants the resulting expiation or purification from sin.[141] Certainly the priest is the subject of the action, but the person or object being cleansed is the direct object, and God the indirect.

First John 1:7 introduces the same idea by its use of the verbal form καθαρίζει. Similarly in 2:2 God removes or *expiates* sin after the appropriate action, confession of sin (1:9), is performed. And God's forgiveness of sin is through *God's* gift of the cleansing blood of the Son (1:7). This is not analogous to Genesis 22:13 where a ram is provided by God as a sacrifice in place of Abraham's son Isaac. In 2:2a ἱλασμός does capture the idea of sacrifice on the Day of Atonement in Leviticus 25:9, as indicated

---

[137] Belousek, *Atonement, Justice and Peace*, 249; *sed contra* Culy, *I, II, III John: A Handbook on the Greek Text*, 22.
[138] Burridge, *Imitating Jesus*, 301–2.
[139] Commenting on 2.2, Brown contends that "there is no doubt that the sacrifice of Christ on the once-for-all Christian Day of Atonement described in Hebrews is more an expiation than a propitiation" (Brown, *The Epistles of St John*, 221), noting interestingly that the Dominican scholar Ceslas Spicq lists sixteen parallels between Hebrews and the Johannine writings (C Spicq, *L'Epître aux Hébreux* (2 Vols; Paris: Gabalda, 1952), 1, 109–38) but it is no part of this study to contend that parallels with non-Johannine writings can determine the meaning of Greek words in 1 John.
[140] So indeed Brown, *Epistles of John*, 220. The usual translation, "atonement", is in reality neutral.
[141] Levine, *In the Presence of the Lord*, 65–6.

by the use of περί.¹⁴² Indeed in 2:2a ἱλασμός does connote sacrifice for sin, but one must not think of it in the usual way, the giving of "life for life".¹⁴³ It is not God's gift of the Son so *we* can appropriate his death as propitiation of God's own self as an angry Father. It is God's free gift of the Son, whose cleansing blood provides forgiveness or expiation, ἱλασμός of sin, as in Psalm 130:4.

In 2:2b-c the corrective statement in 2:2a is extended to "the world": οὐ περὶ τῶν ἡμετέρων δὲ μόνον ἀλλὰ καὶ περὶ ὅλου τοῦ κόσμου. Jesus Christ *is* ἱλασμός – not offered *as* ἱλασμός – and is thereby the expiation, not only for "our" sins, that is those of John's believing community, but for those of the whole world. There are many negative statements about ὁ κόσμος, "the world" in 1 John (e.g. 2:15-17, 3:1, 4:1, 4:4-5 – but cf. 4:9, 4:14). One might say that the author recognises the world's corruption but also affirms God's love for the world and God's willingness to offer the Son as its means of cleansing. The thought in 2:2b-c is that the members of John's community do not themselves hold the key to expiation of sin – only God does, and then only after confession and repentance. It is a strong corrective to the exclusivism of the secessionists.

Summarising 1:5–2:2, there is a stepped build-up, beginning with the opening assertion that God is light (1:5), through the secessionists' boasts or claims and their negative consequences (1:6, 8, 10) and the rejoinders to them (1:7, 9 and 2:1), to the final theological climax in 2:2a that Jesus Christ is ἱλασμός, the expiation, for our sins, and indeed for those of the whole world (2:2b). This triumphant claim is inextricably linked to 1:7-9 that the blood of Jesus is the cleansing agent for our sin.

Not only is the idea of cleansing of sin by blood in 1:7 picked up in 2:2a: so also is the idea of divine forgiveness and cleansing in 1:9. Viewed that way, ἱλασμός in 2:2a is used in the same way, to connote cleansing or covering of sin, as we find in many of its occurrences in the LXX where it translates כָּפַר words. Viewed against the background of first-century Jewish thought, available to the author of 1 John, there is a strong likelihood that ἱλασμός in 2:2a conveys not the idea of propitiation of divine wrath, but of covering or cleansing of sin in the LXX sense we have traced.

As we have seen, the idea often conveyed by Ἱλασμός in the LXX is cleansing, often by cultic sacrifice involving bloodshedding, but on occasion by forgiveness as a divine act, unprompted by any human rite (cf. Psalm 130:4; Daniel 9:9). Those who would make the leap from this idea of cleansing or covering of sin to a substitution of Jesus as propitiatory victim to slake God's anger for the animals sacrificed in the OT do not satisfactorily explain why ἱλασμός is frequently used in the LXX to connote divine forgiveness.

The true meaning of 1 John 2:1-2a is that the Father freely gives the Son in love. This is an idea which becomes much clearer in 4:10 where ἱλασμός again appears. Thus by the Son's gift of his life he becomes an advocate, a παράκλητος with the Father, for sinful humanity – not to assuage divine anger, but to extend forgiveness by his

---

[142] Hans-Josef Klauck, *Der Erste Johannesbrief* (Zürich und Braunschweig: Benziger Verlag AG, 1991), 106; similarly Olsson, *A Commentary on the Letters of John*, 104.
[143] Ernst Gaugler, *Die Johannesbriefe* (Zürich: Evz-Verlag, 1964), 66.

own bloodshedding. To postulate that the Father's anger is propitiated by the Son's death not only ignores the absence of any reference to divine wrath at 2:1-2a (and for that matter in the whole unit, 1:5-2:2) but also breaks apart the loving cooperation between the Father and the Son which is implicit in 2:1-2a. We shall come shortly to the profound implications of these conclusions for a peacemaking, non-violent hermeneutic of 1 John.

(ii) 1 John 4:10

Most scholars see 1 John 4:10 as part of a unit devoted to God's character as love, although they vary as to its boundaries.[144] Westcott and Painter see it as running from 4:7 to the end of the chapter, 4:21.[145] With deference to many who see this unit as extending from 4:7 to 5:4, Painter's argument, that a new section may be recognised at 5:1 because the focus shifts more directly to Christology,[146] is convincing. From 4:7 to 4:21, apart from 4:15, we do not find any explicit reference to Jesus' true nature, as opposed to God's gift of the Son in love (4:9-10).

But at 5:1 a new note – apart from a side reference in 4:15 – is struck: the necessity of belief in Jesus as the Christ, ὁ χριστὸς, God's anointed one. This is followed by an extended statement in 5:2-5 of the connection between Christological belief and love of one another, shown by love of God and obedience to God's commandments, and victory over the world through Christological faith. It is appropriate then to see 4:10 as part of an extended discussion of the relationship between human and divine love in 4:7-21. Within that unit, 4:7-12 stands as a subunit proclaiming that God's love is the *fons et origo*, the source and origin of love for one another. This can be seen from the change of subject at 4:13, to the assurance that we know that we abide in God and God in us because of the gift of the Spirit, whereas 4:12 speaks of God's love perfected in us by love of one another. It is appropriate therefore to see where 4:10 sits in the context of this subunit, 4:7-12.

The subunit begins with 4:7a, where we are commanded: Ἀγαπητοί, ἀγαπῶμεν ἀλλήλους, ὅτι ἡ ἀγάπη ἐκ τοῦ θεοῦ ἐστιν, "beloved ones, let us love one another, because love is from God". The *point* of mutual love is that we share with each other the love God has for us. This is confirmed in 4:7b, καὶ πᾶς ὁ ἀγαπῶν ἐκ τοῦ θεοῦ γεγέννηται καὶ γινώσκει τὸν θεόν, "everyone who loves is born of God and knows God". This completes the triangular relationship: God loves us, and in loving one another, we are children of God and we know who God truly is.[147]

Next in 4:8 comes the converse, negative statement, ὁ μὴ ἀγαπῶν οὐκ ἔγνω τὸν θεόν, ὅτι ὁ θεὸς ἀγάπη ἐστίν, "the one who does not love does not know God, because God is love". There can be no knowledge of God without love of one's fellow, because

---

[144] Law, *Tests of Life*, 16 (4:7–5:3a), Schnackenburg, *Johannine Epistles*, 206 (4:10–5:4), Brown, *Epistles of John*, 513 (4:7–5:4a), Strecker, *Johannine Epistles*, 142 (4:7–5:4a), Smalley, *1, 2, 3 John*, 232 (4:7–5:4), Lieu, *I, II & III John*, 175 (4:7–5:4).
[145] Westcott, *Epistles of St John*, xlvii, Painter, *1, 2, and 3 John*, 265.
[146] *Ibid*, 265–72.
[147] Similarly Lieu, *I, II, & III John*, 179.

God's own nature is loving. The yoking together of γεγέννηται and γινώσκει in 4:7b with ἔγνω in 4:8 forms a linkage between the ideas of birth and knowledge: new birth in God brings knowledge of God as love and love for one another.

At 4:9 we read ἐν τούτῳ ἐφανερώθη ἡ ἀγάπη τοῦ θεοῦ ἐν ἡμῖν, ὅτι τὸν υἱὸν αὐτοῦ τὸν μονογενῆ ἀπέσταλκεν ὁ θεὸς εἰς τὸν κόσμον ἵνα ζήσωμεν δι' αὐτοῦ: "In this manner the love of God was shown among us, that God sent his Son into the world so we may live through him." The linkage between 4:8 and 4:9 is that in 4:8 we read that God is love, and in 4:9 that God showed forth his love in sending the Son as a gift of life. The aorist passive ἐφανερώθη in 4:9a indicates that here we are dealing with a past event, the Incarnation, the earthly life of Jesus in its totality.[148] So God's present, enduring love for us, was shown by the life and death of the Son ἐν ἡμῖν, among us. This grammatical inference is supported by the statement in 4:9b: there the Son is sent *into the world*, rather than sent simply to die, even though that is a dimension of being in the world.

Again ἱλασμὸς marks a climax, this time in 4:10b. But first in 4:10a we read, ἐν τούτῳ ἐστὶν ἡ ἀγάπη, οὐχ ὅτι ἡμεῖς ἠγαπήκαμεν τὸν θεόν, ἀλλ' ὅτι αὐτὸς ἠγάπησεν ἡμᾶς, "in this is love, not that we loved God but that he loved us". It is striking that the perfect tense ἠγαπήκαμεν is used to convey the past continuous, that we "were loving" God, which implies an incomplete action, whereas the aorist ἠγάπησεν portrays God's action as a single, decisive past event, of which we as mere humans are incapable. The idea is that God loved us once and for all, in a single saving act.[149]

What that act was is revealed in 4:10b, καὶ ἀπέστειλεν τὸν υἱὸν αὐτοῦ ἱλασμὸν περὶ τῶν ἁμαρτιῶν ἡμῶν, "and sent his Son to be the expiation for our sins". The use of περὶ here rather than ὑπὲρ is significant. The word ὑπὲρ appears twice in 3:16, which affirms that Jesus gave up his life ὑπὲρ ἡμῶν, "for us", so that we ought to give up our lives ὑπὲρ τῶν ἀδελφῶν, "for the [our] brother". This suggests that the idea in 4:10b is different from that in 3:16. In 4:10b the thought is that Jesus as ἱλασμὸν περὶ τῶν ἁμαρτιῶν ἡμῶν is an agent who has an effect on something. This is consistent with the author's use of ἱλασμὸς in 2:2a. The idea is of Jesus *cleansing* us from sin. First John 4:10b makes explicit what is implicit in 2:1-2: that God in loving cooperation gives the Son as ἱλασμὸς for our sins. First John 4:10 is also in a sense *epexegetical*: that is, it elaborates upon and clarifies 4:9. The "sent" statements in 4:9, 10 and 14 make divine love and life the context for interpreting ἱλασμὸς in 4:10b. Indeed the ἱλασμὸς statement in 4:10b, καὶ ἀπέστειλεν τὸν υἱὸν αὐτοῦ ἱλασμὸν περὶ τῶν ἁμαρτιῶν ἡμῶν, appears to be in synchrony with the wording of the soteriological statement in 4:9b, ὅτι τὸν υἱὸν αὐτοῦ τὸν μονογενῆ ἀπέσταλκεν ὁ θεὸς εἰς τὸν κόσμον ἵνα ζήσωμεν δι' αὐτοῦ.[150] One must not, however, miss the dimension in 4:10b of the "scandal of the cross": the misunderstanding of liberal theology has often been to under-emphasise

---

[148] Culy, *I, II, III John: A Handbook on the Greek Text*, 107; Dodd, *The Johannine Epistles*, 38; Klauck, *Der Erste Johannesbrief*, 251.

[149] Again one is aware of Stagg, "The Abused Aorist", 222–31, but the point made here is not that the aorist suggests that Jesus' death is a past, saving act, but rather that *since* it is obviously in the past and is a single event, the use of the aorist is unsurprising.

[150] Morgen, *Les épîtres de Jean*, 169.

God's own sacrifice in the sending of the Son and to see it *only* as the proclamation of God's love.[151]

In fact 1 John 4:10b is somewhat reminiscent of "you atoned for our iniquities", τὰς ἀσεβείας ἡμῶν σὺ ἱλάσε, in Psalm 64(65):3 in the LXX, noted in the preceding chapter. In both clauses God is the *subject*, not the object of the action, and in both, ἱλασμὸς or a cognate refers to a divine gift to effect forgiveness of sin. In both clauses *God* provides atonement for sin – not humankind.

In 4:11 we find ἀγαπητοί, εἰ οὕτως ὁ θεὸς ἠγάπησεν ἡμᾶς, καὶ ἡμεῖς ὀφείλομεν ἀλλήλους ἀγαπᾶν, "because God loved us so much, we too ought to love one another". The aorist ἠγάπησεν here again implies, once and for all, a finished act of love by God. This echoes the aorist ἀπέστειλεν in 4:10b. The next clause, καὶ ἡμεῖς ὀφείλομεν ἀλλήλους ἀγαπᾶν, returns us to the present. The explicit nominative subject pronoun ἡμεῖς highlights the connection between God's actions and those of the letter's audience.[152] The idea is that God's expiation of sin by sending the Son is the founding act of love, which binds us to love one another. This is connected with the theme of *life* through God's sending the Son into the world in 4:9.

In 4:12a we find θεὸν οὐδεὶς πώποτε τεθέαται, "no-one has ever seen God". The point is that we have not known the Father first-hand: our means of knowledge of God the Father is through the Son. The perfect τεθέαται suggests that no one has ever seen God *so far*, so that *at this time* our only knowledge of God comes through the Son. Realised eschatology is the theme, but this does not exclude direct knowledge of God at some future time. Use of the verb θεάομαι here, rather than the simpler ὁράω (cf. 1:1; 1:2, 1:3), suggests not simple observation but seeing with *insight*. The idea is that no one has ever *understood* God by direct experience.

So in 4:12b we read ἐὰν ἀγαπῶμεν ἀλλήλους, ὁ θεὸς ἐν ἡμῖν μένει καὶ ἡ ἀγάπη αὐτοῦ ἐν ἡμῖν τετελειωμένη ἐστιν, "if we love one another, God abides in us, and his love is made perfect in us". This recalls the idea in 4:7b, καὶ πᾶς ὁ ἀγαπῶν ἐκ τοῦ θεοῦ γεγέννηται καὶ γινώσκει τὸν θεόν, "whoever loves is born from God and knows God". The additional idea in 4:12b is that ἡ ἀγάπη αὐτοῦ ἐν ἡμῖν τετελειωμένη ἐστιν. This implies that it is possible for God's love to be perfectly reflected in our love for one another, not in the sense of producing perfect behaviour, but connoting love's completion in our conduct to one another.[153] Here the passive (or middle) present participle τετελειωμένη[154] implies an external actor, other than ourselves – none other than God himself. So the additional idea here is that God has enabled his love to be made perfect in us by our mutual love. How? By God's own final act of love, spoken of in 4:10b, ἀπέστειλεν τὸν υἱὸν αὐτοῦ ἱλασμὸν περὶ τῶν ἁμαρτιῶν ἡμῶν, "he sent his Son to be the expiation for our sins".[155] Thus the idea of expiation of sin through the gift

---

[151] Gaugler, *Die Johannesbriefe*, 228.
[152] Culy, *I, II, III John: A Handbook on the Greek Text*, 110.
[153] David Rensberger, "Completed Love" in *Communities in Dispute: Current Scholarship on the Johannine Epistles* (ed. R Alan Culpepper and Paul N Anderson; Atlanta: SBL Press, 2014), 237–71, 247.
[154] *Ibid*, 111.
[155] The masculine pronouns are used here only for textual accuracy.

of the Son is inextricably linked with the obligation of mutual love. This is the moral outworking of the divine gift of the Son to give life through him (4:9).

The context in which ἱλασμὸς is used in this subunit therefore suggests strongly that the idea is not propitiation of divine wrath – which is nowhere mentioned – but a cleansing of sin by a loving deity through the sending of the Son, including the self-giving, self-sacrificial death of the Son, releasing humanity to love one another and allow God to make his love perfect in us.

Conclusion

After a reasonably extensive, but necessarily selective overview of scholarship on ἱλασμὸς in 1 John 2:2 and 4:10, we have seen that much the same evidence has been interpreted in different ways, as is so often the case. Our own investigation of the use of ἱλασμὸς and some of its cognates in the LXX in Chapter 2 does not yield a predominantly propitiatory meaning for this term. Its predominant use in the LXX is to connote cleansing, or expiation of sin, by God, not by humanity.

More help comes from the immediate literary context in which ἱλασμὸς occurs in 1 John 2:2 and 4:10 than from the LXX evidence, and we have dealt with that in our exegesis. Context *always* influences the meaning of a word, and words always have context, from which their precise meaning may often be determined. However this does not mean that the LXX evidence provides no guidance. Rather, it provides the Jewish LXX background, of which the author must undoubtedly have been aware, against which the term ἱλασμὸς is used in 1 John. Although this LXX background does not by itself determine the literal meaning of ἱλασμὸς, and still less the theology it expresses, it provides some potent clues as to the author's possible intentions in his use of this word.

We have seen how Judith Lieu argues that where 1 John refers to the undeserved death of God's faithful ones (in the LXX), "the traditional language of sacrifice was being recast without any detailed reflection on why and how their deaths might be efficacious".[156] As noted, this view is persuasive because, as with Perkins and Edwards, Lieu holds that the debate over whether ἱλασμὸς in 1 John 2:2 or 4:10 refers to propitiation or expiation is less important than recognition of the Father's love in sending the Son to be the means of our reconciliation with God by dealing with our sin (4:10).

This leads to the argument espoused by Marianne Meye Thompson that 1 John 2:2 is to be read *in light of* 4:10. Many interpreters have tended to read 4:10 through a propitiatory grid, having arrived at this by noting the use of Ἱλασμός in 2:2, concluding then that its use there is propitiatory after uncovering what they say are LXX examples of such use. Morris and Hill are prime representatives of this viewpoint. However our reading of 2:2 in light of 1:7 and 1:9, as explained above, undoes this reading of ἱλασμὸς in 2:2 and 4:10.

---

[156] Lieu, *I, II, and III John*, 64.

But in fact the use of ἱλασμός in 4:10 sheds light on its use in 2:2. In opening with the statement ἐν τούτῳ ἐστὶν ἡ ἀγάπη, is not John affirming in 4:10 that God's sending the Son as ἱλασμὸν περὶ τῶν ἁμαρτιῶν ἡμῶν is the ultimate act of costly, self-denying love? No wrathful Father is in view in 4:10 – so why should this idea be read into 2:2, when again the idea of reassuring love is introduced by 2:1? Jesus is portrayed in 2:1 as a παράκλητον … πρὸς τὸν πατέρα, followed by the reassurance in 2:2a that καὶ αὐτὸς ἱλασμός ἐστιν περὶ τῶν ἁμαρτιῶν ἡμῶν. This affirms that the loving bond between us and the Father is not broken by sin, because we have a παράκλητος, a "friend at court" (2:1b), in Jesus, God's Son, who cleanses us from all sin (1:7b, 9). The idea of the gift of the Son in 2:1-2 is further expanded and explained by 4:10. There it is explicit that God's gift of Jesus as ἱλασμὸν περὶ τῶν ἁμαρτιῶν ἡμῶν is an act of divine love. First John 4:10b also makes explicit another thought that is implicit in 2:1-2: that God in loving cooperation gives the Son as ἱλασμὸς for our sins. We may surely maintain a degree of "reverent agnosticism" as to precisely *by what mechanism* Jesus in 2:2a is the ἱλασμὸν … περὶ τῶν ἁμαρτιῶν ἡμῶν, while emphasising God's costly love in sending the Son to cleanse God's undeserving people of their sin.

What is notable from the literary contexts in which ἱλασμός is used in 1 John 2:2 and 4:10 is that nowhere in the surrounding verses is there any reference to divine wrath – still less the need to propitiate it. To summarise the foregoing exegesis of 1 John 1:5-10, the author is mainly dealing with human waywardness and recalcitrant sin. There is characteristic Johannine dualism in several opposing statements. God is light and in God there is no darkness (1:5). We lie if we claim fellowship with God yet walk in darkness (1:6). If we walk in the light, we have fellowship, and Jesus' blood cleanses us from sin (1:7). If we say we have no sin, we deceive ourselves, and the truth is not in us (1:8). If we confess our sin, he (God) who is faithful and just will forgive our sins and cleanse us from unrighteousness (1:9). If we say we have not sinned, we make God a liar, and God's word is not in us (1:10).

What is the antidote? In 2:1-2 the author provides it:

> I am writing these things so you may not sin, but if any one [of you] does, we have an advocate with the Father, Jesus Christ the righteous, and he is the expiation to deal with our sin. And not for ours only, but for those of the whole world.

The antidote is provided not by propitiation of divine wrath provoked by human sin, but because God, who the author later explains *is* love, anticipates our sinning and provides the Son as an atoning sacrifice to *cleanse* us from sin, as 1:7 and 9 foreshadow. God is the actor at all points and not the object of a propitiatory sacrifice to turn aside divine wrath. The object is not God, but rather human sin itself. And this gift is available not only for the author's community, his immediate addressees, but for the *whole world*.

In 1 John 4:7-10, we see similar ideas building on one another. The author urges mutual love in his community, because love is from God, and everyone who loves is born of, and thereby knows, God (4:7). And then comes the contrary statement: whoever does not love does not know God, who *is* love (4:8). How was God's love revealed? In this way: God sent God's only Son into the world that we may live through him (4:9). Love does not consist in our love for God, but in God's love for us, in that God sent God's only Son to be the atoning sacrifice for our sins (4:10). Since God loved us so much, we should love one another (4:11). Again, there is no mention of divine wrath over sin in these verses. Rather, God's love in giving the Son as the atoning sacrifice for sin is made the mainspring of the commandment that we should love one another, *as* God has loved us. We must act as God did. Again, God is the actor, the subject of the action at all points, and the object is human sin.

We have seen that Girard writes that "there is nothing in the Gospels to suggest that the death of Jesus is a sacrifice, whatever definition (expiation, substitution etc.) we may give for that sacrifice".[157] Certainly a *propitiatory* sacrifice whereby Jesus offers himself to the Father as the price of sin, which would otherwise be paid by sinful humanity, should not be read into 1 John 2:2 and 4:10, as many have done. But in the sense that the Father gave the Son, who "for our sake … was crucified" as the Nicene Creed says, Jesus' death is a *sacrificial* one, wrought by both the Father and the Son in love, for the cleansing of sin, as seen in 1 John 2:2 and 4:10.

As noted earlier, Weaver is a proponent of a non-violent, "narrative *Christus Victor*" model of the atonement,[158] laying heavy emphasis on Jesus as the "lamb" of the book of Revelation as a non-violent picture of the Saviour.[159] This view is in part consistent with 1 John 2:2 and 4:10, in that the Father emerges not as an angry, punitive Godhead who requires the death of the Son to pay the price of human sin, but as the giver of the Son. The Son cleanses human sin by his saving life and death. This death is self-sacrificial, and the Son does not resist it. Yet it cleanses us of sin. Jesus is the "lamb of God who takes away the sin of the world": John 1:29. He is the "lamb" of Revelation 5:9 who was "slaughtered" and who "ransomed for God" many from every tribe and language and nation. So he is the *victor* over sin. And he enables us also to triumph over the world by faith in him (cf. 1 John 5:4).

Weaver insufficiently emphasises Jesus' cleansing of sin by his blood (cf. 1 John 1:7) as the ἱλασμός for it, preferring to stress his non-resistance to his fate. Indirectly, the *Christus Victor* model of the atonement fits 1 John 5:1-5, in that conquering ὁ κόσμος, symbolising human sin, occurs through obedience to God's commandments, being born of God, and faith in Jesus as ἱλασμός for sin. But a *sacrificial* model, as distinct from a penal substitutionary one, best fits Jesus' role as ἱλασμός for sin through his cleansing of our sins by his blood (1 John 1:7, 9; 2:2), having been sent by the Father as ἱλασμός for our sins, in love for use (4:10).

Lastly, as we have seen, Aulen maintains that the atonement is at all times to be seen as God's work alone.[160] He seeks to recover from mediaeval speculation about God's "justice" being "satisfied" by Christ's atoning death for human sin, the "classic" view of the atonement. The evil powers of the world are vanquished by Jesus, *Christus Victor*, so that in his victory over the "tyrants" under which humankind is suffering,

---

[157] Girard, *Things Hidden*, 180; similarly Girard, *The Scapegoat*, 199–200.
[158] Weaver, *The Nonviolent Atonement*, 19–69.
[159] *Ibid*, 20–46.
[160] Gustav Aulen, *Christus Victor*, 5.

God reconciles the world to God's own self.[161] The background of this idea is dualistic: Jesus' victory is over powers of evil that are hostile to God's will, and this victory brings to pass in a cosmic drama a relation of *reconciliation*,[162] that is between God and humanity. This atonement model indirectly fits 1 John 5:3-5 analysed above, but the object of our faith, which conquers the world, spoken of in 5:4-5, is Jesus as ἱλασμὸς for sin, cleansing it by his blood (1:7, 9; 2:2) and sent by the Father in love (4:10), and the actions of the Father and Son as portrayed there are best characterised as *sacrificial*.

Peacemaking theology on occasions misses the depth of Jesus' role as expiation of sin by his sacrificial, cleansing death in 1 John, but the picture of God it presents, as loving reconciler of humanity to God's own self, is nevertheless broadly consistent and reconcilable with that in 1 John in the passages we have examined.

---

[161] *Ibid*, 4.
[162] *Ibid*, 4–5.

4

Σφάξω and ἀνθρωποκτόνος in 1 John

Introduction

In 1 John 3:11 the author's audience is enjoined to love one another, and in the very next verse they are told not to be like Cain, who murdered his brother. Cain is the very antithesis of love, and murder is the antithesis of love for the writer of 1 John. The verb σφάξω, although it is usually translated here simply as kill, is used also in 3:15. It carries the sense of violent death or slaughter and is used elsewhere in the NT only in Revelation, where it occurs eight times.[1] It is very significant that of all the evil acts the author could have used to depict as the antithesis of love, the ultimate act of interpersonal violence, murder, is the one chosen.

This linkage has been of great interest for peacemaking theology. As but one example, as we have seen, Girard offers 1 John as a "genuine epistemology of love", citing 1 John 2:10-11. He writes that the love of which John speaks here "reveals the victimage processes that underlie the meanings of culture", which is "no purely 'intellectual' process", because "the very detachment of the person who contemplates the warring brothers is an illusion".[2] He says, "Love is the only true revelatory power because it escapes from, and strictly limits, the spirit of revenge and recrimination."[3] To him, 1 John 3:14-15, "all who hate a brother or sister are murderers", shows that "every negation of the other leads … towards expulsion and murder". He says Cain, mentioned in 1 John just before these verses, says in effect "now I have killed my brother, everyone can kill me".[4] Put another way, my act of ultimate violence on my brother unleashes the possibility of the same act on me.

The word ἀνθρωποκτόνος, "murderer", is also used in 3:15, and its being yoked together with σφάξω in 3:12, intensifying its meaning,[5] makes it clear that in the author's eyes, Cain's act is not simply an impulse killing, which might be regarded as manslaughter, but rather a gross violation of all that Abel had the right to expect

---

[1] Brown, *Epistles of John*, 441.
[2] Girard, *Things Hidden*, 277.
[3] *Ibid*.
[4] *Ibid*, 214.
[5] Maarten J Mencken, "The Image of Cain in 1 John 3:12" in *Miracles and Imagery* in Luke and John (ed. J Verheyden, G Van Belle and JG Van Der Watt; Leuven/Paris/Dudley, MA: Uitgeverij Peeters, 2008), 195–211, 200.

from his brother – in particular, love. Clearly, then, a study of these two words in their context in 1 John 3 will do much to illuminate the author's thought on the whole subject of brotherly love.

The author depicts Cain as one whose deeds were πονηρὰ, evil (3:12b), and provides this as the *reason* for Cain's act in murdering his brother. The author's proposition is not that Cain killed his brother, so his acts were evil, but rather vice versa. That linkage, we shall see, is not found in Genesis 4:4-9, where Cain is angry that the Lord has regard for Abel's offering but not his own, and his face falls, so the Lord warns Cain that sin is lurking at the door, desiring him, but that he must master it, but Cain instead kills his brother in the field. Despite the Lord's curse on Cain (4:10-11) there is no indication of any *prior* disposition in Cain to evil acts, nor any direct association between Cain and Satan, or the forces of evil generally.

Why then does 1 John 3:12b affirm that Cain's acts were evil as the *source* of his action in killing his brother? As we shall see, there is a considerable thought-shift between biblical Cain and Abel story and its being taken up in 1 John, marked by the development of the idea of Cain's failure to master sin, which lurks at the door (Genesis 4:7b), to a point where Cain is *himself* representative of the Evil One and a prototype of all that is evil in humanity. This, as we shall see, is to be seen particularly in the writings of Philo of Alexandria and Josephus in the intertestamental period and in intertestamental pseudepigraphical writing itself. Although there is no proof that the author of 1 John read these works, they reflect the Jewish tradition standing behind 1 John.

To demonstrate this thought-shift, and to assess its influence on the reworking of the Cain and Abel story by the author of 1 John, we need first to look at the meaning of the story in its original Hebrew OT setting and in the LXX. Then we shall examine how it is taken up in a representative sample of pseudepigraphical writing in the intertestamental period, including 1 Enoch, Jubilees and the Testament of Abraham,[6] and still later by Philo and Josephus. Then and only then may we attempt an exegesis of the use of σφάξω and ἀνθρωποκτόνος in 1 John. In so doing we must look at 1 John's appropriation of some words and ideas from the LXX in Genesis 4:1-16, from 1 Enoch, Jubilees and the Testament of Abraham, and from Philo and Josephus.

This tracing of thought-shifts in the Cain and Abel story from the Hebrew OT through the LXX, 1 Enoch, Jubilees, and the Testament of Abraham and the accounts by Philo and Josephus to 1 John 3 has been done many times.[7] The contribution this chapter seeks to make is to assess whether 1 John's reworking of the Cain and Abel story has been validly appropriated in recent peacemaking theology. To do so it is necessary to trace the Jewish tradition lying behind the one specific OT reference in 1 John to the

---

[6] A full survey is impossible here for reasons of space.
[7] See for example Brown, *Epistles of John*, 442–3; similarly Painter, *1, 2 and 3 John*, 233; Grayston, *Johannine Epistles*, 110; and most recently and comprehensively in John Byron, *Cain and Abel in Text and Tradition: Jewish and Christian Interpretations of the First Sibling Rivalry* (Leiden/Boston: Brill, 2011). This chapter is much indebted to Byron's work.

Cain and Abel story and thus to lay bare why it is so necessary to the author's argument to make a direct linkage between hatred and violence, murder of the brother.

Cain and Abel in the Hebrew Bible

Significantly, in Genesis 4:1-16 the story of Cain and Abel is placed straight after the account in Genesis 3 of Adam and Eve's primal act of disobedience by eating of the fruit of the tree in the garden, leading to their expulsion from the Garden. Once again a human, Cain, is presented by the Lord with a choice, to master sin, which is "lurking at the door" (Genesis 4:7),[8] and chooses wrongly. It is seen by many as an expanded genealogy of Adam.[9] Therefore in the past the Cain and Abel story has been seen as purely collective or *aetiological*, relating figuratively the estrangement of Cain's descendants, living on inferior land compared to those of Seth. Gunkel saw Cain as "the progenitor of a people", arguing that the statement that Cain's murder will be avenged sevenfold only makes sense if seen as a "poetic statement that every son of Cain will be avenged": it is part of a legend which "understands peoples as individual persons".[10] More commentators follow Westermann in seeing this story as the account of two prototypical individuals, Cain and Abel; Westermann quotes with approval Cassuto's interpretation of the story that "Cain, who killed his brother, is the prototype of the murderer" and that "all human beings are brothers and whoever sheds human blood sheds the blood of his brother".[11]

Genesis 4:4-5 in the Hebrew provides no reason for the Lord's preference for Abel's offering over Cain's. Although many have speculated that this divine preference was because Abel's sacrifice was of firstlings, first-born animals, whereas Cain's was of the fruit of the ground (4:3),[12] the stronger opinion is that the Lord's choice of Abel's offering over Cain's is but a *manifestation* of divine favour towards Abel rather than Cain.[13] Any different interpretation relies on implication from the text of something that is not there: a reason, satisfying the modern mind's expectation of a just and rational God, why such a deity might favour one brother than the other. In Genesis 4:4, the priestly Pentateuchal source has in general nothing to say about why God "takes knowledge" of sacrifices; God simply "has regard" for them – as Genesis 4:4

---

[8] NRSV translation. This version is unusually close to the original Hebrew and is used throughout this chapter in lieu of the author's own translation unless the contrary is indicated.
[9] Claus Westermann, *Genesis 1–11: A Commentary* (trans. John J Scullion SJ; London: SPCK, 1984), 284; Gordon Wenham, *Genesis 1–15* (Waco, Texas: Word Books, 1987), 97. Cf. Martin Kessler and Karel Deurloo, *A Commentary on Genesis* (Manwah, NJ: Paulist Press, 2004), 58.
[10] Hermann Gunkel, *Genesis* (trans. Mark E Biddle; Macon, Georgia: Mercer University Press, 1997), 47.
[11] Westermann, *Genesis 1–11*, 284. This is very close to Girard's view. Cf. Wenham, *Genesis 1–15*, 100; Kessler & Deurloo, *Genesis*, 58–60.
[12] Cf. Robert Alter, *Genesis* (New York/London: W. W. Norton, 1998), 16; Wenham, *Genesis 1–15*, 103.
[13] Westermann, *Genesis 1–11*, 296. So also Victor P Hamilton, *The Book of Genesis: Chapters 1–17* (Grand Rapids: Eerdmans, 1990), 224; Derek Kidner, *Genesis*, 75; *sed contra* Wenham, *Genesis 1–15*, 104.

puts it, "and he had favour" (וַיִּשַׁע, literally "and he looked upon") for them.[14] Perhaps the most that can be said here is that "acceptance and non-acceptance is directed at both givers and gifts".[15]

A history of interpretation of Genesis 4:4 may be traced, which notes that the Hebrew of 4:4, in describing Abel's sacrifice, uses two words not used to describe Cain's offering, מִבְּכֹרוֹת, "firstlings" (lit. "from the first born of") and וּמֵחֶלְבֵהֶן, "fat portions" (lit. "from fat of them"), but that מִנְחָתוֹ, "his offering", in 4:4 occurs again for the gifts Jacob offered Esau (Genesis 32:14, 19, 21-22; 33:10) and for those which Jacob's sons took to Egypt (Genesis 43:11, 15, 25-26). This term does not occur again in a worship setting, suggesting that it may simply mean "tribute" (cf. 1 Kings 4:21; 10:25).[16] This is to be contrasted with the LXX, in which the ritual fault with Cain's offering *is* stated, suggesting that Cain's and Abel's offerings were specifically cultic actions. We shall return to this later.

A narrative approach may be used to posit connections between Genesis 2-3 and 4:1-14, seeing resemblances between Genesis 4:7b and 3:16b, and 4:11a and 3:17b. In both stories the relationship between humans and the earth is important, and words in the opening verses of 4:1-16 such as עָבַר "work, serve", אִישׁ, "man", and אִשָּׁה "woman", refer back to 2-3.[17]

Verbal and narrative connections between Genesis 2–3 and 4:1-16 may also be found, suggesting that the verbs עָבַר and שָׁמַר in various forms, used in Genesis 4 in association, hark back to the use of these same terms in Genesis 2–3, as they occur together in the Garden of Eden story: they describe the purpose of human life, and the reappearance of שָׁמַר in 4:9, "am I my brother's keeper", suggests a triangular relationship between human beings, the earth and God.[18] In the Garden story in 2:5, "there was no-one to work the ground". That עָבַר may also mean "serve" suggests a human obligation not to do anything that does not benefit the land.[19] In 2:15 God tells the אִישׁ, "man", to עָבַר, "work", and שָׁמַר, "keep", the land, suggesting that the human obligation is to work and guard the Garden reverently.[20]

In 3:23 the Lord God sends the man forth from the Garden to עָבַר, "work", the ground: as the man is no longer in paradise, his obligation is to work in *service* of the land, a more mundane obligation than that which he had in the Garden.[21] Significantly, in 4:2 Cain עָבַר, "works", the soil, but Abel's occupation, *outside* of Eden, is not to שָׁמַר, "keep", sheep, but to רָעָה, "shepherd", them, and therefore Cain's question whether he must שָׁמַר, "keep", his brother may be genuine, in that he must already עָבַר, "work" or

---

[14] Gerhard von Rad, *Old Testament Theology Vol 1* (trans. DMG Stalker; London/Leiden/Louisville: Westminster John Knox Press, 2001), 260–1.
[15] Kenneth M Craig Jr., "Questions Outside Eden (Genesis 4:1-16): Yahweh, Cain and Their Rhetorical Interchange," *JSOT* 86 (1999): 107–28, 112.
[16] Jack P Lewis, "The Offering of Abel (Gen 4:4): A History of Interpretation," *JETS* 37:4: 481–96, 481–2; similarly Westermann, *Genesis 1–11*, 294.
[17] Ellen van Wolde, "The Story of Cain and Abel: A Narrative Study," *JSOT* 52 (1991): 25–41, 25.
[18] Kristin M Swenson, "Care and Keeping East of Eden: Gen 4:1-16 in light of Gen 2-3," *Int* 60:4, 373–84, 373–4.
[19] *Ibid*, 375.
[20] *Ibid*, 376.
[21] *Ibid*, 377.

"serve", the land.[22] There are three clues in Genesis 4:2-3 that Cain's obligation *is* to care for his brother and that this is associated with his obligation to work or serve the land: first, Cain's identification as a "man", אִישׁ; second, Eve's bearing of "his brother, Abel", noting that Abel's name, הֶבֶל, which may also mean "mist" or "vapour" or "something transient" (cf. Ecclesiastes 1:2), hints at Cain's responsibility for his (younger) brother; and third, that Cain must care for the soil.[23] Care for one's brother is an idea we shall meet later in 1 John.

The verb שָׁמַר is also used in Genesis 3:24 to refer to the sword guarding the way to the tree of life, which may have some ritual or reverential significance: either the "tree of life" may either refer to the golden candlestick in the Temple, and the flaming sword to the presence of God,[24] or the tree may represent God's garden, with cherubim preventing human access.[25] But the association of הֶבֶל as Abel's name with its very different use in Ecclesiastes 1:2 may be tenuous: Abel is more likely הֶבֶל, "insubstantial", *because* he is murdered.[26] Overall, the Cain and Abel story is a useful model of human obligation as a combination of respect for the land given by God and refraining from harm to one's brother or sister. This is echoed in 1 John 3:12.

It has been proposed by Reis that in Genesis 4:8 Cain's words (inserted by the LXX but not in the Hebrew text[27]), "let us go out to the field", connote Cain speaking *against* his brother, in symmetry with 4:9, "Cain rose up against his brother", on the ground that אָמַר is to be translated as "spoke", not "said", with the result that Cain's motivation travels inevitably from hatred to murder.[28] Jacobson goes so far as to posit that אָמַר here may have an extended use so as to mean "plot", suggesting that this is a permissible extension of the meaning "propose" or "purpose" or "plan" for this word.[29] This would have the result that Cain planned Abel's murder beforehand. Both interpretations are tenuous on exegetical grounds, however, and may press the meaning of אָמַר beyond acceptable limits. As Craig observes, the problem in Genesis 4:8 indeed turns on אָמַר, "said" or "spoke", and his solution is that אָמַר does not have an object: Cain simply "spoke" to Abel, and what he said or intended is not conveyed (as opposed to the LXX version).[30] If so, the Hebrew text is not to be seen as casting Cain as evil *before* his murder of Abel: the *act* is what is evil.

In Genesis 4:9 Cain's answer to the Lord's question, אֵי הֶבֶל אָחִיךָ, "Where is your brother Abel?", is a lie: לֹא יָדַעְתִּי, "I do not know". Some have seen Genesis 4:9-16 as a judicial process, ending in Cain being cursed by God and accepting his punishment, the proceedings beginning at 4:9 where Cain is tried and invited to give his version, which is false.[31] Or Cain's reply may be seen as a repudiation of the OT obligations on

---

[22] *Ibid*, 377–8.
[23] *Ibid*, 378.
[24] Wenham, *Genesis 1–15*, 86.
[25] Westermann, *Genesis 1–11*, 274.
[26] *Ibid*, 292.
[27] Craig, "Questions Outside Eden," 117.
[28] Pamela Tamarkin Reis, "What Cain Said: A Note on Genesis 4:8," *JSOT* 27:1 (2002): 107–13.
[29] Howard Jacobson, "Genesis IV.8," *VT* 55:4 (2005): 564–5.
[30] Craig, "Questions Outside Eden," 119.
[31] The scholars of this view are summarised in Westermann, *Genesis 1–11*, 303–4.

a man's brother to be the first to help him in time of trouble (Leviticus 25:48) and to avenge his blood when he is murdered (Numbers 36:12-28).[32] One way or the other, in the Torah, Cain is simply a foolish man trying to evade responsibility for his evil act by trying to lie his way out of trouble.

The Lord's curse on Cain (Genesis 4:10-11), whose brother's blood is "crying out to me from the ground" (4:10) is the climax of the story.[33] There are "verbal echoes" of God cursing the ground upon which Adam stood (Genesis 3:17).[34] Cain, having polluted the ground by bloodshedding, is driven from it (4:14).[35] As Westermann cogently argues, in 4:10 "the most important word in the sentence is אֵלַי, 'to me'",[36] because there is no such thing as the perfect murder – God will always know of it, so God protects us from complete elimination. God intervenes without a mediator when the blood of the murdered one cries from the ground and "confronts the doer".[37]

Generally the Torah, as we have seen, does not concentrate on Cain's nature in explaining his murder of his brother. Instead, God's favour for Abel's sacrifice sets up a murderous triad, in which Cain, despairing of God's favour, enviously murders the brother who stands in the way of his attaining it. Having done this, instead of achieving God's favour, Cain is cursed by God and expelled from his home to the land of Nod. This is a relatively simple tale which makes no attempt to cast Cain as a representative of cosmic evil, in opposition to God himself, a portrait which emerges in later accounts of the story.

Cain and Abel in the Septuagint

The LXX does not use the more intensive σφάξω, used in 1 John 3:12, to represent Cain's killing of Abel at 4:8.[38] Genesis 4:8 in the LXX uses the simple word ὑπέκτάεινεν, which simply means "kill", to translate the Hebrew וַיַּהַרְגֵהוּ, "and he killed him", which has the same meaning. In the LXX, σφάξω occurs only a few times to translate cognates of the Hebrew root הָרַג, and where it does (Zechariah 11:4, 5, 7; Jeremiah 12:3; 15:3; 19:6), heavy violence (and in Isaiah 22:13 in the LXX, sacrificial slaughter) is the concept conveyed.[39] As we shall see, the word πονηρός (and in one case σφάξω) occurs in later writers' accounts of the incident and represents a thought-shift as to who Cain was and why he did what he did.

However, the LXX does use different words for the Hebrew מִנְחָה, "gift", "offering", used in both Genesis 4:4 and 4:5 for both Cain's and Abel's offerings: Cain's offerings

---

[32] Wenham, *Genesis 1-15*, 107.
[33] Westermann, *Genesis 1-11*, 305; Wenham, *Genesis 1-15*, 107.
[34] Alter, *Genesis*, 18.
[35] Kessler and Deurloo, *Genesis*, 64.
[36] Westermann, *Genesis 1-11*, 305.
[37] Ibid.
[38] Noted in Grayston, *The Johannine Epistles*, 110.
[39] Menken, "The Image of Cain in 1 John 3:12," 200; see also John Byron, "Slaughter, Fratricide and Sacrilege: Cain and Abel Traditions in 1 John 3," *Bib* 88:4 (2007), 526–35, 532.

are a θυσία, "sacrifice", but Abel's are δώροις, "gifts".[40] But it is safer to regard this LXX usage as simply further differentiating Abel's offering from Cain's.[41] Perhaps this difference in the LXX enhances Abel's status as an unambiguous giver compared to the ungenerous Cain.

Also, in the Hebrew text of Genesis 4:4-5 God is said to gaze or not to gaze, שָׁעָה on Cain and Abel and their gifts, but the LXX in 4:4 says God "looked upon", ἐπεῖδεν, Abel and his gifts, but in 4:5 that God "did not pay attention to", οὐ προσέσχεν, Cain and his sacrifice.[42] As שָׁעָה is not translated elsewhere in the LXX as προσέρχομαι, possibly the translators wished to mark a divine rejection of Cain himself.[43] This LXX usage suggests that ἐπεῖδεν conveys the idea of God's providence and care, so that in some sense God appeared to Abel but not to Cain.[44] This may indicate that by implication – though not specifically, as we have seen – the LXX portrays Cain *himself* as evil in God's eyes – not just his act.

Furthermore, the LXX does not translate the difficult Hebrew of Genesis 4:7a, "If you do well, will you not be accepted? And if you do not do well, sin is crouching at the door; its desire is you, but you must master it." Instead, in the LXX text in 4:7a the Lord asks Cain, οὐκ ἐὰν ὀρθῶς προσενέγκῃς, ὀρθῶς δὲ μὴ διέλῃς ἥμαρτες, "Have you not sinned if you have brought it properly, but have not properly cut it up?"[45] This question is not present in the Hebrew text, and it appears to represent an attempt by the LXX translators to rationalise the Lord's preference for Abel's sacrifice over Cain's in terms of an error in ritual sacrifice.[46] This addition in the LXX text, as compared to the original Hebrew, does not clear up *why* Cain did not "divide" his offering properly: it is more likely an attempt to explain God's preference for Abel's offering, rather than a scribal error.[47] This LXX alteration portrays Cain as an impious person, if not a downright evil man.

Also, in 4:7b in the LXX the Lord addresses Cain, ἡσύχασον· πρός σέ ἡ ἀποστροφή αὐτοῦ, καὶ σὺ ἄρξεις αὐτοῦ, "be still, and his obeisance will be to you, and you will rule over him". Therefore, the suggestion in the Hebrew Bible that Cain will rule over *sin* if he "does well" is replaced by one that Abel will then submit to him, and *he* will then rule over Abel.[48] But does this leave the text ambiguous? Is Cain told that sin will haunt him until he conquers it, or is Cain promised supremacy over his younger brother if he conquers sin?[49] The preferable conclusion is that this difference seeks to clear up the ambiguity in the Hebrew Bible, in that Cain's birthright can only be secured if he "does well", but instead, being evil, he forswears it by murdering Abel.

---

[40] Joel N Lohr, "Righteous Abel, Wicked Cain: Genesis 4:10-16 in the Masoretic Text, the Septuagint and the New Testament," *CBQ* 71:3 (2009), 485-96, 486-7.
[41] Byron, *Cain and Abel in Text and Tradition*, 41-2.
[42] Lohr, "Righteous Abel, Wicked Cain," 487.
[43] *Ibid*, 488.
[44] Byron, *Cain and Abel in Text and Tradition*, 51.
[45] Lohr, "Righteous Abel, Wicked Cain," 489.
[46] *Ibid*.
[47] Byron, *Cain and Abel in Text and Tradition*, 49.
[48] Lohr, "Righteous Abel, Wicked Cain," 489-90.
[49] Byron, *Cain and Abel in Text and Tradition*, 54-5.

The LXX version of the Cain and Abel story tends to support Westermann's conjecture that God's address to Cain in Genesis 4:6-7 in the Hebrew Bible is an addition, to ascribe full responsibility to Cain for what he did, by not heeding the Lord's warning[50] – a question outside the scope of this study. But the LXX version of 4:7 may also represent a thought-shift from the Hebrew, in that Cain's act is portrayed, not as a deliberate decision on his part to sin, but as an act predicated by his failure to offer to the Lord an appropriate sacrifice, and to "be still", that is stay his hand, and let the Lord place him over Abel by divine providence. So Cain is perhaps to be seen in the LXX as an archetypal opponent of divine will, which intensifies the evil nature of his action, as compared to the original Hebrew version of Genesis 4:7.

What is notable is that even in the LXX, Genesis 4 does not represent Cain as πουηρός, "evil", as 1 John 3:12 does. However, in the Greek of Wisdom 10:3 in the OT Apocrypha we find another intensification of Cain's evil, where it said that an unrighteous man (Cain) committed the grievous crime of fratricide: he slaughtered, ἀδελφοκτόνοις, his brother in a fit of anger.[51] We shall meet this term again in the writings of Philo and Josephus.

Generally in the LXX Cain is portrayed in somewhat more negative terms than in the Hebrew Bible. By implication, though not explicitly, he is painted as evil by nature. This represents a thought-shift from the Hebrew Bible, where it is Cain's murderous *act* that is evil and attracts God's curse, not Cain himself. In the LXX this thought-shift is incomplete, as we have seen: Cain is not frankly portrayed as evil by nature, although much of the wording in the story points that way.

Cain and Abel in Some Intertestamental Literature

(i) 1 Enoch

The Jewish apocalyptic traditions collected in the Book of Enoch, or 1 Enoch, were largely composed in Aramaic, probably in Palestine, between the fourth century BCE and the turn of the Common Era, but the collection as a whole survives only in a sixth century CE Ethiopic (Ge'ez) text, itself translated from an intermediate Greek translation, although Aramaic fragments exist.[52] The oldest portion, chapters 12–36, from which we shall examine chapter 22, is probably pre-Maccabean in origin, and the Dream Visions in chapters 83–90, from which we shall examine chapter 85, were probably written during Judas Maccabeus' war in 165–161 BCE.[53] Hellenistic influences are often apparent. Unsurprisingly, doubts have been expressed about the reliability of the Ethiopic version as an entirely faithful representation of the content of

---

[50] Westermann, *Genesis 1-11*, 299–300.
[51] Byron, "Slaughter, Fratricide and Sacrilege," 528.
[52] George WE Nickelsburg, *A Commentary on the Book of Enoch, Chapters 1–36; 81–108* (Minneapolis: Fortress Press, 2001), 1; see also *The Book of Enoch*, trans. RH Charles, ix–x. Milik suggests the fifth *or* sixth centuries CE as the date of translation: *The Books of Enoch: Aramaic Fragments of Qumran Cave 4* (ed. JT Milik; Oxford: Clarendon Press, 1976), 88.
[53] *Ibid*, xi.

the original Aramaic text.⁵⁴ This matters. If the author of 1 John had access to 1 Enoch, it would very likely have been to the Greek text. Any conclusions about the influence of 1 Enoch on 1 John must be qualified by this caveat.

At 1 Enoch 22:7, in answer to the writer, the Angel Raphael "answered me, saying, 'this is the spirit which has left Abel, whom Cain, his brother, had killed; it (continues to) pursue him until all of (Cain's) seed is exterminated from the face of the earth, and his seed has disintegrated from among the seed of the people'".⁵⁵ In this exegetical elaboration of Genesis 4:10, Abel's blood, inanimate but personified in Genesis, is the seat of נֶפֶשׁ, "life" or "soul" (Genesis 9:4), which the author identifies as רוּחַ, "spirit", which was an active being, familiar in the Hellenistic world view: here the narrative of Genesis is interpolated with the motif of the dead pleading for vengeance.⁵⁶ Here "eschatology has been built into the universe; rewards and punishments are already in place".⁵⁷ This kind of thinking is not to be found in Genesis 4, either in the Hebrew text or in the LXX.

Furthermore, in 1 Enoch 85:4, we have the visionary symbolism of a black bull, its colour symbolising murder or sin and representing Cain, goring a red one, its colour symbolic of its blood and representing Abel, and pursuing it over the earth.⁵⁸ Omitted from 1 Enoch is any account of the Fall, and in its place we find this episode as the first account of human sin, thus portraying Cain as the first perpetrator of violence.⁵⁹ In this "animal Apocalypse", the omission of the Fall shows that thinkers in the Enoch tradition placed little emphasis on Genesis 3 as explaining the origin of sin: in 1 Enoch the *first* sin is Cain's murder of Abel.⁶⁰

Thus in 1 Enoch the OT picture of Cain in Genesis 4 as an envious killer of his brother intersects with the Hellenistic notion of Abel's immortal spirit or soul pursuing Cain, the original evil-doer, over the earth. Again we see a thought-shift, in which Cain in 1 Enoch is not simply an envious murderer of his own brother, as in Genesis 4, but *the* original evil-doer who will never be free from his brother's spirit, crying for vengeance. Similarly in 1 John 3:12 Cain is the archetypal murderer of his brother, who is "from the evil one".

(ii) Jubilees

The intertestamental, pseudepigraphic Book of Jubilees, probably written in the second century BCE, is sometimes called the "little Genesis".⁶¹ It reflects an expectation of

---

⁵⁴ See for example Knibb, "Interpreting the Book of Enoch," 440–1.
⁵⁵ See Charlesworth's translation: *The Old Testament Pseudepigrapha: Volume 1* (ed. James H Charlesworth; London: Darton, Longman and Todd, 1983), 25. Olsen in a new translation has "killed by his brother Cain" instead of "whom his brother slew," but the sense is the same: Daniel Olson, *Enoch: A New Translation* (North Richland Hills, Texas: Biblical Press, 2004), 59.
⁵⁶ Nickelsburg, *Enoch*, 22.
⁵⁷ James C VanderKam, *Enoch: A Man for all Generations* (Columbia, South Carolina: University of South Carolina Press, 1995), 55.
⁵⁸ *Ibid*, 370–1; Charles (ed.), *The Book of Enoch*, 186.
⁵⁹ Nickelsburg, *Enoch*, 371.
⁶⁰ VanderKam, *Enoch*, 74.
⁶¹ James C VanderKam, *The Book of Jubilees* (London: Sheffield Academic Press, 2001), 11; *The Book of Jubilees or the Little Genesis*, trans. RH Charles, vii.

speedy inauguration of the messianic age but is not a typical apocalypse. It is largely narrative, based on historical narratives in Genesis and Exodus.[62] It was probably composed in Hebrew, known under various titles in Greek, and like 1 Enoch survives only in an Ethiopic text.[63]

Jubilees' most prominent characteristics are the chronological frame within which most events in the patriarchal period are dated, and legal passages added to the rewritten narratives in the book.[64] The scholarly consensus has been that it is a unified work by a single author,[65] though this has been questioned.[66]

The author of Jubilees, like those who wrote the Book of Enoch, is concerned to identify the origin of evil, so as to set out activities and ideas that depart from its order.[67] Jubilees does not pretend to be an entirely new revelation: it has been rightly said that compositions such as Jubilees and the Temple Scroll "seek to provide the interpretative context within which scriptural traditions already acknowledged as authoritative can be properly understood" and that their interpretations "acquire authority through their intermingling with the well-known words of traditions whose authority is already acknowledged".[68] Put another way, Jubilees is "a midrashic insertion of *haggadic* traditions into the biblical narrative in order to anticipate questions, and to solve problems in advance".[69] We shall shortly see some examples.

Initially in Jubilees 4:2-5 Cain and Abel are introduced conventionally, in parallel with the account in Genesis 4, except that it is the angels who do not accept Cain's offering.[70] But in 4:5 we find a citation of Deuteronomy 27:24, "and therefore it is written on the heavenly tablets, 'cursed is the one who strikes his fellow with malice. And all who have seen and heard shall say, "so be it"; and the man who saw it and did not report (it) shall be cursed like him'".[71] The bare account of Cain and Abel in Genesis 4 is taken further in Jubilees 4:5: Cain's sin is made to stand for a supreme act of sin, so heinous that whoever witnesses it but does not disclose it is as guilty as the perpetrator himself. This is an *addition* to Deuteronomy 27:24: the additional point made in Jubilees is that not only is the offender cursed but also the witness who does not disclose the offence.[72] This addition may derive from Leviticus 5:1.[73]

---

[62] *Ibid*, vii-viii.
[63] *Ibid*, ix-x; James C VanderKam, *Textual and Historical Studies in the Book of Jubilees* (Missoula, Montana: Scholars Press, 1977), 1–18.
[64] VanderKam, *The Book of Jubilees*, 12; Michael Segal, "The Composition of Jubilees," 22–35, 24.
[65] *Ibid*, 22.
[66] *Ibid*, 25–9.
[67] Loren T Stuckenbrook, "The Book of Jubilees and the Origin of Evil" in *Enoch and the Mosaic Torah: The Evidence of Jubilees* (ed. Gabrielle Boccaccini and Giovanni Ibba; Grand Rapids/Cambridge, UK: Eerdmans 2009), 294–308, 294.
[68] H Najman, *Seconding Sinai: The Development of Mosaic Discourse in Second Temple Judaism* (JSJ Sup 77; Leiden: Brill, 2003) 46, cited in James C VanderKam, "The Scriptural Setting of the Book of Jubilees," *DSD* 13:1 (2006), 61–72, 61 n.1.
[69] JTAGM van Ruiten, *Primaeval History Interpreted: The Rewriting of Genesis I–II in the Book of Jubilees* (Leiden/Boston/Köln: Brill, 2000), 3 (following Vermes).
[70] VanderKam, *The Book of Jubilees*, 32.
[71] Charlesworth's translation: Charlesworth (ed.), *The Old Testament Pseudepigrapha: Volume 2*, 61.
[72] Van Ruiten, *Primaeval History Interpreted*, 148.
[73] Florentino García Martínez, "The Heavenly Tablets in the Book of Jubilees" in *Studies in the Book of Jubilees* (ed. Matthias Albani, Jorg Frey and Armin Lange: Tübingen: Mohr Siebeck, 1997), 243–0, 245–6.

The doctrine of retributive justice, the *jus talionis*, has been identified in Jubilees: it has been inferred from Jubilees 4:31 that this principle itself springs from the punishment of Cain and is "inscribed on the heavenly tablets".[74] This is cogent: in Jubilees 4:31 we find Cain killed by the stones of his house, which fell on him, because he killed Abel with a stone, and he therefore was killed "in righteous judgment". This suggests the *jus talionis*, even if not executed by Abel. In Jubilees 4:5-6 the author constructs a *halakha* on the *jus talionis* to explain, as Genesis does not, how Cain was killed in retribution for the way he murdered Abel.[75]

In Jubilees 4:7, we find "and for this reason we announce when we have come before the Lord our God all the sin which is committed in heaven and upon earth, and in light and in darkness, and everywhere". The association of sin committed "on earth" with "darkness" here, along with the injunction to "announce", that is acknowledge, sin before God, finds an echo, not necessarily intended of course, in 1 John 1:5-7 with its dualism of light and darkness alongside sin and confession.

Even more significantly, in 4:15, a fragment of Jubilees which survives in Greek, Cain is described as an ἀδελφοκτόνος, the very description we find later in Philo and Josephus.[76] This makes it clear that in the author's eyes, the treacherous attack on the neighbour is even graver because the neighbour is the murderer's brother.

In a Greek fragment, Jubilees preserves the LXX distinction already noted between Cain's and Abel's gifts, describing Cain's as θυσία, "sacrifices", but Abel's as δώροις, "gifts".[77] This suggests that some of the fault is in the giver, not just the gift: again it is Cain's character that is implicitly condemned, not just his offering.

Thus the Cain and Abel story in Jubilees, while mainly following Genesis 4, is presented with some additional elements conveying the ideas of the supreme sin of fratricide, so grave that it must be disclosed by anyone who witnesses it – lest they be equally guilty of it. It presents the elements of light and darkness, in dualistic association with sin and repentance, confession before God. It may have been read and drawn on by the author of 1 John. It is another example of a thought-shift between Genesis 4, in which Cain is presented simply as a cursed sinner who is exiled for murdering his brother, and later literature where there is greater emphasis on the uniquely grave nature of Cain's sin, which springs from rebellion against God and which is committed in a state of darkness, or separation from God. These ideas we find in full flower in 1 John.

(iii) The Testament of Abraham

The Testament of Abraham is dated by Allison as likely composed somewhere near the turn of the Common Era, based on Jewish books adopted by Christians no later

---

[74] John C Endres SJ, *Biblical Interpretation in the Book of Jubilees* (Catholic Biblical Quarterly Monograph Series 18: Washington, DC: Catholic Biblical Association of America, 1987), 231 n.13, citing Harold W Attridge, *Interpretation of Biblical History in the 'Antiquitates Judaici' of Flavius Josephus* (Harvard Dissertations in Religion 7; Missoula: Scholars, 1976), 147 n.1.
[75] Van Ruiten, *Primaeval History Interpreted*, 172.
[76] Byron, "Slaughter, Fratricide and Sacrilege," 528.
[77] Byron, *Cain and Abel in Text and Tradition*, 43.

than the second century CE, with "a strong syntactical and lexical resemblance to the language of the Septuagint and the New Testament".[78] He considers it most likely to be a Jewish work rather than a later Christian composition.[79] Sanders, on the other hand, noting scholarly disagreement even over whether the original text is in Hebrew or Greek,[80] favours a date of c. 100 CE, plus or minus twenty years, on the basis that "it is doubtful if Egyptian, especially Alexandrian Judaism was sufficiently intact after AD 117 to allow the production of such literature, especially a work like the Testament of Abraham, which does not distinguish Jew from Gentile in the judgment."[81] It must be considered as at least doubtful whether it was available to, and potentially read by, the author of 1 John. At best, it is evidence of some ideas within first-century Judaism which *may* have influenced him.

In the Testament of Abraham in its Long Recension in Greek (thought by Allison to be prior to its shorter Recension, also in Greek[82]) at 13.1, Abraham asks the "Commander-in-Chief", a descriptor of God, the identity of a "most marvelous judge", and in 13.2-3 the answer is "the son of the first-formed, the one called Abel, whom the most evil and fratricidal Cain killed", who "sits here to judge all the creation".[83] As we shall see, "the most evil", πονηρότατος, is an adjective applied by Josephus to Cain.[84] We shall come to that later. Allison speculates that Abel's role as judge developed from his status as the first innocent to be murdered.[85]

The most that can be gathered from this single reference is that, consistently with the development of Cain's role in 1 Enoch and Jubilees, his evil nature is made to have eschatological significance. His primeval action in perpetrating the first murder constitutes his victim, his brother Abel, as judge of the world's evil. Symbolically, Cain stands as emblematic of evil incarnate.

Cain and Abel in Philo

Philo of Alexandria – whose exact dates of birth and death we do not know, although it is known that he was born in about 30 BCE – is best described as a philosopher

---

[78] Dale C Allison Jr., *Testament of Abraham* (Berlin & New York: Walter de Gruyter, 2003), 39.
[79] *Ibid*, 28–31. Bauckham notes that a large range of works, including the Testament of Abraham, whose dates and provenance are still doubtful, have in the last few decades been treated by many as of non-Christian, Jewish authorship and sufficiently early to be of relevance to NT research: Richard Bauckham, "The Continuing Quest for the Provenance of Old Testament Pseudepigrapha" in *The Pseudepigrapha and Christian Origins* (ed. Gerbern S Oegema and James H Charlesworth; New York/London: T&T Clark, 2008), 9–29, 9.
[80] EP Sanders. "Testament of Abraham" (translation and commentary) in *The Old Testament Pseudepigrapha* Vol 1, *Apocalyptic Literature and Testaments* (ed. James H Charlesworth, Garden City, New York: Doubleday, 1983), 873–4.
[81] *Ibid*, 875, 874.
[82] Allison, *Testament of Abraham*, 12–15; *sed contra* Sanders, "Testament of Abraham," 871–3.
[83] *Ibid*, 274; see also "The Testament of Abraham," trans. N Turner, in *The Apocryphal Old Testament* (ed. HFD Sparks; Oxford: Clarendon Press, 1989), 393–422, 412.
[84] Allison, *Testament of Abraham*, 280.
[85] *Ibid*, 281.

and theologian, his aim being to justify Judaism as a universal religion, capable of attracting those of all races and lands to it, without, however, abandoning or modifying its fundamental beliefs and practices.[86] At the time of Flaccus, the Roman prefect in Alexandria, Philo led a delegation to Rome, aimed at convincing Caligula that Jewish opposition to worship of images did not indicate hostility to Roman rule itself.[87] Viewed in this historical context, his work may be seen as an attempt to justify Judaism, its faith and institutions, to protect which it seems Philo would have accepted martyrdom, if necessary.[88]

Philo devotes four sections in total, which provide a "running commentary"[89] on the Pentateuch, to the Cain and Abel story, reworking and expanding it to incorporate his own ideas on good and evil in the world. They are *On the Cherubim* ("The Cherubim"), *On the Birth of Abel and the Sacrifices Offered by Him and by His Brother Cain* ("The Sacrifice of Abel and Cain"), *That the Worse Is Wont to Attack the Better* ("The Worse Attacks the Better") and *On the Posterity of Cain and His Exile* ("The Posterity and Exile of Cain").[90]

There are strong parallels between the descriptions of Cain in 1 John 3:12 and in Philo's writings. Byron notes that the bracketing of Cain and anyone else who hates their brother as ἀνθρωποκτόνος in 1 John 3:15 is "not without precedence", exampling, inter alia, Cain's labelling as an ἀδελφοκτόνος no less than ten times, including once each in *The Worse Attacks the Better* (96), *The Posterity and Exile of Cain* (49) and *The Cherubim* (52).[91] Some examination of these and other instances of Philo's view of Cain and their contexts is needed.

In *The Cherubim* Philo indeed refers to Cain as τόν ἀδελφοκτόνον[92] and then as ἐπάρατον, "accursed" (52), but then in the next section he notes that when Cain was born (Genesis 4:1) his male sex is not noted, just his name (53). Philo explains how Cain was from birth associated with the thought that all things were his own possessions (64) and "unreasoning pride" ((54)-(65)). The idea therefore is that Cain was accursed from birth and indeed representative of evil from the beginning.

In *The Sacrifices of Abel and Cain* we find Cain, τὸν φιλαύτος, the "self lover", blamed for making his thank-offering μεθ' ἡμέερας, "after some days". This is contrasted at (53)

---

[86] Kenneth Schenck, *A Brief Guide to Philo* (Louisville: Westminster John Knox Press, 2005) 5–6; Ronald Williamson, *Jews in the Hellenistic World 1ii: Philo* (Cambridge: Cambridge University Press, 1989), 1–3.
[87] Ibid, 7; David T Runia, *Exegesis and Philosophy: Studies on Philo of Alexandria* (Aldershot, Hampshire: Variorum, 1990), 3.
[88] Williamson, *Jews in the Hellenistic World 1ii: Philo*, 17.
[89] This characterisation is Borgen's: Peder Borgen, *Philo of Alexandria, An Exegete for His Time* (Leiden, New York, Cologne: Brill, 1997), 103.
[90] See generally Painter, *1, 2 and 3 John*, 233.
[91] Byron, "Slaughter, Fratricide and Sacrilege," 520. Byron's bracketed references are to the marginal numerals in the Loeb Classical Library translation, *Philo*, Vol II (trans. Revs. FH Colson & GH Whittaker; Cambridge, MA: Heinemann, 1958). The same system will be used in the following discussion of Philo's work with the bracketed references occurring in the text, rather than in footnotes.
[92] Indeed in Byron, "Slaughter, Fratricide and Sacrilege," 528, it is noted that Philo refers to Cain as ἀδελφοκτόνος no less than ten times.

with Deuteronomy 23:21, "if you make a vow, do not be slow to fulfil it", such slowness being a vice which at (54)-(58) Philo associates with forgetfulness, presumption and conviction of one's own merits.[93]

Cain is blamed for not offering πρωτογεννήματα, "first fruits" (52) – another attempt to rationalise the Lord's preference for Abel's sacrifice. Philo explains Cain's action in giving his offering "after some days" as stemming from a desire in a mind seeking ἑαυτὸν προτιμῶν θεοῦ, "to honour itself before God" (72). Thus Philo sees this action as the outworking of Cain's self-love. Philo's thought is that Cain's action in failing to offer first fruits stems from the same fault (72).

In *The Worse Attacks the Better* we find Cain cursed appropriately as an ἀδελφοκτονίας, "fratricide", for the murder of a brother (96). It is earlier made clear by Philo that while Genesis 4:8, where Cain rose up against Abel his brother and slew him, suggests that Abel has been done away with, in reality ὁ Κάιν ὑφ᾽ἑαυτοῦ, Cain has been done away with by himself (47). The picture is of one who is doubly cursed by his own behaviour. Earlier Abel is described dualistically as φιλόθεον δόγμα, "a God-loving creed", whereas Cain is φίλαυτον, "a self-loving creed" (32).[94] A strong parallel exists here with 1 John 3:12b, "and why did he murder him? Because his own deeds were evil and his brother's righteous".

In *The Posterity of Abel and Cain* we see Cain again referred to as ἀδελφοκτόνος (49), in a context where he is characterised as incurring more defiling guilt than an ἀνδροφονίας one, a man-slayer, making it clear that murder of a brother is even more serious than murder per se. Earlier it is made clear that Cain ἐκ προσώπου τοῦ θεοῦ μεταστάστα, left the face of God (12), which suggests a final curse. This contrasts Cain, the "deliberate sinner", from the "wise man, who wants to see God".[95] The thought here is similar to that which yokes together 1 John 3:12 and 15, that Cain was from the evil one and murdered his brother, and all who hate a brother are murderers, who do not have eternal life within them.

To understand Philo's presentation of Cain as evil from birth, and indeed an embodiment of evil itself, in the few examples that space allows in this study, one must understand Philo's philosophical roots. As Berchman says:

> [Philo's] doctrine of the existence of two ontologically distinct realms of being, the authentic and the image, goes back to Plato's *Timaeus*. The epistemological distinction between the opinion (*doxa*) and knowledge (*episteme*) provided the basis upon which Plato based the distinction between the sensible and the intelligible worlds (*Tim.*, 27d-28e). In the *mythos* we are told that the two realms

---

[93] Anita Mèasson and Jacques Cazeaux, "From Grammar to Discourse" in *Both Literal and Allegorical: Studies in Philo of Alexandria's Questions and Answers on Genesis and Exodus* (ed. David M Hay; Atlanta, Georgia: Scholars Press, 1991), 125–226, 219.
[94] As noted in Schnackenburg, *Johannine Epistles*, 179 n.193, Jewish interpretation makes Cain, among other things, a model of unbelief: Schnackenburg instances inter alia Philo in *The Posterity of Cain and Abel* at 38; similarly Menken, "The Image of Cain in 1 John 3:12," 202.
[95] Williamson, *Jews in the Hellenistic World 1ii: Philo*, 185.

are relative as original or pattern (*paradeigma*) to its image or imitation (*eikon*: Tim., 29b; 48e).[96]

Similarly Borgen comments, referring to the scholarly debate as to the degree to which Philo can be placed within the Middle Platonist tradition:

> Philo's views on "ideas" and "logos" can illustrate this interpretation. Philo saw in Genesis a double creation, first that of the *noetic* world as model, then that of the sensible world, which was produced by God from the model. Philo draws here on Platonic thoughts which he has modified. While the model of Plato's *Timaeus* was something independent of the *Demiurge*, the model in Plato's exegesis becomes God's creation.[97]

There is little agreement among scholars as to the extent to which Jewish thought, hellenisation, mysticism and political concerns prevail in Philo.[98] Putting aside the precise relationship between Philo's and Plato's thought (particularly in *Timaeus*, which is outside the scope of this study), it remains useful and necessary to understand Philo through a Middle Platonist lens. Using this approach, it becomes clear that Philo takes the Cain and Abel story from its OT context, where Cain is but an *example* of individual sin and its results, and reinterprets it in Middle Platonist terms so that Cain becomes, for Philo's audience, the *eikon* of sin in the sensible world, in relation to its *paradeigma* or original pattern.

For example, Adam is presented in *The Cherubim* as "mind", which exists before sense-perception (60), but when mind (Adam) joins with body (Eve), bodily perceptions dominate, then Adam names his son Cain, meaning "possession" ((53), (65)-(66)), symbolising that the mind wrongly believes it is self-sufficient.[99] So the teaching in *The Cherubim* is to rid oneself from "Cain" and recognise that God is the cause of the union ((99)-(100)) between body and soul, and the mind must be passive in its migration towards virtue.[100] Cain is here presented as an allegory for sin itself and therefore as evil by his very nature. Even within a framework presenting a human being as "practically the only being who having a knowledge of good and evil chooses the worst" (*Conf.* 176–8), Philo "can speak of bad individuals 'whose nature does not ever allow them to act intentionally in an honest way' (*Mig.* 216-20)".[101] Cain as an allegory for sin itself in *The Cherubim* fits this description.

One therefore must understand also that Philo's whole approach to OT interpretation is *allegorical*: his purpose is to derive from the OT text more general principles of

---

[96] Robert M Berchman, *From Philo to Origen: Middle Platonism in Transition* (Chico, California: Scholars Press, 1984), 24.
[97] Borgen, *Philo of Alexandria*, 7.
[98] DA Carson, "Divine Sovereignty and Human Responsibility in Philo," *Nov T* 23:2 (1981): 148–64, 165.
[99] Fred W Burnett, "Philo on Immortality: A Thematic Study of Philo's Concept of παλιγγενεσία," *CBQ* 46:3 (1984), 447–70, 451.
[100] Ibid.
[101] Carson, "Divine Sovereignty and Human Responsibility in Philo," 154.

theology and ethics by reference to OT stories in which he finds these ideas represented by particular figures and their actions.[102] In *The Cherubim* are themes of "banishment and testing" (1ff.), and "the mistaken idea that what we have is our own and not God's" (40ff.). In *The Sacrifices of Abel and Cain* one finds the "contrasting ideas of man as master and God as master" (1ff.), "the precedence of virtue" (11ff.), the "danger of tardiness and postponement" (52ff.) and "the stable and firm life of virtue" (88ff.).[103] And as Williamson says of Philo's allegorical treatment of the Cain and Abel story in *The Posterity of Abel and Cain*:

> Because of the nature of that method, which allows the exegete to find in the words of scripture meanings which do not appear to reside in them, much of what Philo has to say has nothing to do with 'the posterity of Cain'.[104]

It can be seen from our earlier examples that Philo uses the Cain and Abel story in *The Cherubim*, *The Sacrifices of Abel and Cain*, *The Worse Attacks the Better* and *The Posterity of Cain and His Exile* to set up a more universal conflict between God and sin, of which Cain is the *eikon*, and thus between good and evil.

In summary, in Philo's writings Cain's portrayal has moved from that in the Hebrew Bible where he is a human actor in a drama where he is envious of his brother's favour with God and kills him, and then receives God's curse for his act. It has moved beyond the LXX in which Cain's evil is intensified, largely through changes of wording from the Hebrew to the Greek. In Philo, the picture of Cain reaches a culmination: he is an allegory for evil itself, bad by nature and doomed to eternal struggle with God for mastery over humanity itself, represented by Adam, "the mind". The picture of Cain in 1 John 3 has much in common with such a portrayal.

Cain and Abel in Josephus

Josephus, born in 37 CE was, unlike Philo, primarily an historian, and his overriding concern in his *Judaean Antiquities* was to legitimise, in a historical manner, Jewish faith and practice in the eyes of their Roman overlords.[105] This work was probably written in 93 CE, in the thirteenth year of Domitian's principate.[106] Josephus had by then lost imperial patronage, which he enjoyed during the reigns of Titus and Vespasian, when

---

[102] See generally HAA Kennedy, *Philo's Contribution to Religion* (Edinburgh: Hodder & Stoughton, 1919), 32–4.
[103] Peder Borgen, *Philo, John and Paul: New Perspectives on Judaism and Early Christianity* (Atlanta, Georgia: Scholars Press, 1987), 36.
[104] Williamson, *Jews in the Hellenistic World 1ii: Philo*, 175–6.
[105] Steve Mason, *Josephus and the New Testament* (Peabody, Massachusetts: Hendrickson, 1992), 71.
[106] Louis H Feldman, *Flavius Josephus' Judean Antiquities I–IV: Translation and Commentary* (Boston/Leiden: Brill, 2004), xvii; George Nickelsburg, *Jewish Literature between the Bible and the Mishnah* (Minneapolis: Fortress Press, 2005), 291.

he wrote his *Judaean War*,[107] but he still had significant Roman patronage, probably both Jewish and Gentile.[108]

Unsurprisingly, Josephus' unifying themes in *Judaean Antiquities* are the ἀρχαιολογία, antiquity; πολιτεία, constitution and φιλοσοφία, philosophy of Judaean culture.[109] Josephus' *Judaean Antiquities* is "an all-out campaign to dispel the ridicule and misinformation that characterized literate Roman portrayals of the Jews" and "a massive effort at legitimation, seeking to demonstrate the great antiquity and nobility of Jewish tradition".[110]

Although the precise connection between his thought and Hellenistic philosophy and Jewish tradition is contested in scholarly debate,[111] some Hellenistic influence on Josephus' work is undoubted. Martin notes Josephus' use of the concept of *haemarmene*, "fate" or "destiny", at God's good pleasure in *Judaean Antiquities* at XVIII, 13, among other places, pointing to this belief, held by the Pharisees, as distinguishing them from the Sadducees.[112] Furthermore, the Pharisaic belief in the "immortality of the soul" conditions Josephus' use of Cain as the personification of evil endangering the human soul, as we have seen in Philo's work.

Following Hadas, Yamauchi notes Josephus' use of the full *gamut* of Greek literary style: he is rhetorical, pathetic, glorifying the past and wooing his readers.[113] Yamauchi attributes to Josephus (and Philo) embarrassment at the OT's anthropomorphisms and an intention to tone them down by allegory.[114] Josephus in *Antiquities* (I:52-54),[115] in his reworking of the Cain and Abel story, portrays Cain – not just his deeds – as πονηρότατος, "thoroughly (or most) evil", and Abel as having respect for "justice", δικαιοσύνης – a strong parallel with 1 John 3:12.[116]

In characteristically dualistic manner, Josephus contrasts Abel, the virtuous shepherd, with Cain, the evil plougher of the soil (I:53), and their sacrifices, milk and the firstlings of the flocks and the fruits of the earth (I:54). Here again, as in Philo, we see an a priori characterisation of Cain as evil, in primarily allegorical fashion, so that his deeds might be expected to be evil, rather than vice versa.

---

[107] Feldman, *Flavius Josephus' Judean Antiquities I–IV*, xviii.
[108] *Ibid*, xx; so also Edwin M Yamauchi, "Josephus and the Scriptures," *Fides et Historia* 13:1 (1980), 42–63, 44.
[109] *Ibid*, xxii.
[110] Mason, *Josephus and the New Testament*, 71.
[111] A good discussion of this issue occurs in John R Levinson, "The Debut of the Divine Spirit in Josephus' *Antiquities*," *HTR* 87:2 (1994), 123–38, in the context of Josephus' insertion of three references to the "divine spirit" in his reworking of Numbers 22–24 in *Judaic Antiquities* IV.108: 118, 119 where the Hebrew text has but one (Numbers 24:2), and the possible influence of Plutarch's contemporaneous *De Defectu Oraculorum*.
[112] Luther M Martin, "Josephus' Use of *Heimarmene* in the *Jewish Antiquities* XIII, 171–3," *Numen* 28:2 (1981): 127–37, 127–8.
[113] Yamauchi, "Josephus and the Scriptures," 45.
[114] *Ibid*, 46.
[115] The book and paragraph numbers in parentheses in the text in this chapter again correspond to those in the Loeb Classical Library edition, in this case *Josephus in Nine Volumes: IV, Jewish Antiquities, Books I–IV* (trans. H St J Thackeray; Cambridge, MA: Heinemann, 1967).
[116] Brown, *The Epistles of John*, 443.

Josephus' presentation of Cain as "only interested in gain" (I:61)[117] is consistent with the LXX picture in Genesis 4:7 of Cain's failure to divide properly his offering to God.[118] This last appears to present Cain implicitly as impious by nature.

Josephus uses the more intensive verb κτέινειν, which carries the connotation "put to death", or "put and end to", to depict Cain's slaying of Abel (I:53, 55), which may be somewhat more emphatic than ὑπέκτεινειν which is used in the LXX, as we have seen, and which simply means "kill".

More significantly, Josephus writes that after Cain's denial to God of knowledge of his brother's whereabouts, God accused Cain of being guilty of his brother's murder, φονός, and marvels that Cain cannot tell what has happened to one whom ἀπολώλεκας, "you have destroyed" (I:57), conveying a more intense idea than simple killing, however terrible that may be in itself. The LXX account at Genesis 4:10, following the Hebrew, is that God's address to Cain is "what have you done? Your brother's blood cries out to me from the ground". Josephus omits this account and substitutes a direct accusation by God that Cain is his brother's murderer and has "destroyed" him – an even more intense description of Cain's evil act.

Even more significantly, Josephus writes that Adam's passionate desire for more children arises Ἀβέλον μὲν ἐσφαγμένου, Κάιος δὲ διά τόν ἐκείνου φόνον πεφευγότος, "after the slaughtering of Abel and the resulting escape of Cain his murderer" (I:67). Josephus' use of ἐσφαγμένου here to describe Cain's action is a significant intensification of that action, because σφάζω carries the connotation of "slaughter", as opposed to a simple "killing",[119] and the use here of φόνον conveys the idea of "murder", *unlawful* killing. As we have seen, 1 John 3:12 uses σφάζω to describe Cain's act, rather than the less-intensive ὑπέκτεινειν used in the LXX account in Genesis 4. This is intensified by Josephus' use of the term we have earlier noted in Philo, ἀδελφοκτόνος, "fratricide" (I:65), to describe Cain's act.[120]

With Philo, Josephus tries to rationalise the Lord's preference for Abel's sacrifice over Cain's: Cain brought the fruits of the tilled earth to the Lord in sacrifice, whereas Abel brought milk, and the firstlings of his flocks (I:54). This offering was favoured by God, "who is honoured by things which grow spontaneously and in accordance with natural laws, and not by the products forced from nature by the ingenuity of grasping men" (I:55).[121]

In the Hebrew text of Genesis 4 God may be seen as apparently capricious in preferring Abel's sacrifice to Cain's, without apparent explanation; Josephus provides an explanation, as does Philo, for this divine preference.[122] And Josephus omits the Hebrew of Genesis 4:7.[123] This may suggest that Josephus was using the LXX text: as noted above, it does not contain the Hebrew of 4:7 but *does* offer some explanation for

---

[117] Yamauchi's translation.
[118] Yamauchi, "Josephus and the Scriptures," 46.
[119] Menken, "The Image of Cain in 1 John 3:12," 200.
[120] As noted in Byron, "Slaughter, Fratricide and Sacrilege," 528.
[121] Loeb translation.
[122] Feldman, *Josephus' Judaean Antiquities*, 20 n.117.
[123] *Ibid.*

divine preference for Abel's offering: Cain is told by God, ὀρθῶς δὲ μὴ διέλῃς, "You have not properly cut it up" or "divided it".

Josephus intensifies Cain's rejection by God at (I:59) where God προσέτακεν ἀπιέναι, "*bade* [Cain] depart", as opposed to Genesis 4:16 in the Hebrew, where it is said of Cain, "So he went out", וַיֵּצֵא, from the presence of the Lord, more or less of his own accord.[124]

In summary, Josephus' account of Cain's actions casts Cain as thoroughly evil, in dualistic contrast with Abel, a lover of justice. Cain is depicted intensively, as compared to the bare description of Genesis 4, as the destroyer and violent slaughterer of Abel. God's preference for Abel's sacrifice, a bare statement in Genesis 4, is rationalised by Josephus: Cain brought the products of the earth, but Cain brought firstlings, things that grow spontaneously. Cain's departure was *ordered* by God, not on his own initiative after he was cursed by God, as in Genesis 4. Although, unlike Philo, Josephus probably wrote his *Judaean Antiquities* contemporaneously with, if not after, 1 John, so that its author may not have had potential access to Josephus' work, *Judaean Antiquities* is a useful tool to ascertain the shape of the Jewish tradition of the time, which lies behind 1 John.

Historical Summary

We have seen that there is a considerable thought-shift in depictions of Cain in the Cain and Abel story between the original version in the Torah through the LXX and 1 Enoch and Jubilees, culminating in Philo's portrait of Cain as one who is an ἀδελφοκτόνος, "fratricide", and Josephus' similar portrayal of him as πονηρότατος, thoroughly (or most) evil from the beginning.

An important characteristic of the Hebrew Bible is the *unknowability* of God. God's preference for Abel's offering over Cain's is left unexplained. And the Torah, as we have seen, does not concentrate either on Cain's nature to explain his murder of his brother. Indeed it does not make any statement about Cain's character at all, apart from God cursing him because of his *act*. Instead, God's favour for Abel's sacrifice results in a murderous triad, in which Cain, despairing of God's favour, enviously murders the brother who stands in the way of his attaining it.

In the LXX new ideas are introduced through a rewriting of parts of the Torah's account of the story in Genesis 4:1-16. The LXX does use different words for the Hebrew מִנְחָה, "gift", "offering", used in both Genesis 4:4 and 4:5 for both Cain's and Abel's offerings: Cain's offerings are a θυσία, "sacrifice", but Abel's are δώροις, "gifts". Furthermore, in the Hebrew text God is said to gaze or not to gaze, שָׁעָה, on Cain and Abel and their gifts, whereas in the LXX God "looked upon", ἐπεῖδεν, Abel and his gifts, but God "did not pay attention to", προσέσχες, Cain and his sacrifice. It is arguable that as שָׁעָה is not translated elsewhere in the LXX by the verb προσέσχω, the translator wished to mark a divine rejection of Cain himself.

---

[124] *Ibid*, 21 n.124.

Moreover, the LXX does not translate the difficult Hebrew of Genesis 4:7a, "if you do well, will you not be accepted? And if you do not do well, sin is crouching at the door; its desire is you, but you must master it". Instead, in the LXX text in 4:7a the Lord asks Cain, οὐκ ἐὰν ὀρθῶς προσενέγκῃς ὀρθῶς δὲ μὴ διέλῃς ἥμαρτες, "Have you not sinned if you have brought it correctly, but have not correctly cut it up?" This question is not present in the Hebrew text, and it may represent an attempt by the LXX translators to rationalise the Lord's preference for Abel's sacrifice over Cain's in terms of an error in ritual sacrifice. Also, in 4:7b in the LXX the Lord addresses Cain, ἡσυχασον πρός σὲ ἡ ἀποστροφὴ αὐτοῦ, καὶ σὺ ἄρξεις αὐτοῦ, "Be still, and his obeisance will be to you, and you will rule over him." This difference clears up the ambiguity in the Hebrew Bible, in that Cain's birthright can only be secured if he "does well", but instead, being evil, he forswears it by murdering Abel. In these and other respects, the LXX portrays Cain more negatively than does the Torah. By so doing it provides later writers with a platform on which to expand the Cain and Abel story as an allegory for the ultimate, dualistic struggle between good and evil.

In the pseudepigraphical 1 Enoch, Cain is portrayed in still more negative terms. In 1 Enoch 22:7, in answer to the writer, the Angel Raphael "answered me saying, 'this is the spirit which went forth from Abel, whom his brother Cain slew, and he makes his case against him till his seed is destroyed from the face of the earth, and his seed is annihilated from amongst the seed of men'". In this exegetical elaboration of Genesis 4:10, Abel's blood, inanimate but personified in Genesis, is the seat of נֶפֶשׁ, "life" or "soul" (Genesis 9:4), which the author identifies as רוּחַ, "spirit", which was an active being, familiar in the Hellenistic world view: here the narrative of Genesis is interpolated with the motif of the dead pleading for vengeance. Furthermore, in 1 Enoch 85:4, we have the visionary symbolism of a black bull, its colour symbolising murder or sin and representing Cain, goring a red one, its colour symbolic of blood and representing Abel, and pursuing it over the earth. Omitted from 1 Enoch is any account of the Fall, and in its place we find this episode, portraying Cain as the first perpetrator of human sin – a sin of violence.

Similarly, in the pseudepigraphical Jubilees 4:31 we find Cain killed by the stones of his house, which fell on him, because he killed Abel with a stone, and he therefore was killed "in righteous judgment", which certainly suggests the *jus talionis*, even if it is not executed by Abel himself. In Jubilees 4:7, we find "and for this reason we announce when we have come before the Lord our God all the sin which is committed in heaven and upon earth, and in light and in darkness, and everywhere". The association of sin committed "on earth" with "darkness" here, along with the injunction to "announce", that is acknowledge, sin before God, finds an echo, not necessarily intended of course, in 1 John 1:5-7 with its dualism of light and darkness alongside sin and confession. Similarly, in a fragment of Jubilees which survives in Greek, 4:15, Cain is described as an ἀδελφοκτόνος, the very description we find later in Philo. This makes it clear that in the author's eyes, the treacherous attack on the neighbour is even graver because the neighbour is the murderer's brother.

1 Enoch and Jubilees thus exhibit a rewriting of the Cain and Abel story in symbolic terms in which Cain and Abel serve as ciphers for forces of darkness

and light, with Cain portrayed very darkly indeed as the first human sinner and a progenitor of evil.

In the Testament of Abraham in its earlier Long Recension, Abraham is depicted as asking the "Commander-in-Chief", a descriptor of God, who is "this most marvelous judge", and in 13.2-3 the answer is "the son of the first-formed, the one called Abel, whom the most evil and fratricidal Cain killed", who "sits here to judge all the creation". Abel's role as judge may have developed from his status as the first innocent to be murdered.

The most we can infer from this single reference is that, consistently with the development of Cain's role in 1 Enoch and Jubilees, his evil nature acquires eschatological significance: his primeval action in perpetrating the first murder confers on his victim, his brother Abel, the status of judge of the world's evil, and symbolically, Cain is emblematic of evil personified.

In Philo Abel is described dualistically as φιλόθεον δόγμα, "a God-loving creed", whereas Cain is φίλαυτον, "a self-loving creed". Philo's narration of the story introduces new elements: for example, the teaching in *The Cherubim* is to rid oneself from "Cain" and to recognise that God is the cause of the union ((99)-(100)) between body and soul. Thus Philo uses Cain as a metaphor for evil itself. Cain himself becomes what his actions are taken by Philo to symbolise – ultimate evil.

Similarly Josephus in his reworking of the Cain and Abel story in his *Judaean Antiquities* characterises Cain – not just his deeds – as πονηρότατος, thoroughly evil, and Abel as having respect for justice, δικαιοσύνης. Josephus contrasts Abel, the virtuous shepherd, with Cain, the evil plougher of the soil, and their sacrifices, milk and the firstlings of the flocks and the fruits of the earth, respectively. Here again, as with Philo, we see an a priori characterisation of Cain as evil, in primarily allegorical fashion, though Josephus' focus is historical rather than philosophical, in that he uses this story with many others to explain to Gentile readers the moral and theological foundations of Hebrew religion.

The point of tracing this thought-shift is to demonstrate that the Jewish tradition accessible to the author of 1 John by no means halted at the simple Hebrew narrative of the Cain and Abel story in Genesis 4:1-16. There the narrative runs from God's unexplained preference for Abel's sacrifice over Cain's to Cain's "downcast face" and his murder of his brother in the field and then to God's curse on Cain and Cain's departure to the Land of Nod. By the time 1 John came to be written, Cain and Abel in Jewish thought had come to represent allegorically the primal struggle between good and evil. We may now pass to the manner in which this thought-shift may have affected the author's use of the terms σφάζω and ἀνθρωποκτόνος in 1 John.

Σφάξω and ἀνθρωποκτόνος in 1 John

In 1 John 3:11-12 we read:

Ὅτι αὕτη ἐστὶν ἡ ἀγγελία ἣν ἠκούσατε ἀπ' ἀρχῆς, ἵνα ἀγαπῶμεν ἀλλήλους· οὐ καθὼς Κάϊν ἐκ τοῦ πονηροῦ ἦν καὶ ἔσφαξεν τὸν ἀδελφὸν αὐτοῦ· καὶ χάριν τίνος ἔσφαξεν αὐτόν; ὅτι τὰ ἔργα αὐτοῦ πονηρὰ ἦν, τὰ δὲ τοῦ ἀδελφοῦ αὐτοῦ δίκαια.

This may be translated:

> Because this is the command which you have heard from the beginning, that we should love each other, not like Cain from the evil one who slaughtered his own brother. Why did he slaughter him? Because his deeds were evil and his brother's righteous.

At the outset it bears repeating that the LXX was available to, and used by, Greek-speaking first-century Christians, including the Johannine community, and the Johannine literature contains specific LXX citations,[125] so one may hypothesise that the author of 1 John had these uses well in mind.

We have already noticed that the LXX does not use the more-intensive σφάζω, used in 1 John 3:12, to represent Cain's killing of Abel at 4:8.[126] As already noted, Genesis 4:8 in the LXX uses the simple word ὑπέκτυεινειν, which just means "kill", to translate the Hebrew וַיַּהַרְגֵהוּ, "and he killed him", with the same meaning. We have seen that in the LXX, σφάζω occurs only a few times to translate the Hebrew verb חָרַג, and when it does (Zechariah 11:4, 5, 7; Jeremiah 12:3; 15:3; 19:6), heavy violence (and in Isaiah 22:13 in the LXX, sacrificial slaughter) is the concept conveyed.[127] As we have also seen, Josephus writes that Adam's passionate desire for more children arises Ἀβέλον μὲν ἐσφαγμένου, Κάιος δὲ διὰ τὸν ἐκείνου φόνον πεφευγότος, "after the slaughtering of Abel and the resulting escape of Cain his murderer" (I:67). Josephus' use of ἐσφαγμένου in this passage to describe Cain's action is a significant intensification of that action; σφάζω carries the connotation of "slaughter", as opposed to a simple "killing",[128] and his use of φόνον conveys the idea of "murder", *unlawful* killing. Cain is portrayed in 1 John as the original man-hater and man-murderer, and this retelling of Cain's story goes beyond what is reported in Genesis 4:4-9: Cain's hatred in 1 John is the "original hatred" that comes from darkness.[129]

A reasonable conclusion, therefore, is that the author's use of σφάξω in 1 John 3:12 derives from the tradition available to him, in which Cain's action in killing his brother is intensified from an act of simple killing borne of brotherly jealousy, as portrayed in the Torah, to a manifestation of primeval evil, done by a person who himself stands as the all-time personification of evil itself, such as we find in Philo and Josephus. Furthermore, we have noticed that even in the LXX, Genesis 4:8 uses the simple word ὑπέκτεινειν, which simply means "kill", to translate the Hebrew וַיַּהַרְגֵהוּ, "and he killed him", which has a similar meaning, even if the Greek is slightly intensified compared to the Hebrew. As Morgen notes, the LXX *does* in fact use σφάξω on other occasions, for example, in the story of the sacrifice of Isaac in Genesis 22, and in the directions for the celebration of Yom Kippur in Leviticus 16-17.[130] To relate, as 1 John 3:12 does, that

---

[125] Law, *When God Spoke Greek*, 102, 114.
[126] Noted in Grayston, *The Johannine Epistles*, 110.
[127] Menken, "The Image of Cain in 1 John 3:12," 200; see also John Byron, "Slaughter, Fratricide and Sacrilege," 532.
[128] Menken, "The Image of Cain in 1 John 3:12," 200; Klauck, *Der Erste Johannesbrief*, 205.
[129] Gaugler, *Die Johannesbriefe*, 180.
[130] Morgen, *Les épîtres de Jean*, 139.

Cain ἔσφαξεν τὸν ἀδελφὸν αὐτοῦ, *slaughtered* his brother, is a great step up from the simple LXX statement, ὑπέκτεινεν, and certainly from the original Hebrew, וַיַּהַרְגֵהוּ.

This interpretation of the author's use of σφάξω in 1 John 3:12 is supported by the fact that it is a Johannine term in the NT, elsewhere occurring only in Revelation, and on each occasion is associated with heavy violence, not a simple act of killing. In Revelation 5:6, 9 and 12 the use of the verb σφάξω refers to the "lamb" who was slain, referring back to Isaiah 53:7, where the "lamb" is led to the slaughter without protest or resistance. Granted, the "lamb" metaphor here may have either sacrificial or leadership associations,[131] but also notable is Jesus' non-resistance to the heavy violence against him in his crucifixion and death agonies. In Revelation 6:4 and 9 the same verb, σφάξω, is used in the context of martyrdom for the word of God (6:9): again, the point is the heavy violence to which Christians are subjected in dying for their faith. In Revelation 13:3 the subject is the heavy death blow inflicted on the beast and its miraculous recovery. In Revelation 13:8 the subject again is the lamb who was slain and his book of life. In Revelation 18:24 the theme is again martyrdom, with the blood of all those slaughtered on earth being associated with that of prophets and saints.

Though the context of these occurrences of the verb σφάξω varies in Revelation, it always connotes heavy violence, slaughter, possibly directed to Christian believers.[132] Because of linguistic differences, this text is seen, according to reasonably common scholarly consensus, as written in the last decade of the first century of the common era, not by the same author as John's Gospel (or of 1 John, whether or not they are the same person), but as composed within a Johannine circle with dependence on the same earlier traditions as John's Gospel and 1 John.[133] Nevertheless, the same connotation as that in Revelation, heavy violence, appears to be the intention in using σφάξω in another Johannine work, 1 John 3:12.[134]

Even so, the author of 1 John is not as concerned with Cain's act as with the explanation for it, indicated by the rhetorical question in 3:12b, καὶ χάριν τίνος ἔσφαξεν αὐτόν. What we find in the answer provided in 1 John 3:12 is a straight identification of Cain as ἐκ τοῦ πονηροῦ and his deeds as πονηρά. We have seen that Josephus in *Antiquities* (I:52-54), in his reworking of the Cain and Abel story, characterises Cain himself as πονηρότατος, thoroughly evil. This again suggests adoption by the author of 1 John of the view of Cain developed in the later Jewish tradition he inherited and which we have outlined. Furthermore, the use of πονηρά in 3:12b, which is introduced by ὅτι, suggests inevitability, but not necessarily in the way the modern mind thinks of it, that is in terms of causality.[135] It is better to think of this phrase simply as *litotes*,

---

[131] David E Aune, *Revelation 1-5* (Dallas, Texas: Word Books, 1997), 368–9.

[132] GK Beale, *The Book of Revelation* (Grand Rapids/Cambridge, UK, Carlisle: Paternoster Press, 1999), 379–80; similarly Ian Boxall, *The Revelation of St John* (London/New York: Hendrickson Publishers/A & C Black, 2006), 109; Robert H Mounce, *The Book of Revelation* (Grand Rapids, Michigan/Cambridge, UK: Eerdmans, rev. ed. 1998), 143.

[133] Aune, *Revelation 1-5*, lv; similarly Beale, *The Book of Revelation*, 43–36; Boxall, *The Revelation of St John*, 7; Mounce, *The Book of Revelation*, 14–15.

[134] Brown, *Epistles of John*, 441; Painter, *1, 2 and 3 John*, 233.

[135] I am indebted to my doctoral supervisor, David Neville, for this suggestion; *sed contra*, Culy, *I, II, III John: A Handbook on the Greek Text*, 81, who considers ὅτι to be causal here.

in which the affirmative is expressed by the negative of the contrary.[136] What is the logic of this train of thought? Can we elucidate it in causal terms? Does 3:12 just mean what it says, and as many have thought in the past, that because Cain murdered his brother, inevitably his works were evil? We must place "evil" and "evil one" in a larger literary context and seek a more satisfactory meaning than this traditional one. The Jewish tradition inherited by the author, as already discussed, may provide precisely that literary context. May it indicate that in 1 John 3, "the whole sphere of Cain's life was evil"?[137]

Thatcher argues that Lohr[138] "just stops short" of asking why the LXX translators and the NT writers interpreted the Cain and Abel story in Genesis as they did, and in the case of the NT, enquiring "what factors shaped Christian memory of these tragic figures from the ancient past, and what rhetorical purposes did the evocation of Cain and Abel serve".[139]

This question is right at the heart of our discussion of the role of the Cain and Abel story in 1 John 3. Thatcher correctly suggests that the LXX (and the NT) have gone far beyond the Hebrew Bible in portraying Cain's offering and *character* as flawed, the NT perspective being coloured by the LXX reading.[140] Why? Because present groups tend to present situations by "keying" them, as Thatcher puts it, to events in the past, and secondly because the remembered past helps a group form and maintain its collective identity.[141] Therefore, in 1 John 3:12 we see that "the mnemonic potential of Cain and Abel is refracted through the lens of doctrinal conflicts" within a Christian community.[142]

Elsewhere Thatcher explains further how this phenomenon works. He argues that "John's understanding of his ethical obligations towards Jews, antichrists and others outside his community was not based on a fixed set of maxims drawn from the Mosaic law or Jesus tradition, but rather on a sacred past that provides an interpretative framework for current experience".[143] Thus Thatcher explains the extended reference in 1 John 3:8-15 to the Cain and Abel story as "driven by the Johannine premise that actions reveal spiritual pedigree".[144] Hence, "building on this ancient precedent, the Elder characterizes failure to love as a Satanic sin with moral consequences": "those who hate their brother remain in death" (3:14) and "no murderer has eternal life abiding in him" (3:15).[145] In that John identifies the antichrists with Cain, the original

---

[136] Brown, *Epistles of John*, 441.
[137] *Ibid*.
[138] See Lohr, "Righteous Abel, Wicked Cain," 485–96, n.61 *supra*.
[139] Tom Thatcher, "Cain and Abel in Early Christian Memory: A Case Study in 'The Use of the Old Testament in the New'," *CBQ* 72:4 (2010), 732–51, 733.
[140] *Ibid*, 736.
[141] *Ibid*, 737.
[142] *Ibid*, 745–6.
[143] Tom Thatcher, "Cain the Jew the Antichrist: Collective Memory and the Johannine Ethic of Loving and Hating" in *Rethinking the Ethics of John* (ed. Jan G Van der Watt and Ruben Zimmerman, Tübingen: Mohr Siebeck, 2012), 350–73, 351.
[144] *Ibid*, 352.
[145] *Ibid*, 353.

murderer, Thatcher argues that "early Christians embraced and extended the premises of the Septuagint reading when applying Genesis 4 to current experience".[146]

Precisely; we are mistaken if we look for complete logical consistency between John's admonition to love one another and his hostility to the secessionists, the antichrists. John's point in reaching imaginatively for the Cain example and viewing it through the grid of his community's current experience is that its solidarity is threatened from without by hostility and dissent, and that mutual love in imitation of Jesus himself is the only antidote.

The "sacred past", as Thatcher calls it,[147] upon which John calls in 1 John 3:12 in the Cain example to illustrate ultimate evil, is not merely the unadorned story in the Torah in Genesis 4. This may be illustrated by the way the author explains in 1 John 3:13 why he appropriates the dire example of Cain in 3:12 ("because his own deeds were evil") to illuminate the simple, yet profound point that his community will survive only if they love one another. In 3:15 the author deftly adds another equation: whoever is μισῶν, a hater of his brother, is ἀνθρωποκτόνος, a murderer.

As already noted, in a fragment of Jubilees, 4:15, which survives in Greek, Cain is described by a related term, ἀδελφοκτόνος. Furthermore, in Philo's *The Worse Attacks the Better* we find Cain cursed similarly as an ἀδελφοκτόνος, "fratricide", for the murder of a brother (96). In fact, as we have seen, the bracketing of Cain and anyone else who hates their brother as ἀνθρωποκτόνος in 1 John 3:15 is not without similar precedent: see, for example, Philo's labelling of Cain as an ἀδελφοκτόνος no less than ten times, including once each in *The Worse Attacks the Better* (96), *The Posterity and Exile of Cain* (49) and *The Cherubim* (52).[148] We have also seen Josephus' use in his *Judaean Antiquities* of the same term, ἀδελφοκτόνος, "brother's murderer" (I:65) to describe Cain.

Why does 1 John's author use the related term, ἀνθροποκτόνος, to describe Cain? The thought development we have traced makes it clear that in the tradition available to the author of 1 John, Cain, by his very act of murdering his brother, demonstrates his origin: he is thereby proven to be from the evil one. As Beutler writes, he is dualistically classified as evil because of his action, by which he becomes the "tribal father" ("Stammvater") of evil teaching.[149] It is notable that for the author, as for Philo, Josephus and the intertestamental pseudepigraphical writers, Cain does evil *because* he is from the evil one, not vice versa. His acts demonstrate his origins.[150] By contrast, the original Cain in the Hebrew in Genesis 4 was cursed by God (Genesis 4:11) *because* of his evil act. There is no suggestion in the Torah that he was inspired or directed in it by the evil one.

Some parallels with – though not necessarily influenced by – the Dead Sea Scrolls may exist here. As noted in Chapter 1, in *IQS* 3:15-4:25 a very clear distinction is drawn

---

[146] *Ibid*, 367.
[147] *Ibid*, 351.
[148] Byron, "Slaughter, Fratricide and Sacrilege," 520.
[149] Johannes Beutler, *Die Johanesbriefe* (Regensburg: Verlag Friedrich Pustet, 2000), 94.
[150] Van der Watt, "On Ethics in 1 John," 208.

between the "two spirits" of light and darkness, truth and falsehood, in which initiates into the community had to be thoroughly instructed.[151] Indeed at *IQS* 3.21-22 we read:

> Darkness is total dominion over the sons of deceit; they walk on paths of darkness. From the Angel of Darkness stems the corruption of all the sons of justice, and all their sins, their iniquities their guilts and their offensive deeds are under his dominion.[152]

This language and these ideas greatly resemble those in 1 John 3:12 where Cain is described as "from the evil one". Indeed Charlesworth suggests positive influence on the Johannine literature from the Qumran documents, noting the common dualistic themes of darkness/light, evil/truth, love/hate and perishing/eternal life.[153]

The influence of the Dead Sea scrolls in 4Q252 (where in 4Q252 2.8 the giving of the land to Abraham[154] and in 4Q252 2.11 Abraham's entry into the land[155] are narrated, in apparent rehearsal of Genesis 15) has been detected in John 8. These passages have been seen as evidence of conflict within Judaism at the time, joined in by the NT writers, as to who was entitled to inherit the promise of Abraham.[156] John 8:44, previously noticed, implicitly denies to the Jewish leaders the title of Abraham's children (cf. 8:39b). John 8:44 may show the influence of the Dead Sea Scrolls in 4Q252 referred to above.

As already noted, in *IQS* 3.32-4.15, the two spirits of truth and falsehood are described. Brown sees *IQS* 3.17-22 as underlying 1 John 1:5-2:2, because they share a remarkable number of themes: "a dualism of light and darkness, truth and perversion; walking in light and not in darkness; a prince of light who enables the sons of righteousness (justice) to walk in light; the relation of truth to light; the ability of darkness to deceive; cleansing of sin; atonement; *koinonia*".[157] A similar sharing of themes, though not as pronounced – the descent of the sons of darkness from the evil one – occurs between Q252 and *IQS* 3.32-4.15 and 1 John 3:12.

One might add that the Aramaic text, *4QVisions of Amran* 1.12-1, referring to the "sons of light" going to "everlasting happiness" and the "sons of darkness" to "the shades, to death"[158] is yet another reference in the Qumran literature to cosmic conflict between the forces of good and evil, with ultimate victory going to the latter, which may underlie John's demonisation of Cain as a source of ultimate evil.

---

[151] See *The Dead Sea Scrolls: Study Edition*, Vol 1, 76–9; Vermes, *Dead Sea Scrolls*, 48, 90, 105.
[152] *The Dead Sea Scrolls: Study Edition*, Vol 1, 74–5.
[153] James H Charlesworth, "The Fourth Evangelist and the Dead Sea Scrolls: Assessing Trends over Nearly Sixty Years" in *John, Qumran and the Dead Sea Scrolls,* 161–81, 168.
[154] *The Dead Sea Scrolls Study Edition* Vol 1, 502–3.
[155] Ibid.
[156] George J Brooke, *The Dead Sea Scrolls and the New Testament* (Minneapolis: Fortress Press, 2005), 185.
[157] Brown, *Epistles of John,* 243; see also Joseph A Fitzmyer SJ, "Qumran Literature and the Johannine Writings" in *Life in Abundance: Studies of John's Gospel in Tribute to Raymond E Brown* (ed. John R Donahue; Collegeville, Minnesota: Liturgical Press, 2005), 117–33, 122 for similar parallels between 1 John 1:6-7 and *IQS* 3:20-21.
[158] *Dead Sea Scrolls Study Edition* Vol 2, 1094–5.

The inherited tradition of "demonisation" of Cain may well also explain the use by 1 John's author of the intensive ἀνθρωποκτόνος to describe Cain. This is supported by the fact that the *only* other use of ἀνθρωποκτόνος in the NT is also from the Johannine tradition, in John 8:44 where Jesus says to the Jews of τοῦ διαβόλου that ἀνθρωποκτόνος ἦν ἀπ' ἀρχῆς, "he is a man-killer from the beginning". John 8:44, as John 3:12 does, associates murder with the evil one.[159] The author of 1 John in 3:12 may have had John 8:44 in mind.[160] John 8:44, in saying of the devil that ἐν τῇ ἀληθείᾳ οὐκ ἔστηκεν, "he does not stand in the truth", also parallels 1 John 3:19 where the author's audience is assured that by mutual love, the opposite of hatred, they will know they are from the truth. First John intensifies the portrait of Cain in Genesis 4:9 where, as we have seen, he is a simple human being who tries to lie his way out of trouble by denying that he is his brother's keeper, by associating him as a liar with the evil one, as in John 8:44 where the devil is condemned: ὅτι ψεύστης ἐστὶν καὶ ὁ πατὴρ αὐτοῦ, "he is a liar and the father of lies." This would fit with the tradition we have observed of characterising Cain as the embodiment of human evil.

Between 1 John 3:12 and 3:15 comes 3:13-14, where we read:

καὶ μὴ θαυμάζετε, ἀδελφοί, εἰ μισεῖ ὑμᾶς ὁ κόσμος. ἡμεῖς οἴδαμεν ὅτι μεταβεβήκαμεν ἐκ τοῦ θανάτου εἰς τὴν ζωήν, ὅτι ἀγαπῶμεν τοὺς ἀδελφούς· ὁ μὴ a ἀγαπῶν μένει ἐν τῷ θανάτῳ.

This may be translated:

> Do not be shocked, brothers, if the world should hate you. We know that we have crossed over from death to life, because we love our brothers. Whoever is not loving remains in death.

Here in 3:13-14 the author takes up the verb used in the preceding verse, μισέω, to equate the hatred of Cain for his brother with the attitude of the world towards the author's audience. The same verb, μισέω, occurs in 1 John 2:9, to make a similar point. Those who hate a brother, while saying they are in the light, are confuted: they remain in darkness, in the same way as those who fail to love in 3:13 remain in death. Conversely, those who have crossed over from death to life must expect hatred from the world (3:13), but their consolation is that by mutual love they are in life – which, as indicated by the perfect tense of the verb, μεταβεβήκαμεν, is a permanent change from one state to another[161] – and whoever does not, remains in death. The two steps in this uncompleted syllogism lead to the conclusion that the world remains in death. This further equates hatred with death. Why? The answer again is in 3:15, those who hate are murderers.

---

[159] Brown, *The Gospel According to John I–XII*, 365; Painter, *1, 2 and 3 John*, 233.
[160] Coombes, *1 John*, 135.
[161] D Edmond Hiebert, "An Exposition of 1 John 3:13-24, *B Sac* (1989): 301–19, 303; Culy, *I, II, III John: A Handbook on the Greek Text*, 84.

What overall narrative purpose does 1 John 3:12-15 therefore serve in the pericope on mutual love in 1 John 3? Despite many differing scholarly opinions, the best view is that this passage runs from 3:11 right through to 3:24.[162] The word ἀγάπη and its cognates recur from 3:11 to 3:18, where we find a stepped exposition of hatred as identification with Cain, who was from the evil one (3:12), and of mutual love as identification with Jesus himself, who laid down his life for us (3:16). And the series of further steps in 3:19-24 are all predicated on ἀγάπη, love. By mutual love we will know that we are from the truth, and it will reassure us when our hearts condemn us (3:19-20). Whenever our hearts condemn us, God is greater than our hearts and knows everything, so if our hearts do not condemn us and we have boldness before God, we will receive all we ask because we obey God's commandments and do what pleases God (3:20-22). God's commandment is that we believe in the name of Jesus Christ *and* love one another, as he has commanded (3:23). All who obey God's commandments abide in God, and God in them, and by this we know that God abides in us, by the Spirit given us (3:24). All of these stepped propositions – part of a "test of life", to use Law's phrase, adopted by Painter and others – proceed from the love command in 3:11 (cf. 2:7ff.).

Conclusion

As we have seen, Thatcher rightly suggests that even the LXX (and certainly 1 John 3:12) goes far beyond the Hebrew Bible in portraying Cain's offering and *character* as flawed, the NT perspective being coloured by the LXX reading.[163] There is a thought-shift, which moves from the simple portrayal of Cain in the Torah as his brother's killer as a result of envy to a tradition portraying Cain as the archetype of evil itself in the world, representative of Satan himself. The Jewish tradition which embodied this thought-shift was available to 1 John's author, and the way he in turn portrays Cain and his actions and origins suggests that he employed this tradition.

Thatcher thinks this kind of use of the Cain example by the author of 1 John occurs firstly because present groups tend to reach present situations by "keying" them to events in the past and secondly because the remembered past helps a group form and maintain its collective identity.[164] Therefore, in 1 John 3:12, says Thatcher, we see that "the mnemonic potential of Cain and Abel is refracted through the lens of doctrinal conflicts" within a Christian community.[165]

---

[162] JE McDermond, *1, 2, 3 John* (Harrisonburg, Virginia/Waterloo, Canada: Herald Press, 2011), 180; *sed contra*, Schnackenburg, *Johannine Epistles*, 177 (3:11-20); Painter, *1, 2 and 3 John*, 232 (3:11-18); Strecker, *Johannine Letters*, 107 (3:11-18); Marshall, *Epistles of John*, 188 (3:11-18); Smalley, *1, 2, 3 John*, 176 (3:10-24); Grayston, *Johannine Epistles*, 108 (3:11-18); Lieu, *I, II, and III John*, 146 (3:13-18); Von Wahlde, *Gospel and Letters of John, Volume 3*, 122 (3:11-18).
[163] Thatcher, "Cain and Abel in Early Christian Memory," 736.
[164] *Ibid*, 737.
[165] *Ibid*, 745–6.

This is convincing, because it is reasonably clear from 1 John 2:18-20 that the situation with which the author was dealing involved sectarian, doctrinal strife, emanating in his eyes from secessionists who had left the author's community.[166] There is no reason to suppose that the secessionists were engaged in *actual* killing, like Cain, but by accusing those remaining of not knowing God (a charge which may be implied from the ὁ λέγων slogans in 1 John, e.g. 2:9) they were striking at the identity and eternal life of those remaining.[167] The example of Cain, interpreted by the tradition inherited by 1 John's author, lay at hand as a potent tool with which to argue the disastrous and indeed eschatological consequences of hatred and division in the Johannine community. Furthermore, if in 1 John 3:12 the author had John 8:44 in mind, two consequences may follow: murder, the summit of human violence, which for the author is the ultimate result of hatred, is the ultimate embodiment of evil, and lying to evade responsibility for it is just as much condemned by the author as the act of murder itself.

This hermeneutical appropriation of OT scripture by 1 John's author is imaginative and vivid. It does not merely use the Cain and Abel story to drive home the evils of enmity and hatred; it is a mnemonic literary device to awaken in the imagination of his predominantly Jewish community the slaughter resulting from Cain's hatred of his brother – and perhaps also the even more horrifying slaughter the early Christians faced in the more or less contemporaneous reign of Domitian.[168] These consequences will destroy the Johannine community if mutual love is not the rule. It is this very use of a biblical tradition by 1 John's author in an imaginative, hermeneutical way, in his mnemonic appropriation of the thought-shift over the centuries in the depiction of Cain, which legitimises the hermeneutical use of 1 John 3:12-15 by modern peacemaking theologians to suggest that all violence is inherently evil because it lies at the root of hatred – the opposite of mutual love. Thus John's use of the Cain story permits peacemaking theology to appropriate 1 John's use of it hermeneutically as a similar mnemonic device to drive home the consequences of violence. Peacemaking theology may make this move without being tied hermeneutically – as distinct from exegetically – to the hostility 1 John's author shows to his secessionist opponents. It need not be tied to the author's largely negative vision of ὁ κόσμος, "the world"[169] – entirely understandable in the situation his community faced – as hostile and to be opposed, or to the notion that the love command therefore only applies within the Christian community. Of course ὁ κόσμος is often hostile to Christians and the ideas they propagate – but this poses the question whether Christians must therefore be hostile to it in return. Jesus, of whom 1 John 2:2 says καὶ αὐτὸς ἱλασμός ἐστιν περὶ τῶν ἁμαρτιῶν ἡμῶν, οὐ περὶ τῶν ἡμετέρων δὲ μόνον ἀλλὰ καὶ περὶ ὅλου τοῦ κόσμου, extended to the whole world his expiation of sin, and he provides a model for us to imitate in loving the whole world.

---

[166] Schnackenburg, *Johannine Epistles*, 132–3, 139–44; Brown, *Johannine Epistles*, 338–42; Painter, *1, 2 and 3 John*, 197–9.
[167] Brown, *Johannine Epistles*, 469.
[168] Schnackenburg, *Johannine Epistles*, 179.
[169] But see 1 John 2:2c and 4:9b.

To reinforce the love command, 1 John's author uses the positive results of mutual love – that we will know we are from the truth (3:19), and we will receive all we ask from God (3:22) and he will abide in us and we in him (3:24)[170] – and the negative consequences of disobeying the love command. Using σφάξω and ἀνθρωποκτόνος as alarming descriptors of Cain's actions and very nature, he shows how disobedience of the love command affects not only what we do, but *who we are*. If we disobey it, we shall then be from the evil one, like Cain, and be murderers – not literally, but the reasoning of this pericope is that if we do not love, we will embrace its opposite – hatred, the origin of murder. We risk mutual destruction if we do not love one another, in obedience to 1 John's commandment. Unsurprisingly, 1 John commands mutual love within a community riven with sectarian strife. Hermeneutically, for the modern mind, in a world disfigured by cruelty and war, an equally strong warning is sounded by peacemaking theology – love one another or perish violently, by our own hands. The polar opposite of 1 John's love command is Cain's false defence in Genesis 4:9, that he is not his brother's keeper: in 1 John, we *are* our brother's and sister's keepers, whoever they may be, and we must not do violence to them, or we will be destroyed in a never-ending cycle of retribution.

---

[170] The masculine pronoun is used solely for textual accuracy.

5

Ἀγαπάω and ἀδελφός in 1 John

Introduction

The ideas of love and brotherhood,[1] as they appear in 1 John, are embodied in John's use of the verb ἀγαπάω and the noun ἀδελφός and their derivatives. In 1 John we find ἀγαπάω used throughout the letter, in 1 John 2:10, 2:15 (twice), 3:10, 3:11, 3:14 (twice), 3:18, 3:23, 4:7 (twice), 4:8, 4:10 (twice), 4:11 (twice), 4:12, 4:19 (twice), 4:20 (three times), 4:21 (twice), 5:1 (twice) and 5:2 (twice). Apart from John's Gospel, 1 John uses this term more frequently than any other book in the NT. The noun ἀγάπη occurs in 1 John 2:5, 2:15, 3:1, 3:16, 3:17, 4:7, 4:8, 4:9, 4:10, 4:12, 4:16 (three times), 4:17, 4:18 (three times) and 5:3. It occurs more often in 1 John than in any other NT work, including John's Gospel. Similarly, ἀδελφός is found frequently in 1 John, at 2:9, 2:10, 2:11, 3:10, 3:12 (twice), 3:13, 3:14, 3:15, 3:16, 3:17, 4:20 (twice), 4:21 and 5:16. Frequency of usage proves nothing, except that it shows that 1 John is shot through with the ideas these words convey, and that they are not confined to any one unit, although the author's command that his audience love one another has its own pericope, 1 John 3:11-24. Love and brotherhood are the mainsprings of the letter. These ideas are appropriated in peacemaking theology, as commands of universal love and solidarity. This chapter asks whether 1 John itself justifies such uses, exegetically or hermeneutically. Are its love and brotherhood commands directed at the world at large, or confined to the author's community?

Yet again we should remind ourselves that the LXX was available to, and used by, Greek-speaking first-century Christians, including the Johannine community, and that the Johannine literature contains specific LXX citations,[2] so it may be inferred that the author of 1 John had the LXX well in mind. Might a study of the Hebrew equivalents of the LXX words ἀγαπάω and ἀδελφός therefore aid any decision whether 1 John's author intended them to embody universal commands, or directed them purely to the author's own community? This chapter studies the use of these words in the OT, in Leviticus and in Deuteronomy, to see if it helps answer the question whether the commands they embody are of universal love and brotherhood, or whether they were

---

[1] For the sake of brevity, and fidelity to the Greek text, "brother" and consequently "brotherhood" occur in this study to denote both brotherhood and sisterhood – no sexist assumptions should be read into this usage.

[2] Law, *When God Spoke Greek*, 102, 114.

limited to fellow Israelites. We shall then examine the use of these words in 1 John itself to see whether or not they embody universal commands.

This approach has its limitations. Again we must note Barr's warning that while it is often essential to undertake comparative etymological study to unlock the meaning of Hebrew words, etymology cannot impose a meaning on known usage of Hebrew terms, and etymological associations which appear to be theologically attractive cannot be allowed to assume command of the whole task of interpretation, without attending to the semantic context of the word in the passage under consideration.[3] This chapter simply seeks to uncover ideas beneath particular words in selected OT passages which *may* underlie ideas conveyed by certain terms in 1 John. The Hebrew meaning of a word cannot, without regard for its context, decide the meaning of an apparently corresponding Greek word whose meaning is also context-dependent.

As we have seen in Chapter 1, the better view is that 1 John was probably written by someone steeped in Jewish scripture, who wrote using Jewish thought patterns, and who did not hesitate to reach for the one OT citation in 1 John, the story of Cain and Abel, as an example of deadly hatred which would be familiar to his audience, as the antithesis of the love and brotherhood which he sees as the antidote to conflict in his community. So for that reason also, it is legitimate to examine the use of the Hebrew equivalents of the LXX verb, ἀγαπάω, and noun, ἀδελφός, in Leviticus and in Deuteronomy, to decide whether they embody universal or particular commands, so as to gain some insight into their use in 1 John – always remembering their very different historical and theological contexts there.

Leviticus

Leviticus,[4] especially chapters 17 to 26, has been aptly described as "emphasizing the holiness of God as the most important theological motif".[5] But in the process, human obligations to one's fellows receive emphasis too, notably in chapter 19.

In Leviticus 19:17[6] we find in v.17a a prohibition of hating a brother, the same idea as we find in 1 John 3:15, where hatred of a brother is equated to murder. The Hebrew אָח, "brother" is rendered in the LXX by ἀδελφός, and שָׂנֵא, "hate" by μισέω, the same Greek words used in 1 John 3:15. The idea appears to be similar.

Hatred of a brother *in one's heart*, forbidden in Leviticus 19:17a, is not just an emotion, but a mental activity: it is to be compared to the prohibition in Zechariah

---

[3] Barr, *Semantics of Biblical Language*, 158–9.
[4] This short excursus on Leviticus does not pretend to any analysis of its structure, themes or theology: its purpose is confined to illuminating possible parallels between the ideas of love and brotherhood in a representative chapter in Leviticus and in 1 John. This limitation, with all the defects resulting from it, is necessary for reasons of space. These caveats of course apply to the next section in this chapter, which examines these same ideas in Deuteronomy.
[5] Paul L Redditt, "Leviticus" in *Theological Interpretation of the Old Testament* (ed. Kevin J Vanhoozer; Grand Rapids: Baker Academic/London: SPCK, 2005), 52–8, 57.
[6] "You shall not hate your brother in your heart: you shall reprove your neighbour, or you will incur guilt yourself".

8:17a[7] showing the equivalence of וְאִישׁ אֶת־רָעַת רֵעֵהוּ אַל־תַּחְשְׁבוּ, "do not plot evil in your hearts" and שָׂנֵא, "hate", so that Leviticus 19:17a implies plotting counter-measures.[8] Such counter-measures obviously might include murder. The point of 19:17a is not mere avoidance of an emotion: it is that hatred begets *action*. The idea in 1 John 3:15 is the same. The use of אָח, "brother", in v.17a makes clear that even when wronged by an antagonist, one must still think of them as a brother.[9] Or as Lockshin paraphrases Leviticus 19:17, following Rashbam, "don't brood with anger against your friend in your heart; confront your friend and explain what troubles you".[10]

The use of the infinitive absolute before the verb in 19:17b in the phrase הוֹכֵחַ תּוֹכִיחַ (literally "you rebuke, to rebuke", better translated "rebuke frankly"), makes this a very emphatic command, contrasting with the prohibition on hatred in 19:17a, which does not use that construction.[11] This literary feature suggests that 19:17b is building towards a climax, a "command of commands" which sums up the whole unit. Leviticus 19:18b appears to be that climax.

Leviticus 19:17b is the natural corollary of v.17a: instead of hating the brother, one must reprove one's neighbour or bear guilt oneself. This accords with Proverbs 27:5: "better is open rebuke than hidden love".[12] An interesting shift from אָח, "brother", ἀλεφός in the LXX, to עָמִית, "kindred" or "neighbour" occurs in v.17b, πλησίος in the LXX, which can also mean "fellow man". The commands in vv.17a and 17b are connected: we see two forms of behaviour, one prohibited and the other commanded, although towards different categories of people. It may still be that אָח and עָמִית carry the same or a similar idea.[13]

However, the command in the following verse, 19:18, to love one's neighbour, uses yet another different word from אָח or עָמִית: it reads לְרֵעֲךָ (lit. "to neighbour of you"). It is possible that אָח is used in a figurative, non-literal sense to mean "fellow man" (or woman) in 19:17a. If so, the command not to hate one's brother in this verse would extend to all who are members of one's own community, or even beyond it. If the Hebrew intended this equation, it would be equally arguable that in the LXX, ἀδελφός and πλησίον carry the same idea. If so, 1 John 3:15 may possibly be read as prohibiting hatred of the ἀδελφός, brother, including πλησίον, "neighbour" or "fellow man" (or woman) in one's community as well. But for reasons which follow, this is tenuous.

To sum up, we have noted the shift from אָח, "brother", ἀδελφός in the LXX, in Leviticus 19:17a to עָמִית, "kindred" or "neighbour" in v.17b, rendered in the LXX by

---

[7] "Do not contrive evil in your hearts against your fellow man".
[8] Jacob Milgrom, *Leviticus 17-22* (New York: Doubleday, 2000), 1646; similarly John W Kleinig, *Leviticus* (Saint Louis: Concordia Publishing House, 2001), 412.
[9] *Leviticus: A New Translation with a Commentary from Talmudic, Midrashic and Rabbinical Sources* (translation and commentary by Rabbis Nosson Scherman and Hersh Goldwurm; Brooklyn NY: Mesorah Publications Ltd, 1990), 347.
[10] *Rashbam's Commentary on Leviticus and Numbers*, 105 n.26.
[11] Kleinig, *Leviticus*, 397.
[12] Wenham, *The Book of Leviticus* (Grand Rapids, Michigan: Eerdmans, 1979), 268; see also Milgrom, *Leviticus 17-22*, 1647.
[13] Martin Noth, *Leviticus* (London: SCM Press, first English ed., 1965), 141.

πλησίον, which can also mean "fellow man". We have seen that the commands in vv.17a and 17b appear connected, in that we are given two forms of behaviour, one prohibited and the other commanded, although to different categories of people, but אָח and עָמִית may still carry the same or a similar idea.[14]

Leviticus 19:18[15] contains the classical formulation of the command to practise love towards one's neighbour, לְרֵעֲךָ. A different word from עָמִית in 19:17b, which has more the sense of "kindred", is used in 19:18. This may suggest that 19:18 extends the love command in 19:17a beyond one's immediate kindred. The injunction "you shall love your neighbour as yourself" has been seen by Rabbi Akiva as the most important principle in the Torah.[16] In 19:18 the Hebrew וְאָהַבְתָּ is rendered in the LXX by the Greek verb ἀγαπάω – the same verb as we find in the many citations with the meaning "love" in 1 John listed at the beginning of this chapter.

Brueggemann refers to the concentration of Torah teaching in Leviticus about the need to "maintain an order of sacrifices and a holy priesthood that are pure enough to function effectively in the presence of the holy God". He also notes a second tradition of interpretation taking as its *leitmotif* the concept of "neighbourly justice", and taking as its key reference point the delivery of the Jews from slavery in Egypt. To Brueggemann, this suggests that the obedience of Israel to the same holy God requires "a neighbourly economy in which the exploitative practices of Pharaoh would be excluded", referring particularly to Leviticus 19:34, 36; 35:38, 42, 55; and 26:13, 45.[17] But who is the "neighbour", לְרֵעֲךָ spoken of there?

A common Christian view of Leviticus 19:18 is that it is a universal love command, not confined to one's own community or even Israel itself. Wenham sees the words "love" and "neighbour" in 19:18 as being "as wide-ranging in their scope and meaning in Hebrew as the corresponding English terms".[18] Boyce writes of 19:18 that "such love leaves vengeance and grudges and seeks for our neighbour what we so all covet for ourselves".[19] Willis says 19:18 commands a "holiness" which "involves someone's behaviour towards the poor and the handicapped, and even toward foreigners with whom they are unfamiliar", arguing, with Brueggemann, that this disposition assumes a creator God who has delivered people from death and slavery to life and righteousness, so that they will react by imitating the righteousness shown them.[20] But to Porter, unlike the NT in Luke 10:25-37, Leviticus 19:18 "means the sense of brotherhood which should be felt with every member of the Israelite sacral community", and that "it does not have the universal application that Jesus gives it".[21]

---

[14] Noth, *Leviticus*, 141.
[15] "You shall not take vengeance or bear a grudge against any of the sons of your people, but you should love your neighbour as yourself: I am the Lord".
[16] So Rabbi Sydney Schwartz, *Judaism and Justice: The Jewish Passion to Repair the World* (Woodstock, Vermont: Jewish Lights Publishing, 2006), 42.
[17] Brueggemann, *Old Testament Theology*, 211.
[18] Wenham, *The Book of Leviticus*, 269.
[19] Richard N Boyce, *Leviticus and Numbers* (Louisville/London: Westminster John Knox Press, 2008), 73; similarly Kleinig, *Leviticus*, 412.
[20] Timothy M Willis, *Leviticus* (Nashville: Abingdon Press, 2009) 171–2.
[21] JR Porter, *Leviticus* (Cambridge: Cambridge University Press, 1976), 155.

Some Jewish scholars are more convinced by Porter's view. For Milgrom, the Hebrew לְרֵעֲךָ, "to your neighbour", in Leviticus 19:18 does not "embrace everyone, including non-Israelites", as it "clearly" does in Exodus 11:2, pointing to Leviticus 19:34, which commands love for הַגֵּר, "the alien", as yourself; he suggests that in 19:18 לְרֵעֲךָ, "to your neighbour", means "fellow-Israelite".[22] Levine renders 19:18 as "love your fellow as yourself", noting a negative paraphrase by Hillel, "what is hateful to you, do not do to your comrade", suggesting that the command is limited to one's own community.[23] He sees Leviticus 19 as a *midrash* on the Decalogue.[24]

Might a resolution to this disagreement, in determining whether the command to love the neighbour in Leviticus 19:18b is universal, be found by examining how this verse is related to other religious and ethical laws in Leviticus 19? The chapter is remarkable for combining cultic, ritual laws and other, non-cultic laws extending more generally to human behaviour. Scholars have discerned a common thread between these apparently disparate law groupings. Milgrom links religious duties together in vv.2b-10, after an introduction in vv.1-2a, then ethical duties in vv.11-18, then miscellaneous duties in vv.19-37.[25] This grouping works, provided the duty to honour one's parents and the Sabbath in v.3 is seen as primarily religious. This seems justified, for two reasons. First, the injunction from the Lord there is to honour *my* Sabbath. Second, the command to honour one's earthly parents comes straight after the injunction to honour one's heavenly parent, the Lord, on the Lord's own day, the Sabbath.

Similarly Marx sees all of these commands in Leviticus 19 as related in two ways. Firstly, it propounds an ethic founded on two main principles, limiting Israelites in their dealings with fellow countrymen in not taking advantage of a dominant position, and in the religious sphere, prohibiting all contact with spiritual beings other than God, and secondly, the authors consider sacrificial worship and social ethics to be related areas, governed by the same principles.[26] This linkage is convincing. One example is illustrative. The prohibition in v. 10 on stripping one's vineyard bare, with the associated command to leave the fallen grapes for the poor and the alien, is primarily a religious duty, but also an ethical one. So as Kaminsky puts it, "Leviticus conceptualises holiness as a unity of proper ritual and ethical conduct and also affirms that religion is not a private matter between each individual and God."[27] Another unifying characteristic in Leviticus 19, to which Kline points, is the association between God-oriented material in each of its units with material not so oriented.[28] A convincing example, offered by

---

[22] Milgrom, *Leviticus 17-22*, 1654; similarly Joel S Kaminsky, "Loving One's (Israelite) Neighbour: Election and Commandment in Leviticus 19", *Int* 62.2 (2008): 123–32, 123–4; *Rashbam's Commentary on Leviticus and Numbers*, 107 n.32; *Leviticus: A New Translation*, 348.

[23] Levine, *Leviticus*, 130; similarly Alfred Marx, "The Relationship between the Sacrificial Laws and the Other Laws in Leviticus 19", *The Journal of Hebrew Scriptures* 8.9 (2008): 2–11, 4.

[24] Levine, *Leviticus*, 124; similarly Marx, "The Relationship between the Sacrificial Laws and the Other Laws in Leviticus 19", 4.

[25] Milgrom, *Leviticus 17-22*, 1596–7.

[26] Marx, "The Relationship between the Sacrificial Laws and the Other Laws in Leviticus 19", 11.

[27] Kaminsky, "Loving One's (Israelite) Neighbour", 125.

[28] Moshe Kline, "'The Editor Was Nodding': A Reading of Leviticus 19 in Memory of Mary Douglas", *The Journal of Hebrew Scriptures* 8.17 (2008): 2–59, 33.

Kline, is the unexpected association in 19:35 between honest weights and measures and "the Lord your God, who brought you out of the land of Egypt".

Thus there is broad scholarly consensus that the cultic and ethical commands in the later chapters of Leviticus march together, and are interdependent, firstly because ethical practice in the ancient world of Leviticus is seen to be underpinned by community solidarity conferred by common ritual observance, and secondly because such interdependence arises since both ethical practice and ritual observance are commanded by God, and each solidifies the Israelites' relationship with God in an inseparable way. As Trevaskis puts it, "the idea of 'wholeness' appears common to the ideas of holiness and ethics" in Leviticus.[29]

These features apply particularly to Leviticus 19:18 in its immediate context in chapter 19. We have seen that Milgrom groups religious duties, after an introduction in vv.1-2a, together in vv.2b-10, then ethical duties in vv.11-18, then miscellaneous duties in vv.19-37, and that this taxonomy is useful and cogent.[30] But even within the ethical injunctions in Leviticus 19:11-18, there are sometimes interspersed religious ones. For example, in 19:11, stealing, dealing falsely and lying are proscribed, and in 19:12 profaning the Lord's name is forbidden. In 19:13 fraud, stealing and keeping back one's labourer's wages are interdicted, and in 19:14 mistreating the deaf and blind are proscribed, and fear of the Lord is enjoined.

Leviticus 19:18 fits this pattern, for taking vengeance is first forbidden, which is in reality a religious prohibition, because it constitutes a usurpation of the divine prerogative.[31] Then love of neighbour, an ethical duty, is enjoined. In 19:18 there is an inextricable link between a religious prohibition on presuming to do what God alone can do, by avenging oneself against the neighbour, and the command to love that neighbour instead. What we see in 19:18 is nothing less than two inextricable religious and ethical commands, a ban on private violence against the neighbour, punishment of past wrongs being God's business, not ours, and a command to love the neighbour instead, even if they have wronged you.

Despite this, Leviticus 19:33-34, commanding love of the alien as oneself, are still needed, because in 19:18 it is "to your neighbour", לְרֵעֶךָ, that love is commanded, whereas in 19:34 it is owed to הַגֵּר, "the alien", which suggests that they are different categories. One must reluctantly disagree with the common Christian view that the love command in 19:18 is universal: if it were, why would 19:34 be needed at all? On the other hand, reading 19:18 together with 19:34, one notes that the same verbal construction, וְאָהַבְתָּ, "and you shall love", translated in the LXX by ἀγαπάω, is used in both verses. The effect is to extend the love command, first "to your neighbour", לְרֵעֶךָ, and then to הַגֵּר, "the alien", so that taken overall, and reading it with the other "holiness" obligations in Leviticus 19, the love command in the chapter, read as a whole, is universal, or very nearly so.

---

[29] Leigh M Trevaskis, *Holiness, Ethics and Ritual in Leviticus* (Sheffield: Sheffield Phoenix Press, 2011), 219.
[30] Milgrom, *Leviticus 17-22*, 1596-7.
[31] *Ibid*, 1651.

How then may Leviticus 19 impinge on NT interpretation? Allbee sees a "hermeneutical bridge" between Leviticus 19:11-18 and the NT: he proposes that the same love of neighbour that is explicit in Jesus' command in Mathew 22:34-40 and Mark 12:28-34, described by him as the unifying foundation of the law and the prophets, is already implicitly recognised as such in Leviticus 19:11-18.[32] Allbee correctly concedes there is not perfect symmetry, because the NT gives love the priority over law (cf. Romans 13:8; Galatians 5:13), whereas the OT puts love in a legal context, thus giving law the priority.[33] Leviticus 19:18 is a good example. Albee points out that Leviticus 19:11-18 falls within the "holiness code" section (chapters 18–20) and that the statement "you shall be holy, for I the Lord your God am holy" in 19:2 (cf. 20:26) is the context for 19:11-18, as well as for the rest of the Code.[34] Another way of putting it is that to be קְדֹשִׁים, "holy ones" (19:2) is to keep God's law, including God's ethical commands, and especially that in 19:18b, to love one's neighbour as oneself.

Coming to the command "but you shall love your neighbour as yourself", Allbee notes, importantly, that 19:18b, "you shall love your neighbour as yourself", begins with the conjunction ו used adversatively ("but", "on the other hand"), and its wording, וְאָהַבְתָּ לְרֵעֲךָ כָּמוֹךָ (literally "but you love to neighbour of you as yourself") uses the injunctive use of the imperfect, expressing a strong command.[35] Wenham sees v.18b as a theological climax to the whole passage,[36] and Allbee agrees, suggesting that love of neighbour at least minimally prevents infringement of any of the various prohibitions in 19:11-18, as it is the common concern of all of them.[37] Thus love of neighbour, says Allbee, is not just another single command in this pericope, 19:11-18, but *the foundation and unifying principle of all of the laws in it*.[38] Allbee argues that "but you shall love", וְאָהַבְתָּ in 19:18 also has its positive side, firstly because in 19:17 the command to "reprove" is linked to the love command in the very next verse, and secondly in that in 19:34, the command to love "the alien", הַגֵּר, as oneself, as with 19:18b, requires practical concern for those not as well placed as oneself.[39] Even if one sees this last concept as restricted to "resident alien", that is an alien living within Israel's borders, as Milgrom suggests,[40] the love command in Leviticus 19 is near-universal.

Allbee's argument is convincing. Firstly, the syntax of the command suggests that it is very strong. Secondly, 19:18b falls at the end of the unit from 19:11 to 19:18 containing ethical commands (using Milgrom's useful classification noted above) and it is easy to see it as a climax, purely because of its position. Thirdly, each of the prohibitions from v.11 to v.18 – dishonesty (vv.11-13), cruelty to the disabled (v.14),

---

[32] Richard A Allbee, "Asymmetrical Continuity of Love and Law between the Old and New Testaments: Explicating the Implicit Side of a Hermeneutical Bridge, Leviticus 19:11-18", *JSOT* 31.2 (2006): 147–66, 147–8.
[33] Ibid, 148.
[34] Ibid, 149.
[35] Ibid, 163.
[36] Wenham, *Leviticus*, 267.
[37] Allbee, "Asymmetrical Continuity of Love and Law between the Old and New Testaments", 163–4.
[38] Ibid, 164.
[39] Ibid, 165.
[40] Milgrom, *Leviticus 17-22*, 1704–5.

failure to do justice (v.15), slander and profiting at one's neighbour's expense (v.16), hatred, with a command to reprove instead (v.17) and vengeance, with a command to love instead (v.18) are indeed sins against one's neighbour: if one loves one's neighbour, one is unlikely to infringe any of these prohibitions. Finally, and very significantly, "and you shall love", וְאָהַבְתָּ indeed surfaces again in 19:34, this time directed not just at the other, the neighbour, but at one who is at once not related by ties to oneself and less fortunate than oneself, "the alien", הַגֵּר.

To sum up, the command to love the "neighbour" in 19:18b may be restricted to one's fellow Israelite, only to be extended in 19:34 to one who clearly does not fit this category, the "alien". This recurrence of "and you shall love", וְאָהַבְתָּ, in 19:34 suggests that since the same attitude is required "to your neighbour", לְרֵעֲךָ in 19:18b as to "the alien", הַגֵּר in 19:34, the love command in Leviticus 19, read as a whole, is universal or nearly so, not particular and limited to one's own people.[41] Allbee shows convincingly that love of neighbour is indeed the foundational principle behind the Torah's ethical principles in Leviticus 19:11-18, and that it is not limited to one's own people. In that Leviticus 19:18, read with 19:34, embodies a universal love command, or very nearly so, he is essentially correct. Thus, as Allbee says, 19:18b may form a "hermeneutical bridge" to Jesus' love command in Matthew 22:34-40 and Mark 12:28-34. It may be argued that it forms a similar hermeneutical bridge to the ἀγάπη theme which recurs so frequently in 1 John, as noted above, noting again that ἀγαπάω is the LXX's verb where it translates וְאָהַבְתָּ, "but you shall love", in Leviticus 19:18b and 19:34. Such a bridge may help to discern whether its love commands towards one's brother are universal.

In the Qumran material we find in the Damascus Document at *CD* VI:20-21 direct references to Leviticus 19[42] in a passage containing interspersed ritual instructions and rules for daily life: at VI:18, for example, keeping the Sabbath "according to its exact interpretation" and the festivals is enjoined; at VI:19 the day of fasting must be kept; at VI:20 "holy portions according to their exact interpretation" must be set aside; and at VI:20-21 each must "love his brother like himself" and "strengthen the hand of the poor, the needy and the foreigner (גֵּר)".[43]

So in *CD* VI:20 we find a command to love the אָח, "brother", as ourselves[44] – the same association found in 1 John 3:11-17 – not a "neighbour". *CD* VI:20 contains an obvious echo of Leviticus 19:18b. But *CD* VI:20 does not necessarily use "brother" interchangeably with "neighbour". Might the author of 1 John 3:11-17 have intended such interchangeability? Eisenman cogently notes that after this reference to "loving the brother", we find "God-fearers" and "fearing God's name" referred to in *CD* VIII:42-43; he says the context is *exactly* that in 1 John 4:18,[45] which is one of "loving one's neighbour", "being built up" or "fortified", and "perfection".[46]

---

[41] Wenham, *Leviticus*, 273.
[42] Brooke, *The Dead Sea Scrolls and the New Testament*, 4.
[43] *The Dead Sea Scrolls Study Edition*, Vol 1, 559.
[44] *Ibid*; see also *The Damascus Document Reconsidered* (ed. Magen Broshi; Jerusalem: Israel Exploration Society and the Shrine of the Book, Israel Museum, 1992), 21.
[45] "In love there is no fear, for perfect love casts out fear; for fear is concerned with punishment, and whoever fears has not attained perfection in love".
[46] Robert Eisenman, *The Dead Sea Scrolls and the First Christians* (Shaftsbury, Dorset: Element Books, 1996), 314.

Importantly, in *CD* the word ברית, covenant, appears some forty times, and as Collins notes, "the Damascus Rule is concerned with the Law of Moses as it should apply to all Israel, but it is also concerned with an elite group within Israel, who recognise that the Law is not being properly observed".[47] *Ex hypothesi*, the Law of Moses includes Leviticus 19:17-18, so the proposal that the author of 1 John in 3.11 sees these very verses as an ἐντολὴ, commandment, ἀπ᾽ ἀρχῆς, "from the beginning", in that it comes from the Law of Moses, but is not being properly applied – the same concern that we see in the Damascus Document – becomes the more cogent.

Similarly we find Leviticus 19:17 and 19:18a referred to in *CD* IX:8-9, probably connected with the prohibition on "tale-bearing" in Leviticus 19:16.[48] This is a passage of legal *midrash* aimed at holding grudges and taking vengeance, and requiring instead, reproof of one's neighbour.[49] This may be the same idea as that of hating the brother, contained in 1 John 3:15. The connection between "tale-bearing" in 19:16, hatred of the neighbour (19:17), taking vengeance (19:18a) and loving the neighbour (19:18b) is obvious: the first three phenomena are all instances of failure to love the neighbour. Hatred of the brother is such a failure.

However any suggestion that Leviticus 19:18 was interpreted by the Qumran community as a universal command must take into account the fact that this community was essentially sectarian in character, and that the Damascus Document was so directed.[50] The emphasis on separation, seen in the Damascus Document in part of the passage we have already noted, *CD* VI.19, "according to what was discovered by those who entered the new covenant in the land of Damascus",[51] suggests that the neighbour-love injunction from Leviticus 19:18b, reiterated at *CD* VI.20-21, was intended to apply as between the members of the community in which it was written, not to the world at large, from which the community members were so keen to separate themselves, in the interests of perfection. This is also reflected in the Rule of the Community, at *1QS* I:8-11, where we find the commands to "be united in the counsel of God and walk in perfection in his sight, complying with all revealed things concerning the regulated times of their stipulations; in order to love all the sons of light, each according to his lot in God's plan, *and to detest the sons of darkness, each one in accordance with his guilt in God's vindication*".[52] This same problem may *seem* to arise in relation to the community

---

[47] John J Collins, "The Nature and Aims of the Sect Known from the Dead Sea Scrolls" in *Flores Florentino: Dead Sea Scrolls and Other Early Jewish Studies in Honour of Florentinto Gárcia Martínez* (Leiden/Boston: Brill, 2007), 31–52, 36–7.

[48] Charlotte Hempel, *The Laws of the Damascus Document* (Leiden: Brill, 1998), 32–3; similarly Aharon Shemesh, "Scriptural Interpretations in the Damascus Document and Their Parallels in Rabbinic Midrash" in *The Damascus Document: A Centenary of Discovery – Proceedings of the Third International Symposium of the Orion Centre, 4–8 February 1998* (ed. Joseph M Baumgarten, Esther G Chazon and Avital Pinnick; Leiden: Brill, 2000), 161–76, 174.

[49] Steven D Fraade, "Looking for Legal Midrash at Qumran" in Biblical Perspectives: Early Use & Interpretation of the Bible in Light of the Dead Sea Scrolls – Proceedings of the First International Symposium of the Orion Centre, 12–14 May 1996 (ed. Michael E Stone and Esther G Chazon; Leiden: Brill, 1998), 59–80, 69.

[50] Timothy H Lim, "Towards a Description of the Sectarian Matrix" in *Echoes from the Caves: Qumran and the New Testament* (ed. Florentino Garcia Martinez; Leiden/Boston: Brill, 2009), 7–32, 22.

[51] *Dead Sea Scrolls Study Edition*, Vol 1, 558–9.

[52] Ibid, 70–1 (italics added).

in which 1 John was written. But as Fitzmyer correctly notes, the hatred found in the Qumran literature (e.g. at *IQS* 1:10-11, where the Essenes were made to swear to detest the "sons of darkness", is not found in the teachings of Jesus recorded in the Johannine writings,[53] nor, one might add, in 1 John.

A balanced view of the relationship between the Qumran literature generally and the Johannine literature is still that of Brown, who comments that "the prevalence of the theme of brotherly love in both the Qumran and the Johannine literature is not a conclusive proof of interrelationship", but that "it is certainly remarkable that the New Testament writer who shares so many other ideological and terminological peculiarities with Qumran should also stress the particular aspect of charity which is emphasized more at Qumran than anywhere else in Jewish literature before Christ."[54]

Leviticus 19:18b is best seen as a command to love one's neighbour as oneself where the "neighbour" may be one's kinsman, one's fellow Israelite. Reading 19:18b with 19:34, Leviticus 19, read as a whole, may present a truly universal love command, or nearly so. Leviticus 19:18b alone is cited in Matthew and Luke in that way. Did the Johannine community know of the Levitical love command, and may it underlie the love commands in 1 John? We shall come to this later.

Deuteronomy

Some years ago Weinfeld described Deuteronomy's laws as having a "humanist tone". Following Driver, Weinfeld writes that of the three constituent elements in the book, historical, legislative and paraenetic, the most important and characteristic is the third. To him, underlying Deuteronomy's law and history is a "humanistic-moral outlook which forms the basis of the book as a whole".[55] It may be that this emphasis occurs because in a traditional society such as Israel, the economic system had to stand within the legitimating effect of cultural traditions, in order to meet problems in social systems in Judean society.[56] And these problems in Israel's society have to be met, according to Deuteronomy, by its people's actions, in co-operation with their Lord, not by a permanent connection in which the Lord is permanently obliged to ensure fertility and plenty.[57]

---

[53] Fitzmyer, "Qumran Literature and the Johannine Writings", 125.
[54] Raymond E Brown, "The Qumran Scrolls and the Johannine Gospel and Epistles" in *The Scrolls and the New Testament* (ed. Krister Stendahl; New York: Crossroads, 1992), 183–207, 199. This essay was first published at *CBQ* 17 (1955): 403–19, 559–74. But for criticism of even such a nuanced and cautious statement of the putative relationship between the Qumran and the Johannine literature see Jörg Frey, "Recent Perspectives on Johannine Dualism" in *Text, Thought and Practice in Early Christianity – Proceedings of the Ninth International Symposium of the Orion Centre for the Study of the Dead Sea Scrolls and Associated Literature, Jointly Sponsored by the Hebrew University Centre for the Study of Christianity, 11–13 January 2004* (ed. Ruth A Clements and Daniel R Schwartz; Leiden: Brill, 2009), 127–60, 137–43.
[55] Moshe Weinfeld, "The Origin of the Humanism in Deuteronomy", *JBL* 80.3 (1961): 241–7, 1–2.
[56] ADH Mayes, "On Describing the Purpose of Deuteronomy", *JSOT* 58 (1993): 13–33, 27.
[57] Alexander Rofé, *Deuteronomy: Issues and Interpretation* (London/New York: T&T Clark, 2002), 12.

Over the years other scholars have followed this trend in Deuteronomic interpretation. To Deere, the book's main thought is "obedience through love", so that its supreme command is to "love Yahweh and one's neighbour with all the heart and soul".[58] Toombs writes that Deuteronomy's Covenant shows a triangle of relationships, between God and Israel, Israel's response to God's initiative, and the relationship of members of the Covenant community to one another.[59] Consequently, "in the thought of the Deuteronomist, justice and love are closely akin, *for justice is nothing less than love with its coat off, in action in society*".[60]

Deuteronomic love, with its origins in divine love for Israel and its working out in social obligations, is well explicated in a representative passage, Deuteronomy 10:12-22. This unit begins with the question to Israel, "what does the Lord require of you", and is bound together by a sustained linkage between God's "love", לְאַהֲבָה (lit. "to love") for Israel (v.15) and its obligations to others, entailed by God's love itself. The command to love, וַאֲהַבְתֶּם (lit. "so you love") "the stranger", הַגֵּר is in v.19, and we may usefully trace how vv.10-18 lead up to and are connected with it.

In vv.12-13 we see the commandment to love, וּלְאַהֲבָה (lit. "and to love") and serve God with all one's heart and soul, and to keep God's original commandments, and also those given "today", in this passage. The commands of 10:12-22 cancel out the Golden Calf incident and are a reinstatement of the *Shema*; they are a full renewal of Israel's covenant after her sin.[61] In v.12, and in all those subsequent to it in Deuteronomy 10:11-22 using the Hebrew word אָהַב in verbal form, it is rendered in the LXX by the Greek verb ἀγαπάω – the same verb as we find in the citations in 1 John listed at the beginning of this chapter.

The foundation for the command in vv.12-13 to love God and keep God's commandments is found in vv.14-15 where God's majesty over heaven and earth is affirmed, and God's action in setting God's heart on Israel's ancestors and their descendants alone is proclaimed. Next comes in v.16 the curious command to "circumcise the foreskin of your heart", and to be "stubborn no longer". The idea of circumcision here is suggested by the election of Abraham in Genesis 17, and is used figuratively here to denote setting a mark of God's election on spirit and soul.[62] Then in v.17 the "God of Gods and Lord of Lords", the "great, mighty and awesome", who is not "partial" and "does not take a bribe" is introduced. A hymnic, liturgical expression is used to link God's majesty with God's characteristics of impartiality – God has no need of offerings to change God's behaviour: though God has chosen Israel, God does not discriminate in judgement between his people and others.

Therefore (v.18) God grants justice to the orphan and widow, and loves, and provides food and clothing for, the "stranger". Such a person is to be distinguished from the true Israelite, in that the stranger is not subject to the religious obligation, for example, not to eat anything that has died a natural death: the Israelite is enjoined

---

[58] Derward W Deere, "An Introduction to Deuteronomy", *SJT* 57.3 (1964): 7–16, 10.
[59] Lawrence E Toombs, "Love and Justice in Deuteronomy", *Int* 19.4 (1965): 399–411, 403.
[60] *Ibid*, 407–8 (emphasis in original).
[61] So Paul A Barker, *The Triumph of Grace in Deuteronomy* (Carlisle: Paternoster Press, 2004), 103.
[62] Moshe Weinfeld, *Deuteronomy 1-11* (New York: Doubleday, 1991) 437.

to give it "to a stranger", לַגֵּר or "to a foreigner", לְנָכְרִי (Deuteronomy 14:21).[63] Weinfeld proposes that the wording of v.18 signifies that God gives justice to the stranger too.[64] Tigay sees "to a stranger", לַגֵּר as referring to resident aliens[65] – and since the context is human behaviour towards those one meets in one's daily life, this may well be so – but the fact that "love", אָהֵב, is extended by God not only to Israel (v.15) but also to the resident alien is a sign that it extends farther than God's elected people might have supposed. God's love is more than impartiality between the claims of his people and those of the stranger – God loves both, without distinction. Vv. 17-18 do not connote God as a judicial figure sitting in judgement: rather is God a ruler, granting help to the weak and poor.[66]

In v.19 we find the crowning human obligation to "love", אָהֵב, the "stranger" or "sojourner", גֵּר,[67] precisely *because* the Israelites, to whom the command is addressed, were "strangers", גֵּרִים, in the land of Egypt: needy, vulnerable outsiders.[68] Strangers were vulnerable, being unprotected by clan and family,[69] and if unprotected may end up as slaves, as indeed the Israelites did in their Egyptian captivity.[70] Hence the command not to do them harm, indeed to love them, *as God does* (v.18). This command is ultimately grounded in the Covenant relationship established by God (Exodus 22:21-24, and see Leviticus 19:33-34, noted above).[71] Here, instructions for worship and service of God are inseparable.[72]

Lapsley takes up the connection which we have seen in Deuteronomy 10:12-22 between God's love, אָהֵב, and justice, rightly suggesting that the command in v.16 to "circumcise the foreskin of your heart" is needed, not only because of God's sovereignty and majesty, but because of God's concern for justice: the love shown by God in this way manifests itself, not only in practical concern for food and clothing for "strangers", but in deep and empathic love for them.[73] Israel must love the stranger (v.19), firstly because God does: the controlling factor in Deuteronomy 10:12-23 in understanding the five occurrences of אָהֵב is the nature of *God's* love.[74] She then suggests perceptively that the second motivation to love the stranger in v.19, the remembrance that the Israelites themselves were strangers in Egypt, does not operate through intellectual

---

[63] Weinfeld, *Deuteronomy*, 32.
[64] *Ibid*, 439; similarly SR Driver, *A Critical and Exegetical Commentary on Deuteronomy* (Edinburgh: T&T Clark, 1902), 126; Walter Brueggemann, *Deuteronomy* (Nashville: Abingdon Press, 2001), 130–1.
[65] Jeffrey H Tigay, *Deuteronomy* (Philadelphia: Jewish Publication Society, 1996), 108.
[66] Weinfeld, *Deuteronomy 1-11*, 439; similarly Brueggemann, *Deuteronomy*, 131; Peter Craigie, *The Book of Deuteronomy* (Grand Rapids, Michigan: Eerdmans, 1976), 207.
[67] Driver, *Deuteronomy*, 126; ADH Mayes, *Deuteronomy* (Grand Rapids: Eerdmans/London: Marshall, Morgan & Scott Publ. Ltd., 1979), 211.
[68] Brueggemann, *Deuteronomy*, 131.
[69] Weinfeld, *Deuteronomy 1-11*, 440.
[70] Brueggemann, *Deuteronomy*, 131.
[71] Ray Carlton Jones, "Deuteronomy 10:12-22", *Int* 46.3 (1992): 281–5, 283.
[72] Beth Laneel Tanner, "Deuteronomy 10:2-22", *Int* 55.1 (2001): 60–3, 62.
[73] Jacqueline E Lapsley, "Feeling Our Way: Love for God in Deuteronomy", *CBQ* 65.3 (2003): 350–69, 361.
[74] *Ibid*, 362.

recall alone: the empathic response required to the "stranger" in Israel is part of an emotional identification with the stranger.[75] This may be the corollary of the injunction to "love", אָהֵב, God with all one's heart and soul (v.12), with which this passage begins, and which is its mainspring.

Vogt proposes that because the alien, widow and orphan are *never* referred to as "poor" in Deuteronomy, nor bracketed with them (cf. Zechariah 7:10), they are considered to be people who, like the Levites, are ordinarily landless, and are to be integrated fully into the life of the nation: like the Levites, they were to serve as a "barometer" of the nation's obedience.[76] This is convincing, and consistent with Deuteronomy 10:18-19: *God* loves the "stranger", גֵּר. This imposes a direct, divinely ordained obligation for Israel also to do so – it is not a matter of charity, but of a *duty* to give the stranger, the alien within its gates, loving support.

This intimate connection between the command to love the stranger in Deuteronomy 10:19 and God's own love of the stranger in 10:18 is reinforced by vv.20-22 following it, in which we see Israel commanded to fear the Lord, to worship him alone and to swear by his name, because he is their praise, and their God who has done great and awesome things which their own eyes have seen, so that from their seventy ancestors who went down to Egypt, God has made them as numerous as the stars in heaven. This vivid religious poetry makes it crystal clear that the obligation to love strangers in v.19 is of a piece with the rest of their worship – God loved them, and so must Israel love the strangers in their midst.

The term "brother", אָח, is not found in Deuteronomy 10:12-23, but it is used repeatedly in Deuteronomy 15:1-11, not in the sense of "male sibling" but of "fellow Israelite". Here, as we shall see, there is strong emphasis on the obligation of generosity to the needy brother, used in this sense – but here, we shall also see, it does not extend to the נָכְרִי, "foreigner".[77]

Deuteronomy 15, as part of the Deuteronomic Code, stands on a secular foundation: dealing with loans and debts, it stands with other chapters dealing, at least in part, with secular themes, such as chapters 16 (the judiciary), 17 (the monarchy), 20 (the military), 21, 22 and 24 (the family and inheritance), 25 (litigation and quarrels), and 19 (trespassing and false testimony): in this, says Weinfeld, it "stands in contrast to the Priestly document".[78] We shall limit our study here, for reasons of space, to Deuteronomy 15:1-11, mandating particular obligations to the אָח, "brother".

This unit begins with laws concerning the "Sabbatical year", occurring every seven years. It imposes an obligation in vv.1-2 to remit debts every seven years against a אָח, "brother", but v.2 extends this obligation also בְּרֵעֵהוּ, "to his fellow/neighbour". Tigay sees אָח and רֵעַ as equivalent terms, "fellow, that is, kinsman", comparing this verse with v.12, where, he says, "fellow Hebrew" is literally "Hebrew kinsman".[79] Brueggemann

---

[75] *Ibid*, 363.
[76] Peter T Vogt, "Social Justice and the Vision of Deuteronomy", *JETS* 51.1 (2008): 35–44, 38, 39.
[77] See 15:3, and note also 23:20.
[78] Moshe Weinfeld, *Deuteronomy and the Deuteronomic School* (Oxford: Oxford University Press, 1972), 188.
[79] Tigay, *Deuteronomy*, 146.

sees both categories as signifying "fellow members of the covenanted community", that is Israel.[80] Are these obligations to the brother, אָח, and "fellow", רֵעַ, limited to fellow Israelites? We have noted the permission in v.3 to exact a debt, rather than remitting it in the Sabbatical year, against a נָכְרִי, "foreigner". In Deuteronomy נָכְרִי, "foreigner", does not necessarily carry the same idea as "alien", גֵּר: Deuteronomy 14:21[81] makes this clear.[82] In Deuteronomy 15:1-18 can a גֵּר, "alien" still be an אָח, "brother" or a רֵעַ, "fellow or neighbour"? This is best answered by looking at the context in which אָח and רֵעַ appear in this unit.

In vv.4-6 we read that in fact there will be no-one in need among the Israelites because the Lord is sure to bless them in the land in which they have divine permission to live, if only they obey the whole command given them. We read that when the Lord their God has blessed them as promised, they will give birth to many nations, but will not borrow, but rather rule over many nations, who will in turn not rule over the Israelites. In face of such a protean promise to the Israelites, if they obey God, who among them could be in need? But in vv.7-8 we find the command to the Israelites that if any אָחִיךָ, "brother of you", who is בְּךָ, "among you", is in need, they should not be hard-hearted or "tight" with them, but should open their hands, willingly.[83] Who is the אָח here? Certainly not the "foreigner", נָכְרִי. Such a person passes through Israel, and is not integrated into the community, and is not recommended as the subject of Deuteronomic charity here.[84] Such a one could not be said to be בְּךָ, "among you", that is the Israelites. Surely it is not likely that in strict exegetical terms the command here includes the "alien", גֵּר, in view of the inclusion of this term with "foreigner", נָכְרִי in Deuteronomy 14:28?[85]

However Driver, an earlier but much-respected commentator, suggests that the *spirit* in which these verses are conceived is in accord with the philanthropic motive apparent elsewhere in Deuteronomy,[86] and that possibly vv.7-11 are meant to apply *generally*: "the prospect of a reduced income in the near future is not to check the Israelite's liberality towards any that solicit from him pecuniary aid".[87] This finds little favour among more modern commentators, but may gain some support from Deuteronomy 10:18 where we find side by side God's justice for the orphan and widow and provision of food and clothing for the "stranger" or "alien", גֵּר. As noted above, to Weinfeld, the wording of 10:18 signifies that God also gives justice to (i.e. makes just provision for) the stranger.[88]

---

[80] Brueggemann, *Deuteronomy*, 164.
[81] "You shall not eat anything that has died a natural death: give it to the stranger or to the foreigner".
[82] Mayes, *Deuteronomy*, 248.
[83] Tigay, *Deuteronomy*, 147.
[84] Mayes, *Deuteronomy*, 248.
[85] Anthony Phillips, *Deuteronomy* (Cambridge: Cambridge University Press, 1973), 104; similarly Tigay, *Deuteronomy*, 147; RE Clements, *Deuteronomy* (Sheffield: JSOT Press, 1993), 56; Patrick D Miller, *Deuteronomy* (Louisville: John Knox Press, 1990), 136.
[86] Driver, *Deuteronomy*, 180.
[87] Ibid, 181.
[88] Weinfeld, *Deuteronomy 1-11*, 439; similarly Driver, *Deuteronomy*, 126; Brueggemann, *Deuteronomy*, 130-1.

In v.9 we find a dire warning not to think meanly that the seventh year is approaching, and therefore be hostile towards one's needy אָח, "brother", giving them nothing, lest they cry out to the Lord, so one incurs guilt. The idea is that guilt builds and leads to punishment, as merit leads to reward; cf. 6:25.[89] Finally, in vv.10-11 we find a correlative assurance that generous and ungrudging giving leads to divine blessing, and a command to Israelites to open their hand to the poor and needy אָח, "brother", in their land, where there will always be needy people. In the end, it would seem an over-strict exegesis of the text here to suppose that its generous benefactions are not to extend at least to the גֵּר, the resident alien. The theme of brotherhood serves Deuteronomy's deeper concern that Israel respond properly to God's generosity towards it.[90] An obligation to respond by "open-handed" giving (v.11) to the גֵּר, the resident alien, too, best fits with this theology.

To Von Rad, from the first sentence to the last, Deuteronomy in its preaching is concerned to "make the old cultic and legal traditions relevant for their time".[91] The law of remission (Deuteronomy 15:1-2) does not have social or economic roots: it is a *sacral* obligation.[92] The lawgiver, once the apodictic command in 15:1-2 is given, turns to preaching: the recipient of the law must realise that it is not the law which drove them to adopt an anti-social attitude to the poor.[93] Lapsley, following Anderson, rightly criticises Von Rad's approach as appealing to a higher "spiritual" love of God, and as exemplifying a tendency in Christian scholarship to characterise the Jewish scriptures as containing "overly punctilious behavioural norms".[94] Von Rad's exegesis of 15:1-11 does miss the intimate connection between vv.1-2 and 3-11: remission of debt is as much an expression of open-handed, divinely commanded generosity as is giving to one's needy brother. Deuteronomy 15:1-2 is as much an expression of the "secular foundation"[95] of the Deuteronomic Code as is 15:3-11.

To sum up, Deuteronomy 15:1-11 is a seamless series of commands to the Israelites based on divine concern for the debt-ridden and needy. It is based on pure human obligation, even though it warns of divine justice, at the behest of the spurned brother, if its injunctions are ignored (v.9). The "brother", אָח, is probably not limited to the full citizen of Israel: it may well include the resident alien. The mainspring of this obligation is supplied by 15:7: as God has given his people the land in which their towns are situated and they ought not therefore be themselves "hard-hearted" or "tight-fisted", so in 15:8 are they commanded, in love and obedience, to respond to the needy and powerless in their own land with generous giving which is "open-handed". The wording of 15:8, פָּתֹחַ תִּפְתַּח אֶת־יָדְךָ, literally "hand of you, you open", contrasted in 15:7 by תִקְפֹּץ אֶת־יָדְךָ, literally "fist of you, you tighten", is so powerful that it has spawned the modern

---

[89] Tigay, *Deuteronomy*, 147; Brueggemann, *Deuteronomy*, 166.
[90] JG McConville, *Deuteronomy* (Sheffield: JSOT Press, 1984), 19.
[91] Gerhard Von Rad, *Deuteronomy* (London: SCM Press, 1966), 23.
[92] *Ibid*, 105.
[93] *Ibid*, 106.
[94] Lapsley, "Feeling Our Way", 365, quoting Gary Anderson, *A Time to Mourn, a Time to Dance: The Expression of Grief and Joy in Israelite Religion* (University Park, PA: Pennsylvania State University Press, 1991), 54.
[95] Weinfeld, *Deuteronomy and the Deuteronomic School*, 188.

opposing phrases, "open handed" and "tight fisted". Deuteronomy 15:1-11 links Israel's generosity to their poorer brothers with their relationship with God. Israel's obligation to be generous is reciprocal: as God has been generous to them, so must they be to the needy brother.

Possible Influence of Leviticus and Deuteronomy on 1 John

Often in 1 John we find ἀγαπάω used, and apart from John's Gospel, 1 John uses this term more frequently than any other book in the NT. Ἀγάπη also occurs very frequently in 1 John, and is used more frequently there than in any other NT text, including John's Gospel, and similarly, ἀδελφός is found very frequently in 1 John.

Again it is worth repeating that that the LXX was available to, and used by, Greek-speaking first-century Christians, including the Johannine community, and the Johannine literature contains specific LXX citations,[96] so one may suggest that the author of 1 John had various LXX uses of ἀγαπάω and ἀδελφός well in mind. Again we note that in the LXX the Hebrew verb אהב, "love" is translated in Leviticus 19:11-18 and in Deuteronomy 10:12-22 by ἀγαπάω, and in Leviticus 19:11-18 and in Deuteronomy 15:1-11, the noun אח, "brother", is translated as ἀδελφός. Might the usage and context of these Hebrew words and their Greek equivalents, and the ideas underlying them, cast light on the ideas conveyed by their Greek equivalents as used in 1 John? Again Barr's warning must be heeded, that while it is often essential to undertake comparative etymological study to unlock the meaning of Hebrew words, etymology cannot impose a meaning on known usage of Hebrew terms: thus theologically attractive etymological associations cannot assume command of the whole task of interpretation.[97] This is even more so when we trace the recurrence of LXX words in a NT context, noting the very different situation and context in which the Greek terms ἀγαπάω and ἀδελφός are used in 1 John.

Still, the basal principle in 1 John 4:11,[98] with its καθώς theology, its imitation of God as a basis for ethics, is close in thought to Leviticus 19:2 and Deuteronomy 10:18-19, discussed above, and also Deuteronomy 15:15.[99] Thus οὕτως, "so", in 1 John 4:11 has a double meaning: not only should you love one another *in the same way* as God has loved us, but also we must do so *because* God loved you so much.[100] The idea in Deuteronomy 10:18-19 is similar: you were strangers in Egypt, so you must love the stranger, *because* God loves the stranger, and also *in the same way*.

---

[96] Law, *When God Spoke Greek*, 102, 114.
[97] Barr, *Semantics of Biblical Language*, 158–9.
[98] "My beloved ones, if God so loved us, we also ought to love one another".
[99] David L Baker, *Tight Fists or Open Hands? Wealth and Poverty in Old Testament Law* (Grand Rapids, Michigan/Cambridge UK: Eerdmans, 2009), 214 n.54. Deuteronomy 15:15 may be translated "remember you were a slave in the land of Egypt, and the Lord your God redeemed you: this is why I am giving you this command today".
[100] Painter, *1, 2, and 3 John*, 270.

First John has its own pericope devoted to mutual love, 3:11-24. One may profitably look at the ideas of love and brotherhood developed in this unit alongside their use in Leviticus 19:17-18 and in Deuteronomy 10:12-23 and 15:1-11, using the Hebrew אָהֵב and אָח, rendered both in the LXX and in 1 John by ἀγαπάω and ἀδελφός.

Comparing Leviticus 19 and 1 John 3:11-22, we find in both texts *halakah*, instructions for daily living, interspersed and interconnected with theological material, *haggadah*, in which God's ways towards humankind as set out in scripture are interpreted and explained. In Leviticus 19:18b the Hebrew verb אָהֵב is rendered in the LXX by the Greek verb ἀγαπάω – the same verb we find in the many citations in 1 John listed at the beginning of this chapter. The Hebrew עָמִיר , "neighbour", in Leviticus 19:18 becomes πλησίον in the LXX. Although love of the "neighbour", πλησίον is not found as a command in 1 John, might it be that the command to love one another in 1 John 3:13 is not necessarily inconsistent with this idea?

We find in 1 John 3:11 the message heard from the beginning, that we must love one another, ἀγαπῶμεν ἀλλήλους. Leviticus 19:18[101] contains the classical OT command to love one's neighbour. We have traced the arguments that the command in 19:18 to show love "to your neighbour", לְרֵעֶךָ, is extended in 19:34 to הַגֵּר, "the alien". Might they apply to the love command in 1 John 3:13? Such a proposition appears tenuous. 1 John displays remarkable hostility to sectarian opponents, those who "went out from us" (2:19). Their slogans are repeatedly condemned (cf. 1:8, 4:20) and they are characterised as ἐκ τοῦ κόσμου, "from the world" (4:5). Moreover, τὰ ἐν τῷ κόσμῳ, "the things of the world" are condemned as unworthy of love (2:15-17). And the secessionists themselves are characterised as ἀντίχριστοι, "antichrists" (2:18). First John is structured around a series of "tests of life", each of which involves rejecting the teaching of the secessionists by refuting their slogans.[102] How could a faithful Christian love the opponents in 1 John?

But as Painter writes, true it is that we do not find any injunction to love one's neighbour, as distinct from one's brother, in 1 John, but the epistle affirms that God's love is for the *world*, ὁ κόσμος, and God's will is to save it (1 John 2:2, 4:14; cf. John 3:16; 4:42; 17:20-26; 20:21).[103] First John 2:15-17 does *not* require hatred of those who are not believers: it expresses a clash of values within the believers' community in relation to "the world".[104] But hatred of the world *itself* is not commanded. How could it be? Jesus is the expiation, not only of the sins of the believers, but of those of *the whole world* (2:2), and the Father has sent the Son as saviour of *the world* (4:14). But shot through the epistle is hostility to the things of the world, its impermanence and hatred, over which Jesus must triumph (2:15-17; 3:1, 13, 17; 4:1, 3, 4, 5, 17; 5:4, 5, 19).

---

[101] "You shall not take vengeance or bear a grudge against any of the sons of your people, but you should love your neighbour as yourself: I am the Lord".
[102] Law, *Tests of Life*, 5–6; similarly Dodd, *Johannine Epistles*, xxxiv; Schnackenburg, *Johannine Epistles*, 70–1; Smalley, *1, 2, 3 John*, xxxi; Brown, *Epistles of John*, 92–3; Painter, *1, 2, and 3 John*, 3–6; Grayston, *Johannine Epistles*, 14–18; Marshall, *Epistles of John*, 15–16; Stott, *Letters of John*, 44–7.
[103] Painter, *1, 2, and 3 John*, 182.
[104] Ibid. Similarly Popkes sees John as not founding a sectarian grouping, but rather restoring the faith and love of his community despite a grave breakdown: see EE Popkes, *Die Theologie der Liebe Gottes in den johanneischen Schriften* (Tübingen: Mohr Siebeck, 2005), 136–61.

In 1 John, ὁ κόσμος is regarded ambiguously. The world might hate the believer (3:13), but that does not require reciprocal hatred of the world by the believer – far from it. The author's response is counterintuitive: far from hating the world in return, his community is enjoined to *love* one another.

Certainly in 1 John 3:11 the author's main concern is ensuring solidarity within the believing community against the secessionists by mutual love. But this is not inconsistent with God's wish that the world – including the secessionists – be saved by the gift of the Son as ἱλασμός, the expiation (2:2, 4:10) for its sin. Love of the neighbour, πλησίον is not found as a command in 1 John. Even so, the command to love one another in 1 John 3:13 is not necessarily inconsistent with this idea.

In Leviticus 19:17,[105] hating a brother is prohibited, which is of course the same idea as one finds in 1 John 3:15, where hatred of a brother is equated to murder. In Leviticus 19:17 the Hebrew אָח, "brother", there is rendered in the LXX by ἀδελφός, and שָׂנֵא, "hate" by μισέω, the same Greek words as are used in 1 John 3:15. The idea appears similar, except for the identification of hatred with murder.[106] But who is the ἀδελφός, "brother", in 1 John 3:15, whom one must not hate? The equation with Cain, who murdered his brother, in 3:12 (discussed in Chapter 4, above) suggests one who is close, and possibly the author is referring in 3:15 to the secessionists' failure to love their (former) brothers,[107] perhaps before they left.[108]

But the converse does not necessarily apply: 1 John 3:15 does not contain a command to hate the secessionists *themselves*. Could it be that the secessionist is still an ἀδελφός in 3:15, whom the believers must not hate? Against this is the reference in 2:19 to those who "went out from us" and hence did not "belong to us". But 3:15 can still be read as teaching against hatred of *former* brothers, while remaining hostile to the ideas they propagate: certainly it does not *require* such hatred. Condemnation of hatred by the Cain analogy in 3:12 and identification of hatred with murder in 3:15 are so strong that they are not to be read as mere condemnation of the secessionists' attitude to those who remain in the community. The idea is that *all* hatred is corrosive, and has drastic consequences, and is at *all* times to be avoided. It can be argued that 1 John does not counsel hatred of the secessionists, and may even condemn it. But as there is no command to love "the stranger" or "the alien", גֵּר – translated by the LXX as προσήλυτον in Leviticus 19:34 – in 1 John 3:13-24, it still appears unlikely that the command ἀγαπῶμεν ἀλλήλους, "we must love one another", in 1 John 3:11 is universal – if only because ἀλλήλους must be taken to refer only to the writer's community.

What of the possible influence of Deuteronomy 10:12-22 and 15:1-11 in 1 John 2:11-24? In 1 John 1:1 we find a declaration to the reader of what was *from the beginning*, ἀπ' ἀρχῆς, and in 3:11 we learn of the message heard *from the beginning*, ἀπ' ἀρχῆς, that we should love one another. This is virtually a copy of 1:5, where we read of the

---

[105] "You shall not hate your brother in your heart: you shall reprove your neighbour, or you will incur guilt yourself".
[106] Grayston, *Johannine Epistles*, 113.
[107] Brown, *Epistles of John*, 472–3.
[108] Smalley, *1, 2, 3 John*, 190.

message we have heard ἀπ' αὐτοῦ, from "him" (referring to his Son Jesus Christ: 1:3).[109] This expression is found eight times in 1 John (1:1; 2:7, 13, 14, 24 (twice); 3:8, 11) and is ambiguous: among other things, it may refer to ἡ ἐντολὴ, "the commandment" (2:7) or to ἡ ἀγγελία, "the message" (3:11) heard ἀπ' ἀρχῆς, "from the beginning".[110] For Schnackenburg, the emphatic solemnity of the message, ἀγγελία here takes on the meaning of a commandment.[111] As noted above, Barker writes that the commands of Deuteronomy 10:12-22 cancel out the Golden Calf incident and are a reinstatement of the *Shema*; they are a full renewal of Israel's covenant after her sin.[112] In a similar way, 1 John 1:1, in a clear echo of the Prologue in John 1:1,[113] restates God's revelation τοῦ λόγου τῆς ζωῆς, "of the word of life", which we have heard ἀπ' ἀρχῆς, *from the beginning*, and similarly 1 John 3:11 reinstates a commandment heard ἀπ' ἀρχῆς, *from the beginning*, that we must love one another. There are Deuteronomic echoes in the use of ἐντολὴ, "commandment" in 2:7, which becomes the ἀγγελία, "message" in 3:11, to love one another. The idea of a commandment is *covenantal* – to love because we are loved: since God loved us so much, we ought to love one another (4:11). Porousness is a characteristic of the way love functions in interpersonal relationships: love flowing from God "passes through" the believer to others, and is a way or returning love to God.[114] That same mainspring of the love commands in Deuteronomy 10, divine love, occurs at 10:15, that God set God's heart on the people's ancestors alone. Similarly the mainspring of the love commands in Deuteronomy 15 is divine love, at 15:15, that God redeemed the people, who were slaves in the land of Egypt.

What of the possible influence of the command in Deuteronomy 10:18-19 to love "the stranger", הַגֵּר, in 1 John 3:13-24? In Deuteronomy 10:18 God is portrayed as giving justice to the orphan and the widow, and loving the stranger, and in 10:19 the Israelites are commanded likewise to love the stranger, as they were strangers in the land of Egypt. In 1 John 3:16, we find a similar idea of imitative love: Jesus laid down his life for us, and we ought to lay down our lives for one another. But we must still ask, how can the ἀδελφός, the object of the love enjoined in 1 John 3:16, include "the stranger", הַגֵּר, of Deuteronomy 10:18-19 (translated by the LXX as προσήλυτον) or even the secessionists who are not strangers, but known opponents?

There is another possible parallel between Deuteronomy 10:19 and 1 John beyond our pericope, 1 John 3:11-24. In that Deuteronomy 10:19 is intimately connected to 10:15, where we are told that God set the divine heart in love on Israel's ancestors, one might compare it to 1 John 4:7a where we are commanded to "love one another, because love is from God". In the same way, 1 John 3:23-24a commands that its audience *remember* that as God's commandment is that we believe in God's Son and love one another, so all who obey God's commandments abide in him. As noted in Chapter 4, Thatcher argues (in the context of the Cain reference at 1 John 3:12) that

---

[109] Brown, *Epistles of John*, 440.
[110] Painter, *1, 2, and 3 John*, 120, 237.
[111] Schnackenburg, *Johannine Epistles*, 178.
[112] Barker, *The Triumph of Grace in Deuteronomy*, 103.
[113] Smalley, *1, 2, 3 John*, 4.
[114] Van der Watt, "On Ethics in 1 John", 217.

"early Christians embraced and extended the premises of the Septuagint reading when applying Genesis 4 to current experience".¹¹⁵ In a similar way, the command at 1 John 3:23-24a may well be a recollection and reapplication of Deuteronomy 10:19 to the current circumstances of the author's divided community.

Coming to possible parallels between Deuteronomy 15:1-11 and 1 John 3:11-24, the "brother", אח, in Deuteronomy 15:1-11 is probably not limited to the full citizen of Israel: it may well include the resident alien, גר. But the difference is that in 1 John, there is no command to love the "stranger" or "alien", גר, translated by the LXX as προσήλυτον, in 1 John 3:13-24 – or anywhere else. In the absence of such an indication, it may appear difficult to argue on purely *exegetical* grounds that the command ἀγαπῶμεν ἀλλήλους, "we must love one another", in 1 John 3:11 extends to humanity generally, as its use by peacemaking theologians would suggest.

In 1 John 3:17 we find a rhetorical question: how does God's love abide in one who has the world's goods and, seeing a brother, ἀδελφός in need, refuses help? In Deuteronomy 15:7-8 we find a similar command to the Israelites that if any אח, "brother", among them in any of their towns in the land their God is giving them is in need, they should not be hard-hearted or "tight" with them, but should open their hands, willingly. Indeed, as we have seen, in Deuteronomy 15:9 we find a dire warning not to think meanly that the seventh year is approaching, and therefore be hostile towards one's needy אח, "brother", giving them nothing, lest they cry out to the Lord, so one incurs guilt. This is a very similar idea to that in 1 John 3:17, that God's love does not abide in a person who refuses help to the needy brother.

The verb μένειν, "remain", "stay", "abide", used in the rhetorical question in 1 John 3:17, is used earlier in this same pericope in 3:14 to build a crucial antithesis: ἡμεῖς οἴδαμεν ὅτι μεταβεβήκαμεν ἐκ τοῦ θανάτου εἰς τὴν ζωήν, ὅτι ἀγαπῶμεν τοὺς ἀδελφούς· ὁ μὴ a ἀγαπῶν μένει ἐν τῷ θανάτῳ, "we know that we have crossed over from death to life because we love one another, but one who does not love abides in death". It may be that the author is thinking in 3:14c of the secessionists, who are not real believers and so do not gain eternal life.¹¹⁶ But the implied threat in 1 John 3:17 is that one who refuses help to the needy brother, that is fails to love him, abides in death (3:14). And in Deuteronomy 15:9 the cry of the needy brother to the Lord, if he is given nothing, condemns whoever fails to give to a similar fate: divine wrath.

First John 3:18, requiring love in truth and acts, is also in similar vein to Deuteronomy 15:9: the thought in both verses is that what matters to God is the practical demonstration of love, not mere profession. In Deuteronomy 15:9 failure to give, not mere failure to love, is condemned. Similarly, in 1 John 3:18 the author enjoins active, continuing love for needy brothers.¹¹⁷ But in 3:17 the ἀδελφός, "brother", is not necessarily the same person as the אח, "brother", in Deuteronomy 15:9. Again it needs emphasis that there is no indication in 1 John that this concept includes the προσήλυτον, "alien" or "stranger", of Deuteronomy in the LXX.

---

[115] Thatcher, "Cain the Jew the Antichrist", 367.
[116] Brown, *Epistles of John*, 446.
[117] Painter, *1, 2, and 3 John*, 236.

Furthermore, the promise of divine blessing for generous giving to the needy brother in Deuteronomy 15:10 expresses a similar thought to 1 John 3:19-20.[118] It is that if we are generous in love, which involves giving to the needy brother (3:17), we will receive reassurance from God, who knows all. In 3:19, the sentence beginning ἐν τούτῳ does not merely refer back to 3:18, but is a summary of the teaching about the love command at 3:10-18.[119] The end result of love, which implies giving generously, is divine reassurance.

The promise of divine blessing for generous giving to the needy brother in Deuteronomy 15:10 is similar to 1 John 3:19-20[120]: if we are generous in love, which involves giving to the needy brother (3:17), we will receive reassurance from God, who knows all. Both texts tie divine blessing to love in action towards one's fellow.

Conclusion

We have seen that the author of 1 John was probably steeped in Judaism. The style and theology of the letter demonstrate a high degree of Jewish influence, even though it cites the OT only once (the Cain analogy in 3:15), and probably its audience, though not predominantly Jewish, was steeped in the Jewish scriptures. So it is legitimate to look at how two of 1 John's major themes, love and brotherhood, as represented by the words ἀγάπη and ἀδελφος, are treated in three OT passages where the Hebrew equivalents of these LXX words occur, and to ask whether there is similarity in the ideas conveyed by these words in 1 John 3:11-24, the pericope dealing particularly with the need for mutual love of the brother, but remembering the very different situation addressed by 1 John as compared to the three OT texts examined in this chapter. Again it is worth repeating that the LXX was available to, and used by, Greek-speaking first-century Christians, including the Johannine community, and the Johannine literature contains specific LXX citations,[121] so that 1 John's author may well have had LXX uses of ἀδελφός in mind.

There is little doubt that, even exegetically, Leviticus 19:17-18 and Deuteronomy 10:11-19 and 15:1-11 broadly support the theology in each of the citations from peacemaking theologians at the beginning of this study. Leviticus 19:17 contains a direct command not to hate the brother, אָח, *in one's heart*, which requires a change in motivation, not merely attitude, so violence can be stemmed at its source. Leviticus 19:18 enjoins love, אָהַב (ἀγάπη in the LXX) of the neighbour, עָמִית (πλησίον in the LXX) as oneself. Leviticus 19:34 also requires love of the (resident) alien, גֵּר (προσήλυτον in the LXX) as oneself, even though it is not clear that the neighbour, עָמִית, includes the (resident) alien, גֵּר. So too Deuteronomy 10:19, for example, with its command to love

---

[118] "And by this we will know we are in the truth and it will encourage our hearts before him whenever they condemn us; for God is greater than our hearts, and God knows all things".
[119] Smalley, *1, 2, 3 John*, 200.
[120] "And by this we will know we are in the truth and it will encourage our hearts before him whenever they condemn us; for God is greater than our hearts, and God knows all things".
[121] Law, *When God Spoke Greek*, 102, 114.

the alien or stranger, גֵר, *because* the Israelites too were strangers in Egypt (from which God rescued them) clearly enjoins imitative, undiscriminating love, as a reflection of God's own love. As another example, Deuteronomy 15:9-11 warns against denial of the needs of the brother, אָח, lest they cry out to God and bring down guilt on the ungenerous one, and promises divine blessing on the generous giver, and commands open-handed giving. The brother, אָח, may well extend at least to the resident alien, גֵר. The central themes of Leviticus and Deuteronomy in the units surveyed above are, broadly speaking, the need for undiscriminating love, manifested in deeds, in generous giving to those in need, prompted by God's generosity to needy Israel.

Some of these themes reappear in 1 John 3:11-24. Certainly in 1 John 4:11, outside the present unit, there is a καθώς theology, that we must love each other *because* God loves us and *in the same way* as God loves us – just as Deuteronomy 10:18-19 enjoins love of the stranger *because* God loved the people of Israel and delivered them from Egypt. Leviticus 19:18 enjoins love of the neighbour, πλησίον in the LXX – a word not found in 1 John 3:11-24, or elsewhere in the epistle. Instead love for the brother, ἀδελφός is enjoined. Alison, Schwager and Yoder rightly see love for one another in imitation of God's love as a cornerstone of 1 John, but love for the ἀδελφός, brother, in 1 John does not extend to the πλησίον, neighbour, in strict exegetical terms. But in the very different situation we today, of human hostility, not so much intracommunal as national and international, with civil and international war breaking out everywhere, and with refugee flows to more fortunate societies such as our own, is it perhaps legitimate to interpret it hermeneutically in that way?

Certainly 1 John is hostile to the doctrines of the secessionists, the "antichrists" who "went out from us" (2:19), but it does not require hatred of them – its response is rather to embrace mutual love. It proclaims God's Son Jesus Christ as the atoning sacrifice for the sins, not only of the community but of the *whole* world (2:2), and it also affirms that the Father has sent the Son into the world that we might live through him (4:9) who is saviour of the world (4:14). But throughout the epistle we find hostility to the things of the world, its impermanence and hatred of believers, over which Jesus must triumph (2:15-17; 3:1, 13, 17; 4:1, 3, 4, 5, 17; 5:4, 5, 19).

So ὁ κόσμος in 1 John is ambiguous – God loves the world, but not its evils and hostility, and it is over these that Christ must win victory – not its inhabitants, who are included in God's saving love. So the love for one another, enjoined in 1 John 4:7, is *in consequence* of God's love (4:11) – as it is in Deuteronomy 10:18-19. It is natural, given that it is written against the secessionist's errors, as the epistle sees it, that it promotes love, internal solidarity within its community as an antidote to secessionist hostility and division – but the secessionists themselves are not the object of hatred: instead, that is to be avoided. If hatred is the sin of the secessionists, nothing is gained by compounding evil and hating them in return.

First John 3:17, with its command to help the brother, ἀδελφός in need is paralleled in Deuteronomy 15:1-11, with its requirement of "open-handed" giving to the needy brother, אָח, who may include the resident alien, גֵר. In both texts the requirement is theological, and intimately connected with God's attitude to the giver (3:17).

Many scholars now doubt the "Baur consensus" that John's Gospel has little historical value. A convenient summary of that view for present purposes is by Ernst

Haenchen.[122] For a more recent exposition of this view, one may note, for example, Bultmann's famous statements that John "does not consider the task of the Church's proclamation to be the transmitting of the historical tradition about Jesus", and that "John, that is, in his Gospel presents only the fact (das Dass) of the Revelation without describing its content (ihr Wass)".[123]

However many scholars now think that both the narrative and the discourse material in John's Gospel contain some good, early tradition. Dodd sought "a clear and well based conception of the historical facts upon which our religion is founded" from John's Gospel, demonstrating that it is largely not dependent on the Synoptics, but rather on independent, early tradition.[124] This may be so, even though the discourses display Johannine literary style.[125] Moody Smith has written a good, brief summary of Dodd's contribution,[126] as has Koester.[127] Dunn adopts a position not dissimilar to Dodd.[128] More recently Keith has proposed social memory theory, over against the earlier dichotomy proposed by Bultmann and others between the "Jesus of history" and the "Christ of faith", as the only feasible explanation of the manner in which the early church arrived at its picture of the historical Jesus.[129] A full summary and evaluation of this debate are beyond the scope of this study. But it is fair to say that scholarly opinion nowadays tends not to favour a separation between the "Jesus of history" and the "Christ of faith", and to favour the view that John's Gospel does contain (some) good historical material about the sayings and personality of Jesus.

---

[122] Ernst Haenchen, *John 1* (trans. Robert W Funk; Philadelphia: Fortress Press, 1984), 26–37; see also D Moody Smith, *John among the Gospels* (Columbia: University of South Carolina Press, 2nd ed., 2001), 13–15.

[123] Rudolf Bultmann, *New Testament Theology*, Vol II (trans. Kendrick Grobel; London: SCM Press, 1955), 66, 69.

[124] CH Dodd, *Historical Tradition in the Fourth Gospel* (Cambridge: Cambridge University Press, 1963), 432.

[125] As Painter puts it, "here the distinctive nature of the teaching of Jesus in John matches that of the narrator or evangelist, and Jesus speaks the language of the primary human witness to Jesus": John Painter, "The Signs of the Messiah and the Quest for Eternal Life" in *What We Have Heard from the Beginning: The Past, Present and Future of Johannine Studies* (ed. Tom Thatcher; Waco: Baylor University Press, 2007), 233–6, 238.

[126] Moody Smith, *John among the Gospels*, 53–61.

[127] Craig Koester, "Progress and Paradox: CH Dodd and Rudolf Bultmann on History, the Jesus Tradition and the Fourth Gospel" in *Engaging with CH Dodd on the Gospel of John* (ed. Tom Thatcher and Catlin H Williams; Cambridge/New York: Cambridge University Press, 2013), 49–65.

[128] James DG Dunn, *Jesus Remembered* (Grand Rapids/Cambridge: Eerdmans, 2003), 166-7; for a fuller summary of the evidence Dunn marshalls see James DG Dunn, "John and the Oral Gospel Tradition" in *Jesus and the Oral Gospel Tradition* (ed. H Wansbrough; Sheffield: JSOT, 1991) 351–79; see also FJ Moloney, "The Fourth Gospel and the Jesus of History", *NTS* 46 (2000): 42–58, 42–4; John Painter, "The Farewell Discourses and the Jesus of History", *NTS* 7 (1981): 526–43.

[129] Chris Keith, "The Narratives of the Gospels and the Historical Jesus: Current Debates, Prior Debates the Goal of Historical Jesus Research", *JSNT* 38, 4 (2016): 426–55. For a presentation of the manner in which John portrays the "canonical Christ" see also Chris Keith, "Introduction" in *Jesus among Friends and Enemies: A Historical and Literary Introduction to Jesus in the Gospels* (ed. Chris Keith and Larry W Hurtado, Grand Rapids: Baker Academic, 2011), 1–34, 27–9. However Keith ultimately concludes that the "Pericope Adulterae" at 8.1–11 in John's Gospel was most likely inserted by a later redactor to establish Jesus' literacy: Chris Keith, *The Pericope Adulterae, the Gospel of John and the Literacy of Jesus* (Leiden/Boston: Brill, 2009), 257–60.

If this is so, then from the Torah texts we have examined, one may trace a trajectory through Jesus himself in John's Gospel, in the dominical love command, to love as he has loved, contained at John 13:34 and 15:12, to 1 John 3:11-18. This unit bears a strong textual resemblance to John 15:9-16:4.[130] The dominical ἐντολὴ in John 13:34 and 15:12 to love one another becomes the ἀγγελία to the same effect in 1 John 3:11. In both cases a καθὼς ethic emerges. In John 13:34 and 15:12 the connection between divine and human love is direct: the command is to love one another καθὼς ἠγάπησα ὑμᾶς, "as I have loved you". That linkage is not frankly present at 1 John 3:11, but it appears later at 4:11, ἀγαπητοί, εἰ οὕτως ὁ θεὸς ἠγάπησεν ἡμᾶς, καὶ ἡμεῖς ὀφείλομεν ἀλλήλους ἀγαπᾶν. Both John 15:12 and 1 John 3:11 (read with 4:11) reflect the connection between human and divine love seen in both Leviticus and Deuteronomy in the units surveyed above.

Importantly, as Van der Watt explains in an early article, sociologically, in the ancient world, the analogy of the family, and the expectations it creates, provides the model for the relationship between the Father and the Son. Whatever the Father does, the Son does likewise, so that the remarks at John 8:26, 38 and 40 are "isotopes of 8:28, linking hearing to being taught". Thus "education determines behaviour", in the sense that in John 5.19ff it becomes clear that whatever the Father does, the Son does likewise. Thus "this imagery of *education* legitimises Jesus' behaviour".[131] Thus in turn the disciples, and through them *we* are educated by Jesus. As we have just noticed, in John 13:34 and 15:12 the connection between divine and human love is direct: the command is to love one another καθὼς ἠγάπησα ὑμᾶς, "as I have loved you". We are educated *in the same way* at 1 John 4.11.

Van der Watt's thought on ethics in John, and indeed in 1 John, and on the love commands in the Gospel and epistle in particular, developed considerably over time. Early on, in 1999, he writes that in the absence of ethical guidance for people outside the Johannine circle, "family imagery is a key to understanding the ethics in 1 John", and that being a "child of God" is crucial to the statement in 1 John 3.9 that a "child of God cannot sin", and that as we have seen in an earlier chapter, there is only an apparent contradiction between this statement and that in 2.1 beginning "but if anyone does sin".[132] In 2006 Van der Watt writes that "the 'port of entry' into the Gospel material will be the behaviour of actors in the narrative of the Gospel", that, remembering the likely Jewish background of John's audience, "the Jewish law and tradition seems to be the moral bedrock of the value system in the Gospel", and that "this love between believers is patterned on the exemplary love of the Father and the Son", so that "believers should love as (καθὼς) Jesus has loved them" (John 13.34).[133] We have seen that the love command in 1 John 3.11 is textually almost identical. In the same year (2006) Van der Watt writes that "ethics in the letters of John are based on fellowship", that "believers

---

[130] Coombes, *1 John: The Epistle as a Relecture of the Gospel of John*, 131-6.
[131] Jan van der Watt, "Ethics Alive in Imagery" in *Imagery in the Gospel of John*, WUNT 2000 (ed. J Frey, JG van der Watt and R Zimmermann, Tübingen: Mohr Siebeck, 2006), 421-48, 497.
[132] Van der Watt, "Ethics in First John: A Literary and Socioscientific Perspective", 491, 496-7.
[133] Jan G Van der Watt, "Ethics and Ethos in the Gospel According to John", *ZNW* 97 (2006): 147-76, 151, 155, 160.

are part of the family of God and their lives are therefore determined by their mutual relationships of love", and that "there is a strong Christological motivation: believers should abide in Jesus and should behave as he has behaved".[134]

By 2012 Van der Watt perceives that the dominical ethical commands are developed in response to Jesus' opponents, and are contrasted with their behaviour and accusations, developed in response to who Jesus claimed to be, so that, contrary to their accusations, the Law had to be interpreted in a Christological light, according to who Jesus claimed to be.[135] This proposition is as applicable to 1 John as it is to John's Gospel, although there John's opponents are different.

Van der Watt's statement in 2016, that John's political agenda is that believers actively negotiate the incarnation of God's "superior and victorious eschatological kingdom" in opposition to other political powers, preserving the kingdom through love, but opening it up to others by giving life to all in the kingdom through faith,[136] is profound, and expresses well the ambiguity of John's attitude to the world. Finally, by 2019 Van der Watt writes that in view of the love of God the Father in John 3:16, "believers who claim their God is their Father should have the attitude of God towards the world".[137]

Similarly, Anderson argues that in 1 John the author assumes that his audience claims to love God, and that not far from seeking to love God is the command to love one's neighbours, and that such values are "assumed within the Johannine ethos" in view of the Johannine Jesus' gathering sheep that are not of his fold, and that when Greeks come to Jesus, he declares his mission to be complete (John 10:16; 1-18; 12:20-26).[138] Van der Watt makes a similar argument, that John does "open a door" to love of outsiders, and that the absence of a specific command should not be read as a rejection of this idea, because God's love for the world requires the same for believers.[139] Arguably, however, this approach is not without its exegetical difficulties, at least in 1 John.

For those finding in 1 John an ethic of universal love, the problem is that there is no indication that the brother, ἀδελφός, in 1 John includes the neighbour, πλησίον, or the stranger, προσήλυτον. Granted that 1 John does not *require* hatred of the outsiders, the secessionists or *exclude* love for them, as distinct from their ideas, there is nevertheless no positive command to love them – hardly surprising in a situation of dogged opposition to secessionist doctrine and division.

---

[134] Jan G Van der Watt, "Again: Identity, Ethics and Ethos in the New Testament: A Few Tentative Remarks" in *Identity, Ethics and Ethos in the New Testament* BNZW 141 (ed. JG Van der Watt; Berlin: de Gruyter, 2006), 611–32, 628.

[135] Jan G Van der Watt, "Ethics of/and Opponents of Jesus in John's Gospel" in *Rethinking the Ethics of John: "Implicit ethics" in the Johannine Writings* WUNT 291 (ed. JG Van der Watt and R Zimmermann; Tübingen: Mohr Siebeck, 2012), 175–91, 178–9, 190.

[136] Jan G Van der Watt, "Quaestiones Disputatae: Are John's Ethics Apolitical?", *NTS* (2016):493–7, 497.

[137] JG Van der Watt, *A Grammar of the Ethics of John*, Vol 1 (Tübingen: Mohr Siebeck, 2019), 322.

[138] Paul N Anderson, "Identity and Congruence: The Ethics of Integrity in the Johannine Epistles" in *Biblical Ethics and Application* WUNT 384 (ed. Ruben Zimmerman and Stephan Joubert; Tübingen: Mohr Siebeck, 2017), 331–52, 347.

[139] Van der Watt, *A Grammar of the Ethics of John*, Vol 1, 321–2.

However, as Anderson points out, in a context of combatting Gentile, docetic Christology, the author of 1 John finds that the command to simply "love one another" in John's Gospel, repeated substantially in 1 John 2.10, does not hold others accountable, so that it becomes necessary for 1 John's author, teasing out the implications of the love command, to challenge worldly assimilation, urging his audience not to abandon the community, nor to make the heretical claim to be "without sin".[140]

In the end, we may conclude that 1 John marches with John's Gospel, in proclaiming God's love for the *world* in the gift of the Son. Textually, John 3:16-17 does resemble 1 John 4:9-10. In both cases the Son is "sent" by God into the world as a gift of love: the same verb, ἀποστέλλω, conveying the idea of *revelation*,[141] appears in the aorist, ἀπέστειλεν in 1 John 4:10 and in the perfect, ἀπέσταλκεν in 1 John 4:9.[142] If the dominical command in John's Gospel, repeated in 1 John, is to love one another in imitation of divine love, and that divine love is revealed to the world in the sending of the Son, the Johannine love command may surely be used hermeneutically, supporting an ethic of love for the whole world.

The accusation by some scholars that John's Gospel reflects a sectarian hatred of the world, and a love command aimed exclusively at the author's own community,[143] is answered by John's missionary concern: the disciples, like Jesus, are sent into the world (John 17:18) that it might believe than the Father sent the Son (17:21) and has loved it even as the Father has loved the Son (17:23).[144] This accusation also sits ill with the Johannine Jesus' acceptance of the faith of the Samaritan woman (John 4:1-30).[145] Johannine missionary concern is also seen in 1 John at 2:2, where Jesus is the atoning sacrifice περὶ ὅλου τοῦ κόσμου, at 4:9 where Jesus is sent εἰς τὸν κόσμον, and at 5:4-5, referring to conquest of the world by faith in the Son. The conquest is not destruction of the world: the verb νικάω in 5:4-5 occurs also in Jesus' words in John's Gospel at 16:33,[146] where he promises the disciples *peace*, εἰρήνη, despite persecution, assuring them of his conquest of the world.

Up to a point, Girard is right to say that 1 John offers a genuine epistemology of love, provided that we see that this is a hermeneutical, not an exegetical statement: love in 1 John promotes internal solidarity in a community beset by division and hostility from without. Alison's "brother" is any fellow member of the human race: in 1 John, it

---

[140] 290–318, 304–7.

[141] Brown, *Epistles of John*, 517.

[142] Painter, *1, 2, and 3 John*, 266. Again, one is aware of Stegg, "The Abused Aorist", 222–31, but as has been pointed out above, the point is not that the use of the aorist in 1 John 4:9-10 *proves* that Jesus' saving death is a single, past event, but that since it obviously bears that character anyway, the use of the aorist is unsurprising, and only goes to emphasise that it describes a past event. The same may be said of John 3.16-17.

[143] See e.g. Jack Sanders, *Ethics in the New Testament* (London: SCM Press, 1985), 100. Even Reinhartz, while regarding John 15:12 as "the Johannine version of Leviticus 19:18", sees it as "difficult to read this verse as a challenge or corrective to exclusivism": Adele Reinhartz, *Befriending the Beloved Disciple* (New York/London: Continuum, 2001), 142.

[144] Francis J Moloney, *Love in the Gospel of John* (Grand Rapids: Baker Academic, 2013), 207–8.

[145] Robert Kysar, *Voyages with John: Charting the Fourth Gospel* (Waco, Texas: Baylor University Press, 2005), 222.

[146] Brown, *Epistles of John*, 570.

is one's fellow community member, opposing the secessionists. Schwager rightly poses hatred and murder as ultimately identical, but the "haters" in 1 John, stigmatised by the Cain analogy, are the secessionists. Swartley's *shalom* for the neighbour in need extends in 1 John to community members in need, not to the whole world. And Yoder's idea of suffering servanthood is commended in 1 John as a posture towards those within its remaining community, not the world in general.

Nevertheless, overarching all of these reservations, God in 1 John loves the world, as shown by sending the Son as an atoning sacrifice for the sin of the *whole* world (2:2; cf. 4:10), and the Son was sent into the world that we might live through him (4:9). Hermeneutically, 1 John 2:10-11 can be seen as a genuine epistemology of love: ἀγάπη and its cognates appear constantly in 1 John, and in 3:11-24 the connection between God's love and that which must be shown to the brother, ἀδελφός is inextricable. Hermeneutically, if not exegetically, it is not legitimate to offer this pericope as an epistemology of love, leading to peace, *shalom*, and support of the needy other, who need not be a fellow community member, but any fellow member of the human race?

6

Peacemaking in 1 John

Introduction

In a long journey in this study, using certain keywords, we have seen that a peacemaking hermeneutic of 1 John, as practised in some modern peacemaking theology, is not fundamentally inconsistent with its text and what may reasonably be seen as its background in the OT, in some intertestamental literature, and in the Qumran literature – although sometimes peacemaking theologians pay insufficient attention to John's conflict with the secessionists and his resulting rhetoric.

As noted in Chapter 1, the dominical, Johannine formula εἰρήνη ὑμῖν, "peace be with you" (John 20:19, 20:21, 20:26), is not found in 1 John, and neither are the other uses of εἰρήνη in John's Gospel (John 14:27 [twice]; 16:33). The word εἰρήνη appears in 2 John and 3 John, but it appears nowhere in 1 John. First John might seem the very last text on which to build a theology of peacemaking or non-violence. This final chapter argues that while such a proposal has some difficulties, on balance it has firm foundations.

In this short final chapter we shall not bore the reader with long statements of conclusions already drawn and explained in previous chapters. We shall instead attempt to gather together an original peacemaking hermeneutic for reading 1 John. Some repetition of previous material is necessary in order to demonstrate how such a hermeneutic can be constructed from John's use of certain keywords representing themes crucial to his epistle.

As we shall see, John's hostile rhetoric towards his opponents is not inconsistent with a peacemaking hermeneutic approach to 1 John. This question has been lurking below the surface in all of the exegesis of both 1 John and the LXX and other texts which precedes this chapter. It is simply not good enough to extract from the epistle its injunctions concerning God's nature as love, God's love for humankind, and the need for men and women in turn to love each other, just as God has loved us, central though they be to its themes, and build on them alone a peacemaking hermeneutic of the epistle as a whole, without attending to its overall purpose and its literary features – including its polemic. To produce a coherent peacemaking hermeneutic of 1 John, one must anchor it in its text and demonstrate that it is consistent with John's overall purpose and his language, his polemic, as a whole.

To this end, we shall in this final chapter first examine why it is that the theology and ethics of the secessionists – to judge from their boasts or slogans as reported by

John – are seen by him as such a threat to his remaining community. We shall see that to John, these claims threaten not only the theology of his audience – its understanding of God and God's purposes in Jesus – but consequently its cohesion, its fellowship. The very continued existence of John's community is threatened in his eyes. So John 1 needs to isolate the errors of the secessionists. At bottom, the errors stigmatised appear to over-spiritualise Jesus, to misrepresent and minimise his earthly nature, and thus to deny the reality of his humanity and therefore the reality and significance of his earthly life and death, in short, the love for humanity demonstrated by God in Jesus' incarnation and death.

Of course the exact beliefs of the secessionists are hard to pinpoint. History has been written by the victors, and the opponents are known only through their "boasts", as quoted and stigmatised by John.

It is notable that John does not content himself with strong polemic denouncing the errors of his opponents. He moves on to build a positive theology and an ethic, inextricably linked, of divine love necessitating human love. Most of his statements in his epistle are positive exposition of God's love in Jesus and commands to do likewise. The outworkings of these themes involve key concepts represented by the words we have examined in the last three chapters, ἱλασμός, and then σφάξω and ἀνθρωποκτόνος, and their opposing ideas, ἀγαπάω and ἀδελφος. We shall demonstrate, in a recapitulation of the place of these themes in John's overall purpose – to resolve tensions within his community by right belief and mutual love – how they present a theology and an ethic of peacemaking, of mutual love and self-giving. Some more detailed exegeses of these words in their respective contexts in 1 John appear in earlier chapters, but it is necessary to recapitulate these more briefly here for a different purpose, which is to show that a hermeneutic of peacemaking may be derived from 1 John that is truly anchored to the text of the epistle.

Using this approach, we shall see that John's use of the term ἱλασμός, and the concepts underlying it, elaborates a picture of God that is consistent with this theology and ethic of mutual love and self-giving, because God has first shown love and self-giving to humanity. Sin is the problem dividing men and women, both from God and from each other, so self-evidently it must be dealt with. This has already happened, once and for all, by God's gift of the Son as ἱλασμός for sin. This gift works, not by a transaction between the Father and the Son in which the Son by his death pays at his Father's command the violent price due to the Father from humanity for its sin, but by a cleansing of sin by the Son's blood in his life and death, freely given in love for humanity (1 John 4:10), and not just for John's community of believers, but for the whole world (2:2b). In this different sense, Jesus' atoning death is indeed sacrificial. John's aim in expounding this theology is not only to promote its effects on human reconciliation. As God in Jesus achieves a cosmic reconciliation between God and humankind in Jesus' life and death as a cleansing of sin, a model of human behaviour emerges, entailing mutual love, without violence and death-dealing.

John's point to his community is that if one sees Jesus as truly *the* ἱλασμός for sin, the vice of imagining oneself as part of an inner circle of "spiritual" believers who have risen above sin (cf. 1 John 1:8, 10) loses its point – God by the gift of the Son has dealt with sin once and for all, and humanity need only accept the Son's advocacy for us with the Father (2:1) and his atoning sacrifice for us (2:2) to deal with sin. Thus the divisive and love-denying effect of an "in group" of spiritual people, who have a superior claim to righteousness over those without, is eliminated. Peace results from mutual equality under God through the Son's cleansing of *all* sin – the sins of all – by his blood (1 John 1:8).

Similarly we see that John deploys the words σφάξω and ἀνθρωποκτόνος in order to demonstrate the end result, the inevitable concomitant, of hatred of the brother (3:15) or sister. "Disunity is death" is a popular modern political maxim, but it serves here to encapsulate John's teaching that without love, his community will fall apart and devour itself. John associates hatred and murder, not just with other forms of sin, but with the evil one himself: Cain, who murdered his brother, is from the evil one (3:12). So in John's teaching, Cain, the bringer of violent death, is the ultimate personification of evil – not just the one who jealously kills his brother for bringing a gift favoured by God (Genesis 4:4), but the one who commits the ultimate primordial sin, the violent annihilation of a brother. The ultimate opposite of John's ethic of mutual love is murder – violence stemming from hatred of the brother or sister. John's proscription of hatred follows from his demonstration in the Cain example of the manner in which hatred disrupts human relations – on the other hand, peaceful relations are restored by mutual love, the antithesis of hatred.

Next, in this chapter John's use of the words ἀγαπάω and ἀδελφος is shown to be a positive outworking of his theme of mutual love. We have seen that the ideas of mutual love and brotherhood in 1 John 3:11-24 probably have their origin in the Jewish scriptures, in Leviticus and Deuteronomy, through the LXX version available to John and his community. But John's reworking of them in his epistle contains a new element: that Jesus laid down his life for us, so we ought to do the same for one another (3:16). Brotherhood and sisterhood entail this extreme obligation because of John's realised eschatology: we have passed from death into life *because we love one another* (3:14a). Willingness to die for the brother or sister is the ultimate act of love, as murder is the ultimate evil. Peacemaking by willing victimhood for the brother or sister, in imitation of Jesus, is a discernible theme here.

John's Polemic against the Secessionists

John identifies the secessionists as those who broke fellowship with his community: they "went out from us" and "did not belong to us" (1 John 2:19), and he stigmatises them as "antichrists" (2:18b). But it is significant that the epistle does not explicitly introduce them earlier, although they are implicitly present in the ἐάνεἴπωμεν formula at 1:6, 1:8 and 1:10. The epistle starts with the very positive proclamation in the "little prologue" that what is declared is "what we have seen and heard", if not from the earthly Jesus himself, then most likely from those who knew him and/or inherited very early tradition as to his identity and deeds.[1] After the "little prologue", John begins with the theme of God as light (1:5) and κοινωνία, "fellowship" with God which is denied to those walking in darkness (1:6) – a theme immediately extended to fellowship with one another through walking in the light (1:8).

John now uses the polemical language against his opponents: if we say we have fellowship with him but are walking in darkness, we *lie* (1:6); if we say we have no sin we *deceive ourselves*, and the truth is not in us (1:8); if we say we have not sinned, we make him a liar, and his word is not in us (1:10). These ἐὰν εἴπωμεν, "if we say", statements appear at this early point partly in contrast with "what we have seen and heard" (1:3) – that is the true teaching we have inherited – but also to refute his opponents from the very start.

But John's claims in reply to the secessionists' boasts are positive. From the beginning he promises fellowship with one another, through cleansing of humanity's sin by the blood of Jesus, God's Son (1:7). This atonement for sin by cleansing and thus expiating it immediately solidifies John's community as free from the effects of wrongdoing. Reconciliation with God effects reconciliation with one another.

To inoculate his community against the secessionists' boasts, John must first cut the theological ground from under them by strongly polemical, antithetic language. But it is not directed personally against the people making false claims, so much as at the false claims themselves. "Walking in darkness" is a rejection of fellowship with God and therefore with one another. Claiming sinlessness is self-deception – failure to recognise the existence of evil and its consequences. So to say is not to water down the intensity of John's polemic: it is simply to recognise that is directed *primarily* against the ideas underlying the claims themselves, not those making them – although he certainly demonises them, quite literally on occasions, in the process.

This polemic continues in 1 John 2, but still the secessionists themselves go unmentioned. If someone says they have come to know Jesus, but disobeys his commandments, they lie, and the truth is not in them (2:4). Whoever hates a believer walks in darkness (2:11). But in each case a negative is preceded by a positive. In view of this, it is understandable that some distinguished commentators have thought that John's polemic is directed at tendencies within his community, not opponents outside it.[2] However the resumed polemic against the opponents, this time stigmatising them as "antichrists" who "went out from us" (3:18, 19), militates against this view. Even more intensely, the "liar" and the "antichrist" are the ones who deny that Jesus is the Christ and deny the Father and the Son (3:22). But again the intense language is deployed to defend central tenets of the tradition derived from what has been heard and seen (1:1), rather than to blacken the secessionist opponents – although one must acknowledge that it has that effect.

But is John's polemic against sin itself, as making the sinner lawless (3:4) and a child of the devil (3:8), aimed at the secessionists? This time it appears indeed to be aimed

---

[1] The "we" in 1:1 is capable of referring either to eyewitnesses or tradition-bearers: Brown, *Epistles of John*, 160–1; Painter, *1, 2, and 3 John*, 126–7.

[2] Cf. Perkins, "Apocalyptic Sectarianism and Love Commands", 289; Lieu, *I, II and III John*, 9–14; Lieu, *Theology of the Johannine Epistles*, 30.

also at tendencies within John's own community: the words πᾶς, "everyone" beginning 3:4, and the opening words ὁ ποιῶν commencing 3:8, more appositely refer, in context, to *anyone* who does what is stigmatised, not just a particular group who exhibit this behaviour. This strengthens the argument that the polemic in 1 John is aimed primarily at the tendency itself and not so much the opponents themselves – even though they are still active and posing present danger.

The warning against believing "every spirit" and against "false prophets" (1 John 4:1) is however in a different category. Clearly John has particular and present opponents in mind: those who do not "confess that Jesus Christ is come in the flesh" (4:2) and who have "the spirit of the antichrist" (4:3).[3] Of course the opponents do not literally deny Jesus – rather, they do not have a true estimate of him and his nature.[4] But it cannot be said that John is here stigmatising only a wrong tendency in his own community. "They are from the world" (4:5) stigmatises present opponents, not just a wrong tendency. So does "Those saying 'I love God' and hating their brother are liars" (4:20).

Two characteristics in his opponents are condemned by John: their deviant views as to Jesus' nature and their failure to love, their fellowship-breaking. Moreover, these two tendencies are connected in their effects in at least two respects. First, if the earthly Jesus is seen through a docetic lens as only *appearing* to be human, the potency of his example is lost. John's καθώς ethic surfaces at many points in his epistle: "whoever claims to live in him must walk as Jesus did" (2:6); "just as it [Jesus' anointing] has taught you, remain in him" (2:27); "we shall be like him, for we shall see him as he is" (3:2); "he who has this hope in him purifies himself, just as he is pure" (3:3); "he who does what is right is righteous, just as he is righteous" (3:7); "love one another as he commanded us" (3:23); "because in this world we are like him" (4:17). True it is that God, not Jesus, is the exemplar in many of these occurrences of καθώς in 1 John. But the model of divine love in the gift of the Son falls away if Jesus is not at once "Christ" and "come in the flesh" (4:2), because there is no other fully earthly person who is God, on whom to model ourselves.[5]

Second, the negative result of not walking in God's light is to break fellowship with one another and to walk in darkness (1:5-7). Here κοινωνία is not just with one another

---

[3] Connell's suggestion that ἀντιχρίστου here may refer to "those who have anointed with chrism, and who by their separation from the community have opposed or betrayed (*anti* – against) the unifying material of anointing (*-chrism, -christ*), by which they had marked and been marked for life in the church" (Martin F Connell, "On 'Chrism' and 'Anti-Christs' in 1 John 2:18-27: A Hypothesis", *Worship* 83.3 (2009): 212-34, 217-18) is tempting, but given 2:22, identifying the antichrist with the "liar, he who denies that Jesus is the Christ", it seems clear that the antichrist is simply one who denies Jesus' divinity and thus Jesus himself: so ultimately Craig Koester, "The Antichrist Theme in the Johannine Epistles" in *Communities in Dispute: Current Scholarship on the Johannine Epistles* (ed. R Alan Culpepper and Paul N Anderson; Atlanta: SBL Press, 2014), 187-96, 190.

[4] Smalley, *1, 2, 3 John*, 223.

[5] But a cautionary note must be sounded here. That Jesus Christ is ἐν σαρκὶ ἐληλυθότα, "come in the flesh" in 4:2, given that the perfect participle is used, seems simply to employ "come in the flesh" as a given attribute of Jesus as "the Christ", not as a theological assertion: by itself, it may not necessarily signify that the secessionists denied the Incarnation: so Brown, *Epistles of John*, 492-3; Martinus C de Boer, "The Death of Jesus and His Coming in the Flesh (1 John 4:2)", *Nov T* XXXIII, 4 (1991): 326-46, 332-45.

(1:7), but with Jesus himself (1:6).[6] "Walking in darkness" signifies the absence of light, by which the Father is revealed to humanity (cf. John 1:4).[7] The test of being in God's light is loving the brother or sister (2:9-10). The result of this syllogistic reasoning is that God *is* love (4:8). To fail to love one's fellow is to misunderstand God's true nature as embodying love itself.

Seen in this light, John obviously had to undermine the theological underpinning of his opponents' boasts, not only because they denied Jesus' earthly nature, but because this denial had the potential to break fellowship in his remaining community. It is unsurprising, therefore, that in the manner of his time, his rhetoric is vehemently condemnatory.

But John's prescriptions of love and brotherhood, even assuming they were intended by him to be limited to his community, are hardly typical of what we would recognise today as a cult or sect. His quotations and condemnations of the opponents' boasts are not linked to negative rules and proscriptions of various forms of belief and behaviour deployed as boundaries to define who is within the group and who is not. Rather, they are linked to invitations to love and enjoy fellowship within his community, by imitation of the generosity of God in his gift of the Son. John's realised eschatology signifies that all who love God and therefore their fellows are accepted *now* within the divine κοινωνία, by walking in the light and therefore being cleansed from sin by Jesus' blood (1:7), after confession of sin (1:9), which implies not just acknowledgement of sin, but a change of orientation to God.[8]

To illustrate this, one might wonder what reception John might give, or might recommend to his followers, to a former secessionist who sought to rejoin his community. Would it be unforgiving condemnation for past errors, and fear or suspicion lest they be repeated? Or would it be that given to the prodigal son – one of love and acceptance after a recognition of error? Surely an author who links knowledge of God's true nature as love with a commandment to love one another would favour the latter approach, not the former.[9]

Sectarian groups usually define themselves over against "the world", seen as sinful, hopelessly corrupt and doomed to destruction, as opposed to the "chosen" group members, who alone will be saved. The rhetoric of 1 John is sometimes used to reinforce this view. Certainly "the world", ὁ κόσμος, is usually portrayed in negative terms by John. At 1 John 2:15 (twice), 2:16 (twice), 2:17, 3:1, 3:13, 4:4, 4:5 (three times), 5:4 (twice) and 5:19, ὁ κόσμος is presented in unequivocally evil terms, in dualistic

---

[6] Zane C Hodges, "Fellowship and Confession in 1 John 1:5-10", *B Sac* 129 (1972): 48–60, 51.
[7] Charles P Bayliss, "The Meaning of Walking 'in the Darkness' (1 John 1:6)", *B Sac* 149 (1992): 214–22, 217–18.
[8] Interestingly, the verb ὁμολογέω, used in 1:9 with the meaning "confess", is used with its cognate noun in the LXX to translate the Hebrew root rbanf, "offer" (Jeremiah 44:25, Leviticus 22:18), which suggests more than cursory agreement with a truth, so that confession of sin in 1 John 1:9 includes agreement with God about the offensive and unacceptable nature of the sin: Ed Glassock, "Forgiveness and Cleansing according to 1 John 1:9", *B Sac* 166 (2009): 217–31, 220–2.
[9] John's ostracism of Diotrephes in 3 John 9–10 would not seem to conflict with this view: Diotrephes remains an opponent, not acknowledging John's authority and spreading false charges against him, according to John. Certainly there is no indication that Diotrephes seeks reconciliation with John.

contrast to all that God stands for. For example, at its second appearance in the epistle, at 2:15-17, ὁ κόσμος stands as a symbol of all that is evil, in contrast to the love of the Father, which is not in the world, in contrast to those who do the will of God living forever (2:17). In these verses we are mistaken if we try to identify particular types of sin[10] – those connected with sexual desire, wealth and covetousness, for example – because what is castigated here is devotion to the world per se, not particular varieties of worldliness.

But in contrast to these negative occurrences, ὁ κόσμος in its very first appearance in the epistle, 2:2, is used *positively* – Jesus is the ἱλασμός for the sin of the "whole world". In 4:9, Jesus, God's only Son, is sent "into the world, that we might live through him". And in the following verse, 4:10, he is sent by the God who loves us to be the expiation, ἱλασμός, for our sins. In 2:2 and 4:10, therefore, God's embrace excludes no one in its salvific intent, including those in "the world" beyond John's own community – and even including, by implication, the secessionists. Likewise in 1 John 4:14b the Father sends the Son to be the saviour of the world, τὸν υἱὸν σωτῆρα τοῦ κόσμου. How does John know this? The clue is in 4:14a, καὶ ἡμεῖς τεθεάμεθα καὶ μαρτυροῦμεν, "we have seen and we testify". Here the plural "we" most likely signifies John speaking for his community, as tradition-bearers.[11] The use of the perfect τεθεάμεθα lends prominence to the testimony of the writer.[12]

Thus the final picture emerging from John's fierce rhetoric against the secessionists' destructive theology and love-denying ethic is not one of a cult defining itself over against the world, by narrow boundaries, condemning to destruction of all who fall outside it, but one of rejection of destructive theology and ethics, countered by love, and held in tension with such rejection. John wants to condemn with all his breath what he identifies as the secessionists' wrong view of Jesus, as not the true Son of God who was at once truly human, and the lack of mutual love this engenders. But at the same time he wants to affirm as strongly as he can that God, in all-embracing love, has sent the Son to deal finally with sin by expiating it, by cleansing humanity from it by his blood. This free gift is for all – even the secessionists, if they will embrace it by confessing that Jesus is the Son of God who yet came in the flesh and will walk with God by loving all in John's community. Thus peacemaking in John's community, and indeed among those beyond it who will join it in love, is consistent with, and certainly not excluded by, John's rhetoric.

Today we may legitimately derive from 1 John, despite its fierce rhetoric against the secessionists, a peacemaking hermeneutic of love and inclusion of the other, because John's antidote to the exclusive and fellowship-breaking ideas of the secessionists is not the drawing of stricter theological and ethical boundaries between his own community and the secessionists. It is a positive theology, which places at its absolute centre the reality of Jesus' earthly incarnation as truly human, *and* his mission as God's anointed

---

[10] William RG Loader, "The Significance of 2:15-17 for Understanding the Ethics of John" in *Communities in Dispute: Current Scholarship on the Johannine Epistles* (ed. R Alan Culpepper and Paul N Arnderson; Atlanta: SBL Press, 2014), 223–35, 223.

[11] Brown, *Epistles of John*, 522.

[12] Culy, *I, II, III John: A Handbook on the Greek Text*, 113.

one, the Christ. As the Son in his life and death is God's loving gift to us, so we ought to love one another. Such a theology and ethic is thus embracing and inclusive of others, without fear and hatred, or their inevitable result, violent death.

Ἱλασμός and Peacemaking in 1 John

We have seen how 1 John 2:2 and 4:10 portray Jesus as the ἱλασμός, "expiation" or "reconciling sacrifice", for sin.[13] How can this idea provide a basis for a peacemaking hermeneutic of 1 John if, as argued previously, Jesus is the ἱλασμός for sin through cleansing by his blood (cf. 1:7)? The clue lies in the fact that, as already noted, this ἱλασμός is accomplished for the *whole world*.

In 2:2a-b Jesus is the "reconciling sacrifice for our sins", ἱλασμός ἐστιν περὶ τῶν ἁμαρτιῶν ἡμῶν, but lest ἡμῶν be read triumphantly by his community audience, John adds in 2:2c, οὐ περὶ τῶν ἡμετέρων δὲ μόνον ἀλλὰ καὶ περὶ ὅλου τοῦ κόσμου, "not for ours only but for those of the whole world". There is a "conflict that goes beyond semantics"[14] between John's use of κόσμος in 2:2c and the negative uses highlighted above. In 1 John 2:2c the thought is close to John 3:16-17, "for God did not send the Son into the world to condemn the world, but so that the world might be saved through him", and John 12:47, "for I did not come to condemn the world but to save the world". In 1 John 2:2c, God intents to save the *whole* world from sin through Jesus as reconciling sacrifice, to cleanse or expiate its sin.

The same theme emerges in 1 John 4:9, where we read that ἐν τούτῳ ἐφανερώθη ἡ ἀγάπη τοῦ θεοῦ ἐν ἡμῖν, "God's love was revealed in this way among us", that "God's only Son was sent into the world", εἰς τὸν κόσμον, "so we might live through him". As in 2:2c, so in 4:9b the world is included in God's salvific work in the gift of the Son, as ἱλασμός for our sins (4:10). And 4:9 and 2:2c affirm that he is ἱλασμός, not only for the sins of John's audience but for those of the *whole* world.

But how can this positive view of "the world" prevail if "everyone born of God *overcomes* [νικᾷ] the world, and this is the victory that *overcomes* the world, our faith" (5:4), and if "who is it that overcomes [νικῶν] the world", but "the one who believes that Jesus is the Son of God" (5:5), and if "the whole world [ὁ κόσμος ὅλος] is under the rule of the evil one" (5:19)? The answer may be that in 1 John, the ideas of "the world" as at once the demonstration of evil, and in need of, and indeed *worthy of* salvation by God are held in tension. In 1 John the evil of the world – much as John condemns it – is finally responded to by God, not by wrath and rejection, but by a loving gift of the Son as ἱλασμός for the sins of the *whole* world.

This divine gift is indeed fundamental to our picture of the deity in 1 John. First John 2:2, as discussed earlier in this study, functions as the climax to the unit from 1:5 onwards, where the themes of light, standing for God, and fellowship, standing for

---

[13] In Chapter 2 of this study we have engaged in an extended discussion of the origins and uses of the term ἱλασμός and its cognates in the LXX and how it is that it conveys the idea of *expiation*, not *propitiation* for sin. The translation of ἱλασμός in 1 John 2:2 and 4:10 as "reconciling sacrifice" neatly avoids the idea of propitiation but retains that of sacrifice, and so is adopted here.

[14] Brown, *Epistles of John*, 223.

humanity in right relationship with God, are developed to show how walking in the light and fellowship are ensured by God's dealing with sin. There is no hint of divine wrath, which must be assuaged by the blood of the Son. Far from such a theme, 1 John 1:7 simply affirms fellowship with one another through walking in the light and through the blood of Jesus cleansing us from all sin. The secessionist boast of being without sin is condemned, and forgiveness by a "faithful and just" God is promised on confession of sin (1:9).

"He who is faithful and just", πιστός ἐστιν καὶ δίκαιος, conveys two separate notions. The first, faithfulness, refers to God as the keeper of covenant promises: Deuteronomy 7:9, which speaks of "the faithful God who keeps covenant loyalty with those who keep his commandments", comes to mind here.[15] Thus the epithet in 1 John 1:9, πιστός, "faithful", pictures God as loving Father who is with his people always. The second epithet, δίκαιος, "righteous" or "just", is more ambiguous: does it portray God as always merciful to the penitent sinner or as visiting punishment without mercy on the sinner unless divine anger is sated? The context of forgiveness of sin after repentance would suggest the former.

Confession of individual sin is a Christian inheritance from Jewish practice on the Day of Atonement when a sin offering is made (Leviticus 5:5).[16] The action in this cultic observance is that the people, *after* confession of sin, present their sin offering, a sheep or a goat, to be offered by the priest as an atonement for their sin (5:6) and the priest sprinkles the blood of the animal (or bird: 5:7) on the side and base of the altar: *it* (the blood) "is a sin-offering" (5:9c). "The priest shall make atonement on your behalf for the sin you have committed, and you shall be forgiven" (5:10b).

First John 1:7 raises the question of *how* the blood of Jesus cleanses us from all sin, and 1:9 points a way towards the answer, which is given in 2:1-2. If we, contrary to John's hope, do sin, "Jesus Christ the righteous" stands as advocate with the Father (2:1b), and he is the ἱλασμός, the reconciling sacrifice for our sin (2:2a) – *just as* the blood of the sacrifice on the Day of Atonement effects divine forgiveness of sin – in both cases after personal confession. But in the case of Jesus, the new ἱλασμός, the atoning sacrifice, is not provided by humanity at all, but by God in the gift of Jesus.

It is a mistake to read 1 John 1:7–2:2 as signifying simple substitution by the Father of the Son as sin-offering in place of the OT animal or bird on the Day of Atonement. In 1 John the whole ritual is turned on its head – far from humanity offering Jesus to the Father as a vicarious payment for sin, God instead provides *cleansing* of sin by the blood of the Son, in loving gift of God's own self through the Son. That is a hard concept to grasp, and it is unsurprising that over the centuries Western theologians such as Augustine, Anselm and Aquinas, followed by Luther and Calvin, assimilated it to the doctrine of justification and therefore to notions of divine justice requiring a price for sin, paid not by us, but by Jesus in our stead.[17] But as demonstrated in

---

[15] Smalley, *1, 2, 3 John*, 31; Strecker, *Johannine Letters*, 32 n.30; Brown, *Epistles of John*, 209;

[16] See generally Schnackenburg, *The Johannine Epistles*, 82.

[17] See generally Alister McGrath, *Justitia Dei* (Cambridge University Press: Cambridge, 3rd ed., 2005) 38–54 (on Augustine), 57–72 (on Anselm, Aquinas and others) and 208–57 (on Luther and Calvin); see also Paul S Fiddes, *Past Event and Present Salvation* (London: Darton, Longman and Todd, 1989), chapter 5, "The Demands of Justice", 83–111 and DM Baillie, *God Was in Christ* (London: Faber and Faber, 1948) chapter 7, "Why Atonement", 157–71.

Chapter 3, such notions are essentially a gloss on 1 John 2:2 and do not represent its original meaning.

This becomes clearer when one sees how the other occurrence of ἱλασμός in 1 John 4:10 functions in its immediate context, 4:7-12, which is part of a larger unit, 4:7-21, devoted to the Father's love in the gift of Jesus and its result, the divine command to love one another. "Let us love one another" in 4:7a really functions as an introduction to the meat of the verse in 4:7b, "*everyone* who loves is born of God and knows God".[18] The word ὅτι, beginning 4:7b is causative: we must love one another "*because* love is from God".[19] Hermeneutically, mutual love emerges as an inevitable concomitant, for the Christian, of God's love for humanity. God's sending of the Son as the ἱλασμός for our sins (4:10), to which this passage builds up, is the ultimate expression of this love. That God loved *us* (rather than the other way about) in 4:10 asserts that the proof of God's love is the gift of the Son as ἱλασμός.[20] This word signifies God's love, not satisfaction of God's wrath.

Σφαξω, ἀνθρωποκτόνος and Peacemaking in 1 John

First John 3:12 urges John's community not to be like Cain, who was from the evil one and murdered, ἔσφαξεν, his brother. First John 3:15 proclaims that the one who hates a brother is a murderer, ἀνθρωποκτόνος, and all murderers do not have everlasting life abiding in them. These verses function within a subunit from 3:11 to 3:18 depicting the contrast between love and hatred.[21]

First, 1 John 3:11 identifies the command to love one another as the message, ἡ ἀγγελία, which his audience has heard *from the beginning*, ἀπ' ἀρχῆς. This may refer simply to the beginning of the tradition handed on by its bearers, or it may recall 1:1, what was ἀπ' ἀρχῆς, from the beginning. Even assuming the former, less exalted meaning, John's intention is to associate the love command with what has been the tradition "from the beginning". Elsewhere in the Johannine corpus, it is indeed a dominical command (John 13:34-35, 15:12, 17). It is therefore absolutely central to Christian proclamation, and it is *the* antidote offered in 1 John to the division in the author's community and the pivot on which the epistle turns.

Then in 3:12a we find the negative statement: "We must not be like Cain who was from the evil one and murdered his brother." Being *like* Cain does not simply connote

---

[18] Schnackenburg, *Johannine Epistles*, 207.
[19] Painter, *1, 2, and 3 John*, 265, 268.
[20] "Vv. 9 and 10 are pure gold, enshrining the very heart of Christianity": Victor Bartling, "We Love because He Loved us first (1 John 4:7-21)", *CTM* 23 no 12D (1952): 868–83, 878.
[21] Although many scholars see this unit as commencing at 3:10 (e.g. Smalley, *1, 2, 3 John*, 179), 3:10 is better seen as the culmination of the previous unit, dealing with the children of God. Then 3:11 marks a change of subject, where the demonstrative ὅτι begins the explanation in 3:11-18 of *why* it is that the one who does not love their brother and sister does not do righteousness and is not of God (3:10): Painter, *1, 2, and 3 John*, 232. This subunit is best seen as ending at 3:18, because 3:19 introduces a new subject, the grounds for confidence before God: *ibid*, 244. The larger unit, dealing with the whole subject of mutual love, extends on to 3:24.

having a similar personality to Cain's or committing a similar crime. As we have seen in Chapter 4, by the time 1 John was written, Cain had come to be associated in Jewish intertestamental and in contemporary writings by Philo and Josephus as *the* embodiment of evil. This is confirmed by the further statement in 3:12 that Cain was "from the evil one", ἐκ τοῦ πονηροῦ. For John, evil is to be resisted and overcome, not by violent means, but by faith (5:4-5).[22]

The question in 3:12b, "and why did he murder him?", which answers itself, "because his own deeds were evil and his brother's were righteous", might appear tautological, but it is not. Neither is it a psychological explanation, which might be anachronistic. Rather, it refers to Cain's moral defects as against his righteous brother Abel, in a brief *midrash* on Genesis 4, continuing the theme of the children of God and the children of the devil in 3:1-10. For those who are children of the devil, sin is not merely a symptom, but the *root* of their being.[23]

The following statement, "brothers, do not be surprised that the world hates you", in 3:13 is connected to 3:12b: the intention is to associate the world's hatred with that of Cain, which is diabolically inspired. Here, ὁ κόσμος is best seen as referring, not to worldly temptations or desires (cf. 2:15), but to unbelieving humanity in its rejection, first of Jesus and then his disciples (cf. John 15:18; 17:14).[24]

The contrast is made in 3:14 between life and death, using the criterion of mutual love. Loving here has present eschatological consequences, as does failure to do so. The reverse, hatred, is again associated in 3:15 with murder: "The one who hates the brother is a murderer [ἀνθρωποκτόνος] and all murderers do not have eternal life abiding in them." This is an astonishing and, at first sight, an exaggerated association. But John's thought here is still associated with the example of Cain, who hated his brother to the point of death-dealing.[25]

In 3:16, John commends the converse of murder, laying down one's life for another. In love, Jesus laid down his life for us, so we ought to do the same for one another. Here John takes the Cain story and reverses it: far from hatred to others, which leads to violence and murder, we ought to practise mutual love and be prepared in love to lay down our lives for one another. So love is extended at 3:17 to practical consequences, in the rhetorical question, "If the one who has the good things of the world looks on their brother needing things but shuts out any feeling towards him, how can the love of God abide in them?" This leads to the more general statement in 3:18, "Little children, let us love, not in word or speech, but in truth and action."

From 1 John 3:11 to 3:18 we see a stepped argument, first commanding love for one another and then tracing Cain's example of hatred leading to murder, resulting from his evil nature, associating it with the world's hatred, then urging in its stead mutual love, with a final reminder that all who hate are murderers without eternal life abiding

---

[22] True it is that 1 John contains no equivalent of the Matthean command in 5:39 not to resist evil: see generally John Piper, *Love Your Enemies* (Wheaton, Illinois: Crossway, 2012), 53, 188n.109. But that does not signify that violence is invited by John here.
[23] Schnackenburg, *Johannine Epistles*, 179.
[24] *Ibid*, 180.
[25] Brown, *Epistles of John*, 447.

in them. Then John illustrates the consequences of mutual love – laying down one's life for the brother or sister and sharing the world's goods with them. This is a powerful condemnation of violence and advocacy of love and sharing, even to the point of death, in a realised eschatology[26] which brings the sharer and life-giver into harmony with God, by their practice of Jesus' love.

John's condemnation of hatred and murder also carries a prophetic word to the church of today, which it must receive and pass on. It must stand in solidarity with the victims of hatred, violence and murder, denouncing these evils, even if perpetrated by the church itself. The church must be a faithful tradition-bearer and guard the revelation entrusted to it, regardless of the world's values and beliefs. But if it succumbs to fear of the world outside, that fear will beget hatred. The violent persecutions of opponents by the church were founded in fear, lest it be contaminated by opposing ideas. In totalitarian and semi-totalitarian societies the church has, in fear for its survival and in reprehensible accommodation of an evil state apparatus, often stood beside oppressors, instead of courageously proclaiming God's love in Jesus and the need to love one another – even dying for one's fellow.

Ἀγαπάω, ἀδελφος and Peacemaking in 1 John

The "love commandment" first occurs in 1 John in the subunit extending from 2:7 to 2:11.[27] John's identification of it as an "old commandment" (2:7) which we have had from the beginning, ἀπ' ἀρχῆς. may again be a reference back to 1:1, where John refers to the tradition which was passed on "from the beginning": John's "we" in 1:1-4 claims the prerogative of the tradition bearer.[28] Or 2:7 may be a reference to Jesus' self-revelation during his ministry,[29] for, as we have seen, in the Johannine tradition it is a dominical command (John 13:34-35, 15:12, 17).

Ironically, as indicated by the adverb πάλιν, "yet" in 2:8, intended to introduce a statement contrasting with the "old commandment" one in 2:7, the love command is for John also a "new commandment that is true in him and in you, because the darkness is disappearing and the true light already shines".[30] Again the reference to a "new commandment" may be to its being dominical: Jesus himself called it "new" (John 13:34).[31] Certainly the motivation created by divine sacrifice, requiring human love (1 John 3:16; cf. 4:11), *appears* new. But the consequence of such love, which is

---

[26] The term "realised eschatology" is used here to refer to the entry into human history of Jesus and his revelation, by which the believer is brought into a present or *realised* relationship with God – or in Johannine terms, ἐν τῷ φωτί, "in the light" (cf. 1 John 1:7).

[27] The preferable view is that the second unit in 1 John 2 starts at 2:3 (Brown, *Epistles of John*, 277) but there is a change of subject at 2:7, from knowing God by keeping God's commandments to the "old commandment" to love one another.

[28] Wendy E Sproston, "Witnesses to What Was ἀπ' ἀρχῆς: 1 John's Contribution to Our Knowledge of Tradition in the Fourth Gospel", *JSNT* 48 (1992): 43–65, 52–3.

[29] Schnackenburg, *Johannine Epistles*, 104; Brown, *Epistles of John*, 265.

[30] Smalley, *1, 2, 3 John*, 56; Culy, *I, II, III John: A Handbook on the Greek Text*, 32.

[31] Schnackenburg, *Johannine Epistles*, 105.

help for the needy brother (3:17), reflects the Deuteronomic command of generosity to the fellow community member (Deuteronomy 15:7) and needy neighbour (15:10) in consequence of divine redemption (15:15). The reference to "darkness" and "light" here refers to "the world" which is "passing away" (2:17) and to God as "light" (1:5).[32] God's light is revealed now, in Jesus' coming.

In 2:9-10 we see the contrasting statements that "the one who says 'I am in the light' but hates a brother is still in darkness" and "the one who loves a brother lives in the light, and in him there is no stumbling block". The hypocrisy inherent in hatred coexisting with claiming to be "in the light", that is in harmony with God, is seen by John in 2:9 as characteristic of the secessionists. John's use of the ὁ λέγων formula in 2:9 makes this clear. His point is that hatred of a co-religionist, a "brother", is inconsistent with harmony with God, symbolised by "light". On the other hand, in 2:10 loving a brother means walking in the light, in harmony with God: "stumbling block" or "cause for stumbling", σκάνδαλον in 2:10 makes it clear that John is thinking of the blinding effect of darkness as a cause for stumbling.[33]

The subunit culminates in 2:11 with the statement that "the one who hates a brother is in the darkness, walks in the darkness, and does not know where to go, because the darkness has brought blindness to him". This is a reference back to the "stumbling block" of 2:9 – in darkness there is a stumbling block, caused by moral blindness. John hints at the loss of direction of the secessionists who have left the community.[34]

The thread of John's argument in 2:7-11 is that an old and yet new commandment is that his audience should love one another, because it is consistent with knowledge of, and harmony with, God, whereas hatred, characteristic of the secessionists, is not. Again John combats dissension in his community by pointing out that hatred has eschatological consequences: by practising it, we risk lasting disharmony, not only with our fellow but with God. Here John's close identification of love with the divine nature, later made explicit (4:8), makes hatred of the brother, the co-religionist, out of the question for the true Christian believer. *Peace and harmony* in John's community is not just an ideal, not just the true badge of the believer, but eschatologically essential. This applies both to the present, and in the future, in eternal life (1:2, 2:25, 5:11, 5:13, 5:20).

Apart from 1 John 2:7-11, John uses the words ἀγαπάω and its cognates and ἀδελφός very frequently in his epistle. We have just examined their use in 1 John 3:11-18. More particularly, we have noticed that John advocates, in response to the world's hatred, predicted for his community,[35] not hatred and rejection in return, but holding in tension a prophetic judgement on the world's evil and violence, and mutual love, generosity and preparedness to lay down one's life for the brother or sister.

First John carries a prophetic word for the church today, in its proclamation that all Christians must practise ἀγάπη towards one another and see one another as true

---

[32] Painter, *1, 2, and 3 John*, 171.
[33] Schnackenburg, *Johannine Epistles*, 108; Painter, *1, 2, and 3 John*, 173.
[34] Brown, *Epistles of John*, 275.
[35] Cf. John 15:18. See James A Kelhoffer, *Persecution, Persuasion and Power: Readiness to Withstand Hardship as a Corroboration of Legitimacy in the New Testament* (Tübingen: Mohr Siebeck, 2010), 255n.5.

ἀδελφοί, brothers and sisters. John confronts the fellowship-breaking hatred and exclusivism of the secessionists, not with hatred and rejection in return, but with inclusive love and brotherhood. The church must practise these virtues too, not only as between its diverse components with their many variants in doctrine and practice, but towards those of other world faiths, or none.

But in practising love and brotherhood with all, it must not lose its catholicity – its proto-creedal proclamation of Jesus as the one who truly came in the flesh *and* is the Christ, God's anointed Son who is the ἱλασμός for sin, and of the need to walk with God in love for one another and in acceptance of God's cleansing or expiation of sin by the blood of Jesus. A purely exemplarist model of the atonement risks missing this divine dimension of God's love in Jesus, the Christ. Such a model does not require Jesus as the Christ, the divine gift, at all, and is equally valid if Jesus is purely human, without any divine attributes at all. First John tells as strongly against such accommodation as it does against Jesus as spirit only, devoid of genuine human attributes and suffering.

Conclusion: A Peacemaking Hermeneutic of 1 John

Two cautionary notes must first be sounded here. The first is that this study makes no pretence at dealing with wider themes in NT theology which do not appear in 1 John, such as the Pauline teaching on justification and the divine covenant with humanity. The second is that this study does not presume either to affirm or deny the traditional divine attributes of wrath and judgement, so prominent in the Johannine book of Revelation, because the emphasis in 1 John is on realised eschatology – unity with God in the here and now. Divine judgement, which is *potentially* final, is certainly present as a prominent theme in 1 John – witness, for example, the frequent references to "darkness" (1:6, 2:8, 9, 11), "death" (3:14, 5:16, 17) and "eternal life" (1:2, 2:25, 3:15, 5:11, 13, 20) – but judgement is not actually final. "Walking in the light" (1:7), confession of sin (1:9), reliance on Jesus as παράκλητος (2:1) and ἱλασμός (2:2), love (3:14), and God-given life (5:16) are the remedies.

A peacemaking hermeneutic is used here to mean one displaying the characteristics of love, reconciliation, forgiveness and abstinence from violence. Does this fit 1 John? This study provides an affirmative answer to this question. Little further summary of how this is so is attempted at this final point, in view of the extensive discussion at the end of our chapters, dealing with the ideas conveyed by our keywords, of the manner in which they are consistent with, and supportive of, the use of 1 John by certain peacemaking theologians, and, by close analysis of the ideas they represent in the LXX and elsewhere, with a peacemaking hermeneutic of 1 John. So we shall leave behind our various citations of 1 John by these theologians and offer only a short recapitulation of our major findings in previous chapters.

First, we have seen in our study of the keyword ἱλασμός and the ideas it represents in 1 John that in the LXX, God is more often the subject, rather than the object of the action. Where God is not the subject, the direct object of the action is usually the person, place or object being cleansed, and God is the indirect object. The person, place or object is cleansed *before* God, so they are rendered once again holy in God's sight. We have seen that there is mutual illumination in the uses of ἱλασμός in 1 John 2:2 and 4:10. In opening with the statement ἐν τούτῳ ἐστὶν ἡ ἀγάπη, John is proclaiming at 4:10 that God's act in sending the Son as ἱλασμὸν περὶ τῶν ἁμαρτιῶν ἡμῶν was the ultimate act of costly, self-giving love. The wrathful Father is not in view in 4:10, so this idea should not be read into 2:2, when the idea of reassuring love is introduced by 2:1: παράκλητον ἔχομεν πρὸς τὸν πατέρα. Then comes the reassurance, καὶ αὐτὸς ἱλασμός ἐστιν περὶ τῶν ἁμαρτιῶν ἡμῶν. The loving bond between us and the Father is not broken by sin, because we have a παράκλητος, a "friend at court" (2:1b), in Jesus, God's Son, who cleanses us from all sin (1:7b). The idea of the gift of the Son in 2:1-2 is further expanded by 4:10. There it is explicit that the Father's gift is of Jesus, who ἱλασμός ἐστιν περὶ τῶν ἁμαρτιῶν ἡμῶν, is an act of divine love. Then 4:10b makes explicit another thought implicit in 2:1-2: that the Father gives the Son as ἱλασμός for our sins.

Second, we have seen from our tracing of the treatment of the Cain and Abel story from Genesis 4 in the Hebrew Bible, through our study of the keywords σφάξω and ἀνθρωποκτόνος and the ideas they convey; how even the LXX and certainly the NT in 1 John 3:12 have gone far beyond the Hebrew Bible in portraying Cain's offering and *character* as flawed; the NT perspective being coloured by the LXX reading, and possibly by the treatment of the Cain and Abel story in the OT pseudepigrapha, Philo, Josephus and the Qumran literature. This is the result of a thought-shift, moving from the simple portrayal of Cain in the Torah as his brother's killer as a result of envy to a tradition which portrays Cain as the archetype of evil itself in the world: a representative of the evil one himself. The tradition embodying this thought-shift clearly influenced the writer of 1 John, and the way in which he in turn portrays Cain and his actions and origins suggests that he employed this tradition. By his use of σφάξω and ἀνθρωποκτόνος as alarming descriptors of Cain's actions and very nature, John illustrates how our failure to love affects not only what we do, but *who we are* – our very identity. These words depict the polar opposite of what John enjoins – mutual love in imitation of the divine love that gave us the gift of the Son.

Third, in our study of the keywords ἀγαπάω and its cognates and ἀδελφος, we have seen that 1 John 3:17, with its command to help the brother in need, finds a parallel in Deuteronomy 15:1-11 with its requirement of "open-handed" giving to the needy brother, χ)ϝ, who may well include the resident alien, גר. In both texts the requirement is theological and intimately linked with God's attitude to the giver (diving blessing in Deuteronomy 15:10, God's love abiding in the giver in 1 John 3:17). But for an ethic of universal love and caring in 1 John, the problem is that there is no indication there that the brother, ἀδελφος, includes the neighbour, πλησίον, or the stranger, προσήλυτον. First John does not *require* hatred of the secessionists or *exclude* love for them, as distinct from their ideas, but there is still no positive command to love them – hardly surprising in a situation of dogged opposition to secessionist doctrine and division.

As argued previously, however, even though there is no command to love the secessionists, 1 John may be used hermeneutically, employing the love command in

John's Gospel and supporting an ethic of love extending even to one's enemies. First John throws up great exegetical difficulty in the path of an ethic of universal love derived from it, but hermeneutically this is a valid solution. Certainly John condemns unequivocally the polar opposite of such love, which is hatred and killing of one's enemies. This is the very essence of a peacemaking hermeneutic of 1 John. Let the final word go to John, in 3:15a: πᾶς ὁ μισῶν τὸν ἀδελφὸν αὐτοῦ ἀνθρωποκτόνος ἐστίν.

Bibliography

Adam, Peter, "The Atoning Saviour." Pages 15–34 in *Christ Died for Our Sins: Essays on the Atonement* (ed. Michael R Stead; Canberra: Barton Books, 2013)
Akin, Daniel A, *1, 2, 3 John* (Nashville: Broadman & Holman Publishers, 2001)
Alexander, Neil, *The Epistles of John* (London: SCM Press, 1962)
Allison, Dale C Jr., *Testament of Abraham* (Berlin & New York: Walter de Gruyter, 2003)
Alison, James, *Knowing Jesus* (Springfield, IL: Templegate Publishers, 1993/London: SPCK 1993)
Alison, James, *Raising Abel: The Recovery of the Eschatological Imagination* (New York: Crossroads, 1996)
Alison, James, *The Joy of Being Wrong: Original Sin through Easter Eyes* (New York: Crossroad, 1998)
Allbee, Richard A, "Asymmetrical Continuity of Love and Law between the Old and New Testaments: Explicating the Implicit Side of a Hermeneutical Bridge, Leviticus 19: 11-18," *JSOT* 31.2 (2006): 147–66
Allen, Leslie C, *Ezekiel 20-48* (Dallas, TX: Word Books, 1990)
Alter, Robert, *Genesis* (New York/London: W. W. Norton, 1998)
Alter, Robert, *The Book of Psalms* (New York: W. W. Norton, 2007)
Andersen, Francis L and Freedman, David Noel, *Amos* (New York: Doubleday, 1989)
Anderson, Gary, *A Time to Mourn, a Time to Dance: The Expression of Grief and Joy in Israelite Religion* (University Park, PA: Pennsylvania State University Press, 1991)
Anderson, Paul N, "Discernment-Oriented Leadership in the Johannine Situation." Pages 290–318 in *Rethinking the Ethics of John: "Implicit Ethics" in the Johannine Writings* (ed. JG Van der Watt and R Zimmermann; Tübingen: Mohr Siebeck, 2012)
Anderson, Paul N, "Identity and Congruence: The Ethics of Integrity in the Johannine Epistles." Pages 331–52 in *Biblical Ethics and Application* WUNT 384 (ed. Ruben Zimmermann and Stephan Joubert; Tübingen: Mohr Siebeck, 2017)
Andrews, James A, *Hermeneutics and the Church: In Dialogue with Augustine* (Notre Dame, IN: Notre Dame Press, 2012)
Anstall, Kharalambous, "Juridical Justification Theology and a Statement of the Orthodox Teaching." Pages 482–503 in *Stricken by God? Nonviolent Identification and the Victory of Christ* (ed. Brad Jersak and Michael Hardin; Grand Rapids, MI: Eerdmans, 2007)
Attridge, Harold W, *Interpretation of Biblical History in the "Antiquitates Judaici" of Flavius Josephus* (Harvard Dissertations in Religion 7; Missoula: Scholars, 1976)
Auld, AG, *Amos* (Sheffield: Sheffield Academic Press, 1995)
Aulen, Gustav, *Christus Victor: An Historical Study of the Three Main Types of the Idea of Atonement* (trans. AG Herbert; London: SPCK, 1931; repr. Eugene, OR: Wipf and Stock, 2003)
Aune, David E, *Revelation 1-5* (Dallas, TX: Word Books, 1997)
Baillie, DM, *God Was in Christ* (London: Faber and Faber, 1948)
Baker, David L, *Tight Fists or Open Hands? Wealth and Poverty in Old Testament Law* (Grand Rapids, MI/Cambridge, UK: Eerdmans, 2009)

Barker, Paul A, *The Triumph of Grace in Deuteronomy* (Carlisle: Paternoster Press, 2004)
Barth, Karl, *Church Dogmatics*, IV/1 (trans. GW Bromiley; Edinburgh: T&T Clark, 1956)
Barr, James, *The Semantics of Biblical Language* (Oxford: Oxford University Press, 1961)
Bartling, Victor, "We Love Because He Loved Us First (1 John 4: 7-21)," *CTM* 23.12D (1952): 868–83
Bauckham, Richard, *Jesus and the Eyewitnesses: The Gospels as Eyewitness Testimony* (Grand Rapids, MI: Eerdmans, 2006)
Bauckham, Richard, "The Continuing Quest for the Provenance of Old Testament Pseudepigrapha." Pages 9–29 in *The Pseudepigrapha and Christian Origins* (ed. Gerbern S Oegema and James H Charlesworth; New York/London: T&T Clark, 2008)
Bauckham, Richard, "The Fourth Gospel as the Testimony of the Beloved Disciple." Pages 120–39 in *The Gospel of John and Christian Theology* (ed. Richard Bauckham and Carl Mosser; Grand Rapids, MI: Eerdmans, 2008)
Bauer, Walter, *Orthodoxy and Heresy in Earliest Christianity* (London: SCM Press, 1972)
Bayliss, Charles P, "The Meaning of Walking" in the Darkness' (1 John 1:6), *B Sac* 149 (1992) 214–22
Beale, GP, *The Book of Revelation* (Grand Rapids, MI/Cambridge, UK, Carlisle: Paternoster Press, 1999)
Beasley-Murray, George R, *John* (New York: Thomas Nelson Inc., 2nd ed., 1999)
Belousek, Darrin W Snyder, *Atonement, Justice and Peace: The Message of the Cross and the Mission of the Church* (Grand Rapids: Eerdmans, 2012)
Berchman, Robert A, *From Philo to Origen: Middle Platonism in Transition* (Chico, CA: Scholars Press, 1984)
Bergsma, John S, "The Relationship between Jubilees and the Early Enoch Books." Pages 36–51 in *Enoch and the Mosaic Torah: The Evidence of Jubilees* (ed. Gabriele Boccaccini and Giovanni Ibba; Grand Rapids, MI/Cambridge, UK: Eerdmans, 2009)
Beutler, Johannes, *Die Johhanesbriefe* (Regensburg: Verlag Friedrich Pustet, 2000)
Block, Daniel I, *The Book of Ezekiel Chapters 25-48* (Grand Rapids, MI: Eerdmans, 1998)
Borgen, Peder, *Philo, John and Paul: New Perspectives on Judaism and Early Christianity* (Atlanta, GA: Scholars Press, 1987)
Borgen, Peder, *Philo of Alexandria, An Exegete for His Time* (Leiden, New York, Cologne: Brill, 1997)
Bowen, Nancy R, *Ezekiel* (Nashville: Abingdon Press, 2010)
Boxall, Ian, *The Revelation of St John* (London/New York: Hendrickson Publishers/A & C Black, 2006)
Boyce, Richard N, *Leviticus and Numbers* (Louisville/London: Westminster John Knox Press, 2008)
Braun, Roddy, *1 Chronicles* (Waco, TX: Word Books, 1986)
Briggs, Charles Augustus, *A Critical and Exegetical Commentary on the Book of Psalms Vol II* (Edinburgh: T&T Clark, 1925)
Brown, Raymond E, *The Community of the Beloved Disciple* (London: Geoffrey Chapman, 1979)
Brown, Raymond E, *The Gospel According to John, I-XII* (New York: Doubleday, 1966)
Brown, Raymond E, "The Qumran Scrolls and the Johannine Gospel and Epistles." Pages 183–207 in *The Scrolls and the New Testament* (ed. Krister Stendahl; New York: Crossroads, 1992)
Brown, Raymond E, *The Epistles of John* (New Haven & London: Yale University Press, paperback edition, 2006)

Brooke, AE, *A Critical and Exegetical Commentary on the Johannine Epistles* (Edinburgh: T&T Clark, 1912)
Brooke, George J, *The Dead Sea Scrolls and the New Testament* (Minneapolis: Fortress Press, 2005)
Bruce, FF, *The Epistles of John* (London: Pickering & Inglis, 1970)
Brueggemann, Walter, *Deuteronomy* (Nashville: Abingdon Press, 2001)
Brueggemann, Walter, *Old Testament Theology* (Nashville: Abingdon Press, 2008)
Budd, Ohilip J, *Numbers* (Waco, TX: Word Books, 1984)
Bultmann, Rudolf, *New Testament Theology* Vol II (trans. Kendrick Grobel; London: SCM Press, 1955)
Bultmann, Rudolf, *The Gospel of John: A Commentary* (trans. GR Beasley-Murray; Oxford: Basil Blackwell, 1971)
Bultmann, Rudolf, *The Johannine Epistles* (trans. PP O'Hara with LC McGaughy and RW Funk; Philadelphia: Fortress Press, English translation 1973 from the 2nd German edition, 1967)
Burge, Gary M, "Spirit-Inspired Theology and Ecclesial Correction: Charting One Shift in the Development of Johannine Ecclesiology and Pneumatology." Pages 179–85 in *Communities in Dispute: Current Scholarship on the Johannine Epistles* (ed. R Alan Culpepper and Paul N Anderson; Atlanta: SBL Press, 2014)
Burge, Gary M, *The Anointed Community: The Holy Spirit in the Johannine Tradition* (Grand Rapids, MI: Eerdmans, 1987)
Burge, Gary M, *The Letters of John* (Grand Rapids, MI: Zondervan, 1996)
Burnett, Fred W, "Philo on Immortality: A Thematic Study of Philo's Concept of παλιγγενεσία," *CBQ* 46.3 (1984): 447–70
Burridge, Richard, *Imitating Jesus: An Inclusive Approach to New Testament Ethics* (Grand Rapids, MI/Cambridge, UK: Eerdmans, 2007)
Byron, John, *Cain and Abel in Text and Tradition: Jewish and Christian Interpretations of the First Sibling Rivalry* (Leiden/Boston: Brill, 2011)
Byron, John, "Slaughter, Fratricide and Sacrilege: Cain and Abel Traditions in 1 John 3," *Bib* 88.4 (2007): 526–35
Campbell, Constantine R, *1, 2 and 3 John* (Grand Rapids: Zondervan, 2017)
Carson, DA, "Divine Sovereignty and Human Responsibility in Philo," *Nov T* 23.2 (1981): 148–64
Cassuto, U, *A Commentary on the Book of Exodus* (trans. Israel Abrahams; Jerusalem: The Magnes Press, The Hebrew University, 1967)
Charlesworth, James A, "The Fourth Evangelist and the Dead Sea Scrolls: Assessing Trends over Nearly Sixty Years." Pages 161–81 in *John, Qumran and the Dead Sea Scrolls: Sixty Years of Discovery and Debate* (ed. Mary L Coloe and Tom Thatcher; Atlanta: Society of Biblical Literature, 2011)
Charlesworth, JH, *The Pseudepigrapha and Modern Research* (Missoula, MT: Scholars Press, 1976)
Charlesworth, RH, "Can We Determine the Composition Date of the Parables of Enoch?" Pages 450–68 in *Enoch and the Messiah Son of Man* (ed. Gabriele Boccaccini; Grand Rapids, MI/Cambridge, UK: Eerdmans, 2007)
Charlesworth, RH, *The Old Testament Pseudepigrapha and the New Testament* (Cambridge: Cambridge University Press, 1985)
Clark, Gordon H, *First John: A Commentary* (Jefferson: Trinity Foundation, 1980)
Clavier, Henri, "Notes sur un Mot-clef du Johannisme et de la Soteriologie Biblique: Ἱλασμός," *Nov T* 10 (1968): 287–304

Clements, RE, *Deuteronomy* (Sheffield: JSOT Press, 1993)
Collins, John J, *Daniel* (Minneapolis: Fortress Press, 1993)
Collins, John J, "The Nature and Aims of the Sect Known from the Dead Sea Scrolls." Pages 31-52 in *Flores Florentino: Dead Sea Scrolls and Other Early Jewish Studies in Honour of Florentinto Gárcia Martínez* (ed. Florentino garcia Martinez; Leiden/Boston: Brill, 2007)
Connell, Martin F, "On 'Chrism' and 'Anti-Christs' in 1 John 2: 18-27:A Hypothesis," *Worship* 83.3 (2009): 212-34
Cooke, GA, *A Critical and Exegetical Commentary on the Book of Ezekiel* (Edinburgh: T&T Clark, 1936)
Coombes, Malcolm, *1 John: The Epistle as a Relecture of the Gospel of John* (Preston, VIC: Mosaic Press, 2013)
Cosgrove, Charles A, *Appealing to Scripture in Moral Debate: Five Hermeneutical Rules* (Grand Rapids, MI: Eerdmans, 2002)
Craig Jr., Kenneth M, "Questions Outside Eden (Genesis 4: 1-16): Yahweh, Cain and Their Rhetorical interchange," *JSOT* 86 (1999): 107-28
Craigie, Peter, *The Book of Deuteronomy* (Grand Rapids, MI: Eerdmans, 1976)
Culy, Martin M, *I, II, III John: A Handbook on the Greek Text* (Waco, TX: Baylor University Press, 2004)
Curtis, Edward Lewis and Madsen, Albert Alonzo, *The Book of Chronicles* (Edinburgh: T&T Clark, 1910)
Davenport, Gene L, *The Eschatology of the Book of Jubilees* (Leiden: EJ Brill, 1971)
Davies, Glenn N and Stead, Michael R, "Atonement and Redemption." Pages 35-58 in *Christ Died for Our Sins: Essays on the Atonement* (ed. Michael R Stead; Canberra: Barton Books, 2013)
Davis, Peter H, "The Use of the Pseudepigrapha in the Catholic Epistles." Pages 228-45 in *The Pseudepigrapha and Early Biblical Interpretation* (ed. JH Charlesworth and Craig A Evans; Sheffield: Sheffield Academic Press, 1993)
De Boer, Martinus C, "The Death of Jesus and His Coming in the Flesh (1 John 4:2)," *Nov T* XXXIII.4 (1991): 326-46
Deere, Derward W, "An Introduction to Deuteronomy," *SJT* 57.3 (1964), 7-16
Denney, James, *The Death of Christ* (London: Hodder and Stoughton, 1951)
Dodd, CH, *Historical Tradition in the Fourth Gospel* (Cambridge: Cambridge University Press, 1963)
Dodd, CH, "HILASKESTHAI, Its Cognates, Derivatives and Synonyms, in the Septuagint," *JTS* 32 (1931): 352-60
Dodd, CH, *The Bible and the Greeks* (London: Hodder & Stoughton, 1935)
Dodd, CH, *The Johannine Epistles* (London, Hodder & Stoughton, 1946)
Doering, Lutz, "Purity and Impurity in the Book of Jubilees." Pages 261-75 in *Enoch and the Mosaic Torah: The Evidence of Jubilees* (ed. Gabriele Boccaccini and Giovanni Ibba; Grand Rapids, MI/Cambridge, UK: Eerdmans, 2009)
Driver, SR, *A Critical and Exegetical Commentary on Deuteronomy* (Edinburgh: T&T Clark, 1902)
Duguid, Iain M, *Daniel* (Phillipsburg, NJ: P & R Publishing, 1998)
Dunn, James DG, *Jesus Remembered* (Grand Rapids/Cambridge: Eerdmans, 2003)
Dunn, James DG, "John and the Oral Gospel Tradition." Pages 351-79 in *Jesus and the Oral Gospel Tradition* (ed. H Wansbrough; Sheffield: JSOT, 1991)
Durham, John C, *Exodus* (Nashville: Thomas Nelson, 1987)

Eisenman, Robert, *The Dead Sea Scrolls and the First Christians* (Shaftsbury, Dorset: Element Books, 1996)
Ellis, E Earl, *The World of St John: The Gospel and Epistles* (Grand Rapids, MI: Eerdmans, 1984)
Endres SJ, John C, *Biblical Interpretation in the Book of Jubilees* (Catholic Biblical Quarterly Monograph Series 18; Washington, DC: Catholic Biblical Association of America, 1987)
Eynikel, Erik, "The Qumran Background of Johannine Ethics." Pages 102-13 in *Rethinking the Ethics of John* (ed. Jan G Van Der Watt and Ruben Zimmerman; Tübingen: Mohr Siebeck, 2012)
Feder, Yitzhaq, "On *Kupperu, Kipper* and Etymological Sins That Cannot be Wiped Away," *VT* 60 (2010): 535-45
Feldman, Louis H, *Flavius Josephus' Judean Antiquities I-IV: Translation and Commentary* (Boston/Leiden: Brill, 2004)
Fiddes, Paul S, *Past Event and Present Salvation* (London: Darton, Longman and Todd, 1989)
Fisch, Rabbi Dr S, *Ezekiel* (London & Bournemouth: Socino Press, 1950)
Fitzmyer SJ, Joseph A, "Qumran Literature and the Johannine Writings." Pages 117-33 in *Life in Abundance: Studies of John's Gospel in Tribute to Raymond E Brown* (ed. John R Donahue; Collegeville, MN: Liturgical Press, 2005)
Fraade, Steven D, "Looking for Legal Midrash at Qumran." Pages 59-80 in *Biblical Perspectives: Early Use & Interpretation of the Bible in Light of the Dead Sea Scrolls— Proceedings of the First International Symposium of the Orion Centre, 12-14 May 1996* (ed. Michael E Stone and Esther G Chazon; Leiden: Brill, 1998)
Frey, Jörg, "Recent Perspectives on Johannine Dualism." Pages 127-60 in *Text, Thought and Practice in Early* Christianity—*Proceedings of the Ninth International Symposium of the Orion Centre for the Study of the Dead Sea Scrolls and Associated Literature, Jointly Sponsored by the Hebrew University entre for the Study of Christianity, 11-13 January 2004* (ed. Ruth A Clements and Daniel R Schwartz; Leiden: Brill, 2009)
Gane, Roy, *Cult and Character: Purification Offerings, Day of Atonement, and Theodicy* (Winona Lake, IN: Eisenbrauns, 2005)
Gaugler, Ernst, *Die Johannesbriefe* (Zürich: Evz-Verlag, 1964)
Girard, Réne, *Battling to the End: Conversations with Benoît Chantre* (trans. Mary Baker; East Lancing: Michigan State University Press, 2010)
Girard, Réne, *I See Satan Fall Like Lightning* (trans. James G Williams; Maryknoll, New York: Orbis Books, 2009)
Girard, Réne, *The Girard Reader* (ed. James G Williams; New York: Crossroad, 1996)
Girard, Réne, *The Scapegoat* (trans. Y Freccero; Baltimore: Johns Hopkins University Press, 1986)
Girard, Réne, *Things Hidden since the Foundation of the World* (trans. Stephen Bann and Michael Metteer; Stanford, California: Stanford University Press, 1987)
Girard, Réne, *Violence and the Sacred* (trans. Patrick Gregory; New York and London: Johns Hopkins University Press, paperback edition, 1979)
Girard, Réne, with Antonello, Pierpaolo and Rocha, João de Castro, *Evolution and Conversion: Dialogues on the Origin of Culture* (London: T&T Clark, 2007)
Glassock, Ed, "Forgiveness and Cleansing according to 1 John 1:9," *B Sac* 166 (2009): 217-31
Glenny, W Edward, *Finding Meaning in the Text: Translation Techniques and Theology in the Septuagint of Amos* (Leiden/Boston: Brill, 2009)

Goff, Matthew, "Male and Female, Heaven and Earth: Claude Lévi-Strauss's Structuralist Approach to Myth and the Enochic Myth of the Watchers." Pages 77–91 in *The Dead Sea Scrolls and the Study of the Humanities* (ed. Pieter B Hartog, Alison Schofield and Samuel I Thomas; Leiden/Boston: Brill, 2018)

Goldwurm, Hersh and Rabbi Hersh, *Daniel* (Brooklyn, NY: Mesorah Publications Ltd, 1998)

Gore, Charles, *The Epistles of St John* (London: John Murray, 1920)

Gore-Jones, Lydia and Llewellyn, Stephen, "The Parting of the Ways." Pages 158–83 in *Into All the World: Emergent Christianity in Its Jewish and Greco-Roman Context* (ed. Mark Harding and Alanna Nobbs; Grand Rapids: Eerdmans, 2017)

Gorman, FH, *The Ideology of Ritual: Space, Time and Status in the Priestly Theology* (Sheffield: Sheffield Academic Press, 1990)

Grayston, K, *The Johannine Epistles* (London: Marshall, Morgan & Scott, 1984)

Greenhill, William, *Ezekiel* (Edinburgh, Banner of Truth Trust, first published 1645–67, 1863 edition, reprinted, 1994)

Griffith, Terry, "A Non-Polemical Reading of 1 John: Sin, Christology and the Limits of Johannine Christianity," *Tyn Bul* 49.2 (1998): 253–76

Gunkel, Hermann, *Genesis* (trans. Mark E Biddle; Macon, Georgia: Mercer University Press, 1997)

Haenchen, Ernst, *John 1* (trans. Robert W Funk; Philadelphia: Fortress Press, 1984)

Hamilton, Victor P, *The Book of Genesis: Chapters 1–17* (Grand Rapids, Michigan: Eerdmans, 1990)

Harrington, Hannah K, "Purification in the Fourth Gospel in light of Qumran." Pages 117–39 in *John, Qumran and the Dead Sea Scrolls: Sixty Years of Discovery and Debate* (ed. Mary L Coloe and Tom Thatcher; Atlanta: Society of Biblical Literature, 2011)

Harris, R Laird, "The Meaning of 'Kipper', Atone," *JETS* 4.1 (1961): 3

Hartog, Paul A, "The Opponents of Polycarp, *Philippians* and 1 John." Pages 375–91 in *Trajectories through the New Testament and the Apostolic Fathers* (ed. A Gregory and C Tuckett; Oxford: Oxford University Press, 2005)

Hauerwas, Stanley, *The Peaceable Kingdom: A Primer in Christian Ethics* (London, SCM Press, 1983)

Hayes, John H, "Atonement in the Book of Leviticus," *Int* 52.1 (1998): 5–15

Hays, Richard B, *The Moral Vision of the New Testament* (New York: HarperCollins, 1996)

Heckel, Theo C, "Die Historisierung der Johanneischen Theologie im Ersten Johannesbrief," *NTS* 50.3 (2004): 425–43

Hempel, Charlotte, *The Laws of the Damascus Document* (Leiden: Brill, 1998)

Hiebert, D Edmond, "An Exposition of John 3: 13-24," *B Sac* (1989): 301–19

Hill, Charles E, *The Johannine Corpus in the Early Church* (Oxford: Oxford University Press, 2004)

Hill, D, *Greek Words and Hebrew Meanings* (Cambridge: Cambridge University Press, 1967)

Hodges, Zane C, "Fellowship and Confession in 1 John 1:5-10," *B Sac* 129 (1972): 48–60

Holtzmann, HJ, *Briefe und Offenbarung des Johannes* (Freiburg und Leipzig, 1893)

Holy Bible: New Revised Standard Version (London: HarperCollins, 1998)

Houlden, JL, *A Commentary on the Johannine Epistles* (London: A & C Black, 1973)

Hullinger, Jerry M, "The Function of the Millennial Sacrifices in Ezekiel's Temple, Part 1," *B Sac* 167 (2010): 40–57

Hunsinger, George, "The Politics of the Non-Violent God: Reflections on René Girard and Karl Barth," *SJT* 51.1 (1998): 61–85

Jacobson, Howard, "Genesis IV.8," *VT* 55.4 (2005): 564–5
Janzen, David, *The Social Meaning of Sacrifice in the Hebrew Bible* (Berlin/New York: Walter de Gruyter, 2004)
Japhet, Sara, *I and 11 Chronicles* (London: SCM Press, 1993)
Jeanrond, Werner, *Theological Hermeneutics: Development and Significance* (London: SCM Press, 1994)
Jensen, Matthew D, *Affirming the Resurrection of the Incarnate Christ: A Reading of 1 John* (Cambridge: Cambridge University Press, 2012)
Jensen, Matthew, "The Structure and Argument of 1 John," *JSNT* 35.1 (2012): 54–73
Jenson, Robert, *Ezekiel* (Grand Rapids, MI: Brazos Press, 2009), 318
Jobes, Karen H, *1, 2, and 3 John* (Grand Rapids, MI: Zondervan, 2014)
Johnson, TF, *1, 2, and 3 John* (Peabody, MA: Hendrickson, 1993)
Jones, Peter Rhea, *1, 2 and 3 John* (Macon, GA: Smith and Helwys, 2009)
Jones, Ray Carlton, "Deuteronomy 10:12-22," *Int* 46.3 (1992): 281–5, 361
Josephus in Nine Volumes: IV, Jewish Antiquities, Books I-IV (trans. H St J Thackeray; Cambridge, MA: Heinemann, 1967)
Kaminsky, Joel S, "Loving One's (Israelite) Neighbour: Election and Commandment in Leviticus 19," *Int* 62.2 (2008): 123–32
Kaufman, Gordon, *God, Mystery, Diversity: Christian Theology in a Pluralistic World* (Minneapolis: Fortress Press, 1996)
Kaufman, Gordon, *In the Beginning...Creativity* (Minneapolis: Fortress Press, 2004)
Kaufman, Gordon D, *The Face of Mystery: A Constructive Theology* (Cambridge, MA: Harvard University Press, 1993)
Keener, Craig S, *The Gospel of John: A Commentary, Vol* II (Peabody, MA: Hendrickson Publishers, 2003)
Keith, Chris, "Introduction." Pages 1–34 in *Jesus among Friends and Enemies: A Historical and Literary Introduction to Jesus in the Gospels* (ed. Chris Keith and Larry W Hurtado; Grand Rapids: Baker Academic, 2011)
Keith, Chris, "The Narratives of the Gospels and the Historical Jesus: Current Debates, Prior Debates and the Goal of Historical Jesus Research," *JSNT* 38.4 (2016): 426–55
Keith, Chris, *The Pericope Adulterae, the Gospel of John and the Literacy of Jesus* (Leiden/Boston: Brill, 2009)
Kelhoffer, James A, *Persecution, Persuasion and Power: Readiness to Withstand Hardship as a Corroboration of Legitimacy in the New Testament* (Tübingen: Mohr Siebeck, 2010)
Kennedy, HAA, *Philo's Contribution to Religion* (Edinburgh: Hodder & Stoughton, 1919)
Kessler, Martin and Deurloo, Karel, *A Commentary on Genesis* (Manwah, NJ: Paulist Press, 2004)
Kidner, Derek, *Genesis* (London: Tyndale Press, 1968)
Kidner, Derek, "Sacrifice: Metaphors and Meaning," *Tyn Bul* 33 (1982): 119–36
Kiuchi, N, *The Purification Function in the Priestly Literature: Its Meaning and Function* (Sheffield: JSOT, 1987)
Klassen, William, "'Love your Enemies': Some Reflections on the Current Status of Research." Pages 1–31 in *The Love of Enemy and Nonretaliation in the New Testament* (ed. Willard M Swartley; Louisville, KY: Westminster/John Knox Press, 1992)
Klauck, Hans-Josef, *Der Erste Johannesbrief* (Zürich und Braunschweig: Benziger Verlag AG, 1991)
Klauck, Hans-Josef, "Internal Opponents: the Treatment of the Secessionists in the First Epistle of John." Pages 55–65 in *Truth and Its Victims* (ed. Wim Beuken, Sean Freyne

and Anton Weiler; English language editor James Aitken Gardiner; Edinburgh: T&T Clark, 1988)

Klein, Ralph W, *1 Chronicles* (Minneapolis: Fortress Press, 2006)

Kleinig, John W, *Leviticus* (Saint Louis: Concordia Commentary, Concordia Publishing House, 2001)

Kline, Moshe, "'The Editor was Nodding': A Reading of Leviticus 19 in Memory of Mary Douglas," *The Journal of Hebrew Scriptures* 8.17 (2008): 2–59

Knibb, Michael A, "Interpreting the Book of Enoch: Reflections on a Recently Published Commentary," *JSJ* (2002) 33.4: 437–50

Knohl, Israel, "The Guilt Offering of the Holiness School (Num. V 5-8)," *VT* 54.4 (2004): 516–26

Knoppers, Gary N, *1 Chronicles 10-29* (New York: Doubleday, 2009)

Koester, Craig, "Progress and Paradox: CH Dodd and Rudolf Bultmann on History, the Jesus Tradition and the Fourth Gospel." Pages 49–65 in *Engaging with CH Dodd on the Gospel of John* (ed. Tom Thatcher and Catlin H Williams; Cambridge/New York: Cambridge University Press, 2013)

Koester, Craig, "The Antichrist Theme in the Johannine Epistles." Pages 187–96 in *Communities in Dispute: Current Scholarship on the Johannine Epistles* (ed. R Alan Culpepper and Paul N Anderson; Atlanta: SBL Press, 2014)

Kostenberger, Andreas J, *A Theology of John's Gospel and Letters* (Grand Rapids, MI: Zondervan, 2009)

Kruse, Colin G, *The Letters of John* (Grand Rapids, MI: Eerdmans/Leicester: Apollos, 2000)

Kugel, James A, "On Hidden Hatreds and Open Reproach: Early Exegesis of Leviticus 19:17," *HTL* 80.1 (1987): 43–61

Kysar, Robert, *The Maverick Gospel* (Atlanta: John Knox Press, 1976)

Kysar, Robert, *Voyages with John: Charting the Fourth Gospel* (Waco, TX: Baylor University Press, 2005)

Lapsley, Jacqueline E, "Feeling Our Way: Love for God in Deuteronomy," *CBQ* 65.3 (2003): 350–69

Law, Robert, *The Tests of Life* (Edinburgh: T&T Clark, 1909)

Law, Timothy Michael, *When God Spoke Greek: The Septuagint and the Making of the Christian Bible* (Oxford/New York: Oxford University Press, 2013)

Levin, Schnier, "Cain versus Abel," *Judaism* 53.1-2 (2004): 51–4

Levine, Baruch A, *In the Presence of the Lord* (Leiden: EJ Brill, 1974)

Levine, Baruch A, *Leviticus* (Philadelphia/New York/Jerusalem: The JPS Torah Commentary, Jewish Publication Society, 1989)

Levine, Baruch A, *Numbers 1–20* (New York: Doubleday, 1993)

Levinson, John R, "The Debut of the Divine Spirit in Josephus' *Antiquities*," *HTR* 87.2 (1994): 123–38

Leviticus: A New Translation with a Commentary from Talmudic, Midrashic and Rabbinical Sources (translation and commentary by Rabbis Nosson Scherman and Hersh Goldwurm; Brooklyn, NY: Mesorah Publications Ltd, 1990)

Lewis, Jack P, "The Offering of Abel (Gen 4:4): A History of Interpretation," *JETS* 37.4 (1994): 481–96

Lewis, Scott M, *The Gospel According to John and the Johannine Letters* (Collegeville, MN: Liturgical Press, 2005)

Lindars, Barnabas, *The Gospel of John* (London: Marshall, Morgan and Scott, 1972)

Lieu, JM, *The Theology of the Johannine Epistles* (Cambridge: Cambridge University Press, 1991)
Lieu, JM, "Us or You? Persuasion and Identity in 1 John," *JBL* 127.4 (2008): 805-19
Lieu, Judith, *I, II, & III John* (Louisville/London: Westminster John Knox Press, 2008)
Lieu, JM, *Neither Jew Nor Greek?* (London & New York: T&T Clark, 2002)
Lim, Timothy H, "Towards a Description of the Sectarian Matrix." Pages 7-22 in *Echoes from the Caves: Qumran and the New Testament* (ed. Florentino Garcia Martinez; Leiden/Boston: Brill, 2009)
Loader, W, *The Johannine Epistles* (London: Epworth Press, 1992)
Loader, William RG, "The Significance of 2: 15-17 for Understanding the Ethics of John," Pages 223-35 in *Communities in Dispute: Current Scholarship on the Johannine Epistles* (ed. R Alan Culpepper and Paul N Anderson; Atlanta: SBL Press, 2014)
Lohr, Joel N, "Righteous Abel, Wicked Cain: Genesis 4: 10-16 in the Masoretic Text, the Septuagint and the New Testament," *CBQ* 71.3 (2009): 485-96
McConville, JG, *Deuteronomy* (Sheffield: JSOT Press, 1984)
McDermond, JE, *1, 2, 3 John* (Harrisonburg, Virginia/Waterloo, Canada: Herald Press, 2011)
McGrath, Alister, *Justitia Dei* (Cambridge: Cambridge University Press, 3rd ed., 2005)
McHugh, John, "'In Him was Life': John's Gospel and the Parting of the Ways." Pages 123-58 in *Jews and Christians: The Parting of the Ways* (ed. JDG Dunn; Grand Rapids, MI: Eerdmans, 1992)
McNamara MSC, Martin, *Intertestamental Literature* (Wilmington, DE: Michael Glazier Inc., 1983)
Marshall, IH, *The Epistles of John* (Grand Rapids, MI: Eerdmans, 1978)
Martin, Luther M, "Josephus' Use of *Heimarmene* in the *Jewish Antiquities* XIII, 171-3," *Numen* 28.2 (1981): 127-37
Martinez, Florentino Garcia, "The Heavenly Tablets in the Book of Jubilees." Pages 243-60 in *Studies in the Book of Jubilees* (ed. Matthias Albani, Jorg Frey and Armin Lange; Tübingen: Mohr Siebeck, 1997)
Martyn, J Louis, *History and Theology in the Fourth Gospel* (Louisville, KY: Westminster John Knox Press, 3rd ed., 2003)
Marx, Alfred, "The Relationship between the Sacrificial Laws and the Other Laws in Leviticus 19," *The Journal of Hebrew Scriptures* 8.9 (2008): 2-11
Mason, Steve, *Josephus and the New Testament* (Peabody, MA: Hendrickson, 1992)
Mayes, ADH, *Deuteronomy* (Grand Rapids, MI: Eerdmans/London: Marshall, Morgan & Scott Publ. Ltd., 1979)
Mayes, ADH, "On Describing the Purpose of Deuteronomy," *JSOT* 58 (1993): 13-33
Méasson, Anita and Cazeaux, Jaques, "From Grammar to Discourse." Pages 125-226 in *Both Literal and Allegorical: Studies in Philo of Alexandria's Questions and Answers on Genesis and Exodus* (ed. David M Hay; Atlanta, GA: Scholars Press, 1991)
Mencken, Maarten J, "The Image of Cain in 1 John 3, 12." Pages 195-211 in *Miracles and Imagery* in Luke and John (ed. J Verheyden, G Van Belle and JG Van Der Watt; Leuven/Paris/Dudley, MA/Uitgerverij Peeters, 2008)
Milgrom, Jacob, "A Prolegomenon to Leviticus 17:11," *JBL* 90 (1971): 150-1
Milgrom, Jacob, *Leviticus 1-16* (New York: Doubleday, 1991)
Milgrom, Jacob, *Leviticus 17-22* (New York: The Anchor Bible, Doubleday, 2000)
Milgrom, Jacob, *Numbers* (Philadelphia: Jewish Publication Society, 1990)
Miller, Patrick D, *Deuteronomy* (Louisvile: John Knox Press, 1990)
Moloney, FJ, "The Fourth Gospel and the Jesus of History," *NTS* 46 (2000): 42-58

Moloney, FJ, *Love in the Gospel of John* (Grand Rapids: Baker Academic, 2013)
Moloney, FJ, *The Gospel of John* (Collegeville, MN: Liturgical Press, 1998)
Montgomery, James A, *A Critical and Exegetical Commentary on the Book of Daniel* (Edinburgh: T&T Clark, 1927)
Morgen, Michéle, *Les Epîtres de Jean* (Paris: Les Editions du Cerf, 2005)
Morris, Leon, *The Apostolic Preaching of the Cross* (Leicester: IVP 3rd ed., 1965, repr. 1976)
Morris, Leon, *The Gospel According to John* (rev ed.; Grand Rapids: Eerdmans, 1995)
Mounce, Robert H, *The Book of Revelation* (Grand Rapids, MI/ Cambridge, UK: Eerdmans, rev ed., 1998)
Najman, H, *Seconding Sinai: The Development of Mosaic Discourse in Second Temple Judaism* (JSJ Sup 77; Leiden: Brill, 2003) 46
Neufeld, Dietmar, *Reconceiving Texts as Speech Acts: An Analysis of 1 John* (Leyden/New York/Köln: EJ Brill, 1994)
Nickelsburg, George, *Jewish Literature between the Bible and the Mishnah* (Minneapolis, Fortress Press, 2005)
Nickelsburg, George WE, *A Commentary on the Book of Enoch, Chapters 1–36; 81–108* (Minneapolis: Fortress Press, 2001)
Nickelsburg, George WE, and Vanderkam, James C, *1 Enoch* (Minneapolis: Fortress Press, 2004)
Nickelsburg, George WE, and Vanderkam, James C, *1 Enoch 2* (Minneapolis: Fortress Press, 2012)
Nicole, Roger R, "CH Dodd and the Doctrine of Propitiation," *Tyn Bul* 17.2 (1955): 117-57
Nihan, Christophe, *From Priestly Torah to Pentateuch* (Tubingen: Mohr Siebeck, 2007)
Northey, Wayne, "The Cross: God's Peace Work—Towards a Restorative Peacemaking Understanding of the Atonement." Pages 356-77 in *Stricken by God? Nonviolent Identification and the Victory of Christ* (ed. Brad Jersak and Michael Hardin; Grand Rapids, MI: Eerdmans, 2007)
Noth, Martin, *Leviticus* (London: SCM Press, First English ed., 1965)
Novum Testamentum Graece (ed. Barbara and Kurt Aland, Johannes Karavidopoulos, Carlo M Martini, Bruce M Metzger; Deutsche Bibelgesellschaft: Münster/Westphalia, 28th rev ed., 2012)
Olson, Daniel, *Enoch: A New Translation* (North Richland Hills, Texas: Biblical Press, 2004)
Olsson, Birger, *A Commentary on the Letters of John: An Intra-Jewish Approach* (trans. Richard J Erickson, Eugene, OR: Pickwick Publications, 2013)
O'Neill, JC, *The Puzzle of 1 John* (London: SPCK, 1966)
Painter, J, *John: Witness and Theologian* (Melbourne: Beacon Hill Books, 3rd ed., 1986)
Painter, J, *1, 2, and 3 John* (Collegeville, MN: Liturgical Press, 2008)
Painter, J, "The Farewell Discourses and the Jesus of History," *NTS* 7 (1981): 526-43
Painter, J, *The Quest for the Messiah* (Edinburgh: T&T Clark, 2nd ed., 1993)
Painter, J, "The Signs of the Messiah and the Quest for Eternal Life." Pages 233-56 in *What We Have Heard from the Beginning: The Past, Present and Future of Johannine Studies* (ed. Tom Thatcher; Waco: Baylor University Press, 2007)
Paul, Shalom M, *Amos* (Minneapolis: Fortress Press, 1991)
Perkins, Pheme, "Apocalyptic Sectarianism and Love Commands: The Johannine Epistles and Revelation." Pages 287-96 in *The Love of Enemy and Nonretaliation in the New Testament* (ed. Willard M Swartley; Louisville, KY: Westminster/John Knox Press, 1992)

Perkins, Pheme, "*Koinōnia* in 1 John 1: 3-7: The Social Context of Division in the Johannine Letters," *CBQ* 45.4 (1983): 631-41
Perkins, Pheme, *The Johannine Epistles* (Dublin: Veritas Publications, 1979)
Philo, Vol II (trans. Revs. FH Colson and GH Whittaker; Cambridge, MA: Heinemann, 1958)
Phillips, Anthony, *Deuteronomy* (Cambridge: Cambridge University Press, 1973)
Piper, John, *Love Your Enemies* (Wheaton, Illinois: Crossway, 2012)
Popkes, EE, *Die Theologie der Liebe Gottes in den johanneischen Schriften* (Tübingen: Mohr Siebeck, 2005)
Porter, JR, *Leviticus* (Cambridge: Cambridge University Press, 1976)
Propp, William HC, *Exodus 19-40* (New York: Doubleday, 2006)
Rashbam's Commentary on Leviticus and Numbers (ed. and trans. Martin I Lockshin; Providence: Brown Judaic Studies, 2001)
Redditt, Paul L, "Leviticus." Pages 52-8 in *Theological Interpretation of the Old Testament* (ed. Kevin J Vanhoozer; Grand Rapids, MI: Baker Academic/London: SPCK, 2005)
Reinhartz, Adele, *Befriending the Beloved Disciple* (New York/London: Continuum, 2001)
Rensberger, D, *1 John, 2 John, 3 John* (Nashville: Abingdon Press, 1997)
Rensberger, D, "Completed Love." Pages 237-71 in *Communities in Dispute: Current Scholarship on the Johannine Epistles* (ed. R Alan Culpepper and Paul N Anderson; Atlanta: SBL Press, 2014)
Ricoeur, Paul, *Hermeneutics and the Human Sciences: Essays in Language, Action and Interpretation* (ed. and trans. John B Thompson; Cambridge: Cambridge University Press, 1981)
Ricoeur, Paul, "Thou Shalt Not Kill: A Loving Obedience." Pages 111-40 in André LaCocque and Paul Ricoeur, *Thinking Biblically: Exegetical and Hermeneutical Studies* (trans. David Pellauer; Chicago and London: The University of Chicago Press, 2016)
Ringren, Helmer, *The Faith of Qumran: Theology of the Dead Sea Scrolls* (trans. Emilie T Sander; Philadelphia: Fortress Press, 1963)
Rofé, Alexander, *Deuteronomy: Issues and Interpretation* (London/New York: T&T Clark, 2002)
Romerowski, Silvain, "Old Testament Sacrifices and Reconciliation," *Euro J Th* 16.1 (2007): 13-24
Rowland, Christopher and Roberts, Jonathan, "Introduction," *JSNT* 33.2 (2010): 131-6
Runia, David T, *Exegesis and Philosophy: Studies on Philo of Alexandria* (Aldershot, Hampshire: Variorum, 1990)
Sanders, EP, "Testament of Abraham" (translation and commentary). Pages 871-902 in *The Old Testament Pseudepigrapha* Vol 1, *Apocalyptic Literature and Testaments* (ed. James H Charlesworth; Garden City, NY: Doubleday, 1983)
Sanders, Jack, *Ethics in the New Testament* (London: SCM Press, 1985)
Sanders, JN, *The Fourth Gospel in the Early Church: Its Origins and Influence on Christian Theology up to Irenaeus* (Cambridge: Cambridge University Press, 1942)
Schenck, Kenneth, *A Brief Guide to Philo* (Louisville, KY: Westminster John Knox Press, 2005)
Schiffman, Lawrence H, "The Case of the Day of Atonement Ritual." Pages 181-8 in *Biblical Perspectives: Early Use and Interpretation of the Bible in Light of the Dead Sea Scrolls* (ed. Michael E Stone and Esther G Chazon; Leiden/Boston/Cologne: Brill, 1997)
Schmid, Hansjörg, *Gegner im 1. Johannesbrief?* (Stuttgart: Verlag W Kohlhammer, 2002)

Schnackenburg, Rudolf, *The Johannine Epistles* (trans. R & I Fuller; New York, Crossroad, 1992)
Schnelle, Udo, "Ethical Theology in 1 John." Pages 321–39 in *Rethinking the Ethics of John* (ed. Jan G Van Der Watt and Ruben Zimmerman; Tübingen: Mohr Siebeck, 2012)
Schuchard, Bruce C, *1-3 John* (Saint Louis: Concordia Publishing House, 2012), 89
Schwager, Raymund, *Jesus in the Drama of Salvation: Towards a Biblical Doctrine of Redemption* (trans. James G Williams and Paul Haddon; New York: Crossroads, 1999)
Schwager, Raymund, *Must There Be Scapegoats? Violence and Redemption in the Bible* (trans. Maria L Assad; New York: Gracewing, 1987)
Schwartz, Rabbi Sydney, *Judaism and Justice: The Jewish Passion to Repair the World* (Woodstock, VT: Jewish Lights Publishing, 2006)
Segal, Michael, "The Composition of Jubilees." Pages 22–35 in *Enoch and the Mosaic Torah: The Evidence of Jubilees* (ed. Gabriele Boccaccini and Giovanni Ibba; Grand Rapids, Michigan/Cambridge, UK, 2009)
Shemesh, Aharon, "Scriptural Interpretations in the Damascus Document and their Parallels in Rabbinic Midrash." Pages 161–76 in *The Damascus Document: A Centenary of Discovery—Proceedings of the Third International Symposium of the Orion Centre, 4–8 February 1998* (ed. Joseph M Baumgarten, Esther G Chazon and Avital Pinnick; Leiden: Brill, 2000)
Smalley, Steven S, *1, 2, 3 John* (Waco, TX: Word Books, 1984)
Smith, D Moody, *First, Second and Third John* (Louisville: John Knox Press, 1991)
Smith, D Moody, *John among the Gospels* (Columbia: University of South Carolina Press, 2nd ed., 2001)
Spicq, C, *L'Epitre aux Hebreux* (2 Vols; Paris: Gabalda, 1952)
Sproston, Wendy E, "Witnesses to What Was ἀπ' ἀρχῆς John's Contribution to Our Knowledge of Tradition in the Fourth Gospel," *JSNT* 48 (1992): 43–65
Stassen, Glen and Gushee, David P, *Kingdom Ethics: Following Jesus in Contemporary Context* (Downers Grove: IVP, 2003)
Stegg, Frank, "The Abused Aorist," *JBL* 91 (1972): 221–34
Stiver, Dan R, *Theology after Ricoeur: New Directions in Hermeneutical Theology* (Louisville/London/Leiden: Westminster John Knox Press, 2001)
Stott, John RW, *The Letters of John* (Downers Grove, IL: IVP Academic, 2nd ed., 1988)
Strecker, G, *The Johannine Letters* (trans. LM Maloney; Minneapolis: Fortress Press, English translation 1995 from the German edition, 1989)
Stuckenbrook, Loren T, "The Book of Jubilees and the Origin of Evil." Pages 294–308 in *Enoch and the Mosaic Torah: The Evidence of Jubilees* (ed. Gabrielle Boccaccini and Giovanni Ibba; Grand Rapids, MI; Cambridge, UK: Eerdmans 2009)
Swartley, Willard M, *Covenant of Peace: The Missing Peace in New Testament Theology and Ethics* (Grand Rapids, MI: Eerdmans, 2006)
Swartley, Willard M, "Discipleship and Imitation of Christ/Suffering Servant: The Mimesis of New Creation." Pages 218–45 in *Violence Renounced: René Girard, Biblical Studies and Peacemaking* (ed. Willard M Swartley; Telford, PA: Pandora Press U.S., 2000)
Swenson, Kristin M, "Care and Keeping East of Eden: Gen 4: 1-16 in light of Gen 2–3," *Int* 60.4 (2006): 373–84
Talbert, Charles, *Reading John: A Literary and Theological Commentary on the Fourth Gospel and the Johannine Epistles* (London: SPCK, 1992)
Tamarkin Reis, Pamela, "What Cain Said: A Note on Genesis 4:8," *JSOT* 27.1 (2002): 107–13
Tanner, Beth Laneer, "Deuteronomy 10: 2–22," *Int* 55.1 (2001): 60–3

Tehillim Vol 2 (trans. Rabbi Avrohom Chaim Feuer in association with Rabbi Nosson Scherman, commentary by Rabbi Avrohom Chaim Feuer; Brooklyn, NY: Mesorah Publications)

Thatcher, Tom, "Cain and Abel in Early Christian Memory: A Case Study in 'The Use of the Old Testament in the New,'" *CBQ* 72.4 (2010): 732–51

Thatcher, Tom, "Cain the Jew the Antichrist: Collective Memory and the Johannine Ethic of Loving and Hating." Pages 350–73 in *Rethinking the Ethics of John* (ed. Jan G Van der Watt and Ruben Zimmerman; Tübingen: Mohr Siebeck, 2012)

The Apostolic Fathers: Greek Texts and English Translations (ed. and trans. Michael W Holmes; Grand Rapids, MI: Baker Academic, 3rd ed., 2007)

The Book of Enoch (trans. RH Charles; London: SPCK, 1917)

The Books of Enoch: Aramaic Fragments of Qumran Cave 4 (ed. JT Milik; Oxford: Clarendon Press, 1976)

The Book of Jubilees or the Little Genesis (ed. RH Charles; London, SPCK, 1917)

The Damascus Document Reconsidered (ed. Magen Broshi; Jerusalem: Israel Exploration Society and The Shrine of the Book, Israel Museum, 1992)

The Dead Sea Scrolls: Hebrew, Aramaic Texts with English Translations, Vol 1, Rule of the Community and Related Documents (ed. James A Charlesworth et al.; Tubingen: JCB Mohr/Louisville: Westminster John Knox Press, 1994)

The Dead Sea Scrolls: Study Edition, Vols 1 and 2 (ed. and trans. Florentino García Martinez and Eibert JC Tigghelaar; Leiden/New York/Ko+ln, Brill, 1997)

The Interlinear NIV Hebrew–English Old Testament (ed. John R Kohlenberger III; Grand Rapids: Zondervan, 1987)

The Old Testament Pseudepigrapha: Volume 1 (ed. James H Charlesworth; London: Darton, Longman and Todd, 1983)

"The Testament of Abraham." Pages 393–422 in *The Apocryphal Old Testament* (ed. HFD Sparks and trans. N Turner; Oxford: Clarendon Press, 1989)

Thomas, John Christopher, "The Literary Structure of 1 John," *Nov Test* 40.4 (1998): 369–81

Thompson, Marianne Meye, *1–3 John* (Downers Grove, IL: InterVarsity Press, 1992)

Thornton, TGD, "Propitiation or Expiation," *Exp Tim* 80 (1968–9): 53–5

Tigay, Jeffrey H, *Deuteronomy* (Philadelphia: Jewish Publication Society, 1996)

Toombs, Lawrence E, "Love and Justice in Deuteronomy," *Int* 19.4 (1965) 399–411

Torrance, TF, *The Mediation of Christ* (Edinburgh: T&T Clark, 1992)

Trevaskis, Leigh M, *Holiness, Ethics and Ritual in Leviticus* (Sheffield: Sheffield Phoenix Press, 2011)

Van der Watt, JG, *A Grammar of the Ethics of John*, Vol 1 (Tübingen: Mohr Siebeck, 2019)

Van der Watt, JG, "Again: Identity, Ethics and Ethos in the New Testament: A Few Tentative Remarks." Pages 611–32 in *Identity, Ethics and Ethos in the New Testament* BNZW 141 (ed. JG Van der Watt; Berlin: de Gruyter, 2006)

Van der Watt, JG, "Ethics Alive in Imagery." Pages 421–48 in *Imagery in the Gospel of John* WUNT 200 (ed. J Frey, JG Van Der Watt and R Zimmermann; Tübingen: Mohr Siebeck, 2006)

Van der Watt, JG, "Ethics and Ethos in the Gospel According to John," *ZNW* 97 (2006): 147–76

Van der Watt, JG, "Ethics in First John: A Literary and Socioscientific Perspective," *CBQ* 61 (1999): 491–511

Van der Watt, JG, "Ethics of/and Opponents of Jesus in John's Gospel." Pages 175-91 in *Rethinking the Ethics of John: "Implicit Ethics" in the Johannine Writings* WUNT 291 (ed. JG Van der Watt and R Zimmermann; Tübingen: Mohr Siebeck, 2012)

Van der Watt, JG, "On Ethics in 1 John." Pages 197-222 in *Communities in Dispute: Current Scholarship on the Johannine Epistles* (ed. R Alan Culpepper and Paul N Anderson; Atlanta: SBL Press, 2014)

Van der Watt, JG, "Quaestiones Disputatae: Are John's Ethics Apolitical," *Nov Test Stud* (2016): 493-7

Vanderkam, James C, "Biblical Interpretation in 1 Enoch and Jubilees." Pages 96-125 in *The Pseudepigrapha and Early Biblical Interpretation* (ed. JH Charlesworth and Craig A Evans; Sheffield: Sheffield Academic Press, 1993)

VanderKam, James C, *Enoch: A Man for All Generations* (Columbia, SC: University of South Carolina Press, 1995)

VanderKam, James C, *Textual and Historical Studies in the Book of Jubilees* (Missoula, MT: Scholars Press, 1977)

VanderKam, James C, "The Manuscript Traditions of Jubilees." Pages 3-21 in *Enoch and the Mosaic Torah: The Evidence of Jubilees* (ed. Gabriele Boccaccini and Giovanni Ibba; Grand Rapids, MI/Cambridge, UK, 2009)

VanderKam, James C, "The Scriptural Setting of the Book of Jubilees," *DSD* 13.1 (2006): 61-72

Van Ruiten, JTAGM, *Primaeval History Interpreted: The Rewriting of Genesis I-II in the Book of Jubilees* (Leiden/Boston/Koln: Brill, 2000)

Van Wolde, Ellen, "The Story of Cain and Abel: A Narrative Study," *JSOT* 52 (1991): 25-41

Vermes, Geza, *The Dead Sea Scrolls: Qumran in Perspective* (London: Collins, 1977)

Vogt, Peter T, "Social Justice and the Vision of Deuteronomy," *JETS* 51.1 (2008): 35-44

Von Balthasar, Hans Urs, *Theo-Drama: Theological Dramatic Theory*, Vol IV, "The Action" (trans. G Harrison; San Francisco: Ignatius Press, 1994)

Von Rad, Gerhard, *Deuteronomy* (London: SCM Press, 1966)

Von Rad, Gerhard, *Old Testament Theology Vol 1* (trans. DMG Stalker; London/Leiden/Louisville: John Knox Press, 2001)

Von Wahlde, Urban C, *The Gospel and Letters of John: Vol 3, Commentary on the Three Johannine Letters* (Grand Rapids, MI: Eerdmans, 2010)

Von Wahlde, Urban C, *The Johannine Commandments: 1 John and the Struggle for the Johannine Tradition* (New York/Manwah: Paulist Press, 1990)

Vouga, François, *Die Johannesbriefe* (Tübingen: JCB Mohr (Paul Siebeck), 1990)

Watson, Duane F, "Amplification Techniques in 1 John: the Interaction of Rhetorical Style and Invention," *JSNT* 16 (1993): 99-123

Watson, Duane F, "1 John 2: 12-14as *Distributio, Conduplicatio,* and *Expolitio*: A Rhetorical Understanding," *JSNT* 11 (1989): 97-110

Weinfeld, Moshe, *Deuteronomy 1-11* (New York: Doubleday, 1991)

Weinfeld, Moshe, *Deuteronomy and the Deuteronomic School* (Oxford: Oxford University Press, 1972)

Weinfeld, Moshe, "The Origin of the Humanism in Deuteronomy," *JBL* 80.3 (1961): 241-7

Wenham, Gordon, *Genesis 1-15* (Waco, TX: Word Books, 1987)

Wenham, Gordon J, *The Book of Leviticus* (Grand Rapids, MI: Eerdmans, 1979)

Westermann, Claus, *Genesis 1-11: A Commentary* (trans. John J Scullion SJ; London: SPCK, 1984)

Westcott, Brook Foss, *Epistles of St John* (Cambridge and London: Macmillan & Co., 1886)

Wevers, John William, *Notes on the Greek Text of Leviticus* (Atlanta, GA: Scholars Press, 1997)
Williamson, Ronald, *Jews in the Hellenistic World 1ii: Philo* (Cambridge: Cambridge University Press, 1989)
Willis, Timothy M, *Leviticus* (Nashville: Abingdon Press, 2009)
Wright, Daniel P, "Holiness in Leviticus and Beyond," *Int* 50.4 (1999): 351-64
Yamauchi, Edwin M, "Josephus and the Scriptures," *Fides et Historia* 13.1 (1980): 42-63
Yarbrough, Robert W, *1-3 John* (Grand Rapids, MI: Baker Publishing Group, 2008)
Young, Norman H, "CH Dodd, 'Hilaskesthai' and His Critics," *Ev Q* 48.2 (1976): 67-78
Yoder, John H, *The Politics of Jesus* (Grand Rapids, MI: Eerdmans, 2nd ed., 1994)
Yoder, John H, *Christian Attitudes to War, Peace and Revolution* (ed. Theodore J Koontz and Andy Alexis-Baker; Grand Rapids, MI: Baker Publishing Group, 2009)
Zimmerli, Walther, *Ezekiel* 2 (trans. James D Martin; Philadelphia: Fortress Press, 1983)

Author Index

Adam, P. 103 n.91
Akin, D. A. 37 n.36, 103 n.91
Alexander, N. 96 n.55
Alison, J. 4, 10–11, 174
Allbee, R. A. 159–60
Allen, L. C. 71 n.59, 71 n.61
Alter, R. 70 n.47, 125 n.12, 128 n.34
Andersen, F. L. 72 n.70, 73 n.76, 73 n.79
Anderson, G. 167
Anderson, P. N. 44 n.106, 111 n.132, 118 n.153, 177–8, 185 n.3
Andrews, J. A. 2 n.6
Anstall, K. 17
Attridge, H. W. 133 n.74
Auld, AG. 73 n.78
Aulen, G. 28–9, 121
Aune, D. E. 145 n.131, 145 n.133

Baillie, DM. 189 n.17
Baker, D. L. 168 n.99
Barker, P. A. 163 n.61, 171
Barr, J. 64, 154 n.3, 168 n.97
Barth, K. 2–3, 26, 28, 30
Bartling, V. 190 n.20
Bauckham, R. 36–7, 134 n.79
Bauer, W. 59
Bayliss, C. P. 186 n.7
Beale, GP. 145 nn.132–3
Beasley-Murray, G. R. 1 n.1, 37 n.36
Belousek, D. W. S. 21–2, 71 n.63, 96 n.55, 114 n.137
Berchman, R. A. 136, 137 n.96
Bergsma, J. S. 76 n.102
Beutler, J. 147
Block, D. I. 71 n.56
Borgen, P. 135 n.89, 137, 138 n.103
Bowen, N. R. 71 n.57, 74 n.85
Boxall, I. 145 nn.132–3
Boyce, R. N. 156
Braun, R. 68 n.37
Briggs, C. A. 70 n.45, 74 n.87

Brooke, AE. 37, 41, 43–4, 46–7, 49, 55, 57, 60, 92
Brooke, G. J. 148 n.156, 160 n.42
Brown, R. 32–3, 35, 38–9, 40–1, 43, 47, 49–52, 54, 56–8, 60, 94 n.37, 95–6, 111–12, 114 nn.139–40, 116 n.144, 124 n.7, 148, 149 n.159, 162, 169 n.102, 185 n.5
Brueggemann, W. 33 n.10, 70 n.50, 74 n.83, 156, 164 n.66, 165–6
Budd, O. J. 68 n.33
Bultmann, R. 14, 38, 41–2, 111 n.128, 175 n.127
Burge, G. M. 44 n.106, 103 n.91
Burnett, F. W. 137 n.99
Burridge, R. 23–4, 114
Byron, J. 124 n.7, 128 n.39, 135, 135 n.91

Campbell, C. R. 37 n.36
Carson, DA. 137 n.98, 137 n.101
Cassuto, U. 69 n.40, 100 n.85, 125
Cazeaux, J. 136 n.93
Charlesworth, JH. 78 n.118, 148 n.153
Charlesworth, RH. 75 n.94, 76 n.96, 79 n.120, 131 n.55, 132 n.70, 134 nn.79–80
Clark, G. H. 37 n.36
Clavier, H. 97
Clements, RE. 166 n.85
Collins, J. J. 72 n.69, 161
Connell, M. F. 185 n.3
Cooke, GA. 71 n.55, 71 n.58
Coombes, M. 56 n.197, 176 n.130
Cosgrove, C. A. 2 n.6
Craigie, P. 164 n.66
Craig Jr., K. M. 126 n.15
Curtis, E. L. 69 n.39

Davenport, G. L. 79 n.120
Davies, G. N. 67 n.26
Davis, P. H. 76 n.95

De Boer, M. C. 185 n.5
Deere, D. W. 163
Denney, J. 106
Derek Kidner, D. 80 n.128, 103 n.91, 125 n.13
Deurloo, K. 125 n.9, 125 n.11, 128 n.35
Dodd, CH. 37, 41, 43, 48, 92–6, 98–106, 113 n.134, 175
Doering, L. 79 n.124
Driver, SR. 162, 164 n.64, 164 n.67, 166
Duguid, I. 72 n.68
Dunn, J. DG. 32 n.3, 175
Durham, J. C. 69 n.40

Eisenman, R. 160
Ellis, E. E. 103 n.91
Endres SJ, J. C. 133 n.74
Eynikel, E. 33, 34 n.14

Feder, Y. 64 n.6
Feldman, L. H. 138 n.106, 139 n.107
Fiddes, P. S. 189 n.17
Fisch, R. Dr S. 71 n.61
Fitzmyer SJ, J. A. 148 n.157, 162
Fraade, S. D. 161 n.49
Freedman, D. N. 72 n.70, 73 n.76, 73 n.79
Frey, J. 132 n.73, 162 n.54

Gane, R. 65 n.10
Gaugler, E. 115 n.143
Girard, R. 5–11, 13–14, 16, 24–6, 29–30, 121, 123, 178
Glassock, E. 186 n.8
Glenny, W. E. 73 n.80
Goff, M. 33
Gore, C. 106
Gore-Jones, L. 32 n.2
Gorman, FH. 65 n.9
Grayston, K. 40, 46 n.119, 96 n.55, 128 n.38
Greenhill, W. 71 n.60
Griffith, T. 50–4
Gunkel, H. 125
Gushee, D. P. 17–18

Haenchen, E. 175
Hamilton, V. P. 125 n.13
Harrington, H. K. 81 n.131
Harris, R. L. 66 n.21

Hartog, Paul A. 60–1
Hauerwas, S. 21
Hayes, J. H. 67 n.30
Hays, R. 3–4, 22–3
Heckel, T. C. 54 n.187
Hempel, C. 161 n.48
Hersh, G. 72 n.67, 155 n.9
Hiebert, D. E. 149 n.161
Hill, C. E. 59, 61
Hill, D. 103–6, 119
Hodges, Z. C. 186 n.6
Holtzmann, H. 90–1
Hort, FJA. 55
Houlden, JL. 41 n.76, 48
Hullinger, J. M. 72 n.64
Hunsinger, G. 4, 25–6, 30

Jacobson, H. 127
Janzen, D. 65 n.9
Japhet, S. 69 n.42
Jeanrond, W. 2 n.2
Jensen, M. 40 n.70, 111 n.129
Jenson, R. 71 n.62
Jobes, K. 37 n.36
Johnson, TF. 40, 46, 96 n.55
Jones, P. R. 40 n.68, 46, 96 n.55
Jones, R. C. 164 n.71
Jones, R. P. 40, 46

Kaminsky, J. S. 157
Kaufman, G. 20
Keener, C. S. 37 n.36
Keith, C. 175
Kelhoffer, J. A. 193 n.35
Kennedy, HAA. 138 n.102
Kessler, M. 125 n.9, 125 n.11, 128 n.35
Kidner, D. 80 n.128, 103 n.91, 125 n.13
Kiuchi, N. 65 n.7
Klassen, W. 14–15
Klauck, H. 44, 115 n.142, 117 n.148, 144 n.128
Kleinig, J. W. 155 n.8, 155 n.11, 156 n.19
Klein, R. W. 69 n.41
Kline, M. 157–8
Knibb, M. A. 76 n.99, 131 n.54
Knohl, I. 68 n.34
Knoppers, G. N. 68 n.38
Koester, C. 175, 185 n.3
Kostenberger, A. J. 107 n.111

Kruse, C. G. 107 n.111
Kysar, R. 44, 178 n.145

Lapsley, J. E. 164, 167
Law, R. 32, 32 n.6, 41, 43, 47, 49, 55, 57–60, 73 n.81, 91
Law, T. M. 87 n.2, 144 n.125
Levine, B. A. 66 n.12, 66 n.23, 67 n.25, 67 n.28, 68 n.35, 74 n.90, 74 n.93, 114 n.141, 157
Levinson, J. R. 139 n.111
Lewis, J. P. 126 n.16
Lewis, S. M. 96 n.55
Lieu, J. M. 32, 34–5, 45, 50–3, 60, 107–9, 111, 113 n.134, 116 n.147, 119, 150 n.162, 184 n.2
Lim, T. H. 161 n.50
Lindars, B. 37 n.36
Llewellyn, S. 32 n.2
Loader, W. 40, 46, 187 n.10
Lohr, J. N. 129 n.40, 129 n.42, 129 n.45, 129 n.48, 146

Madsen, A. A. 69 n.39
Marshall, IH. 33 n.12, 46, 60, 105–6, 111, 150 n.162, 169 n.102
Martinez, F. G. 132 n.73
Martin, L. M. 139, 155 n.13
Martyn, J. L. 35
Marx, A. 157
Mason, S. 138 n.105, 139 n.110
Mayes, ADH. 162 n.56, 164 n.67, 166 n.82, 166 n.84
McConville, JG. 167 n.90
McDermond, JE. 150 n.162
McGrath, A. 189 n.17
McHugh, J. 32 n.3
McNamara, MSC. 78 n.112, 79 n.123
Measson, A. 136 n.93
Mencken, M. J. 123 n.5
Milgrom, J. 64 n.6, 65 n.9, 65 n.10, 66 n.11, 66 n.20, 68 n.35, 74 n.89, 74 n.92, 155 n.8, 157–9
Miller, P. D. 166 n.85
Moloney, F. J. 37 n.36, 175 n.128, 178 n.144
Montgomery, J. A. 72 n.66
Morgen, M. 96 n.55, 117 n.150, 144

Morris, L. 37 n.36, 96 n.55, 99–103, 109, 119
Mounce, R. H. 145 n.132, 145 n.133

Najman, H. 132 n.68
Neufeld, D. 40 n.70
Nickelsburg, G. 76, 77 n.103, 130 n.52, 138 n.106
Nicole, R. R. 98–9
Northey, W. 16
Noth, M. 155 n.13, 156 n.14

Olson, D. 131 n.55
Olsson, B. 32 n.7, 37 n.36, 96 n.55, 115 n.142
O'Neill, JC. 35 n.25, 43

Painter, J. 34, 39–40, 43–7, 49–50, 54, 57–60, 94 n.37, 96–7, 107 n.114, 116, 124 n.7, 150, 169, 175 n.125, 175 n.128, 178 n.142, 184 n.1, 190 n.21
Paul, S. M. 73 n.73
Perkins, P. 15–16, 40, 45, 48–9, 51–3, 109, 119, 184 n.2
Phillips, A. 166 n.85
Piper, J. 191 n.22
Popkes, EE. 169 n.104
Porter, JR. 156–7
Propp, W. HC. 69 n.40, 100 n.85

Redditt, P. L. 154 n.5
Reinhartz, A. 178 n.143
Rensberger, D. 40, 46, 96 n.55, 118 n.153
Ricoeur, P. 2
Ringren, H. 81 n.135, 82 n.140, 82 n.141
Roberts, J. 87 n.1
Rofe, A. 162 n.57
Romerowski, S. 66 n.21
Rowland, C. 87 n.1
Runia, D. T. 135 n.87

Sanders, EP. 134
Sanders, JN. 59, 178 n.143
Schenck, K. 135 n.86
Schiffman, L. H. 81
Schmid, H. 54 n.189
Schnackenburg, R. 34, 38, 42–4, 46, 48–9, 55–6, 58, 60, 94–5, 111 n.128, 116 n.144, 136 n.94, 150 n.162, 151 n.166, 169 n.102, 171

Schnelle, U. 33 n.10
Schuchard, B. C. 37 n.36, 107 n.111
Schwager, R. 4, 11–12, 27, 174, 179
Schwartz, R. S. 156 n.16
Segal, M. 79 n.119, 132 n.63
Shemesh, A. 161 n.48
Smalley, S. S. 35 n.26, 39, 46, 58, 106–7, 111 n.128, 116 n.144, 150 n.162, 169 n.102
Smith, D. M. 96 n.55, 175
Spicq, C. 114 n.139
Sproston, W. E. 192 n.28
Stassen, G. 17–18
Stead, M. R. 67 n.26
Stegg, F. 178 n.142
Stiver, D. R. 2 n.4
Stott, J. RW. 103 n.91, 169 n.102
Strecker, G. 38, 42, 97–8, 111 n.128, 116 n.144, 150 n.162, 189 n.15
Stuckenbrook, L. T. 132 n.67
Swartley, W. M. 4, 12–14, 179
Swenson, K. M. 126 n.18

Talbert, C. 56 n.198, 94 n.41
Tamarkin Reis, P. 127 n.28
Tanner, B. L. 164 n.72
Thatcher, T. 146–7, 150, 171–2
Thomas, J. C. 58
Thompson, M. M. 98, 119
Thornton, TGD. 96 n.55
Tigay, J. H. 164, 165
Toombs, L. E. 163
Torrance, TF. 25, 26–8
Trevaskis, L. M. 158

Vanderkam, J. C. 76, 77 n.103, 78 n.118, 79 n.119, 79 n.121, 79 n.122, 79 n.126, 131 n.57, 131 n.61, 132 n.63, 132 n.64, 132 n.68
Van der Watt, J. G. 111 n.132, 113, 176, 177
Van Ruiten, JTAGM. 132 n.69, 132 n.72, 133 n.75
Van Wolde, E. 126 n.17
Vermes, G. 33 n.12
Vogt, P. T. 165
Von Balthasar, H. U. 4, 25–7, 30
Von Rad, G. 126 n.14, 167
Von Wahlde, U. C. 44, 109–10, 150 n.162
Vouga, F. 96 n.55, 113

Watson, D. F. 50 n.160, 53, 54
Weinfeld, M. 162, 163 n.62, 164–6, 167 n.95
Wenham, G. 125 n.9, 155 n.12, 156, 159
Westcott, B. F. 34, 37, 47, 55, 59, 89–90, 102, 105, 111 n.128, 116
Westermann, C. 125, 126 n.16, 127 n.31, 128, 130
Wevers, J. W. 65
Williamson, R. 135 n.86, 135 n.88, 136 n.95, 138, 138 n.104
Willis, T. M. 156
Wright, D. P. 67 n.25

Yamauchi, E. M. 139, 140 n.117
Yarbrough, R. 107 n.111
Yoder, J. H. 4, 13, 18–20, 174, 179
Young, N. H. 96 n.55

Zimmerli, W. 71 n.59

Index of References

Old Testament
Genesis
2–3	126
2:5	126
2:15	126
3:1–10	191
3:16b	126
3:17	128
3:17b	126
3:23	126
3:24	127
4	195
4:1	135
4:1–14	126
4:1–16	124–6, 143
4:2	126
4:2–3	127
4:3	125
4:4	125–6, 128–9, 141, 183
4:4–5	125, 129
4:4–9	124, 144
4:5	128–9, 132, 141
4:6–7	130
4:7	125, 130, 140
4:7a	129, 142
4:7b	124, 126, 129, 142
4:8	127–8, 136, 144
4:9	126–7, 149, 152
4:9–16	127
4:10	128, 131, 140, 142
4:10–11	128
4:11	147
4:11a	126
4:14	128
4:15	5, 133
4:16	141
4:18	10
4:19	10
4:25–26	6
5:21–24	76
9:4	89, 131, 142
9:4–6	79, 83
17	163
22:1–14	107
22:13	107, 114
32:14, 19, 21–22	126
32:20	101
33:10	126
37:24	80
37:28	80
37:31–35	79–80, 84
37:33	80
43:11, 15, 25–26	126

Exodus
11:2	157
19:8	33
22:21–24	164
24	33
24:1–8	33
24:3, 8	33
24:4	79
24:12	33–4
25:17	69, 100–1
25:18	69
30:10	93
30:12–16	101
32:14	100
32:30	74, 101
32:32	74
34:6	77, 83
39:33, 36	93

Leviticus
4:3	71
4:3–12	65
4:13–21	65
4:14	66
4:20	74

4:22–26	65	19:18a	161
5:1	132	19:18b	155, 157, 159, 160, 161, 162, 169
5:1–7	68		
5:5	189	19:33–34	158, 164
5:6	189	19:34	43, 156, 157, 158, 159, 160, 162, 169, 170, 173
5:7	189		
5:9c	189		
5:10b	189	19:35	158
5:20–26	68	19:36	156
5:22	68	20–21	65
5:25	68	25:8	82
6:1–7	67	25:8–55	64
6:4	67	25:9	64–7, 96, 108–9, 112–14
6:5b	67		
6:7a	67	25:9b	64–5, 67, 114
7:1–10	67	25:48	128
12:6–8	71	26:13	156
12:7	74	26:45	156
14:12–19	71	35:38	156
15:15	71	35:42	156
16	81, 84	35:55	156
16:9	81		
16:10	65, 75, 77, 83	Numbers	
16:14–15	69, 100	5:5–10	68
16:15–16	81	5:5–8	67
16:16	109	5:6	67
16:18–19	66	5:8	67–8, 94, 96–7
16:33	66, 79, 83	5:8a	67
17b	156	6:11–14	71
17:11	112	19:11–19	71
17:11a–b	89	25:3–9, 11–13	101–2
19	157, 159, 160, 162, 169	31:50	101
		35:33	101–2
19:2	159, 168	36:12–28	128
19:11	158		
19:11–18	158, 159, 160, 168	Deuteronomy	
19:11 to 19:18	159	4:31	69
19:12	158	6:25	167
19:13	158	7:9	189
19:14	158	9:21	73
19:16	161	10	171
19:17	154, 155, 159, 161, 170, 173	10:11–19	173
		10:11–22	163
19:17a	154, 155, 156	10:12–22	163, 164, 168, 170, 171
19:17b	155, 156		
19:17–18	161, 169, 173	10:12–23	164, 165, 169
19:18	24, 155, 156, 157, 158, 159, 160, 161, 169, 173, 174	10:15	171
		10:18	165, 166, 171

10:18–19	165, 168, 171, 174	2 Chronicles	
10:19	165, 171, 172, 173	30:18	101–2
12:23	89	30:18–19	102
14:21	164, 166	30:20	102
14:28	166		
15	165, 171	Nehemiah	
15:1–2	167	9:17	108
15:1–11	165, 167, 168, 169, 170, 172, 173, 174, 195	Esther	
		13:17	100
15:1–18	166		
15:3–11	167	Psalms	
15:7	167, 193	2:1–2	87
15:7–8	172	2:8–9	87
15:8	167	24	70
15:9	172	24(25):11	100
15:9–11	174	25:11	70
15:10	173, 193, 195	64	70
15:15	168, 171, 193	64(65):3	118
21:1–9	65, 101, 102	64(65):4	100
23:21	136	65:3	70, 73–4
27:24	132	65:4a	70
31:1–8	69	66:5a	66
31:3	69	77(78):38	100
31:7, 23	69	78:38	73, 101–2
32:41–43	101–2	78:38a	66
		78(79):9	100
Joshua		79:9	73
1:5	69	79:9b	66
		130:4	69–70, 82, 96–8, 106, 108, 115
2 Samuel			
21:1–14	101–2	130(129):4	69–70
1 Kings		Proverbs	
4:21	126	16:6	101–2
10:25	126	27:5	155
2 Kings		Ecclesiastes	
5:18	100	1:2	127
24:3f	100		
		Isaiah	
1 Chronicles		6:6	102
25:21	69	6:7	101–2
28:2	68	6:7b	66
28:20	63, 68–9	22:13	128, 144
28:20b	69	22:14b	66
28:20c	68–9, 82, 100–1	27:9	101–2

27:9a	64	Amos	
40:3	87	8:4	73
47:11	101	8:4–6	73
53:4	6	8:7	73
53:7	145	8:14	72–3, 82, 96
Jeremiah		Zechariah	
12:3	128, 144	7:2	95
15:3	128, 144	7:10	165
18:23	101–2	8:17a	155
18:23b	64, 66	11:4, 5, 7	144
19:6	128, 144		
25:11–12	72	Malachi	
29:10	72	1:9	95
Lamentations		**New Testament**	
3:42	100	Matthew	
		5:17	7
Ezekiel		5:22	14
4:27	96	5:38–48	3
16:59	74, 99	5:39–48	20
16:60	74, 99	5:43–48	14
16:63	66, 73, 99, 101–2	13:35	6
44:11	71	22:34–40	159–60
44:15	71		
44:15–27	71	Mark	
44:15–31	71	12:28–34	159, 160
44:25	71		
44:25–27	71	Luke	
44:26	71	10:25–37	156
44:27	21, 70–2, 82, 94, 97, 106	11:47–48	6
Daniel		John	
7:9	78, 83	1:13	23
7:13	78, 83	1:14	22
9	72	1:15	87
9:2	72	2:10–11	7
9:4–19	72	2:23–25	22
9:9	72, 82, 96–8, 106, 108, 115	3:36	103
		4:1–30	178
9:19	100	4:42	169
9:24	93, 101–2	5.19ff	176
		6	22
Hosea		6:27	78
8:6	73	6:51	13
		6:53	78

6:62	78	19:34	43
7:30	22	20:19	1, 181
8	148	20:21	1, 169, 181
8:26	176	20:26	1, 181
8:39	8	21:24	36
8:39b	148	21:24a	37
8:39–44	34	21:24b	36
8:40	176		
8:42–44	8	Acts	
8:44	8, 11, 148–9, 151	2:37–42	32
8:59	22	10:44–48	32
9:22	23, 35, 39		
10:11–18	12	Romans	
10:16	177	3:25	21, 97
10:1–18	177	5:8	21
11:14–15	22	8:32	107
11:35	22	13:8	159
12:20–26	177	13:10	16
12:23	78		
12:34	78	Galatians	
12:42	23, 35, 39	5:13	159
12:47	188		
13:1	45	Ephesians	
13:3–5	22	5:1–2	19
13:15	24		
13:31	78	Hebrews	
13:34	19, 22, 176, 192	2:17	21, 97
13:34–35	190, 192	4:4	126
14:7	52	4:7	140
14:16	23, 114	7:27	89
14:18–24	45	9–10	96
14:27	1, 181		
15:9–10	45	Peter	
15:9–16:4	176	1:11	76
15:12	176, 190, 192		
15:13	12	1 John	
15:17	190, 192	1:1	61, 111–12, 118, 170, 171, 184, 190, 192
15:18	191	1:1–2	61
16:1–2	35	1:1–4	55, 56, 58, 111, 112, 192
16:2	39	1:1–5	36, 57
16:20	23	1:2	18, 118, 193, 194
16:27	45	1:3	111–12, 114, 118, 171, 184
16:33	1, 178, 181		
17:14	191	1:4	186
17:18	178	1:5	111–14, 170, 184, 188, 193
17:20–26	169		
17:21	178		
17:22–26	45		
17:23	178		

Reference	Pages	Reference	Pages
1:5–2:2	111, 114–16, 148	2:2	11–12, 14–16, 19–21, 23–24, 26, 63, 73, 77–8, 80, 83–5, 87–97, 101, 103–12, 114–15, 119–21, 169, 170, 174, 178, 179, 183, 187, 188, 190, 194, 195
1:5–2:11	38, 51		
1:5–2:17	55		
1:5–2:29	58		
1:5–3:10	56		
1:5–7	13, 18, 33, 58, 133, 142, 185		
1:5–10	120	2:2a	114–15, 117, 120, 189
1–6	120	2:2a–b	188
1:6	13, 50, 111–12, 183, 184, 186, 194	2:2b	10, 19, 96, 115, 182
		2:2b–c	115
1:6–2:1	111	2:2c	12, 188
1:6–2:17	57	2–3	10
1:6–2:27	57	2:3–11	16, 58
1–6–7	111	2:4	18, 45–6, 50, 52, 53, 184
1:6, 8 and 10	44, 115		
1:6–10	36, 45, 49	2:4, 8, 9	44
1:7	21, 25, 92, 94–8, 105, 108, 111–15, 119, 120, 121, 184, 186, 188, 189, 194	2:5	7, 153
		2:6	13, 19, 24, 45–6, 50, 52–3, 185
		2:7	42, 56, 171, 192
1:7a	112	2:7 to 2:11	192
1:7b	23, 89, 94, 112, 114, 195	2:7–3:24	56
1:7–2:2	189	2:7–8	33–4
1:7, 9	115, 121–2	2:7–11	10, 193
1:7–9	90	2:8	192, 194
1:7b, 9	120	2:8–11	33, 35
1:8	18, 105, 109, 111, 112–13, 120, 169, 183, 184	2:9	45, 46, 50, 52–3, 149, 151, 153, 193, 194
		2:9–10	186, 193
1:8–2:2	58	2:9:10	112
1:8, 10	50	2:9–11	15, 44, 50
1:9	111, 113–15, 119–20, 186, 189, 194	2.10	178
		2:10	7, 14, 56, 103, 153, 193
1:9a	112	2:10–11	7, 123, 179
1:9b	113–14	2:11	153, 184, 193, 194
1:10	46, 111, 113, 120, 183, 184	2:11–24	170
		2:12–17	58
1:29	121	2:13	171
1:51	78	2:14	171
2:1	20, 23–4, 97, 103, 106–7, 111, 113–15, 120, 183, 194, 195	2:15	8, 23, 153, 186, 191
		2:15–17	8, 115, 169, 174, 187
		2:16	186
2:1a	113	2:17	186, 187, 193
2:1b	189, 195	2:18	19, 21, 38, 169
2–1b	97, 113, 120	2:18b	183
2:1–2	88, 109, 117, 120, 189, 195	2:18–2:25	52
		2:18	60
2:1–2a	115–16	2:18–3:24	55

2:18–19	8, 39	3:12	9–10, 14, 32, 35, 62, 110, 123, 127, 128, 130–1, 135, 139–40, 144–51, 153, 170, 171, 183, 190, 191, 195
2:18–20	152		
2:18, 22	16		
2:18–25	51		
2:18–27	55, 57		
2:18–29	58	3:12a	190
2:19	38, 41, 43–4, 48, 51–2, 60, 169, 170, 174, 183	3:12b	124, 136, 145, 191
		3:12–15	5, 136, 150–1
2:19c	52	3:12–24	32
2:21	18	3:13	8, 13, 19, 23, 78, 110, 147, 149, 153, 169, 170, 174, 186, 191
2:22	38, 46, 48		
2:22a	53		
2:22ff	43	3:13–14	23, 149
2:24	42, 171	3:13–15	9
2:25	38, 193, 194	3:13–16	13
2:27	185	3:13–24	170, 171, 172
2:28–4:6	57	3:14	11–12, 23, 78, 110, 146, 153, 172, 191, 194
3:1	58, 115, 153, 169, 174, 186		
3:1–3	18, 58	3:14a	183
3:1–5:13	58	3:14c	172
3:2	60, 185	3:14–15	7, 15, 123
3:3	33, 185	3:14–18	12
3:3, 7	24	3:15	7, 11, 78, 83, 110, 123, 135, 146–7, 149, 153, 154, 155, 161, 170, 173, 183, 190, 191, 194
3:3, 7 and 16	24		
3:4	33, 184, 185		
3:4–9	58		
3:4–24	38	3:15a	196
3:5	88	3:15–18	24
3:7	185	3:16	12, 15, 19, 21, 91, 96, 110, 116, 150, 153, 169, 171, 177, 183, 191, 192
3:8	61, 146, 171, 184, 185		
3:8–10	9		
3.9	176		
3:10	56, 57, 58, 153	3:16b	20, 24
3:10–18	173	3:16–17	178, 188
3:10–24	58	3:16–18	22
3:11	22, 32, 42, 56, 110, 123, 150, 153, 161, 169, 170, 171, 172, 176, 190	3:17	14, 110, 153, 169, 172, 173, 174, 191, 193, 195
		3:18	53, 153, 172, 173, 184, 191
3:11–3:18	150, 190, 191		
3:11–5:12	56	3:19	149, 152, 173, 184
3:11–12	11, 33, 143	3:19–20	150, 173
3:11–15	10	3:19–24	150
3:11–16	19	3:20–22	150
3:11–17	61, 160	3:22	32, 152, 184
3:11–18	58, 176, 193	3:22–24	34
3:11–22	169	3:23	32, 39, 150, 153, 185
3:11–24	24, 153, 169, 171, 172, 173, 174, 179, 183	3:23–24a	171, 172
		3:24	32, 56, 57, 58, 150, 152

Reference	Pages	Reference	Pages
4:1	48, 56, 58, 115, 169, 174, 185	4:10–12	28
4:1d	51	4:11	10, 12, 109, 118, 121, 153, 168, 171, 174, 176, 192
4:1–5	16		
4:1–5:17	55	4:12	20, 153
4:1–6	34, 40, 52, 55, 57, 58	4:12a	118
4:2	42–3, 46, 60, 185	4:12b	118
4:2–3	22, 38, 48, 60	4:13	15, 20, 116
4:2b	56	4:13–21	21
4:2b–3a	60	4:14	15, 88, 169, 174
4:3	8, 46, 52, 169, 174, 185	4:14a	187
4:3a	60	4:14b	187
4:4	169, 174, 186	4:15	116
4:4–5	115	4:16	17, 153
4:4–6	48	4:16b	15
4:5	169, 174, 185, 186	4:17	13, 19, 153, 169, 174, 185
4:6	18, 56		
4:7	14, 17, 22, 57, 109, 116, 120, 153, 174	4:18	153, 160
		4:18a	21
4:7a	116, 171, 190	4:18–19	21
4:7b	19, 116–17, 118, 190	4:19	24, 26, 153
4:7–8	20	4:19–21	12
4:7–10	19, 120	4:20	16, 20, 44, 45–6, 50, 52–3, 153, 169, 185
4:7–11	10, 17		
4:7–11, 16, 19	13	4:20–5:3	38
4:7–12	18, 20, 112, 116, 190	4:20–21	15, 50, 53
4:7–21	15, 55, 57, 116, 190	4:21	12, 116, 153
4:7–5:4	58	5:1	116, 153
4:7–5:12	57	5:1–5	15, 57, 121
4:7–5:14	116	5:1–12	55
4:8	17, 112, 116–17, 120, 144, 153, 186, 193	5:2	15, 43, 153
		5:2a	57
4:9	8, 15, 21, 88, 107, 117–19, 121, 153, 174, 178, 179, 188	5:2b	57
		5:2–5	116
		5:3	153
4:9–10	116, 178	5:3–5	122
4:9, 10, 14	117	5:4	121, 169, 174, 186
4:9–11	17	5:4a	15
4:9a	117	5:4b	15
4:9b	117, 188	5:4–5	178, 191
4:10	11–12, 14, 20–1, 26–7, 63, 73, 77–8, 80, 83–5, 87–92, 95–8, 101, 103–11, 116–17, 119–22, 153, 170, 178, 179, 182, 187, 188, 190, 195	5:5	15, 169, 174, 188
		5:5–13	58
		5:6	42–3
		5:6b	57
		5:6–12	57
		5:10	46
		5:11	57, 193, 194
4:10a	117	5:13	57, 193, 194
4:10b	94, 117–18, 120, 195	5:13–21	56, 57
4:10–11	124	5:14–21	58

5:16	49, 153, 194
5:17	194
5:18–21	15, 55
5:19	23, 29, 169, 174, 186, 188
5:20	193, 194
5:21	21
6:27	78
6:53	78
6:62	78
8:28	78, 176
8:31	8
8:39b	148
12:23	78
12:34	78
13:31	78
17:20–26	169
24	42

2 John
7	8
110:11	49

3 John
9–10:12	36
15	1

Jude
14–15	75

Revelation
1:13	78
2:26–27, 12:5, 19:15	87
5:6	145
5:9	121, 145
5:12	145
6:4	145
6:9	145
6:16	103
6:17	103
11:15, 18	87
11:18	103
12:12	103
13:3	145
13:8	145
14:8	103
14:10	103
14:14	78
14:19	103
15:1, 7	103
16:19	103
18:3	103
18:24	145
19:15	103

OT Apocryphal Works
2 Maccabees
3:33	106
6:28	24
6:31	24
7:37–38	108

Wisdom
2:18	107
10:3	130

Pseudepigrapha
1 Enoch
1:9	75
8:1	76–7
8, 9, 10	77
9:1	75
9:6	77
10:4	77
10:4–6	76
12–36	130
22	130
22:7	131, 142
40:6	77
40:9	77
41:2	77–8, 83
45:6	78
46	78
46:2	78
46:5	78
46:6	78
46:13	78
83–90	130
85:4	131, 142

Jubilees
4:2–5	132
4:5	132
4:5–6	133
4:7	133, 142
4:15	142, 147

4:31	133, 142
7:20	79
7:27–29, 30–33	79
21:19–20	79
34:12–19	79, 83
34:18	79

4 Maccabees
6:28f	94
6:29	94
17:21–22	108
17:22–23	24

Testament of Abraham
13.1	134
13.2–5	134

Qumran Literature

Damascus Document
6.19	161
6.20–21	161

Rule of the Community
2.1–7	81
2.8	80

Manual of Discipline
I:8–11	161
1:10–11	162
3.13–4.7	35
3:15–4:25	147
3:17–22	33, 148
3:21–22	148
3:32–4:15	148

Temple Scroll
26.5–7	81

Philo

The Cherubim
1ff.	138
11ff.	138
40ff.	138
52	135
52ff.	138
53	135
54–65	135
60	137
64	135
65–66	137
88ff.	138
99–100	137

The Sacrifices of Abel and Cain
52	136
53	135
54–58	136
72	136

The Worse Attacks the Better
32	136
47	136
96	136

The Posterity of Abel and Cain
12	136
49	136

Josephus

Antiquities
I:52–54	139, 145
I:53, 55	140
I:54	140
I:55	140
I:57	140
I:59	141
I:61	140
I:65	140, 147
I:67	140, 144

Church Fathers

Polycarp
Philippians 7.1	60

www.ingramcontent.com/pod-product-compliance
Lightning Source LLC
Chambersburg PA
CBHW062216300426
44115CB00012BA/2094